JANE'S ARMOURED PERSONNEL CARRIERS

JANE'S ARMOURED PERSONNEL CARRIERS

Christopher F. Foss

JANE'S

First published in the United Kingdom in 1985 by
Jane's Publishing Company Ltd
238 City Road, London EC1V 2PU

ISBN 0 7106 0354 1

Distributed in the Philippines and USA and its dependencies by
Jane's Publishing Inc
135 West 50th Street   5-89 PCB 2200
New York, NY 10020

Typeset by D. P. Media Ltd, Hitchin, Herts

Printed in the United Kingdom by
Biddles Ltd, Guildford, Surrey.

Introduction

Although the tank, or main battle tank (MBT) as it is normally called today, has been around for some 70 years, the armoured personnel carrier is a much more recent development. During the Second World War both the Americans and Germans produced large numbers of half-track armoured personnel carriers of which some are still in service today. The Soviet Union did not place any armoured personnel carriers in production at all and the infantry were forced to go into battle hanging onto the turrets of tanks or on their feet! The British used light carriers and American-supplied half-tracks for the troop carrying role, although there were never enough of these to go around. Towards the end of the war the British and Canadians used tanks with their turrets removed in the troop carrying role and these proved quite successful even though the only means for the troops to enter and leave the vehicle was by climbing over the sides.

After the end of the Second World War the major powers, France, Britain, United States and the Soviet Union all started development programmes for armoured personnel carriers, tracked or wheeled.

As originally conceived the role of the armoured personnel carrier was to transport the infantry from one part of the battlefield to another where they would dismount and fight on foot. Vehicles of this type such as the American M59 and M113, or the British FV432, normally had the engine at the front with the troop compartment at the rear. The infantry entered the vehicle via a ramp (M113) or door (FV432) in the hull rear and no facilities were provided for the infantry to fire their weapons from within the vehicle. A 7.62 mm machine gun was normally mounted for local protection but the gunner was not provided with any protection from small arms fire or shell splinters.

As an interim measure some countries have fitted their M113 type vehicles with turret-mounted 7.62 mm/12.7 mm machine guns or even 20 mm cannon, the latter when firing APDS/AP ammunition enabling the vehicle to engage other enemy light armoured vehicles as well as its normal role of fire suppression. Some full tracked armoured personnel carriers are fully amphibious and are fitted not only with a NBC system but also night driving equipment.

More recently the armoured personnel carrier has been supplemented by the mechanised infantry fighting vehicle (MICV) or infantry fighting vehicle (IFV) as it is also called. This normally has a number of significant advantages over the basic armoured personnel carrier including improved armour protection, greater power-to-weight ratio for improved cross-country mobility, firing and vision blocks to enable the infantry to aim and fire their weapons from within the vehicle, NBC system, night vision equipment for commander, gunner and driver and a heavier armament. The latter can be a 20 mm or 25 mm cannon with a coaxial machine gun, for example as fitted in the two-man turret of the West German Marder, or even heavier armament. The Soviet BMP-1 MICV, which appeared almost 20 years ago, has a one-man power-operated turret armed with a 73 mm gun fed by an automatic loader, 7.62 mm coaxial machine gun and a launch rail over the 73 mm gun for a Sagger ATGW. The latest version of the BMP however has many improvements including a new two-man turret with what is believed to be a 30 mm cannon, 7.62 mm coaxial machine gun and a launcher for a Spandrel fire-and-forget ATGW.

The American Army is now taking delivery of the M2 Bradley Infantry Fighting Vehicle, but this is so expensive that it cannot replace the older M113 on a one-for-one basis. In any case, the M113 is more than adequate for many of the roles that it is required to undertake on the battlefield such as mortar carrier, command post vehicle, ambulance, fire control and so on. The M113 is the most widely used vehicle of its type and since 1960 some 80 000 M113s have been built by the FMC Corporation and sold to some 40 countries. Many users have adopted the vehicle to meet their own unique requirements and further development as a private venture by FMC has resulted in the Armoured Infantry Fighting Vehicle (AIFV) which bridges the gap between the cheap M113 and the very expensive M2 Bradley. The AIFV has already been adopted by Belgium, Netherlands and the Philippines.

The first armoured personnel carrier to enter service with the British Army in the post-war period in large numbers was the Alvis Saracen (6 × 6) which used many automotive components of the Alvis Saracen armoured car. This is still used for internal security duties in Northern Ireland but in the British Army of the Rhine was replaced many years ago by the FV432 of which some 3000 were built. In the next few years FV432 will be supplemented by the MCV-80, also built by GKN, which has better armour protection, mobility and firepower. The latter includes a two-man turret armed with a 30 mm Rarden cannon and a 7.62 mm coaxial machine gun. The vehicle does not have firing ports as this was not a British Army requirement. Also recently introduced into the British Army is the GKN Saxon (4 × 4) armoured personnel carrier. This is used by United Kingdom-based infantry battalions who would deploy to West Germany in time of war.

The West German Army has some 3000 Marder MICVs, the first of which entered service in 1970. Until the introduction of the American M2 Bradley several years ago this was the most powerful vehicle of its type in NATO. Many Marders have now been fitted with a MILAN ATGW launcher to give them an anti-tank capability out to 2000 metres and in the future the 20 mm cannon will be replaced by a 25 mm cannon with much improved capabilities against both air and ground targets. The West German Army also has 996 Transportpanzer 1 (6 × 6) vehicles which are used for a wide range of specialised roles, and over 3000 M113s. In addition to being used for the transport of infantry they are also employed as 120 mm mortar carriers, observation vehicles and artillery command posts.

In recent years the French Army have adopted a different approach as it is now fielding both tracked and wheeled vehicles. The former is the AMX-10P which is the replacement for the older AMX VCI based on the AMX-13 light tank chassis. Main improvements of the AMX-10P over the

AMX VCI can be summarised as improved armour protection, mobility and fire power. It is also fully amphibious, has an NBC system and a full range of night vision equipment. Full tracked vehicles are however expensive to procure, operate and maintain and for this reason the French Army already has large numbers of Renault VAB (4×4) armoured personnel carriers in service; this number is expected to increase to as many as 4000 vehicles in the 1990s. Large numbers of VABs have been built for the export market and a 6×6 version has also been built and sold in some numbers. Like many vehicles today the armoured personnel carrier is only the basic member of the family and other variants include anti-tank vehicles, mortar carriers, internal security vehicles, command vehicles, ambulances and so on.

The Soviets have been fielding a mix of tracked and wheeled vehicles since the early 1950s. The first full tracked armoured personnel carrier was the BTR-50P which had an open top. This was followed by the BTR-50PK with a fully enclosed troop compartment. The Czechoslovakians did not like the basic BTR-50P design so carried out a major redesign which resulted in the OT-62, some versions of which have turret-mounted machine guns for improved firepower and a light anti-tank weapon of the recoilless type. The BMP-1 MICV is now being replaced by the BMP-2 which was first seen several years ago. The first wheeled armoured personnel carrier was the BTR-152 (6×6) which was basically a truck chassis with an armoured body. This was replaced by the BTR-60P (8×8), the first version of which had an open-topped crew compartment. The BTR-60P was followed by the BTR-60PA and finally the BTR-60PB which has a fully enclosed troop compartment and a turret armed with a 7.62 mm and a 14.5 mm machine gun. More recently an improved version of the BTR-60PB has entered service under the designation of the BTR-70. Once again the Czechoslovakians did not like the BTR-60 series so they designed the OT-64, which is used by Czechoslovakia and Poland and also has been exported in significant numbers.

In recent years some manufacturers have designed an armoured personnel carrier that shares many common parts with an armoured car. For example the Renault VBC-90 armoured car shares parts with the VAB, while the Panhard ERC armoured car shares some 90 per cent of its components with the VCR armoured personnel carrier. Some vehicles, such as the American V-150/V-300 Commando and the Dragoon can be used as an armoured car or an armoured personnel carrier. The Brazilian EE-11 Urutu (6×6) armoured personnel carrier is in service with a number of countries fitted with a two-man turret armed with a 90 mm gun for the fire support role. Many countries also use wheeled armoured personnel carriers in the internal security roles. These vehicles are normally provided with special protection against petrol bombs and are often fitted with a special blade at the front of the hull for clearing obstacles such as barricades.

Although most peoples attention is focused on the main battle tank, the armoured personnel carrier or infantry fighting vehicle is an essential and often overlooked vehicle on the battlefield of today and the future. Tanks can take ground but it can only be held by the infantry. Tanks also need the close support of infantry to protect them from enemy infantry armed with deadly anti-tank weapons such as ATGWs.

Jane's Armoured Personnel Carriers covers all wheeled and tracked armoured personnel carriers, mechanised infantry fighting vehicles and internal security vehicles evolved since the Second World War that are in service or under development. Each entry has a development history, detailed description, complete list of variants, full specifications, list of users and current manufacturer.

The author would like to take this opportunity of thanking the many companies, armies and individuals who have provided material for this book. Information and photographs for revised editions should be forwarded to the author via the publisher.

Christopher F Foss
February 1985

British GKN Sakney MCV-80 being tested in the Middle East in 1984. This vehicle was accepted for service with the British Army in November 1984 and is expected to enter service in 1987. Main armament consists of a turret mounted 30 mm Rarden cannon with a 7.62 mm co-axial Hughes Helicopters Chain Gun.

TAM medium tank armed with 105 mm gun (left) and VCTP infantry combat vehicle (right)

VCTP Infantry Combat Vehicle

Development

In mid-1974 the West German company of Thyssen Henschel was awarded a contract for the design and development of a new medium tank for the Argentinian Army under the designation TAM (Tanque Argentino Mediano), as well as an infantry combat vehicle under the designation VCTP (Véhiculo de Combate Transporte de Personal). The contract covered the design, development and construction of three prototypes of both the tank and the VCTP. Argentina has a requirement for 200 TAMs and 300 VCTPs which will be built in Argentina, with some components being supplied from West Germany. Early in 1984 it was announced that Panama had ordered 60 TAMs and a quantity of VCTPs for early delivery.

Description

The VCTP is similar to the Marder MICV but has a more powerful 720 bhp engine, less sophisticated two-man turret armed with a 20 mm cannon and a 7.62 mm roof-mounted machine gun, three gun ports in each side of the troop compartment at the rear, two rectangular roof hatches over the troop compartment that are hinged in the centre and a remote-controlled 7.62 mm machine gun installation which is fitted over the troop compartment at the rear of the hull. Mounted either side of the hull, slightly forward of the turret is a bank of four electrically-operated smoke dischargers firing forwards. The vehicle is fitted with an NBC system which pressurises the crew compartment for a period of three hours. A heating system pre-heats the engine for cold starts as well as heating the crew compartment.

The mortar version of the VCTP is called the VCTM (Véhiculo de Combate Transporte de Mortero) and is fitted with a 120 mm 120LR (Liviano Reforzado) mortar developed in Argentina for which 49 M44/46 high explosive and 12 PEPA/LA long-range projectiles are carried. The mortar has a maximum range of 6150 metres with the M44/M46 bomb or 8380 metres with the PEPA/LA bomb.

The VCTM is now in service with the Argentinian Army and is essentially the VCTP with the turret removed and fitted with a three-part opening in the roof through which the mortar can fire. This model does not have the rectangular roof hatches of the VCTP but has one circular hatch in the right side of the roof and a much larger one instead of the remote-controlled 7.62 mm machine gun.

A detailed description of the Marder MICV is given under Federal Republic of Germany. The VCTP was previously known as the VCI, or Véhiculo Combate Infanteria.

SPECIFICATIONS		
Model	**VCTP**	**VCTM**
CREW	2 + 10	5
WEIGHT	27.5 tonnes	27.5 tonnes
LENGTH	6.79 m	6.79 m
WIDTH	3.28 m	3.25 m
HEIGHT	2.45 m	1.858 m
GROUND CLEARANCE	0.44 m	0.44 m
MAX ROAD SPEED	75 km/h	75 km/h
MAX RANGE		
road	570 km	570 km
road with auxiliary		
fuel tanks	915 km	915 km
FORDING	1 m	1 m
GRADIENT	60%	60%
ENGINE	720 hp diesel	720 hp diesel

Status: In production. In service in Argentina, on order for Panama.

Manufacturer: TAMSE, Avda Rolon 1441/43, 2609, Boulgone sur Mer-Provincia de Buenos Aires, Argentina.

Véhiculo Armado Exploración

The French companies of Panhard and Renault have each built prototypes of a 6 × 6 armoured personnel carrier to meet the requirements of the Argentinian Army under the designation of the Véhiculo Armado Exploración (VAE). It is believed that the prototype selected for production will be manufactured under licence in Argentina. Using the same components both companies have also designed an armoured car designated the Véhiculo de APoyo y Exploración (VAPE). Recent information has indicated that the whole VAE/VAPE project has been suspended for financial reasons.

Status: Prototypes.

AUSTRALIA

Project Waler

In April 1981 the Australian Minister of Defence announced that the Army was starting a long-range project named Waler to replace its light armoured fighting vehicles in the mid-1990s.

Exploratory studies conducted within the Defence Department indicated that Australian industry had the potential to design, develop and manufacture such vehicles provided that suitable overseas technology transfer could be arranged. Characteristics of future light armoured vehicles were broadly determined as a basis for further study.

The first phase of the four-phase project began in September 1982 and consisted of three non-competitive target studies to assess project feasibility. The studies were undertaken by ESAMS Ltd of Sydney, Evans Deakin Industries Ltd of Brisbane and A Goninan and Co Ltd of Newcastle. They were supported respectively by EASAMS and Vickers DSD of the UK, SOFMA and GIAT of France, and FMC of the United States. Each company had to present four options for an infantry vehicle, the army selecting two from each company for further work. This included outline designs for other vehicles in each family, costs and Australian industry involvement. The studies were completed in September 1982 and provided the army with information on which to base realistic vehicle requirements. They covered such aspects as whether the vehicles should be wheeled or tracked, engine,

weapon and armour options, optimum Australian content and proposals for the further development and management of the project.

The selection of the three companies for the target studies does not preclude future involvement of any other Australian company. The second phase, project definition to be based on the staff requirement, would involve calling for new competitive tenders from any Australian organisations capable of writing specifications for, and designing, developing and manufacturing fighting vehicles. Three companies will undertake the first part of project definition, reducing to two when new outline designs have been assessed, then to one when plans for development are considered.

The third phase, development, is to be undertaken by the winning company. It will lead to full-scale production with first deliveries being made in the mid-1990s. It is expected that between 800 and 1000 vehicles will be required to replace the Australian Army's present fleet of M113 series vehicles.

In December 1983 the Australian Minister of Defence said that a year's study by the three Australian companies and their overseas partners had indicated that Australian production of a fleet of armoured fighting vehicles was feasible. Subject to government approval, tenders for the project definition phase of Waler were expected to be called for in August 1984, but as of early 1985 these had not been called for.

AUSTRIA

Steyr 4K 7FA G 127 Armoured Personnel Carrier

Development

The Steyr 4K 7FA G 127 is an uparmoured version of the earlier Saurer 4K 4FA armoured personnel carrier fitted with the engine and transmission of the tank destroyer SK 105 which is also manufactured by Steyr. The first prototype of the 4K 7FA G 127 was completed in 1976 with first production vehicles following in 1977. The Steyr 4K 7FA G 127 is now in service with the Austrian Army and has also been exported to Bolivia, Greece (qv) and Nigeria.

Description

The basic model is designated the 4K 7FA G 127 and is armed with a 12.7 mm (0.50) M2 HB Browning machine gun. The hull is made of all-welded steel and is immune to penetration from 20 mm armour-piercing projectiles over its frontal arc.

The driver sits at the front of the hull on the left side with the engine to his right. He has a two-piece hatch cover that opens to the left and right, in front of which are three periscopes.

The gunner sits behind the driver and has a cupola with a two-piece hatch cover opening left and right which can be

locked vertical to give some protection. There are two observation periscopes in the front part of the cupola. A standard 12.7 mm (0.50) Browning machine gun is mounted on the forward part of the cupola and mounted on the rear of the cupola are four smoke dischargers which point to the rear of

Steyr 4K 7FA G 127 APC armed with 12.7 mm M2 HB machine gun at front and single 7.62 mm machine gun at rear

the vehicle. When unlocked the 12.7 mm machine gun has an elevation from −20 to +35 degrees and when locked of −10 to +7.5 degrees.

The personnel compartment is at the rear of the hull with the eight infantrymen seated on bench seats, four down each side of the hull. The section leader, the first man on the right bench, is provided with a periscope in the forward part of the personnel compartment, on the right side. Two hatches over the roof of the vehicle open outwards. Mounting sockets for the pivot trunnion of an adapter mount for the MG 74 machine guns are provided on the front, right, left and rear side of the hatch, above the personnel compartment. Normal means of entry and exit for the crew is by the twin doors at the rear of the hull.

The torsion bar suspension has five dual road wheels with the drive sprocket at the front, idler at the rear and three track return rollers. The first and last road wheel stations are provided with a hydraulic shock absorber. The Diehl connector tracks are provided with rubber pads and can be fitted with spikes for operation on ice-covered surfaces.

Standard equipment includes a ventilating and heating system. The vehicle has passive night vision equipment for the driver and an individual NBC protection system. If required the Steyr 4K 7FA G 127 can be fitted with firing ports for the Steyr 5.56 mm AUG assault rifle.

Variants

4K 7FA-K SPz Infantry Fighting Vehicle

This is the basic vehicle with two ball mountings for a Steyr AUG assault rifle or Steyr MP 69 in either side of the rear troop compartment, aiming being accomplished via a periscope mounted above. In addition there are two periscopes in the hull rear, plus one for the commander which can be traversed through a full 360 degrees. The infantry sit back to back down the centre of the vehicle rather than along either side of the troop compartment as in the original model of the 4K 7FA.

4K 7FA-KUPz 1/90 Fire Support Combat Vehicle

This is the basic vehicle with a modified hull rear on which a GIAT TS 90 90 mm turret is mounted. The crew of five consists of the driver, commander, gunner and two infantrymen who are seated in the hull rear which retains the two doors. A total of 20 rounds of 90 mm and 2000 rounds of 7.62 mm ammunition are carried in the turret and an additional 44 rounds of ammunition in the hull. Technical specifications are the same as for the basic vehicle except that the combat weight is 16.95 tonnes, the length with turret traversed forwards 6.934 metres, length of hull 5.87 metres, height to top of commander's cupola 2.565 metres, ground pressure 0.63 kg/cm² and a road cruising range of 500 km. This model is not yet in production.

4K 7FA-SP2/300 MICV

The prototype of this was completed in 1984 and is essentially the 4KA 7FA-K SPz fitted with a one-man turret armed with a British 30 mm Rarden cannon and a 7.62 mm coaxial machine gun. Combat weight is 15 900 kg and power-to-weight ratio is 20.1 hp/tonne.

4K 7FA-Fü Command Vehicle

This model, which is in production, has a crew of seven: commander, gunner, two radio operators, two messengers

4K 7FA-K SPz infantry fighting vehicle with all hatches closed

4K 7FA-KUPz 1/90 fire support combat vehicle with TS 90 turret fitted with coaxial and anti-aircraft machine guns

Prototype of the 4K 7FA-SP2/300 MICV fitted with turret-mounted 30 mm Rarden cannon

and the driver. Communications equipment includes two radios with an automatic tuning unit, loud speaker and a crew intercom.

4K 7FA-San Armoured Ambulance

This model is in production and is unarmed. Its crew of two consists of the driver and a medical orderly. It can carry up to

Steyr 4K 7FA G 127 armoured personnel carrier from rear with back doors closed and MG 74 mounted on roof

4K 7FA GrW 81

Mortar carrier with a crew of five (driver, commander, gunner and two mortar men), armed with 81 mm mortar and carrying 78 mortar bombs, in production.

4K 7FA GrW 120 Mortar Carrier

Fitted with 120 mm mortar, project only.

4K 7FA FLA 1/2.20 Twin 20 mm Self-propelled Anti-aircraft System

Uses a modified chassis and is fitted with a French ESD TA 20/RA 20 turret armed with twin 20 mm cannon. The prototype of this system has been completed.

4K 7FA FLA 3/2.30 Twin 30 mm Self-propelled Anti-aircraft Gun System

With Thomson-CSF twin 30 mm turret, has been developed to the prototype stage.

four sitting and two stretcher patients and carries extensive medical equipment.

SPECIFICATIONS

CREW	2 + 8	3rd gear	19.8 km/h	TRANSMISSION	ZF manual with 6 forward and 1 reverse gears
COMBAT WEIGHT	14 800 kg	4th gear	32.3 km/h		
POWER-TO-WEIGHT		5th gear	46.4 km/h	STEERING	hydrostatic split torque
RATIO	21.62 hp/tonne	6th gear	63.6 km/h		type
GROUND PRESSURE	0.55 kg/cm²	reverse	7.4 km/h	CLUTCH	single dry plate
LENGTH HULL	5.87 m	FUEL CAPACITY	360 litres	SUSPENSION	torsion bar
WIDTH	2.5 m	MAX ROAD RANGE	520 km	ELECTRICAL SYSTEM	24 V
HEIGHT (without armament		FORDING	1 m	BATTERIES	2 × 12 V, 180 Ah
but including MG		GRADIENT	75%	ARMAMENT (main)	1 × 12.7 mm MG
support)	1.611 m	SIDE SLOPE	40%	SMOKE-LAYING	
GROUND CLEARANCE	0.42 m	VERTICAL OBSTACLE	0.8 m	EQUIPMENT	4 smoke dischargers on
TRACK	2.12 m	TRENCH	2.1 m		rear of gunner's cupola
TRACK WIDTH	380 mm	ENGINE	Steyr 7FA 6-cylinder		
LENGTH OF TRACK			liquid-cooled 4-stroke		
ON GROUND	3.192 m		turbo-charged diesel		
MAX ROAD SPEED			developing 320 hp at		
1st gear	6.9 km/h		2300 rpm		
2nd gear	12 km/h				

Status: In production. In service with Austria, Bolivia, Greece and Nigeria. In 1981 it was confirmed that Nigeria had taken delivery of a quantity of Steyr 4K 7FA G 127 APCs and that licence production would be undertaken there.

Manufacturer: Steyr-Daimler-Puch AG, Werke Wien, A-1111 Vienna, Austria. It is also being manufactured under licence in Greece where it is known as the Leonidas. Photographs of Greek-built vehicles appear under Greece.

Saurer 4K 4FA Armoured Personnel Carrier

Development

In 1956 Oesterreichische Saurer-Werke (which was taken over by Steyr-Daimler-Puch AG in 1970) of Vienna started development of a full tracked armoured personnel carrier. The first prototype, the 3K 3H, was completed in 1958 and the second, the 4K 3H, the following year, both powered by a Saurer 3H 200 hp diesel engine. Their hull shape was different to the production vehicle's and the suspension consisted of five road wheels with the drive sprocket at the front and the idler at the rear, there being no track return rollers.

The next model, the 4K 2P, had a different hull layout, new suspension and was powered by a 250 hp Saurer 2P diesel engine. In appearance it was similar to the first production vehicles which were completed in 1961 and were designated the 4K 4F. Later production vehicles were the 4K 3FA (230 hp) and the 4K 4FA (250 hp), which differed only in minor details such as their engines.

The Saurer armoured personnel carrier is used only by the Austrian Army which has about 450 vehicles in service,

including variants. Production was finally completed in 1969. The vehicle has now been succeeded in production by a new model, described in the previous entry, called the 4K 7FA which uses the same automotive components as the SK 105 tank destroyer which is also manufactured by Steyr.

Description

The hull of the Saurer armoured personnel carrier is made of all-welded steel armour and is immune to penetration from 20 mm armour-piercing projectiles over its frontal arc.

The driver is seated at the front of the hull on the left side with the engine to his right. He is provided with a two-piece hatch cover that opens to the left and right in front of which are three periscopes.

The gunner is seated behind the driver and on the basic model is provided with a cupola which has a two-piece hatch cover opening left and right and a single observation periscope. A standard 12.7 mm (0.50) Browning machine gun is mounted on the forward part of the cupola and most vehicles are fitted with a shield to give a measure of protection to the gunner. This model is known as the 4K 4FA-G1.

The personnel compartment is at the rear of the hull with the eight infantrymen seated on bench seats, four down each side of the hull. The section leader is the first man on the right seat and is provided with a periscope in the forward part of the personnel compartment roof, on the right side. Access to the personnel compartment is by two doors in the rear of the hull. Two hatches over the roof of the vehicle open to the outside. Mounting sockets for the pivot trunnion of an adapter mount for the MG 42 machine gun are provided on the front, right, left and rear side of the hatch above the personnel compartment.

The torsion bar suspension consists of five dual road wheels with the drive sprocket at the front and the idler at the rear and two track return rollers. The first and last road wheel stations are provided with a hydraulic shock absorber.

The 4K 4FA has no NBC system, night vision equipment or amphibious capability.

Variants

4K 4FA-G2 (Grenadier-Schützenpanzer)

This is similar to the basic 4K 4FA-G1 but is fitted with an Oerlikon GAD AOA turret which is armed with a 20 mm Oerlikon cannon model 204 GK. This is belt-fed and can be used in both the ground and anti-aircraft roles. The weapon is provided with 100 rounds of ready-use ammunition and the empty cartridge cases and links are ejected outside the turret. The 20 mm cannon has an elevation of +70 degrees and a depression of −12 degrees, turret traverse being 360 degrees. Elevation and traverse are manual, gun elevation being 8.1 degrees and turret traverse 5.46 degrees for one revolution of the hand wheel. The gunner is provided with a sight with a magnification of ×6.5 and a 9-degree field of view.

4K 3FA-Fü1 (Command Vehicle) (Führungs-SPz, for Brigade Commander)

4K 3FA-FüA (Artillery Command Vehicle) (Artillerie-Führungs-Schützenpanzer)

4K 3FA-Fü/FlA (Anti-aircraft Command Vehicle) (FlA Führungs-Schützenpanzer)

Saurer 4K 4FA-G1 with 12.7 mm machine gun and cupola hatch covers open (Austrian Army)

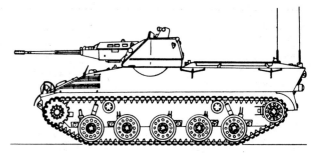

Saurer 4K 4FA-G2 with turret-mounted 20 mm cannon

Saurer 4K 7FA-G2 firing turret-mounted Oerlikon 20 mm cannon (Austrian Army)

4K 3FA-FS (Wireless Teleprinter Vehicle) (Funkfernschreiber Panzer)

4K 4FA-San (Ambulance)

Full designation is 4K 4FA-San (Sanitätspanzer San). This model is unarmed and has a crew of two consisting of the driver and medical orderly, and can carry four sitting and two stretcher patients. The stretchers are carried in the left side of the hull with the four sitting patients on the bench seat down the right side of the hull, strapped in with waist and shoulder straps. There are four stowage containers for medical supplies under the bench seat and other equipment carried includes a heater, oxygen and respirating equipment.

4K 4F GrW1 81 mm Mortar Carrier (Granatwerfer-SPz)

Mounted in the rear of the troop compartment, firing forwards, is an 81 mm mortar. A 120 mm self-propelled mortar was developed to the prototype stage (GrW2) but never entered service.

81 mm Multiple Rocket Launcher

This is the basic APC with an Oerlikon-Bührle 81 mm rocket launcher mounted on a turntable over the rear troop compartment. The launcher consists of two single-barrel launchers each of which has a nine-rocket magazine, mounted on a turntable. The launcher can be elevated from −10 to +50 degrees.

SPECIFICATIONS					
CREW	2 + 8	GROUND CLEARANCE	0.42 m	ENGINE	Saurer model 4FA 4-stroke
COMBAT WEIGHT		TRACK	2.12 m		6-cylinder diesel
with 20 mm turret	15 000 kg	TRACK WIDTH	375 mm		developing 250 hp at
with 12.7 mm MG	12 500 kg	LENGTH OF TRACK			2400 rpm
UNLOADED WEIGHT		ON GROUND	2.9 m	TRANSMISSION	manual with 5 forward
(without turret or		MAX ROAD SPEED			and 1 reverse gears
armament)	11 100 kg	1st gear	11.3 km/h	SUSPENSION	torsion bar
POWER-TO-WEIGHT		2nd gear	18 km/h	ELECTRICAL SYSTEM	24 V
RATIO		3rd gear	28.3 km/h	BATTERIES	2 × 12 V, 180 Ah
20 mm model	16.66 hp/tonne	4th gear	43.8 km/h	ARMAMENT	1 × 12.7 mm MG or
12.7 mm model	20 hp/tonne	5th gear	65 km/h		1 × 20 mm cannon
GROUND PRESSURE	0.52 kg/cm²	FUEL CAPACITY	184 litres	ARMOUR	
LENGTH	5.4 m	MAX ROAD RANGE	370 km	Hull nose	20 mm at 45°
WIDTH	2.5 m	FORDING	1 m	Hull glacis	20 mm at 30°
HEIGHT		GRADIENT	75%	Hull sides	14 mm
including 12.7 mm MG	2.1 m	SIDE SLOPE	50%	Hull top	8 mm
to hull top	1.65 m	VERTICAL OBSTACLE	0.8 m	Hull rear	12 mm
FIRING HEIGHT	1.95 m	TRENCH	2.2 m	Turret front	20–35 mm
				Turret, other surfaces	15–20 mm

Status: Production complete. In service only with the Austrian Army.

Manufacturer: Steyr-Daimler-Puch AG, Werke Wien, A-1111 Vienna, Austria.

BELGIUM

SIBMAS Armoured Personnel Carrier

Development

The SIBMAS (6 × 6) APC was designed as a private venture from 1975 by B N Constructions Ferroviaires et Métalliques. The first prototype was completed in 1976 and has been extensively tested both in Belgium and Malaysia. A second prototype, with improved vision for the driver and a more powerful engine, was completed in mid-1979.

The vehicle has been designed to undertake a wide range of roles including use as an anti-tank vehicle (armed with HOT, TOW and MILAN type ATGWs), APC (carrying a maximum of 16 men depending on the armament installed), internal security vehicle, mortar carrier, reconnaissance vehicle, anti-aircraft vehicle and recovery vehicle. Wherever possible standard MAN automotive components such as the engine, transmission and axles have been used.

Late in 1981 Malaysia placed an order valued at £50 million with the company for 186 vehicles with first deliveries made in June 1983. Two versions have been ordered:
AFSV-90: Armoured Fire Support Vehicle with Cockerill CM-90 turret and 90 mm Mk III gun and an OIP LRS-5 fire-control system; 162 have been ordered.
ARV: Armoured Recovery Vehicle with front and rear spades, weight of 20 000 kg, winch with a capacity of 20 000 kg and a crane with a capacity of 8000 kg; 24 have been ordered.

Description

The hull of the SIBMAS is made of all-welded steel and provides the crew with complete protection against 7.62 mm and 5.56 mm armour-piercing rounds.

The driver sits at the very front of the vehicle and has a single-piece hatch cover over his position that opens to his right, adjustable seat and an adjustable steering wheel. In front and at both sides of the driver are large bullet-proof windscreens that provide excellent vision at all times. If

SIBMAS (6 × 6) armoured recovery vehicle with front and rear stabilising blades lowered as used by Malaysia

SIBMAS (6 × 6) vehicle with Cockerill two-man turret armed with 90 mm gun as used by Malaysia

13

SIBMAS (6 × 6) APC fitted with Vickers turret with twin 7.62 mm machine guns and single 7.62 mm machine gun at rear, and all roof hatches closed

SIBMAS (6 × 6) AFSV fitted with Cockerill two-man turret armed with Cockerill 90 mm gun showing its amphibious capabilities

required these can be quickly covered by armoured shutters which are hinged at the lower part.

The turret is mounted immediately behind the driver and in each side of the hull is a large door that opens forwards.

The troop compartment is to the rear of the turret and the engine at the very rear on the left side. Six of the infantrymen are seated back-to-back down the centre of the vehicle and the remaining three in the aisle between the troop compartment and the rear door. One small and three large hatches are provided over the top of the troop compartment and if required a remote-controlled machine gun can be pintle-mounted over the aisle. There are spherical firing ports and vision blocks in the troop compartment.

The engine can be removed through the roof of the vehicle in 30 minutes by two men. Quick disconnect couplings are provided for both the power and hydraulic circuits. The cooling system is behind and separated from the engine compartment by a waterproof bulkhead. Power is taken from the engine to the transmission, which is under the floor between the first and second axles, by a propeller shaft. The differentials of the front and rear two axles are lockable and a lockable differential between the two rear axles allows them to be longitudinally locked.

The SIBMAS is fully amphibious, being propelled in the water by its wheels at a speed of 4 km/h. The amphibious version has two propellers at the rear of the hull which can be traversed through 360 degrees and give the vehicle a maximum water speed of 11 km/h. The propellers are driven from the PTO on the engine. An advantage of the SIBMAS is that when approaching the river bank the driver can engage first gear and as soon as the front wheels touch the bank maximum tractive effort is available as the propellers are still pushing the vehicle forward. Before entering the water a trim vane is erected at the front of the hull. Two bilge pumps, each with a maximum capacity of 180 litres a minute, are fitted as standard.

The tyres are of the run-flat type. Optional equipment includes infra-red or passive night vision equipment, hydraulic winch mounted at the front of the hull with 60 metres of cable and a maximum capacity of 8000 kg (which can be increased to 16 000 kg with snatch blocks), heater, air-conditioning system and an NBC system.

The SIBMAS can be fitted with a wide variety of armament installations and the following have already been fitted for trials purposes:

Cockerill turret with 90 mm gun, 7.62 mm coaxial and

SPECIFICATIONS

CREW	3 + 11	ANGLE OF APPROACH/ DEPARTURE	50°/46°	TRANSMISSION	fully automatic ZF HP 500, 6 forward and 1 reverse gears, with hydro-dynamic torque converter
CONFIGURATION	6 × 6	MAX ROAD SPEED	100 km/h		
COMBAT WEIGHT	14 500–16 500 kg depending on role	MAX WATER SPEED			
		propelled by wheels	4 km/h	STEERING	power-assisted
UNLOADED WEIGHT	12 500 kg	propelled by propellers	11 km/h	SUSPENSION	longitudinal suspension arms (lower) and wishbone above axle, helical springs and hydraulic shock absorbers
WEIGHT		ACCELERATION			
first axle, loaded	4950 kg*	0–60 km/h	22 s		
second axle, loaded	5650 kg*	FUEL CAPACITY	400 litres		
third axle, loaded	5900 kg*	MAX ROAD RANGE	1000 km		
POWER-TO-WEIGHT		FUEL CONSUMPTION	0.36 litre/km	TYRES	14.00 × 20
RATIO	19.39 hp/tonne*	FORDING	amphibious	BRAKES	
GROUND PRESSURE	2.4 kg/cm²	GRADIENT	70%	main	hydraulic air-assisted
LENGTH HULL	7.32 m	SIDE SLOPE	40%	parking	pneumatic on gearbox
WIDTH	2.5 m	VERTICAL OBSTACLE	0.6 m	continuous	pneumatically-actuated exhaust brake
HEIGHT		TRENCH	1.5 m		
to turret top	2.77 m	TURNING RADIUS	8 m	ELECTRICAL SYSTEM	24 V
to hull top	2.24 m	ENGINE	MAN D 2566 MK 6-cylinder	BATTERIES	4 × 12 V, 100 Ah
GROUND CLEARANCE	0.4 m		in-line water-cooled		
TRACK	2.07 m		turbo-charged diesel	* with a vehicle weight of 16 500 kg	
WHEELBASE	2.8 m + 1.4 m		developing 320 hp at 1900 rpm		

Status: In production. In service with Malaysia.

Manufacturer: SIBMAS, Marketing Department, Rue de Bellecourt, B-6538 Manage, Belgium.

7.62 mm anti-aircraft machine gun (adopted by Malaysia)
ESD anti-aircraft turret with twin 20 mm cannon
Hispano-Suiza Lynx 90 turret with 90 mm gun, 7.62 mm
coaxial and 7.62 mm anti-aircraft machine gun
Hispano-Suiza Serval 60/20 turret with 60 mm breech-
loaded mortar, 20 mm cannon and 7.62 mm machine gun
Vickers turret with twin 7.62 mm machine guns
SAMM TG 120 (recently redesignated the TTB 120) tur-
ret with 20 mm cannon and 7.62 mm coaxial machine gun
SAMM S 365 (recently redesignated the BTM 208) turret
with 12.7 mm and 7.62 mm machine guns

Variants

Command post vehicle with additional communications
equipment and a tent which can be erected at the rear of the
hull
Ambulance vehicle carrying four stretcher and three seated
patients and two medical orderlies
Cargo vehicle with a payload of more than 4000 kg
Recovery vehicle with front and rear stabilising blades,
20 000 kg winch and a 3000 kg crane

BMF production of M113A1/AIFV

In April 1980 the Belgian Government placed an order for
514 FMC Armoured Infantry Fighting Vehicles and 525
M113A1 armoured personnel carriers. These are being built
under licence at Aubange by Belgian Mechanical Fabrication (BMF). This is a joint company established by ASCO
(55 per cent), Cockerill-Sambre (37 per cent) and
Bruxelles-Lambert (eight per cent).

The first two vehicles were handed over in 1982 and it is
expected that production will continue at the rate of 20 to 25
vehicles a month until 1988. In 1983 the Netherlands ordered
26 M113A1 hulls from BMF which will be converted to
recovery vehicles by the Dutch Company RDM.

In the Belgian Army they will replace the old American-
supplied M75s and French-supplied AMX VCI armoured
personnel carriers.

M113A1-B

The Belgian variants of the M113A1 are very similar to the
standard US Army M113A1 but with the following
modifications: suspension system similar to that of the
M113A2, 200-ampere alternator, exterior air intake/exhaust
personnel heater, an NBC system supplying air to each individual, Halon fixed fire-extinguishing system for the engine
compartment and vehicle lights for Belgian and West German roads.

The Belgian vehicle is designated the M113A1-B and two
basic models are produced. The first is the standard two-
holed vehicle with a driver's hatch and a commander's
cupola, the second is a new three-holed vehicle with a driver's
hatch and two transversely adjacent cupolas. The
M113A1-B vehicles are all armed with the standard 12.7 mm
M2 HB machine gun on the commander's cupola, except for
the unarmed ambulance vehicle and the anti-tank vehicle
which has the same weapon in a cupola weapon station. The
manual machine gun has an elevation of +53 degrees, depression of −21 degrees and 360-degree traverse. Additional
weapons, other than personal equipment are detailed in the
variants below.

Variants

M113A1-B-ATK

This is a three-holed vehicle with the 12.7 mm Cupola
Weapon Station (CWS) on the right and an unarmed cupola
on the left. The CWS permits operation of the gun in both
closed hatch remote mode and open hatch, manual flex

M113A1 APC built by BMF at Aubange

mode. Remote operation permits an elevation range of −10 to +50 degrees and complete 360-degree traverse. The flex mode has an elevation range of −21 to +53 degrees with 360-degree traverse. The vehicle has a crew of ten, carries a 7.62 mm machine gun, short range anti-tank weapon and ammunition.

M113A1-B-MIL MILAN
This is a three-holed vehicle which has the 12.7 mm machine gun on the left commander's cupola and a quick disconnect mount on the right cupola for the MILAN ATGW. The missile is fired from its tripod either attached to the cupola mount or in the field. The mount allows for the rapid escape of the vehicle over a limited distance with the launcher still attached to the cupola. Two Bofors Lyran mortar launchers are mounted on the top of the vehicle at the left rear. This model has a crew of five.

M113A1-B-TRG
This is the basic MILAN vehicle with hatches, cupolas, stowage provision and so on and is equipped with two plexi-glass clear canopies, one for the driver and the other for the commander/instructor. Equipment is provided for all weather manoeuvres and the transport of observers. This vehicle can be converted into the M113A1-B-MIL.

Engineer Vehicle M113A1-B-ENG
This is a two-holed vehicle for carrying a demolition team and its equipment; it has a self-recovery winch and a crew of eight.

Command Post Vehicle M113A1-B-CP
This is a two-holed vehicle based on the M113A1, not the M577A1, and is fitted with communications equipment, map boards and other equipment for a mobile command post. It includes an optional side awning or canvas covered exten-sion. The extension is of lightproof construction and may be connected to extensions of the same design on other M113A1-B-CPs. This has a crew of seven.

Recovery Vehicle M113A1-B-REC
This is a two-holed vehicle fitted with a hydraulic winch and fairlead assembly for recovering disabled vehicles. It also has a manual crane mounted on the top left. This model has a crew of four.

AIFV built by BMF at Aubange

Maintenance Vehicle with crane M113A1-B-MTC
This is a two-holed vehicle with an HIAB hydraulic crane on the mid-left top, a self-recovery winch is installed in the engineer vehicle and a portable work bench, special lighting and storage for tools. It has a crew of five.

Ambulance Vehicle M113A1-B-AMB
This is a two-holed vehicle, unarmed and with a crew of three. It can carry four stretcher, two stretcher and three sitting or six sitting patients.

AIFV-B
The Belgian Armoured Infantry Fighting Vehicle is very similar to the Dutch AIFV fully designed in the AIFV entry except that the following major differences are incorporated: suspension is similar to the M113A2's (and identical to the M113A1-B's), external air intake/exhaust personnel heater, NBC system supplying air to each individual, and HALON fixed fire-extinguishing system for the engine compartment and lights for Belgian and German roads. There are three versions of this vehicle.

AIFV-B with 25 mm Oerlikon KBA-BO2 cannon, Enclosed Weapon Station (EWS), AIFV-B-25 mm
This is similar to the Dutch AIFV squad vehicle except that the commander's cupola is fitted with a quick disconnect mount for the MILAN missile launcher. As with the M113A1-B-MIL, the launcher remains fixed to its tripod for use on the quick disconnect mount or in the field. With the launcher attached to the mount, limited distance rapid escape vehicle operations are possible. This model has a crew of seven and two Bofors Lyran launchers are mounted on the top of the vehicle and operated from the turret.

AIFV with 12.7 mm Cupola Weapon Station (CWS), AIFV-B-50
This vehicle is similar to the AIFV-B-25 mm except that the 12.7 mm CWS is used in place of the EWS. This CWS is identical to that used on the M113A1-B-ATK except six grenade launchers are added, as is provision for carrying a 7.62 mm machine gun with a tripod and a short range anti-tank weapon.

AIFV-B-CP Command Post
This vehicle is similar to the Dutch AIFV command post with an M113A1 type of cupola in place of a weapon station on the right. A pintle-mounted 12·7 mm M2 HB machine gun is affixed to this cupola. Special communication equip-ment, map boards and other equipment for operating a mobile command post are provided and a single side awning is included. This verson has a crew of seven.

Status: Production. In service with the Belgian Army.

Manufacturer: BMF, Parc Industriel, 6798 Aubange, Belgium.

BDX Armoured Personnel Carrier

Development
In 1976 the Engineering Division of Beherman Demoen negotiated successfully with the Irish company of Tech-

nology Investments Limited for a licence to produce an improved version of the Timoney (4 × 4) armoured personnel carrier.

The first production order for the BDX was awarded by the Belgian Government in 1977 and called for the delivery of 43 vehicles to the Belgian Air Force for airfield protection duties and 80 vehicles to the Belgian Gendarmerie. The vehicles for the Air Force are armed with a ring-mounted 7.62 mm light machine gun. The Gendarmerie order consisted of 41 APCs without a turret, 26 vehicles with a dozer blade for clearing road obstacles and 13 vehicles fitted with an 81 mm mortar in the rear of the hull. First production vehicles were completed late in 1978 and production was completed for the Belgian Government in February 1981.

BDX has delivered five vehicles to Argentina and the vehicle has also been demonstrated to a number of other countries including Indonesia and Malaysia. Further development of the BDX armoured personnel carrier by Vickers Defence Systems of the United Kingdom has resulted in the Valkyr which is described later under the United Kingdom.

Description

The hull of the BDX is made of all-welded steel which varies in thickness from 9.5 to 12.7 mm and provides complete protection against 5.56 and 7.62 mm armour-piercing projectiles fired at point-blank range and splinters from 105 mm artillery projectiles exploding on the ground ten metres from the vehicle. The BDX will withstand the blast from a 9 kg mine exploding ten metres from the vehicle.

The driver sits at the front of the hull in a central position and has three windscreens, one in front and one on either side, made of multiplex glass 81 mm thick which provides the same degree of protection as the rest of the hull. The large front windscreen has a wiper and can be hinged forward for improved ventilation in a non-combat area.

The crew enters and leaves the BDX by three doors, one in each side of the hull and one at the rear. All the doors open through a full 180 degrees and can be locked half open if required. Ball mounts with vision blocks are provided in each side of the hull to the rear of the side entrance door and in the rear door.

The ten infantrymen are seated on individual seats with waist seatbelts. The interior of the hull is padded to reduce both noise and the internal temperature of the vehicle.

The engine is mounted to the immediate rear of the driver and is coupled to an automatic transmission which in turn provides power to the transfer box at the back of the vehicle. This transmits power to the front and rear axles by a propeller shaft. Both front and rear axles are equipped with a self-locking differential of the 'no-spin' type. The air-inlet and air-outlet louvres are in the roof over the driver's position with the air-outlet louvres located either side of the engine compartment in the roof. Protection against Molotov cocktails can be fitted if required. The exhaust pipes run along the outside of the hull.

The machine gun turret is fitted on the roof of the BDX to the rear of the engine compartment and a further circular hatch cover is provided in the roof at the rear. The vehicle, when fitted with the 81 mm mortar, has two rectangular hatches in the roof that open either side of the hull.

The BDX is fully amphibious and propelled in the water by its wheels. Optionally two water-jets can be fitted to increase its water speed.

Optional equipment includes an air-conditioning system, front-mounted dozer blade for clearing obstacles, heater, NBC system and hull-mounted smoke dischargers.

Variants

In addition to being used as an armoured personnel carrier the BDX can be used for a wide range of other roles such as an ambulance, command vehicle and reconnaissance vehicle. The BDX can be fitted with a turret-mounted 20 mm cannon, turret-mounted 90 mm Cockerill gun, Vickers turret with single or twin 7.62 mm machine guns, Euromissile MCT turret with two MILAN ATGWs in ready to launch position, SNIA BPD FIROS 6 48-round 51 mm multiple rocket system, turret with 81 mm breech-loaded mortar and a coaxial 7.62 mm machine gun or an 81 mm mortar mounted in the hull firing forwards.

Late in 1980 the company completed testing of a BDX APC powered by a General Motors Detroit Diesel model 4V-53T which develops 180 hp at 2800 rpm.

User trials and service reports indicated that certain areas of the vehicle could incorporate new components and methods of construction which would increase the service life

BDX APC used by Belgian Air Force for airfield defence armed with 7.62 mm machine gun and three smoke dischargers either side of hull (C R Zwart)

BDX APC fitted with Vickers turret (but not armed with twin 7.62 mm GPMGs) and smoke dischargers

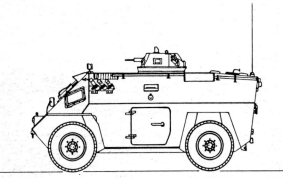

BDX (4 × 4) APC fitted with Vickers turret with twin 7.62 mm machine guns

of the BDX and improve the ride and accessibility for the crew.

A design study has been completed in which the front has been modified to give the driver more room, a more streamlined ballistic shape to the front of the vehicle, a strengthened

suspension system to take a wide variety of weapons and turrets and a redesigned high efficiency air-conditioning system and various other detailed improvements. The new design of the APC, incorporating all the improvements, was named Valkyr. This has been developed and produced by Vickers Defence Systems of the United Kingdom in association with Beherman-Demoen Engineering Division. The higher combat weight of the new vehicle and the concept of the hull and the armour provide considerable space and payload for carrying weapons, stores or troops. For a complete description and specifications refer to the entry under the United Kingdom.

Status: Production complete. In service with Argentina, Belgian Air Force and Gendarmerie.

Note: There is a separate entry for the Timoney armoured personnel carrier.

Manufacturer: Beherman Demoen Engineering (BDX), Motstraat 54, B-2800 Mechelen, Belgium.

SPECIFICATIONS	
CREW	2 + 10
CONFIGURATION	4 × 4
COMBAT WEIGHT	10 700 kg
UNLOADED WEIGHT	9750 kg
POWER-TO-WEIGHT	
RATIO	16.82 bhp/tonne
LENGTH OVERALL	5.05 m
WIDTH	2.5 m
HEIGHT	
overall with twin	
7.62 mm MG turret	2.84 m
to hull top	2.06 m
GROUND CLEARANCE	0.4 m
TRACK	1.93 m
WHEELBASE	3.003 m
MAX ROAD SPEED	
forwards	100 km/h
reverse	18 km/h
FUEL CAPACITY	248 litres
MAX ROAD RANGE	500-900 km
FORDING	amphibious
GRADIENT	60%
SIDE SLOPE	40%
VERTICAL OBSTACLE	0.4 m
TURNING RADIUS	less than 7 m
ENGINE	Chrysler V-8 water-cooled petrol developing 180 bhp at 4000 rpm*
TRANSMISSION	GM Allison AT540 automatic with 4 forward and 1 reverse gears
TRANSFER CASE	2-speed
STEERING	hydraulically-assisted
CLUTCH	hydraulic, torque converter
SUSPENSION	independent wishbone with helical springs and telescopic dampers
TYRES	12.00 × 20
BRAKES	disc (dual circuit)
ELECTRICAL SYSTEM	24 V
BATTERIES	4 × 12 V
ARMAMENT	see text
ARMOUR	
Hull front	12.7 mm
Hull sides	12.7 mm
Hull top	9.5 mm
Hull floor	9.5 mm
Hull rear	12.7 mm

* Diesel engine available if required

Cobra Armoured Personnel Carrier

Development
The Cobra APC has been developed from 1977 as a private venture by the Ateliers de Constructions Électriques de Charleroi (ACEC) in co-operation with the Belgian Army. By 1981 three prototypes powered by a Cummins V-6 diesel developing 143 hp at 3300 rpm had been completed and evaluated by the Belgian Army.

A decision was then taken to build a further prototype with a turbo-charged Cummins diesel developing 190 hp for improved performance and amphibious characteristics. Testing of the fourth prototype was undertaken by the Belgian Army in 1984.

An interesting feature of the Cobra is the electric transmission which enables the conventional mechanical transmission to be dispensed with. Power from the Cummins diesel engine is converted by a compact unit mounted on the engine. The power is then transmitted by cables to the electric motors which drive the sprockets. ACEC also developed the electric transmission of the French Crotale low altitude surface-to-air missile system used by a number of countries.

Description
The all-welded hull of the Cobra provides complete all-round protection from small arms fire, shell splinters and armour-piercing projectiles.

The driver sits at the front of the vehicle on the left, with the gunner/vehicle commander on the right and the engine between them. Both have a bullet-proof vision block to their front, another one to their side and a single-piece hatch cover opening to the outside above their position. The gunner/commander has a bow-mounted flexible 7.62 mm MAG machine gun mounted in the front plate of the vehicle.

The turret is mounted in the centre of the roof to the rear of the engine and is armed with a 12.7 mm (0.50) M2 HB machine gun. The weapon is mounted externally and fired electrically from within the turret. Turret traverse and weapon elevation are controlled by electric motors. Mounted either side of the turret are three smoke-grenade launchers.

Third Cobra prototype undergoing trials in Belgium

Fourth Cobra APC prototype

The turret has a periscopic sight in its forward part, a vision block in either side and a single-piece hatch cover opening to the rear. Other turrets can also be fitted such as the one-man Oerlikon-Bührle GAD-AOA armed with a 20 mm cannon.

The troop compartment is at the rear of the vehicle and the ten infantrymen enter and leave by a large door in the hull rear hinged on the right and with a single vision block. The ten infantrymen sit five each side on bench seats that run down either side of the hull. One of the infantrymen would normally man the 12.7 mm machine gun. In the roof of the troop compartment is a single-piece hatch that opens to the rear.

Power from the Cummins diesel engine is converted by a flywheel-mounted generator fixed on the engine. The power is then transmitted by cables to the electric motors which drive the sprockets at the rear of the vehicle.

The suspension either side consists of five rubber-tyred road wheels, each supported by a helical spring, with the idler at the front and drive sprocket at the rear. There are four track return rollers and the first and last road wheel stations have a hydraulic shock absorber. The noiseless rubber tracks have steel links and rubber road pads.

The Cobra is fully amphibious without preparation, and propelled by electrically-driven hydrojets mounted at the rear of the hull on each side of the door. By pushing the amphibious mode selector switch, the trim vane on the front of the hull is raised automatically, bilge pumps are switched on and the hydrojets are activated.

Optional equipment includes an NBC system, night vision equipment and air-conditioning system.

Variants

The manufacturer has proposed that the basic Cobra could be converted for a number of other roles including fire support vehicle, reconnaissance vehicle, command post, mortar carrier, ambulance and engineer vehicle.

SPECIFICATIONS					
CREW	2 + 10	MAX SPEED		ELECTRICAL SYSTEM	24 V
COMBAT WEIGHT	8500 kg	road	75 km/h	BATTERIES	2 × 12 V
UNLOADED WEIGHT	6700 kg	water (hydrojet)	10 km/h	ARMAMENT	
POWER-TO-WEIGHT		FUEL CAPACITY	309 litres	main	1 × 12.7 mm MG
RATIO	22.35 hp/tonne	MAX ROAD RANGE	600 km	bow	1 × 7.62 mm MG
GROUND PRESSURE	0.49 kg/cm²	FORDING	amphibious	SMOKE-LAYING	
LENGTH OVERALL	4.52 m	GRADIENT	60%	EQUIPMENT	2 × 3 smoke
WIDTH		SIDE SLOPE	45%		dischargers
overall	2.75 m	VERTICAL OBSTACLE	0.7 m		
over tracks	2.72 m	TRENCH	1.6 m	FIRE CONTROL SYSTEM	
HEIGHT		TURNING RADIUS	pivot	Turret power contol	manual/electric
overall	2.4 m	ENGINE	Cummins VT 190	Turret traverse	360°
to hull top	1.76 m		super-charged, water-cooled		
GROUND CLEARANCE	0.42 m		diesel developing 190 hp at		
TRACK WIDTH	425 mm		3300 rpm		
LENGTH OF TRACK		TRANSMISSION	ACEC electrical		
ON GROUND	2.65 m	SUSPENSION	helical springs with		
			shock absorbers		

Status: Four prototypes completed. Not yet in production or service.

Manufacturer: Ateliers de Constructions Électriques de Charleroi (ACEC), Division MCG, Dok Noord, 7, B-9000 Ghent, Belgium.

Moto Pecas Charrua XMP-1 Armoured Personnel Carrier

The Brazilian Army still has about 30 American-supplied M59 APCs in service and Moto Pecas has rebuilt at least one of these with a new armoured hull front, new engine and transmission, refurbished tracks and a new radio. Following tests the Brazilian Army may decide to rebuild its remaining M59s to this new configuration. Moto Pecas has already started to rebuild the Brazilian Army's fleet of 600–700 M113s with a diesel engine.

In 1984 the company built the prototype of a new full tracked APC called the Charrua XMP-1. This has a hull of all-welded steel construction that provides protection against small arms fire and shell splinters. The overall layout of the vehicle is very similar to the M59's with the driver sitting at the front of the hull on the left and the commander/machine gunner on the right. The driver has a single-piece circular hatch cover that opens to the rear and four periscopes, three to the front and one to his left. The machine gun cupola is almost identical to that installed on the M59A1 APC and has a single-piece hatch cover that opens to the rear, vision blocks for all-round observation.

The Saab-Scania DSI 11 six-cylinder diesel, made in Brazil, develops 400 hp and gives the XMP-1 a maximum road speed of 70 km/h and is coupled to an American CD-500 series automatic transmission. The engine compartment is to the rear of the commander and driver. The air-inlet and air-outlet louvres are in the roof. The troop compartment is at the rear and above it are two rectangular roof hatches.

The suspension, wheels and tracks are based on those of the M41 light tank used in large numbers by the Brazilian Army. The suspension either side consists of five dual rubber-tyred road wheels, drive sprocket at the front, idler at the rear and track return rollers.

The XMP-1 is fully amphibious, being propelled in the water at a maximum speed of 6 km/h by two water jets mounted in the hull rear, one either side. Before entering the water the bilge pumps are switched on and the two-part trim vane erected at the front of the vehicle. The XMP-1 has a combat weight of 20 000 kg and can carry 12 fully-equipped troops in addition to its crew of two. Variants under consideration include a command post, mortar carrier and bridgelayer.

Status: Trials.

Manufacturer: Moto Pecas SA, Sorocaba, São Paulo State, Brazil.

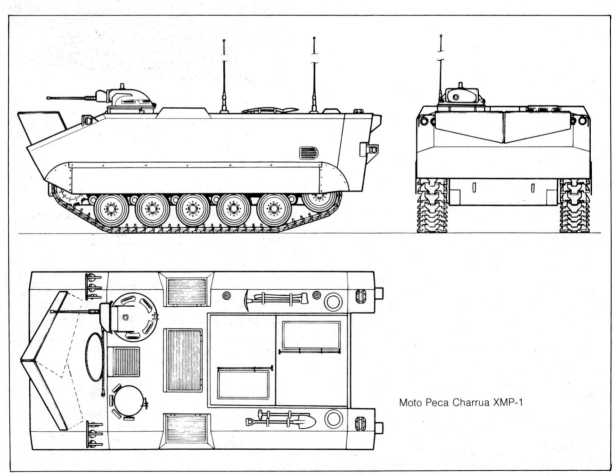

Moto Peca Charrua XMP-1

EE-11 Urutu Armoured Personnel Carrier

Development

The EE-11 Urutu armoured personnel carrier was designed by ENGESA from January 1970 with the first prototype being completed in July the same year. After trials a production order was placed for the EE-11 Urutu by the Brazilian Army which calls the vehicle the Carro de Transporte Sobre Rodas Anfíbio, or CTRA for short, and production began at a new factory at São Jose dos Campos in 1974. The EE-11 shares many common components with the ENGESA EE-9 armoured car which was developed from July 1970 and is also in service with the Brazilian and other armies. By early 1984 total production of the Urutu armoured personnel carrier had reached just over 1500 vehicles.

Description

The hull is of all-welded construction and consists of an outer layer of hard steel and an inner layer of softer steel that are roll-bonded and heat treated to give the maximum ballistic protection. The armour gives complete protection against small arms fire at point-blank range.

The driver sits at the front of the hull on the left side and is provided with a single-piece hatch cover, with three periscopes fitted in the glacis plate forward of the hatch. If required a windscreen can be erected over the driver's position when he is driving with his head out.

The engine compartment is at the front of the vehicle on the right side. The Detroit Diesel 6V-53N engine is coupled to an Allison MT-643 automatic transmission.

The air inlet louvres are on the hull top to the right of the driver while the exhaust outlets are on the right side of the hull.

The troop compartment is at the rear of the hull and bench seats are provided down each side of the vehicle with an additional bench seat behind the driver's seat across the troop compartment.

There are three doors in the hull, one on either side immediately behind the front axle and one at the back which is hinged on the left side. The rear door is automatically operated by the driver.

Two arrangements of firing ports and vision blocks are possible: five ball mount firing ports, two in each side of the hull and one in the rear door, and two glass bullet- and splinter-proof vision blocks in each side door, or eleven firing ports, five on each side of the hull and one in the rear door, and seven bullet- and splinter-proof vision blocks, one in the left door, one in the right door, two in each side of the hull and one in the rear door. Four roof hatches over the troop compartment open towards the outside of the vehicle.

The main armament station is behind the driver, slightly offset to the left of the vehicle's centre line. The basic model EE-11 Urutu APC, is armed with a ring-mounted 12.7 mm (0.50) M2 HB machine gun, but the vehicle can be fitted with many other types of armament installation including a ring-mounted 7.62 mm machine gun, Swedish Hägglunds 20 mm turret, turret-mounted 60 mm Brandt mortar, turret as fitted to the British CVR(T) Scorpion, French ESD TA 20 twin 20 mm anti-aircraft gun system and ENGESA ET-90 turret armed with ENGESA EC-90 mm gun. ENGESA has developed two new turrets that can be fitted to the EE-11 Urutu armoured personnel carrier or the EE-3 Jararaca scout car. Brief details of these are:

ENGESA ET-MD one-man turret armed with a 7.62 mm

ENGESA EE-11 Urutu of Brazilian Marines with snorkels retracted along either side of hull and armed with single 12.7 mm M2 HB machine gun (Ronaldo S Olive)

ENGESA EE-11 Urutu AFSV fitted with ENGESA ET-90 turret armed with ENGESA EC-90 90 mm gun and coaxial 7.62 mm machine gun with trim vane erected

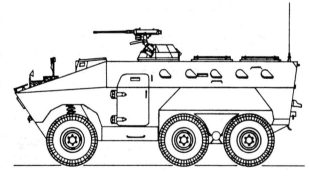

Late production ENGESA EE-11 Urutu APC with 12.7 mm (0.50) M2 HB machine gun

machine gun and a 12.7 mm M2 HB machine gun, both internally-operated

ENGESA ET-20 one-man turret armed with a 20 mm Oerlikon cannon and a 7.62 mm machine gun

The front suspension is independent with helical springs and double-action hydraulic shock absorbers. For amphibious operations, the front and rear axles can be pressurised.

The rear suspension consists of semi-elliptical springs and double-action telescopic shock absorbers. The articulated rear axle is the ENGESA 'Boomerang' type with walking beams and a differential locking system. The 'Boomerang' axles allow the wheels to travel 0.9 metre upwards and downwards and ensure that all wheels are in constant contact with the ground. All tyres are the run-flat type with automatic inflation system. Disc brakes are provided for all wheels. The electrical system has a double 24-volt system, a battery set is used for vehicle operations while a second set is just for engine start to avoid lack of power after long still radio operations. The EE-11 Urutu has been developed for the Brazilian Marines which required a vehicle capable of operating in heavy surf. This vehicle is propelled in the water by two propellers with kort-nozzles and is steered by two rudders at the rear of the hull which are connected to the steering wheel. Before entering the water, a trim vane is erected pneumatically at the front of the hull by the driver.

It has a maximum water speed of 8 km/h and in addition to the electric bilge pumps a hand-operated emergency bilge pump is provided.

Optional equipment includes night vision equipment, various radio installations, winch with a capacity of 6000 kg and a Mercedes-Benz OM-352A (190 hp-SAE) engine with an automatic transmission Allison AT-643 in place of the standard Detroit Diesel 6V-53Ndiesel developing 212 hp. The EE-11 Urutu can be fitted with an NBC system.

Variants

ENGESA has so far produced four distinct models of the EE-11 Urutu, which can be summarised as follows:

Model	I	II	III	IV
ENGINE	Mercedes-Benz 174 hp	Mercedes-Benz 190 hp	General Motors 212 hp	Mercedes-Benz 190 hp
TRANSMISSION	manual	automatic	automatic	automatic
TYRE PRESSURE REGULATION SYSTEM	no	yes	yes	yes

81 mm Mortar Carrier

Mounted in the hull rear is an 81 mm mortar firing through the roof of the vehicle. A 7.62 mm machine gun is fitted for local protection.

Ambulance

This model is unarmed and has a higher roof and can carry between six and eight walking wounded, or a smaller number of stretcher cases. Standard equipment includes an air-conditioning system, breathing equipment and a refrigerator for storing medicines.

Cargo

When being used for cargo the EE-11 can carry 2000 kg.

AFSV

The ENGESA EE-11 Urutu AFSV is an amphibious Armoured Fire Support Vehicle fitted with the ENGESA ET-90 turret armed with the ENGESA EC-90 90 mm gun. This model has a crew of seven: driver, commander, gunner and four infantrymen who are seated at the very rear of the hull. Thirty-six rounds of 90 mm ammunition are carried, 12

ENGESA EE-11 Urutu armoured personnel carrier fitted with ET-MD one-man turret armed with 7.62 mm and 12.7 mm machine guns

Recovery model of ENGESA EE-11 Urutu APC with hydraulic crane in use

rounds ready use in the turret and 24 rounds in the hull. The turret can be fitted with a power traverse system and a gunner's sight with an integral laser rangefinder.

Command Vehicle

Basic vehicle fitted with a special radio set and all the modern requirements for a command post.

Recovery

This model has different roof hatches to permit personnel to work standing upright and is fitted with a front-mounted winch, hydraulic crane, oxy-acetylene welding machine, portable generator, electric welding transformer, electric grinder, complete range of tools and specialised equipment and a tent.

ENGESA EE-11 Urutu riot control vehicle fitted with one-man turret with mount for externally-mounted 7.62 mm machine gun

Riot Control

The ENGESA EE-11 Urutu in the riot control and internal security operation version has the same basic features as the EE-11 Urutu armoured personnel carrier and retains the same mobility and ballistic protection. Mounted at the front of the vehicle is a blade for clearing obstacles. Typical missions of this model would include riot control, internal security, escorting convoys, transport of troops and patrolling airports and other high-risk areas.

Status: In production. In service with the Brazilian Army and Marines, Bolivia, Chile, Colombia, Gabon (including version with 20 mm Hägglund and Söner turret), Iraq (including armoured repair vehicle), Libya, Tunisia (including version with turret-mounted 90 mm gun), United Arab Emirates, Uruguay (including version with 60 mm breech-loaded mortar) and other undisclosed countries.

Manufacturer: Engesa Engenheiros Especializados sa, Avenue Nacões Unidas, 22.833 (Santo Amaro), CEP 04795, PO Box 6637 (CEP 01000), São Paulo, SP, Brazil.

SPECIFICATIONS

CREW	14 (13 + 1)
CONFIGURATION	6 × 6
COMBAT WEIGHT	13 000 kg
UNLOADED WEIGHT	11 000 kg
POWER-TO-WEIGHT	
RATIO	16.5 hp/tonne
LENGTH	6.15 m
WIDTH	2.59 m
HEIGHT	
to top of MG mount	2.72 m
to hull top	2.09 m
GROUND CLEARANCE	0.375 m
TRACK	2.1 m
WHEELBASE	3.05 m
ANGLE OF APPROACH/	
DEPARTURE	60°/60°
MAX ROAD SPEED	90 km/h
MAX WATER SPEED	8 km/h
FUEL CAPACITY	380 litres
MAX RANGE	
road	850 km
water	60 km
FORDING	amphibious
GRADIENT	60%
SIDE SLOPE	30%
VERTICAL OBSTACLE	0.6 m
TURNING RADIUS	7.7 m
ENGINE	Detroit Diesel 6V-53N 6-cylinder water-cooled diesel developing 212 hp at 2800 rpm
TRANSMISSION	Detroit Diesel Allison MT 643 automatic with 5 forward and 1 reverse gears (or Clark manual with 5 forward and 1 reverse gears)
TRANSFER BOX	2-speed
STEERING	ZF integral hydraulic
CLUTCH	single dry plate (manual gearbox only)
SUSPENSION	
front	independent with helical springs and double-action telescopic shock absorbers
rear	as front but with ENGESA 'Boomerang' with walking beams
TYRES	12.00 × 20
BRAKES	
main	air over hydraulic, dual circuit
parking	mechanical on transfer case output
ELECTRICAL SYSTEM	24 V
BATTERIES	4 × 12 V
ARMAMENT	depends on role of vehicle
SMOKE-LAYING EQUIPMENT	2 or 3 smoke dischargers either side of turret (optional)

CANADA

Armoured Vehicle General Purpose

Development

In June 1974 the Canadian Armed Forces issued a requirement for an Armoured Vehicle General Purpose (AVGP) for use in Canada. After an initial study of 14 possible vehicles three were selected for field and engineering tests, as a result of which the Swiss MOWAG Piranha (6 × 6) vehicle was chosen.

In February 1977 the Canadian Minister of Defence signed a contract worth $171 million with the Diesel Division of General Motors Canada Limited for the supply of 350 vehicles manufactured under licence from MOWAG. The first was handed over in January 1979. The original order for 350 vehicles was subsequently increased to 441 units owing to lower production costs, and early in 1981 was again extended by 35 units bringing the total up to 476 units. A further extension of 15 units brought the total order to 491 vehicles. Delivery of this contract was completed by September 1982.

The Canadian vehicles are used by both regular and militia units; have heaters for the engine and crew compartment and are fitted with cold-starting aids. All vehicles

Grizzly Wheeled Armoured Personnel Carrier (WAPC)

The Grizzly APC, of which 261 were originally ordered, is the basic vehicle fitted with a Cadillac Gage one-metre turret armed with a 12.7 mm machine gun and a 7.62 mm machine gun, with four smoke dischargers mounted on either side of the turret. The weapons have an elevation of +55 degrees and a depression of −8 degrees, turret traverse being a full 360 degrees. A total of ten boxes of 12.7 mm and 18 boxes of 7.62 mm machine gun ammunition are carried. The Grizzly WAPC has a crew of three and carries eight fully-equipped infantrymen. The vehicle has firing ports and vision blocks in the hull sides and rear.

Husky Wheeled Maintenance and Recovery Vehicle (WMRV)

Twenty-six of these were originally ordered for field repair and recovery work. The Husky has a crew of three and is fitted with an HIAB 650 crane with a capacity of 1750 kg.

LAV Programme

In September 1981 Diesel Division, General Motors Canada was awarded a $3.1 million contract by the United States Marine Corps for the supply of four 8 × 8 models of the Piranha vehicle, and supporting services, for use in competitive evaluation in the United States Marines Light Armored Vehicle (LAV) programme.

By October 1981 the company had supplied two Light Assault Vehicles fitted with a two-man Arrowpointe turret armed with a 25 mm Hughes Chain Gun, 7.62 mm M240 coaxial machine gun and eight smoke grenade dischargers, and one Assault Gun Vehicle fitted with an Arrowpointe two-man turret armed with a 90 mm Cockerill Mark III gun, 7.62 mm M240 coaxial machine gun and eight smoke dischargers. The second Assault Gun Vehicle was delivered early in 1982.

In September 1982 it was announced that the Diesel Division, General Motors of Canada, had won the LAV competition. The original five-year contract was to have been for 969 LAVs, 680 for the US Army and 289 for the Marine Corps with a total value of $477.8 million, with an option for a further 598 vehicles. The first buy, with fiscal year 1982

Wheeled Armoured Personnel Carrier Grizzly with Cadillac Gage 1-metre turret armed with 12.7 mm and 7.62 mm machine gun (Canadian Armed Forces)

Wheeled Fire Support Vehicle Cougar which has same turret as British Alvis Scorpion CVR(T) (Canadian Armed Forces)

have an AN/VVS-501 passive night driving periscope for the driver. The Canadians have three versions of the Piranha:

Cougar 76 mm Gun Wheeled Fire Support Vehicle (WFSV)

The Cougar, of which 189 were originally ordered, is the basic vehicle fitted with the turret mounted on the British CVR (T) Scorpion and the Australian M113A1 Fire Support Vehicle. The turret is armed with a 76 mm L23A1 gun with a 7.62 mm machine gun mounted coaxially with the main armament and four smoke dischargers mounted on either side of the turret. The weapons have an elevation of +34 degrees and depression of −10 degrees, with 360-degree powered turret traverse. Ten rounds of 76 mm and 220 rounds of 7.62 mm machine gun ammunition are carried in the turret with a further 30 rounds of 76 mm and 15 boxes of 7.62 mm ammunition in reserve in the hull. The Cougar has a crew of three: commander, gunner and driver. It carries an AN-GVS-5 laser rangefinder.

LAV-25 fitted with Arrowpointe two-man turret and armed with Hughes Helicopters 25 mm M242 Chain Gun, 7.62 mm M240 coaxial machine gun and two banks of smoke dischargers

LAV logistics vehicle with roof hatches open

Logistics Vehicle

This has a higher roof with twin hatches for the rapid loading and unloading of cargo, crew of three consisting of commander, driver and third crew member, and a crane for loading and unloading cargo at the left hull rear. Armament consists of a pintle mount with a 7.62 mm or 12.7 mm machine gun and two four-barrelled M257 smoke grenade launchers.

Mortar Carrier

This has a crew of five consisting of commander, driver and three mortar men and can be fitted with an 81 mm mortar (90 rounds carried) or a 107 mm mortar (80 rounds carried). The mortar is mounted in the centre of the vehicle and fires through the three-part roof hatch. It is also armed with a pintle-mounted 7.62 mm or 12.7 mm machine gun and two four-barrelled M257 smoke grenade launchers.

Recovery

This has a crew of five consisting of commander, driver, rigger and two fitters and is armed with a 7.62 mm or 12.7 mm pintle-mounted machine gun and two M257 four-barrelled smoke grenade launchers. Equipment fitted includes a fuel transfer sub-system, portable auxiliary power unit, crane with a capacty of 1814 kg and a rear-mounted winch with a capacity of 13 608 kg. Four stabilisers are fitted to give a more stable platform when the crane is being used.

Anti-tank

This has an Emerson twin TOW launcher mounted on top of the hull above the third wheel station carrying two ready-to-launch missiles and a further ten missiles in the hull. Secondary armament consists of a 7.62 mm or 12.7 mm machine gun on a pintle and two four-barrelled M257 smoke dischargers. A ground mount for TOW is also carried as is a hand-held laser rangefinder. This model has a crew of four: driver, commander, gunner and loader.

Command and Control

This has a similar hull to the logistics vehicle and has extensive communications equipment installed.

LAV anti-tank vehicle with TOW launcher retracted

funding, was for 60 vehicles all of which were for the Marine Corps. The first of these was handed over in October 1983. The second year buy, with fiscal year 1983 funding, was for 170 vehicles of which 134 were for the Marine corps and the remaining 36 for the Army. Early in 1984 the Army withdrew from the programme and the latter vehicles are to be taken over by the Marine Corps.

For fiscal year 1984 the Marine Corps is requesting 236 vehicles at a cost of $170.6 million with the anticipated 1985 request being for 292 vehicles at a cost of $274.8 million.

At the same time the original order was placed the company was awarded a $21.6 millon contract for the development and testing of five specialised versions: 81 mm mortar carrier, logistic support, command and control, maintenance/recovery and anti-tank fitted with an Emerson twin launcher as on the M901 Improved TOW Vehicle (ITV). All of these vehicles had been delivered by early 1984.

The quantities of LAV-25s to be procured by the US Marine Corps between fiscal year 1982 and fiscal year 1985 are as follows:

	FY82	FY83	FY84	FY85	Totals
LAV-25	60	170	123	69	422
LAV(R)	nil	nil	33	13	46
LAV(L)	nil	nil	80	14	94
LAV(M)	nil	nil	nil	50	50
LAV(C)	nil	nil	nil	50	50
LAV(AT)	nil	nil	nil	96	96
TOTAL	60	170	236	292	758

LAV-25(MC)

This is for the US Marine Corps as are all the following variants. The US Army designation for this vehicle was the M1047: this was very similar to the Marine Corps version but had increased ammunition stowage as it was not intended to carry troops.

The LAV-25(MC) has a Delco two-man turret armed with a 25 mm Hughes Helicopters Chain Gun, 7.62 mm M240 coaxial machine gun and a pintle mount for an M60 7.62 mm or M2 12.7 mm machine gun. Mounted either side of the turret is a bank of M257 smoke dischargers.

Assault Gun Vehicle

The future of the Assault Gun version of the LAV remains in doubt as the exact calibre of the armament has yet to be decided. All prototypes of the Assault Gun version were tested with the 90 mm Cockerill Mark III gun but other types of weapon are now under consideration including the IMI HVMS 60 mm weapon system and the ARES 75 mm automatic cannon.

Note: Additional details of the background of the LAV Programme are given under the United States.

SPECIFICATIONS		FIRE-CONTROL SYSTEM		STEERING	power-assisted on front 2
(Grizzly WAPC)		Turret power control	electric/manual		axles
CREW	3 + 6	by commander	no	SUSPENSION	
COMBAT WEIGHT	11 790 kg	by gunner	yes	front four wheels	independent coil springs and
LENGTH HULL	5.968 m	Gun elevation/depression	+55°/−8°		shock absorbers
WIDTH	2.489 m	Turret traverse	360°	rear four wheels	independent torsion bars and
HEIGHT OVERALL	2.629 m	Turret vision devices	1 × M28C sight		shock absorbers
HEIGHT HULL ROOF	1.854 m		8 vision blocks	BRAKES	
GROUND CLEARANCE	0.392 m	ARMOUR		main	8-wheel dual air hydraulic
MAX ROAD SPEED		Hull front upper	8 mm at 23°		drum brake
forward	99.76 km/h	Hull front lower	8 mm at 45°	parking	transmission brake and
reverse	16.89 km/h	Hull sides	10 mm at 55°		transfer case lock
MAX WATER SPEED	9.98 km/h	Turret	9.5 mm	TYRES	11.00 × 16 with Hutchinson
FUEL CAPACITY	204 litres				run-flat inserts
MAX ROAD RANGE	603 km	SPECIFICATIONS		ARMAMENT	
GRADIENT	60%	(LAV-25)		main	1 × 25 mm M242
SIDE SLOPE	30%	CREW	3 + 6		cannon
VERTICAL OBSTACLE	0.381–0.508 m	CONFIGURATION	8 × 8	coaxial	1 × 7.62 mm M240 MG
TRENCH	0.406 m	COMBAT WEIGHT	12 882 kg	anti-aircraft, optional	1 × 7.62 mm M60 or
TURNING RADIUS	6.55 m	UNLOADED WEIGHT	11 099 kg		1 × 12.7 mm M2 HB
ENGINE	GM Detroit Diesel 6V-53,	LENGTH	6.393 m		MG
	6-cylinder diesel developing	WIDTH	2.499 m	smoke dischargers	2 × 4 (M257)
	215 hp	HEIGHT OVERALL	2.692 m	AMMUNITION	
TRANSMISSION	Allison MT-650 automatic, 5	HEIGHT REDUCED	2.565 m	25 mm	210
	forward and 1 reverse gears	MAX ROAD SPEED	100 km/h	7.62 mm	420 [990]
STEERING	power-assisted, front wheels	MAX WATER SPEED	10.46 km/h	FIRE-CONTROL SYSTEM	
SUSPENSION	independent, all wheels	MAX RANGE	668 km	Turret power control	hydraulic/manual
TYRES	11.00 × 16 with Hutchinson	GRADIENT	70%	Elevation/depression	+60°/−10°
	run-flat inserts	VERTICAL OBSTACLE	0.5 m	Turret traverse	360°
		TRENCH	2.057 m	Gun stabiliser	
ARMAMENT		ENGINE	GM Detroit Diesel 6V-53T,	vertical	yes
main	1 × 12.7 mm M2 HB		6-cylinder diesel developing	horizontal	yes
	MG		275 hp at 2800 rpm	Periscopes	7 × M27
coaxial	1 × 7.62 mm C1 GPMG	TRANSMISSION	Allison MT-653 DR	Sights	2 × M36E1
smoke dischargers	2 × 4		automatic, 5 forward and 1		
AMMUNITION			reverse gears		
main	1000	TRANSFER CASE	Rockwell AG-VST (modified)		
coaxial	4400				

Status: Production of the 6 × 6 model has been completed for the Canadian Armed Forces. Production of the 8 × 8 model for the US Marines began in 1983 with first production vehicles completed in October 1983.

Manufacturer: Diesel Division, General Motors Canada Limited, PO Box 5160, London, Ontario N6A 4N5, Canada.

CHILE

Cardoen/MOWAG Armoured Personnel Carriers

Development/Description

Cardoen Industries manufactures 4 × 4 and 6 × 6 versions of the MOWAG Piranha multi-role amphibious vehicle. These are identical to their Canadian and Swiss counterparts except that the 6 × 6 version has a fuel capacity of 400 litres (compared to 250 litres of the original Swiss vehicle) which gives an operating range of some 1200 km compared to the Swiss vehicle's 600 km. It is believed that at least 50 vehicles have been delivered to the Chilean Army.

The 4 × 4 model can be fitted with a variety of light

Cardoen/MOWAG (4 × 4) APC without armament

armament installations while the 6 × 6 model is known to have been fitted with an Oerlikon-Bührle GAD-AOA 20 mm turret, Israeli TCM-20 twin 20 mm anti-aircraft turret, French Hispano-Suiza 90 mm turret and a Brazilian ENGESA ET-90 90 mm turret. In 1984 the company exhibited a Piranha (6 × 6) fitted with a Chilean-designed turret armed with a 90 mm gun. A half-track version of the 6 × 6 model has been developed to meet the requirements of the Chilean Army.

Status: In production. In service with the Chilean Army.

Manufacturer: Industrias Cardoen SA, Avda Providencia 2237–6°p, Santiago, Chile.

Cardoen VTP-1 Orsa Multi-purpose Armoured Vehicle

Development
The VTP-1 Orsa (Killer Whale) multi-purpose armoured vehicle, developed as a private venture by Industrias Cardoen SA, was announced in 1983. The prototype is different in appearance to that in the original drawings released in 1982.

Description
The all-welded steel hull of the Orsa provides complete protection from small arms fire up to 7.62 mm in calibre and shell splinters. The engine compartment is at the front of the hull with air-inlet louvres in the top to allow access to the engine for maintenance. The driver sits to the rear of the engine on the left with the commander to his right, each having a single-piece hatch cover in front of which are three fixed observation periscopes.

The open-topped troop compartment is at the rear of the hull and entry to it is via two doors in the hull rear, the lower part of each door folding down to form a step. The infantry sit on bench seats that run down either side of the hull. A number of 7.62 mm and/or 12.7 mm machine guns are mounted around the top of the troop compartment.

Variants
In addition to its primary role of troop transport, the manufacturer has proposed the vehicle for a number of other roles

Cardoen VTP-1 Orsa multi-purpose armoured vehicle

including ambulance, anti-aircraft, maintenance and anti-tank as well as towing 105 mm or 155 mm howitzers and carrying their crews and ammunition.

SPECIFICATIONS	
CREW	2 + 16
CONFIGURATION	6 × 6
COMBAT WEIGHT	18 000 kg
UNLOADED WEIGHT	13 000 kg
LENGTH	7.84 m
WIDTH	2.5 m
HEIGHT	2.5 m
MAX ROAD SPEED	120 km/h
FUEL CAPACITY	400 litres
MAX RANGE	1000 km
GRADIENT	60%
SIDE SLOPE	30%
ENGINE	General Motors 6V-53T 6-cylinder water-cooled diesel developing 260 hp at 2400 rpm
TRANSMISSION	Allison MT-653-DR automatic, 5 forward and 1 reverse gears
TYRES	14.00 × 20
BRAKES	
main	air
parking	mechanical
ARMOUR	6 mm – 12 mm

Status: Production.

Manufacturer: Industrias Cardoen SA, Avda Providencia 2237–6°p, Santiago, Chile.

Cardoen BMS-1 Alacran Multi-purpose Armoured Vehicle

Development
The BMS-1 Alacran half-track multi-purpose armoured vehicle has been designed as a private venture by Cardoen Industries with the first prototype completed early in 1983.

Description
The all-welded steel hull provides the crew with protection from small arms fire and shell splinters.

The driver sits at the front of the hull on the left side and has a single-piece hatch cover above his position opening to the left, forward of this are three periscopes.

The engine compartment is to the right of the driver with the air-inlet and air-outlet louvres in the roof and the exhaust pipe along the right side of the hull. Access panels are provided in the glacis plate for the engine. The prototype is powered by the Cummins V-555 diesel engine developing 225 hp at 3000 rpm. The Alacran can however be powered by the Detroit Diesel 6V-53T engine developing 300 hp at 2800 rpm which is already fitted to the Cardoen/MOWAG Piranha APC.

The commander sits to the rear of the driver and has a cupola that can be traversed through a full 360 degrees, on the forward part of this is a pintle mount for a 7.62 mm or 12.7 mm machine gun. The cupola has a single-piece hatch cover opening to the rear and observation periscopes. In addition there is a rearward opening door in the lower part of the hull between the front wheel and the rear half-track unit.

A wide range of armament installations can be fitted on the roof in the centre of the vehicle including ATGWs, 25 mm or 30 mm anti-aircraft cannon, 90 mm, 75 mm or 60 mm guns, and a 40-round 70 mm multiple rocket launcher has already

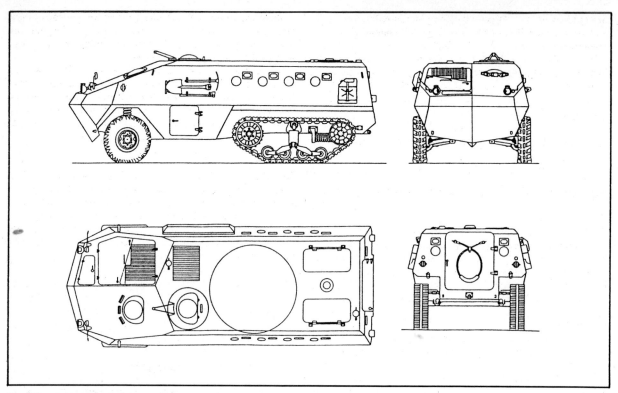

Provisional drawing of Cardoen BMS-1 Alacran half-track multi-purpose armoured vehicle released in August 1983 (not to 1/76th scale)

Cardoen BMS-1 Alacran multi-purpose armoured vehicle fitted with 70 mm multiple rocket system

SPECIFICATIONS	
CREW	2 + 12
CONFIGURATION	half-track
COMBAT WEIGHT	10 500 kg
UNLOADED WEIGHT	8000 kg
POWER-TO-WEIGHT	
RATIO	21.4 hp/tonne
LENGTH	6.37 m
WIDTH	2.38 m
HEIGHT WITHOUT	
ARMAMENT	2.03 m
TRACK	
front	2.175 m
rear	1.99 m
WHEELBASE	3.555 m
ANGLE OF APPROACH/	
DEPARTURE	40°/38°
MAX ROAD SPEED	70 km/h
FUEL CAPACITY	350 litres
MAX RANGE	900 km
FORDING	1.6 m
GRADIENT	70%
ENGINE	Cummins V-555
	turbo-charged diesel
	developing 225 hp at
	3000 rpm
TRANSMISSION	Allison MT-653 automatic, 5
	forward and 1 reverse gears
BRAKES	
main	air/hydraulic
parking	mechanical
TYRES	11.00 × 16 XL
	(run-flat)

been mounted for trials purposes. A mortar carrier is proposed.

The troop compartment is at the rear of the hull and entry to this is via a large door in the rear that opens to the right. Either side of this is a vision block with a circular firing port underneath.

In the left side of the hull are four vision blocks and four firing ports while in the right side of the hull are four vision blocks and three firing ports. Over the top of the troop compartment are two oblong roof hatches that open either side and between these is a single domed ventilator.

Power is transmitted to the front axle and rear half-tracks which are similar to those of American half-tracks of the

Second World War. When travelling on roads the front axle and drive can be disengaged. The front suspension consists of a spiral spring and hydraulic shock absorber.

The BMS-1 can also be used for a wide range of roles including ambulance, troop carrier, anti-aircraft, anti-tank, communications, recovery and workshop.

Status: Prototype.

Manufacturer: Industrias Cardoen SA, Avda Providencia 2237–6° p, Santiago, Chile.

Cardoen VTP-2 Armoured Personnel Carrier

Development
The VTP-2 was designed as a private venture by Industrias Cardoen SA, the first prototype being completed in 1981–82. This was tested by the Chilean Army in 1982 and unconfirmed reports have indicated that it has placed an order for an undisclosed number of vehicles. The VTP-2 is also known as the Escarabajo, or insect.

Description
The vehicle is available with a fully enclosed body (as shown in the photographs) or with an open truck type body. The all-welded steel body can be built with one of two thicknesses of armour, 6 mm which gives a body weight of 2500 kg or 8 mm which gives a body weight of 3300 kg. The vehicle is based on the chassis of the Mercedes-Benz Unimog cross-country vehicle so spare parts are available worldwide.

The engine compartment is at the front of the vehicle with an access hatch in the bonnet, the commander and driver are in the centre with the troop compartment at the rear.

The commander and driver have a bullet-proof windscreen to their front and either side of their position is a shallow door that opens to the rear. In the upper part of this is a bullet-proof window that can be covered by an armoured shutter hinged at the bottom when in a combat area.

The troop compartment is at the rear of the hull and entry to this is via a large door in the hull rear that opens to the right. Either side of this is a vision block with a firing port underneath and in either side of the hull are a further three firing ports and a similar number of vision blocks. The troops are seated on bench seats that run down either side of the hull with individual seats for the commander and driver. In the forward part of the roof is a circular mounting on which a 7.62 mm or 12.7 mm machine gun can be installed or a variety of other weapons systems such as an Oerlikon-Bührle 20 mm one-man turret. In the rear part of the hull roof are two oblong roof hatches that are hinged to the outside and can be locked in the vertical position.

The VTP-2 can also be delivered with two doors in the hull rear, each with a vision block and firing port. In this model the troops are seated on bench seats that run down the centre of the vehicle facing outwards and the commander and driver have single-piece hatch covers. The manufacturer has also proposed that a version could be built with doors in either side of the hull and periscopes in the roof for use by the commander and driver if the vehicle were fitted with an armoured shutter for the front windscreen. One model has also been built with the rear entrance consisting of two doors that open either side each having a lower part that folds down to form a step.

Standard equipment includes a forced ventilation system. The interior of the body is covered with a thermal and acoustic insulating material. Optional equipment includes a heater and air-conditioning system.

In 1984 the company announced that the VTP-2 was being offered with a Detroit Diesel 4-53 turbo-charged diesel developing 170 hp at 2800 rpm coupled to an Allison MT-653 automatic transmission. This would also have reinforced axles, hydraulic steering and an improved braking system.

Variants
According to the manufacturer the VTP-2 can be adopted for a wide range of roles including ambulance, 81 mm mortar vehicle, fire-control vehicle, internal security vehicle, anti-tank with HOT, MILAN or TOW ATGWs, anti-tank with 106 mm M40 recoilless rifle, command post with extensive communications equipment and anti-aircraft with TCM-20 twin 20 mm system.

VTP-2 armoured personnel carrier with single rear door open

VTP-2 APC with infantrymen using roof hatches

CREW	12 (2 + 10)	MAX RANGE	600 km	STEERING	hydraulic
CONFIGURATION	4 × 4	GRADIENT	70%	TYRES	12.50 × 20
WEIGHT		SIDE SLOPE	35%		(bullet-proof)
loaded, 8 mm armour	7800 kg	VERTICAL OBSTACLE	0.5 m	NUMBER OF TYRES	4
loaded, 6 mm armour	7800 kg	TURNING RADIUS	6.45 m	BRAKES	
empty, 8 mm armour	6600 kg	ENGINE	Mercedes-Benz OM-352	main	disc on all 4 wheels
empty, 6 mm armour	5800 kg		6-cylinder water-cooled	parking	mechanical on rear
LENGTH	5.37 m		diesel developing 120 hp at		2 wheels
WIDTH	2.32 m		2800 rpm	ELECTRICAL SYSTEM	24 V
HEIGHT	2.22 m	TRANSMISSION	manual, 4 forward and 1	BATTERIES	2 × 12 V, 110 Ah
GROUND CLEARANCE	0.44 m		reverse gears		
MAX ROAD SPEED	100 km/h	CLUTCH	single dry plate		
FUEL CAPACITY	150 litres	TRANSFER CASE	2-speed		

Status: Probably in production.

Manufacturer: Industrias Cardoen SA, Avda Providencia 2237–6°p, Santiago, Chile.

Makina Multi 163 Armoured Personnel Carrier

Development/Description

The Multi 163 has been designed by the Makina Company primarily for internal security operations and for patrolling airfields and other high risk areas. It is based on a modified commercial chassis and fitted with a fully armoured body. The commander and driver are seated at the front of the vehicle, each with a windscreen which can be covered by an upward opening hatch cover. The troop compartment is at the rear with doors, firing ports, two rectangular roof hatches and one circular roof hatch. The circular hatch is towards the front of the vehicle and can be fitted with a 7.62 mm machine gun or similar weapon.

Variants

Suggested variants include an ambulance, anti-aircraft vehicle, command post and an 81 mm or 105 mm mortar carrier.

Makina Multi 163 APC fitted with roof-mounted 7·62 mm machine gun, commander's and driver's hatches open

CREW	2 + 8
CONFIGURATION	4 × 2
WEIGHT	
loaded	5000 kg
empty	3300 kg
LENGTH	5.057 m
WIDTH	2.23 m
HEIGHT	2.1 m
WHEELBASE	3.327 m
GROUND CLEARANCE	0.325 m
FUEL CAPACITY	114 litres
RANGE	450 km
MAX ROAD SPEED	110 km/h
ENGINE	Chrysler 8-cylinder petrol developing 180 hp
TRANSMISSION	manual, 4 forward and 1 reverse gears
TRANSFER CASE	none
TYRES	9.50 × 16.50
ELECTRICAL SYSTEM	12 V

Status: Believed to be in production.

Manufacturer: Makina Company, Chile.

Model 531 Armoured Personnel Carrier

Development
The Model 531 APC was developed in the late 1960s and at various times has been called the K-63, M1967 and M1970. The official Chinese designation for this vehicle is the Type 63 but within the Chinese Army it is referred to as the Model 531. It has seen combat in Viet-Nam (used by both China and Viet-Nam), in Angola by Zaïrean forces and by Tanzania against Uganda in their 1978 October–November border war. In 1983 a quantity of these vehicles was delivered to Iraq by China. Each Chinese armoured division has one battalion of 85 Type 531 APCs, which are assigned to the transport company of the mechanised infantry regiment.

The vehicle has a crew of four which consists of the commander, gunner, loader and driver and can carry ten fully-equipped infantrymen. The Australian Army has tested one example of the Model 531 and reports have indicated that it has excellent cross-country mobility.

Description
The hull of the Model 531 is made of all-welded steel. The driver sits at the front of the hull on the left side and has a single-piece domed hatch cover that opens to the left, in front of which are two periscopes. The commander sits at the front of the hull on the right side and has a single-piece hatch cover that opens to the right with an integral periscope which can be traversed through 360 degrees. The engine is behind the commander with the air-inlet and air-outlet louvres in the roof and the exhaust outlet in the right side of the roof. The third crew member is seated behind the driver and has a single domed hatch cover that opens to the left, with an integral periscope which can be traversed through 360 degrees.

The gunner's position is to the rear of the vehicle in the roof. Mounted on the forward part of the gunner's hatch is a 12.7 mm Type 54 heavy machine gun (the Soviet DShKM weapon manufactured in China). The gunner also has a single-piece hatch cover that opens to the rear.

Model 531 APC with rear door open showing folded-up seat on door (Tank Magazine)

Type 70 19-barrel multiple rocket launcher (Tank Magazine)

Model 531 APC showing gap-crossing capabilities during trials in Australia (Paul Handel)

The infantrymen enter and leave the vehicle by a door in the rear of the hull which is hinged on the right side. A single firing port is provided in each side of the hull. The torsion bar suspension consists of four single rubber-tyred road wheels with the drive sprocket at the front and the idler at the rear. There are no track return rollers as the top of the track rests on the top of the road wheels.

The Model 531 is fully amphibious, being propelled in the water by its tracks. Before entering the water a trim board, which is stowed on the glacis plate when travelling, is erected at the front of the hull. As far as is known the Model 531 has no NBC system or night vision equipment, although the driver can have a TVN-2 night vision device.

Recent Chinese documents have also referred to the Model 531 as the Type YW531 with at least three sub-variants which may well be specialised command vehicles. Differences between these are given below:

Name	Radio set		Intercom set		Firing port		
	Model	Number	Model	Number	left	right	rear
YW531C	889	2	803	1	2	1	1
YW531D	889	1	803	1	1	1	1
YW531E	889	1	803	1	1	1	1
	892	1					

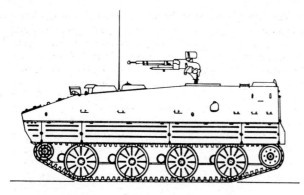

Model 531 APC armed with 12·7 mm machine gun

Variants

Ambulance: This has the Chinese designation of the YW750 and has a crew of two plus two doctors and can carry four stretcher or eight seated patients.

122 mm SPH: This is called the 122 mm Type 54-1 self-propelled howitzer by the Chinese and is a longer and slightly wider Model 531 fitted with a 122 mm howitzer in an open-topped troop compartment. Powered by a Model 6150 L 6-cylinder, 4-cycle, water-cooled diesel developing 260 hp at 2000 rpm.

Rocket launcher: This is called the 130 mm Type 70 19-barrel multiple rocket launcher and has the same engine as the 122 mm self-propelled howitzer.

Mortar: Believed developed to prototype stage.

Psychological warfare: Fitted with roof-mounted loudspeakers.

SPECIFICATIONS	
CREW	4 + 10
COMBAT WEIGHT	12 600 kg
POWER-TO-WEIGHT	
RATIO	29.39 hp/tonne
GROUND PRESSURE	0.57 kg/cm²
LENGTH	5.476 m
WIDTH OVERALL	2.978 m
HEIGHT	
overall	2.563 m
to hull top	1.887 m
GROUND CLEARANCE	0.433 m
TRACK	2.464 m
TRACK WIDTH	433 mm
LENGTH OF TRACK	
ON GROUND	3.095 m
MAX SPEED	
road	65 km/h
water	6 km/h
FUEL CAPACITY	450–480 litres
MAX ROAD RANGE	500 km
GRADIENT	60%
SIDE SLOPE	40%
VERTICAL OBSTACLE	0.6 m
TRENCH	2 m
ENGINE	BF8L 413F, 4-cycle turbocharged and inter-cooled V-8 diesel developing 320 hp at 2500 rpm
TRANSMISSION	manual, 5 forward and 1 reverse gears
SUSPENSION	torsion bar
ELECTRICAL SYSTEM	24 V
MAIN ARMAMENT	1 × 12.7 mm MG
elevation	0° to 90°
traverse	360°
AMMUNITION	1120 rounds

Status: Probably still in production. In service with Albania, China, Iraq, North Korea, Sudan, Tanzania, Viet-Nam and Zaïre.

Manufacturer: Chinese state arsenals.

Type 56 Armoured Personnel Carrier

Development/Description

In the early 1950s the Soviet Union supplied China with a quantity of BTR-152 (6 × 6) armoured personnel carriers. It is possible that production was subsequently undertaken in China under the designation Type 56. As far as is known the Type 56 has similar characteristics to the original Soviet vehicle but may well have detailed differences such as a different engine and transmission. There are no known variants of the Type 56 but it is quite probable that an anti-aircraft model is in service fitted with the Soviet twin 14.5 mm ZPU-2 system which is manufactured in China as the Type 58 anti-aircraft gun. It is also possible that late production Type 56s are fitted with an armoured roof over the troop compartment, similar to that of the Soviet BTR-152K. Command versions of the Type 56 may also exist.

Status: Production of the Type 56 is probably complete. It is known to be in service with China, Kampuchea, Tanzania and Viet-Nam and has probably been supplied to other countries that have received Chinese military assistance.

Manufacturer: Chinese state arsenals.

Type 55 Armoured Personnel Carrier

Development/Description

In the early 1950s the Soviet Union supplied China with a quantity of BTR-40 (4 × 4) armoured personnel carriers, it is possible that production was then undertaken in China under the designation Type 55. As far as it is known the Type 55 has similar characteristics to the original Soviet vehicle but may well have detailed differences such as a different engine. There are no known variants of the Type 55 but it is quite probable that an anti-aircraft model is in service fitted with the Soviet twin 14.5 mm ZPU-2 system which is manufactured in China as the Type 58 anti-aircraft gun.

Status: Production of the Type 55 is probably complete. It is known to be in service with China, Kampuchea, Tanzania and Viet-Nam and has probably been supplied to other countries that have received Chinese military assistance.

Manufacturer: Chinese state arsenals.

Type WZ 501 Infantry Fighting Vehicle

This is almost a direct copy of the Soviet BMP-1 mechanised infantry fighting vehicle, the only major differences being a slight reduction in weight and maximum road speed.

Main armament of the Type WZ 501 is a 73 mm smooth-bore gun with 40 rounds of ammunition and a 7.62 mm coaxial machine gun with 2000 rounds. The original Soviet vehicle has a Sagger wire-guided ATGW mounted above the 73 mm gun with an additional four missiles being carried internally for manual reloading. The Chinese WZ 501 carries four Red Arrow ATGWs which are assumed to be copies of the Sagger as China is known to have produced this for some years. In addition to seven 7.62 mm SMGs and two 7.62 mm LMGs, a new 40 mm man-portable rocket launcher is carried plus a man portable surface-to-air missile called Red Tassel, probably a copy of the Soviet SA-7 Grail. The WZ 501 is fully amphibious and is fitted with an NBC system and infra-red night vision equipment for the commander, driver and gunner.

Status: Not certain.

Manufacturer: Chinese state arsenals.

Type 77 Armoured Personnel Carrier

Development
The Type 77 armoured personnel carrier is very similar to the Soviet BTR-50PK armoured personnel carrier but has a much more powerful engine which gives an improved road and water speed as well as higher power-to-weight ratio. Many of the automotive components of the Type 77 armoured personnel carrier are also used in the Type 63 light amphibious tank.

Description
The hull of the Type 77 is of all-welded steel construction with the crew compartment at the very front, troop compartment in the centre and the engine compartment at the rear.

Type 77-2 armoured personnel carrier with side door open

Type 77-1 armoured personnel carrier from rear with loading ramps in position

The driver is seated at the front on the left side and has a single-piece hatch cover that opens to the right and three forward-facing periscopes. The commander sits in a projecting bay at the front on the right side and has three periscopes for forward observation and a single circular hatch cover that opens to the rear. At the commander's station is mounted the 12.7 mm heavy machine gun which is a copy of the Soviet DShKM weapon; no protection is provided for the commander while firing this weapon.

The troop compartment has hatches in the roof and a single forward-opening door in the right side. Three firing ports are provided, two in the left and one in the right side. The troop compartment is provided with a ventilating system and a white light searchlight is mounted in the roof at the front left which can be operated from within the vehicle.

The suspension is of the torsion bar type and consists of six rubber tyred road wheels with the idler at the front and drive sprocket at the rear. There are no track return rollers.

The Type 77 is fully amphibious, being propelled in the water by two water jets at the rear of the hull. The only preparation that is required is to erect the trim vane at the front of the hull and switch on the two electric bilge pumps. There is a manual bilge pump for emergency use.

Variants
In addition to being used as an armoured personnel carrier, the Type 77 can also be used as an ambulance, command post, fuel resupply vehicle and load carrier. The Type 77-1 has three loading ramps that can be positioned at the rear to enable an 85 mm Type 56 gun (with a crew of eight and 30 rounds of ammunition to be carried) or a 122 mm Type 54 howitzer (with a crew of eight and 20 rounds of ammunition) to be carried.

SPECIFICATIONS	
CREW	2 + 16
COMBAT WEIGHT	15 500 kg
POWER-TO-WEIGHT	
RATIO	25.8 hp/tonne
LENGTH	7.4 m
WIDTH	3.2 m
HEIGHT OVERALL	2.436 m
TRACK	2.8 m
TRACK WIDTH	400 mm
LENGTH OF TRACK	
ON GROUND	4.44 m
MAX ROAD SPEED	60 km/h
MAX WATER SPEED	11/12 km/h
FUEL CAPACITY	416 litres
MAX RANGE	
(road)	370 km
(water)	120 km
FORDING	amphibious
GRADIENT	60%
SIDE SLOPE	40%
VERTICAL OBSTACLE	0.87 m
TRENCH	2.9 m
ENGINE	Type 12150L-2A, 4-cycle, compression ignition, direct injection, water-cooled diesel developing 400 hp at 2000 rpm
TRANSMISSION	manual
STEERING	clutch and brake
SUSPENSION	torsion bar
ELECTRICAL SYSTEM	24 V
ARMAMENT	1 × 12.7 mm MG
AMMUNITION	500

Status: Production. In service with Chinese Army.

Manufacturer: Chinese State Arsenals.

OT-64C(1) APC

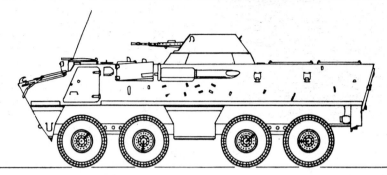

OT-64 Armoured Personnel Carrier

Development

The OT-64 (Obrneny Transporter) was jointly developed from 1959 by Czechoslovakia and Poland and is used by them in place of the similar Soviet BTR-60 (8 × 8) APC. There is a possibility that the vehicle has also been assembled in Poland. The vehicle, which uses many automotive components of the Tatra 813 series of 8 × 8 high-mobility trucks, entered service in 1964 and has since been widely exported outside the Warsaw Pact. The Polish designation for the vehicle is the Średni Kolowy Opancerzny Transporter.

Description (OT-64C (1))

The hull of the OT-64 is made of all-welded steel with the crew compartment at the very front, engine immediately behind and the troop compartment at the very rear.

The driver is seated at the front of the vehicle on the left side with the commander to his right, both with a single-piece rear-opening door beside them. The driver has a single-piece hatch cover that opens to the rear and three periscopes for vision to his front and sides. The commander has a single-piece hatch cover that opens forwards with a periscope in its forward part which can be traversed through 360 degrees. In the roof, between the driver's and commander's positions, is a searchlight which can be operated from inside the vehicle.

The engine is behind the commander and driver with the air inlet and air outlets on the top of the hull and the exhaust pipes on either side of the hull.

The turret is in the centre of the vehicle and is mounted on an eight-sided plinth to enable the weapon to have some degree of depression.

The troop compartment is at the rear of the vehicle and the troops enter and leave by two doors in the rear of the hull, each of which has a firing port. Over the top of the troop compartment are four roof hatches, each with a firing port, hinged on the outside. If required, the roof hatches can be locked vertical. There are two firing ports in each side of the troop compartment. The infantrymen are seated down each side of the vehicle on seats which can be folded up to allow the vehicle to be used for cargo.

Steering is powered on the front four wheels and all eight tyres are provided with a tyre pressure regulation system which allows the driver to adjust the tyre-pressure to suit the

OT-64C(1) SKOT-2A with single Sagger ATGW mounted either side of turret

OT-64C(1) with roof hatches open

OT-64C(2) which has same armament as OT-64C(1) but mounted in new turret

OT-64A with Sagger ATGWs mounted over top of personnel compartment

type of ground being crossed. The vehicle is fully amphibious, being propelled in the water by two propellers mounted at the rear of the hull. Before entering the water a trim vane is erected at the front of the vehicle; when travelling it is stowed on the glacis plate. Standard equipment on all vehicles

includes an over-pressure NBC system, winch mounted at the front of the hull and bilge pumps.

The one-man manually-operated turret is similar to those fitted to the Soviet BRDM-2 (4 × 4) reconnaissance vehicle and BTR-60PB (8 × 8) APC and is armed with a 14.5 mm KPVT machine gun with a 7.62 mm PKT machine gun mounted to the right of the main armament and the sight to the left. The weapons have a maximum elevation of +29 degrees, depression of −4 degrees and 360-degree turret traverse. Some models have been observed with a single Sagger ATGW mounted on each side of the turret with lateral armour protection.

Variants

OT-64A (SKOT)
This is the basic member of the series. Those used by Czechoslovakia are unarmed while those used by Poland are fitted with a pintle-mounted 7.62 mm machine gun. There are five hatches over the troop compartment: two open to the left and right of the vehicle, the centre one opens forwards and the last two open to the left and right. All of them can be locked vertical. Some OT-64As have been observed with two Sagger ATGWs mounted over the top of the troop compartment. A total of four Sagger ATGWs are carried.

OT-64B (SKOT-2)
This model has been used only by Poland and has a square plinth with a pintle-mounted 7.62 mm or 12.7 mm machine gun which has a shield which gives front and side protection to the gunner, but has an open top and is open at the rear. The OT-64B has three hatches over the troop compartment: the first one opens forwards and the other two open either side. This was probably a temporary expedient pending the delivery of turrets.

OT-64C(1) (SKOT-2A)
This is the model described in the detailed description earlier.

OT-64C(2) (SKOT-2AP)
This is used only by Poland and is similar to the OT-64C(1) except that it has a new turret with a curved top. It is armed with a 14.5 mm KPVT machine gun with a 7.62 mm PKT machine gun mounted to the right of the main armament and the sight to the left. The weapons have a depression of −4 degrees and an elevation of +89.5 degrees which allows them to be used against helicopters and aircraft. Some vehicles have been observed with a single Sagger ATGW mounted either side of the turret. This turret is also installed on the OT-62C tracked armoured personnel carrier.

OT-64 Command Vehicle
There are at least two command models of the OT-64 which are designated the R-2 and R-3. They have additional communications equipment and additional radio antennas.

OT-64 Recovery Vehicle
A recovery vehicle based on the OT-64 is known to be in service with Poland. This is armed with a 7.62 mm PKT machine gun and is provided with a light crane for changing components in the field. Its official designation is Armoured Repair and Maintenance Vehicle SKOT-WPT.

Model	OT-64A SKOT	OT-64C(1) SKOT-2A
CREW	2 + 18	2 + 15
CONFIGURATION	8 × 8	8 × 8
COMBAT WEIGHT	14 300 kg	14 500 kg
UNLOADED WEIGHT	12 300 kg	12 800 kg
POWER-TO-WEIGHT		
RATIO	12.58 hp/tonne	12.41 hp/tonne
LENGTH	7.44 m	7.44 m
WIDTH	2.55 m	2.55 m
HEIGHT		
to turret top	n/app	2.71 m
to hull top	2.06 m	2.06 m
FIRING HEIGHT	n/a	2.5 m
GROUND CLEARANCE	0.46 m	0.46 m
TRACK	1.86 m	1.86 m
WHEELBASE	1.3 m + 2.15 m + 1.3 m	1.3 m + 2.15 m + 1.3 m
ANGLE OF APPROACH/		
DEPARTURE	42°/43.5°	42°/43.5°
MAX SPEED		
road	94.4 km/h	94.4 km/h
water	9 km/h	9 km/h
FUEL CAPACITY	320 litres	320 litres
MAX ROAD RANGE	710 km	710 km
FUEL CONSUMPTION		
(road)	0.45 litre/km	0.45 litre/km
FORDING	amphibious	amphibious
GRADIENT	60%	60%
SIDE SLOPE	30%	30%
VERTICAL OBSTACLE	0.5 m	0.5 m
TRENCH	2 m	2 m
ENGINE		
model	Tatra 928-14	Tatra 928-18
type	V-8 air-cooled diesel developing 180 hp at 2000 rpm	
TRANSMISSION	semi-automatic dual-range 5-speed plus over-drive providing 20 forward and 4 reverse gears	
STEERING	power-assisted	
SUSPENSION	telescopic springs and hydraulic shock absorbers	
TYRES	13.00 × 18	13.00 × 18
ELECTRICAL SYSTEM	24 V	24 V
BATTERIES	4 × 12 V	4 × 12 V
ARMAMENT		
main	1 × 7.62 mm MG	1 × 14.5 mm MG
coaxial	n/app	1 × 7.62 mm MG
AMMUNITION		
main	1250	500
coaxial	n/app	2000
FIRE-CONTROL SYSTEM		
Turret power control	n/app	manual
Gun elevation/depression	+23.5°/−6°	+29°/−4°
Weapon traverse	90° (pintle)	360° (turret)
ARMOUR		
Hull	10 mm (max)	10 mm (max)
Turret	n/app	14 mm

Status: Probably still in production. In service with Czechoslovakia, Hungary, India, Iraq, Libya, Morocco, Poland, Sudan, Syria and Uganda.

Manufacturer: Czechoslovak state arsenals.

OT-62 Armoured Personnel Carrier

Development

The OT-62 is the Czechoslovak equivalent of the Soviet BTR-50PK APC and in appearance is almost identical to the BTR-50PU model 2 command vehicle, but the Soviet vehicles have a distinct chamfer between the top and side of their hulls. The main improvements over the Soviet vehicle are a more powerful engine which gives the vehicle a higher road and water speed, a fully-enclosed troop compartment with an NBC system, and, in the case of some members of the OT-62 family, fully-enclosed armament installations rather than a simple pintle-mounted machine gun.

The OT-62 (Obreny Transporter 62) entered service with

Czechoslovakia in 1964 and with Poland in 1966. The Polish Army calls the vehicle the TOPAS (Transporter Obrneny Pasovy). In both countries the vehicle is normally used by the tank divisions while the motorised rifle divisions use the OT-64 (8 × 8) armoured personnel carrier.

Description (OT-62A)

The hull of the OT-62 is all-welded with the crew compartment at the front and the engine compartment at the rear.

The commander is seated at the front of the vehicle in the left projecting bay and is provided with a cupola that can be traversed through 360 degrees by hand. Mounted in the forward part of his cupola is a periscope. His single-piece hatch cover opens forwards and can be locked vertical. The commander is also provided with three observation periscopes in the front part of the projecting bay.

The driver is seated to the right of the commander and is provided with a single-piece hatch cover in the front of the vehicle that opens upwards on the outside and has an integral vision block. The driver is provided with three periscopes below his hatch cover.

The right projecting bay is equipped with three observation periscopes but does not normally have a hatch cover. In the case of the OT-62B, the main armament installation is on the right projecting bay.

The troops enter and leave by the large door in either side of the vehicle which also has a circular observation/firing port. There is an additional observation/firing port in front of the side door in each side of the hull. Over the troop compartment are two large rectangular doors that open to the outside of the vehicle.

The engine is immediately behind the troop compartment with the cooling system on the left, the fuel and oil tanks on the right and the transmission at the rear. There are access panels in the top of the hull for maintenance.

The power train consists of the engine, master clutch, transmission, steering clutch, inner reduction gear, neutral steering clutch, final drive, water-jet propeller and mechanical water drainage pump drive. Power is transmitted through the transmission to the left and right inner reduction gears to the final drives which connect directly to the track drive sprockets.

The OT-62 is fitted with a fire-extinguishing system which automatically or manually extinguishes fires in the engine and transmission compartment. When activated the exting-

OT-62C which has same turret as OT-64C(2) 8 × 8 APC

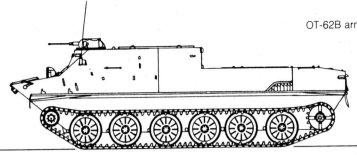

uisher is operated, engine stopped automatically, forced blowers are started and, if required, the second bottle of fire-extinguishing agent is also used.

The torsion bar suspension consists of six road wheels with the idler at the front and the drive sprocket at the rear. There are no track return rollers. The first and last road wheel stations are provided with a hydraulic shock absorber. Track tension can be adjusted from the driver's compartment.

The OT-62 is fully amphibious, being propelled in the water by two water jets at the rear of the hull. Before entering the water a trim vane is erected at the front of the hull and the bilge pumps for which the outlets are on the top of the hull at the rear are switched on. The vehicle is fitted with an over-pressure NBC system, consisting of an electrically-operated blower, two filter elements, control box, inlet port and hoses. It is on the right forward side of the troop compartment and in case of electrical failure can be hand operated. An infra-red driving light is mounted at the front of the vehicle on the right side.

Variants

OT-62A (or Model 1)
This was the first model to enter service and is unarmed. It is also known as the TOPAS. If required an M59A 82 mm recoilless gun can be carried and fired from the rear deck. Full

details of the M59A are given in the following entry for the Czechoslovak OT-810 half-track armoured personnel carrier.

OT-62B (or Model 2)
The OT-62B is used by the Czechoslovak Army and is fitted with a small turret on the right projecting bay. This manually-operated turret is identical to that fitted to the OT-65A (4 × 4) amphibious scout car and is armed with a 7.62 mm M59T machine gun with an elevation of +20 degrees, depression of −10 degrees, and turret traverse of 360 degrees. Mounted externally on the right side of the turret is an 82 mm T-21 Tarasnice recoilless gun, which can be aimed and fired from inside the turret but can be reloaded only from the outside. The T-21 fires a HEAT projectile weighing 2.13 kg with a muzzle velocity of 250 metres a second, which will penetrate 230 mm of armour. Maximum range is quoted as 2500 metres but its range against a moving target is 300 metres. When being fired when the vehicle is afloat, the water-jet propulsion system must be in operation to stop the vehicle from drifting backwards. A total of 1250 rounds of 7.62 mm and 12 rounds of 82 mm recoilless ammunition are carried. Mounted to the right of the T-21 recoilless gun is an infra-red search light. It is assumed that this moves in elevation with the armament. This model is also known as the TOPAS-2A.

OT-62B used for training by US Army clearly showing 82 mm T-21 Tarasnice recoilless gun mounted externally on turret (US Army)

OT-62C (or Model 3)

This is a Polish version and is officially called the TOPAS-2AP. Mounted in the centre of the hull is a manually-operated turret identical to that fitted to the OT-64C(2) (8 × 8) armoured personnel carrier. This is armed with a 14.5 mm KPVT machine gun with a 7.62 mm PKT machine gun mounted coaxially to the right. The weapons have an elevation of +89.5 degrees, depression of −4 degrees, and turret traverse of 360 degrees. The OT-62C is also used to carry two 82 mm mortar squads, each squad with a crew of four and an 82 mm mortar.

SPECIFICATIONS

Model	OT-62B	OT-62C
CREW	2 + 18	3 + 12
COMBAT WEIGHT	15 000 kg	16 390 kg
POWER-TO-WEIGHT RATIO	20 hp/tonne	18.3 hp/tonne
GROUND PRESSURE	0.53 kg/cm²	0.55 kg/cm²
LENGTH	7.08 m	7 m
WIDTH	3.14 m	3.225 m
HEIGHT (including turret)	2.23 m	2.725 m
GROUND CLEARANCE	0.37 m	0.425 m
TRACK	2.74 m	2.74 m
TRACK WIDTH	360 mm	360 mm
LENGTH OF TRACK ON GROUND	4.08 m	4.08 m
MAX SPEED		
road	58.4 km/h	60 km/h
water	10.8 km/h	10.8 km/h
FUEL CAPACITY	417 litres	520 litres
MAX ROAD RANGE	460 km	570 km
FUEL CONSUMPTION	0.9 litre/km	0.9 litre/km
GRADIENT	65%	65%
SIDE SLOPE	40%	40%
VERTICAL OBSTACLE	1.1 m	1.1 m
TRENCH	2.8 m	2.8 m
ENGINE	PV-6 6-cylinder super-charged water-cooled diesel developing 300 hp at 1800 rpm	
TRANSMISSION	manual with 5 forward and 1 reverse gears	
SUSPENSION	torsion bar	torsion bar
ELECTRICAL SYSTEM	24 V	24 V
BATTERIES	2 × 12 V	2 × 12 V
ARMAMENT		
main	1 × 7.62 mm MG	1 × 14.5 mm MG
coaxial	none	1 × 7.62 mm MG
anti-tank	1 × 82 mm	none
SMOKE-LAYING EQUIPMENT	diesel fuel injected into exhaust system	
AMMUNITION		
14.5 mm	none	500
7.62 mm	1250	2000
82 mm	12	none
FIRE-CONTROL SYSTEM		
Turret power control	manual	manual
Gun elevation/depression	+20°/−10°	+89.5°/−4°
ARMOUR		
Hull front upper	8 mm at 83°	8 mm at 83°
Hull front lower	10 mm at 53°	10 mm at 53°
Hull side upper	10 mm at 0°	10 mm at 0°
Hull side lower	9 mm at 0°	9 mm at 0°
Hull rear upper	7 mm at 0°	7 mm at 0°
Hull rear lower	6 mm at 42°	6 mm at 42°
Hull top	7 mm at 86°	7 mm at 86°
Belly front	6 mm	6 mm
Belly rear	6 mm	6 mm

Status: Production complete. In service with Angola, Bulgaria, Czechoslovakia, Egypt, India, Iraq, Israel, Libya, Morocco, Poland (Army and Marines) and Sudan.

Manufacturer: Czechoslovak state arsenals.

OT-62 Command Vehicle

It is known that there are both ambulance and command versions of the OT-62 in service; some of the latter are fitted with additional communications equipment.

WPT-TOPAS Recovery Vehicle

This is a Polish development and is used for recovery of damaged and disabled vehicles during amphibious operations. In appearance it resembles an OT-62A but is fitted with a winch with a capacity of 2500 kg, small hand-operated crane with a capacity of 1000 kg and other specialised equipment. Armament comprises a 7.62 mm PK machine gun, RPG-7 anti-tank weapon and 12 F-1 fragmentation grenades.

OT-810 Armoured Personnel Carrier

Development

During the Second World War the German Sd Kfz 251 half-track was manufactured at the Pilsen plant of Skoda in Czechoslovakia for the German Army. After the end of the war Czechoslovakia continued production of the vehicle for its own Army for a short period and subsequently carried out a number of modifications to the basic vehicle. These included the replacement of the original 120 hp petrol engine with a Tatra 120 hp diesel and the addition of overhead armour protection to the troop compartment which previously had an open top. The OT-810 was replaced in the 1960s as an armoured personnel carrier by the OT-64 (8 × 8) and many of the half-tracks were then converted into anti-tank vehicles and remain in use in this role today.

Description

The hull of the OT-810 is made of all-welded steel with the engine at the front, commander and driver in the centre and the troop compartment at the rear.

The driver sits on the left with the vehicle commander to his right. Both have a small observation flap that opens upwards on the outside to their front, and a similar flap to their sides. The commander has a single-piece hatch cover over his position that opens to the rear, in front of which is a pintle-mounted 7.62 mm M59 machine gun. It should be noted that neither the commander nor driver is provided with a door in the side of the hull and they have to enter and leave the vehicle by the troop compartment at the rear of the hull, entry to which is by the twin doors in the hull rear. The troop compartment is provided with two roof hatches that open either side of the hull, in each side of which are two firing/observation ports.

Basic OT-810 armoured personnel carrier

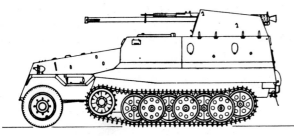

OT-810 with 82 mm M59A recoilless gun

degrees, elevation of +25 degrees and a depression of −5 degrees. It can also be removed from the vehicle and used in the ground role when it has an elevation of +25 degrees, depression of −13 degrees, and traverse of 360 degrees at 0 degrees elevation and 60 degrees at 25 degrees elevation. The twin doors in the rear of the basic OT-810 have been replaced in this version by a single hatch which unfolds into the horizontal to provide additional space for the gun crew. Ammunition is stowed in ready-use lockers at the rear of the hull, on either side of the rear hatch.

The M59A can be used in both the direct and indirect roles as it is provided with a PBO-4K sight. It can fire HE or HEAT projectiles; the former weighs 6 kg, has a muzzle velocity of 565 metres a second and a maximum range in the indirect fire role of 7560 metres, while the HEAT projectile weighs 6 kg, has a muzzle velocity of 745 metres a second and will penetrate 250 mm of armour at a range of 1000 metres. Forty rounds of 82 mm ammunition are carried. The M59A is the only recoilless gun in the Warsaw Pact that is provided with a spotting rifle similar to that mounted on Western recoilless weapons such as the American 106 mm M40. The M59A has a 12.7 mm ZH 59 spotting rifle mounted on the right side of the barrel which is fed from a small magazine.

The OT-810 has no NBC system or night vision equipment and has no amphibious capability.

Variants

The OT-810 was widely used to tow the 82 mm M59A recoilless gun, but in recent years the vehicle has been modified to allow the weapon to be carried on and fired from the vehicle.

The M59A is mounted in the troop compartment and is provided with front and side armour shields which can be quickly folded down when the weapon is required for use. When mounted in the vehicle it has a total traverse of 90

SPECIFICATIONS					
CREW	2 + 10	LENGTH OF TRACK ON GROUND	1.8 m	TRANSFER BOX	2-speed
COMBAT WEIGHT	8500 kg	MAX ROAD SPEED		TYRES (front)	7.50 × 20
POWER-TO-WEIGHT		forwards	52.5 km/h	SUSPENSION	
RATIO	14.18 hp/tonne	FUEL CAPACITY	160 litres	front	coil springs with non-driving axle
GROUND PRESSURE	0.843 kg/cm²	MAX ROAD RANGE	320 km		
LENGTH	5.8 m	FUEL CONSUMPTION	0.5 litre/km	rear	6 road wheels, overlapping 3 inner and 3 outer
WIDTH	2.1 m	FORDING	0.5 m		
HEIGHT		GRADIENT	50%	ARMAMENT	1 × 7.62 mm MG
(without armament)	1.75 m	VERTICAL OBSTACLE	0.255 m	ARMOUR	
GROUND CLEARANCE	0.3 m	TRENCH	1.98 m	Hull front	12 mm
TRACK		ENGINE	Tatra 928-3 V-8 air-cooled diesel developing 120 hp	Hull sides	7 mm
wheels	1.65 m				
track	1.6 m	TRANSMISSION	manual with 4 forward and 1 reverse gears		
width	300 mm				

Status: Production complete. In service in Czechoslovakia. **Manufacturer:** Skoda plant, Pilsen, Czechoslovakia.

EGYPT

Fahd Armoured Personnel Carrier

Development

The Fahd (4 × 4) armoured personnel carrier has been developed by the Kadar Factory of the Arab Organisation for Industrialisation to meet the requirements of the Egyptian Army based on their experiences in recent Middle East conflicts.

Following trials with a prototype vehicle production is expected to commence late in 1985 with first production vehicles being completed in 1986. In the Egyptian Army it will replace Egyptian-built Walid (or Waleed as it is also called) (4 × 4) armoured personnel carriers designed and built some 20 years ago but still in service in significant numbers.

The Fahd is already being offered for export and in November 1984 it was reported that Jordan was showing a strong interest in the vehicle.

The Fahd essentially consists of a Daimler-Benz LAP 1117/32 truck chassis fitted with an armoured body. Wherever possible standard and proven commercial components are used in the construction of the vehicle.

Description

The hull of the Fahd is of all-welded steel armour construction which provides complete protection from attack from 7.62 × 54 mm armour-piercing projectiles and shell splinters.

The driver is seated at the front of the vehicle on the left side with the commander to his right. Both are provided with

Fahd (4 × 4) armoured personnel carrier from front with 5000 kg capacity winch installed (Christopher F Foss)

Fahd (4 × 4) armoured personnel carrier with driver's and commander's doors open (Christopher F Foss)

a large bullet-proof windscreen to their front which can be covered by a shutter hinged at the top and a side door that opens to the front. The latter has a window in its upper part which can be covered by a shutter if required. Above the driver's and commander's position is a single-piece hatch cover that opens to the rear. The driver has a forward-facing roof-mounted periscope which can be replaced by an infra-red or passive periscope for driving at night.

The troop compartment is at the rear of the hull with the infantry entering via a door in the rear, the upper part of which folds upwards and the lower part downwards to form a step. Over the top of the troop compartment are two rectangular roof hatches hinged in the centre which can be locked in the vertical position. The infantry are seated on individual bucket seats down the centre of the vehicle facing outwards. In either side of the troop compartment are four firing ports with a vision block above to enable the troops to fire their weapons from within the vehicle. Either side of the rear hatch is another vision block with a firing port underneath.

The engine is mounted towards the front of the vehicle with ventilation for the engine and cooling system being provided through an opening with armoured shutters at the front of the vehicle. The air inlet for the engine is in the roof of the vehicle.

The Fahd is fitted with a central tyre pressure regulation system that allows the driver to adjust the tyre pressure to suit the type of ground being crossed. The driver can select front or rear tyres, or both together. The central tyre pressure system stops automatically after reaching the maximum or minimum tyre pressure selected by the driver. Low pressure run-flat tyres are fitted as standard and allow the vehicle to travel a distance of 50 km at a speed of 30 km/h in the event of a puncture. Power assisted steering is fitted as standard and there is a differential lock between the front and rear axles.

Up to three machine guns can be mounted on the roof of the Fahd to provide suppressive fire.

Optional equipment includes a front-mounted hydraulic winch with a capacity of 5000 kg, NBC and ventilating system, passive night vision equipment and smoke dischargers mounted either side of the hull.

Variants

The design of the Fahd is such that a wide range of armament installations can be mounted on the hull top such as a one-man turret with single or twin 7.62 mm machine guns or a 20 mm cannon. Other variants suggested by the manufacturer include ambulance, anti-tank with ATGWs, command, multiple rocket launcher, recovery, reconnaissance and a weapon supply carrier.

SPECIFICATIONS	
CREW	2 + 10
COMBAT WEIGHT	10 900 kg
UNLOADED WEIGHT	9100 kg
POWER-TO-WEIGHT	
RATIO	15.4 hp/tonne
LENGTH	6 m
WIDTH	2.45 m
HEIGHT HULL TOP	2.1 m
GROUND CLEARANCE	0.31 m to 0.37 m
ANGLE OF APPROACH/	
DEPARTURE	35°/35°
WHEELBASE	3.2 m
MAX ROAD SPEED	90 km/h
MAX ROAD RANGE	800 km
FORDING	0.7 m
GRADIENT	70%
SIDE SLOPE	30%
TRENCH	0.8 m
ENGINE	Mercedes-Benz OM-352 A 6-cylinder direct injection turbocharged water-cooled diesel developing 168 hp at 2800 rpm
TRANSMISSION	fully automatic
TRANSFER CASE	2-speed
STEERING	power-assisted
ELECTRICAL SYSTEM	24 V

Status: Development complete. Expected to enter production in 1985.

Manufacturer: Kadar Factory for Developed Industries, Orouba Street, Heliopolis, POB 287, Arab Republic of Egypt.

Walid Armoured Personnel Carrier

Development

The Walid armoured personnel carrier was designed and developed by the NASR Automotive Plant at Helwan and was used in combat for the first time in the 1967 Middle East campaign. It basically consists of a West German Magirus Deutz chassis, which was manufactured under licence in

Walid (4 × 4) armoured personnel carrier (Christopher F Foss)

Egypt, fitted with an armoured body. The vehicle is very similar in appearance and performs a similar role to the Soviet BTR-40 armoured personnel carrier which is also used by the Egyptian Army. The BTR-40 can be distinguished from the Walid by vertical rather than sloped sides to the troop compartment.

Description

The hull of the Walid is made of all-welded steel with the engine at the front, driver and commander in the centre and the troop compartment at the rear. The driver sits on the left with the commander to his right, both with a door in the side of the hull, the upper part of which folds down on the outside for increased visibility. Both the commander and driver have an individual windscreen to their front which when in action can be covered by an armoured shutter hinged at the top.

The open-topped troop compartment is at the rear of the hull and entry to it is by a door on which the spare wheel and tyre are carried. Three observation/firing ports are provided in each side of the hull with a further two at the rear of the hull, one either side of the spare wheel.

The Walid has no NBC system, no night vision equipment and no amphibious capability. A central tyre pressure regulation system is fitted as standard.

The basic model is armed with a 7·62 mm pintle-mounted machine gun but additional weapons can be mounted around the top of the hull. Israel has also used the Walid for internal security operations and some Israeli vehicles have been fitted with an armour-plated seat which is mounted on arms well away from the front of the vehicle. A man sits here to examine the road for any traces of recently laid mines.

It was reported in 1977 that the chassis for the Walid was supplied by the NASR Automotive Plant and the body was made by the Kadar plant which also undertakes final assembly of the vehicle. In March 1980 the United States announced that it was to sell to Egypt 550 M113A2 APCs worth US$82·8 million. The contract also covered the provision of related test equipment, training, armament, ammunition, spare parts, special tools and other services. The first M113A2s were delivered to Egypt late in 1980 and some have been fitted with the Hughes TOW ATGW system. There is a possibility that the M113 will be made under licence in Egypt.

Variants

The Egyptian Army is known to have at least two versions of this vehicle in service, a minelayer and a multiple rocket launcher that launches smoke rockets.

SPECIFICATIONS	
CREW	2 + 8/10
CONFIGURATION	4 × 4
MAX PAYLOAD	2800 kg
LENGTH	6.12 m
WIDTH	2.57 m
HEIGHT	2.3 m
ENGINE	168 hp diesel
MAX ROAD SPEED	66 km/h
MAX ROAD RANGE	800 km

Status: Production complete. In service with Algeria, Burundi, Egypt, Israel, Sudan and the Yemen Arab Republic (North).

Manufacturer: NASR Automotive Plant, Helwan, Egypt.

FINLAND

Sisu XA-180 Armoured Personnel Carrier

Development

The Finnish Army operates about 60 Soviet-supplied BTR-60PB (8 × 8) APCs but has a requirement for between 300 and 400 new wheeled APCs. To meet this requirement Sisu built the XA-180 (6 × 6) and Valmet the model 1912–16 (6 × 6), with both prototypes completed in 1982.

Following trials with these vehicles in December 1983 the Finnish Government placed an initial order for 59 Sisu XA-180 APCs at a cost of FM 42 million, with deliveries taking place over a three-year period. Of the initial order, 50 will be for the Finnish Army and the remaining nine will be used by the Finnish United Nations Battalion.

A major reason in the decision to select the Sisu XA-180 was that this vehicle uses many automotive components of the new Sisu SA-150 VK (4 × 4) 6500 kg truck already in service with the Finnish Army.

Description

The hull of the XA-180 is of all-welded steel armour construction that provides the crew with protection from small arms fire and shell splinters. The commander and driver sit at the very front of the vehicle and have an entry door in either side, in the upper part of which is a bullet-proof window. Forward observation is provided by a bullet-proof window which can be covered in a combat area by a shutter hinged at the top. Both the commander and driver also have a roof hatch, and the former can operate a Soviet type infra-red searchlight from within the vehicle.

The engine compartment is to the rear of the front compartment on the left side with an aisle being provided to connect with the troop compartment at the rear of the hull. The troop compartment has roof hatches and two doors in the rear, the left one of which has a vision block and firing port.

The suspension of the XA-180 consists of leaf springs and hydraulic shock absorbers, steering is power-assisted on the front two axles. The vehicle is fully amphibious, being propelled in the water by two propellers mounted under the hull rear, one either side. Before entering the water a trim vane is erected at the front of the vehicle.

Variants

It is anticipated that command post, mortar carrier and anti-aircraft versions will be built.

SPECIFICATIONS						
CREW	2 + 10	WIDTH	2.89 m	TRANSMISSION	semi-automatic, 4 forward and 4 reverse gears, 2-speed power divider
CONFIGURATION	6 × 6	HEIGHT	2.47 m		
COMBAT WEIGHT	15 000 kg	GROUND CLEARANCE	0.45 m		
UNLOADED WEIGHT	12 000 kg	MAX SPEED		STEERING	power-assisted, front two axles
PAYLOAD		road	105 km/h		
road	6500 kg	water	10 km/h	SUSPENSION	leaf springs, hydraulic shock absorbers
cross-country	3000 kg	MAX ROAD RANGE	800 km		
swimming	3000 kg	ENGINE	Valmet 6-cylinder turbo-charged diesel developing 245 hp		
LENGTH	7.35 m				

Status: In production. In service with the Finnish Army.

Manufacturer: Sisu-Auto Ab, PO Box 307, 00101 Helsinki 10, Finland.

FRANCE

AMX-10P Mechanised Infantry Combat Vehicle

Development

The AMX-10P was developed from 1965 by the Atelier de Construction d'Issy-les-Moulineaux to meet a French Army requirement for a vehicle to replace the older AMX VCI based on the chassis of the AMX-13 light tank. The first prototypes were completed in 1968 and were powered by a Hispano-Suiza multi-fuel engine which developed 250 hp and gave the vehicle a maximum road speed of 65 km/h.

Production began at the Atelier de Construction Roanne (where the AMX-30 MBT is produced) in 1972 and first vehicles were delivered to the 7th Mechanised Brigade at Rheims in 1973. Since then over 2000 vehicles have been produced for the French Army and for export. The largest export order to date is for 300+ vehicles for Saudi Arabia. The 1981 French defence budget included funding for 115 AMX-10P and APX-10PC vehicles, 55 in 1982 and 43 in 1983.

Description

The hull of the AMX-10P is made of all-welded aluminium with the driver's compartment at the front of the vehicle on the left, engine compartment to his right and the troop compartment at the rear of the hull. The driver has a single-piece hatch cover that opens to the rear, in front of which are three periscopes, the centre one of which can be replaced by a passive periscope for driving at night.

The engine compartment is provided with a fire-extinguishing system and the complete powerpack can be replaced in two hours. The air-inlet and air-outlet louvres are in the top of the hull and the exhaust outlet is in the right side of the hull. The transmission consists of a torque converter with an electro-magnetically operated clutch and a steer/drive unit comprising a gearbox, steering mechanism and a PTO for the waterjets.

The two-man Toucan II turret is mounted in the centre of the vehicle, offset slightly to the left of the vehicle's centre line, with the gunner seated on the left and the commander on the right. Both the commander and the gunner have a single-piece hatch cover that opens either side of their posi-

AMX-10P MICV with Toucan II turret

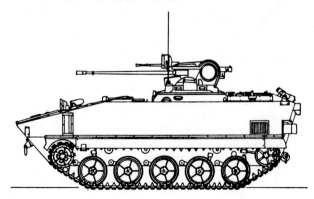

AMX-10P MICV (ECP Armées)

tion. The commander has an M371 sight with a magnification of ×1 and ×6, a direct sight for anti-aircraft use and an external sight for direct fire. The gunner has an OB 40 day/night periscope, which has a day magnification of ×6 (10-degree field of view) and a night magnification of ×5 (7-degree field of field). The vehicle can also be delivered with the gunner's OB 40 sight replaced by an M406 day sight with a magnification of ×2 and ×6, which is replaceable by an OB 37 image intensification sight with a magnification of ×6. The commander and gunner also have seven periscopes for all-round observation.

The 20 mm cannon is mounted externally on the turret and has a dual-feed system allowing the gunner to select either HE or AP projectiles, and a burst selector. The cyclic rate of fire of the 20 mm cannon is 700 rpm and the maximum effective range is 1500 metres. Of 325 rounds of 20 mm ready ammunition carried in the turret, 260 are HE and 65 AP.

Mounted coaxially above and to the right of the 20 mm M693 cannon is a 7.62 mm machine gun, which has a cyclic rate of fire of 900 rpm and a maximum effective range of 1000 metres. Of 900 rounds of ammunition for the machine gun carried in the turret, 200 are for ready use. Mounted coaxially with the 20 mm cannon and 7.62 mm machine gun is a PH 9A searchlight and mounted on either side of the forward part of the turret are two electrically-operated smoke dischargers.

If required the vehicle can be delivered with the 20 mm M693 replaced by a similar weapon such as the West German Rheinmetall Rh 202, or fitted with other turrets such as the one-man Toucan I or GIAT Capre 20.

The eight infantrymen are seated on individual bucket seats in the troop compartment at the rear. One man is seated forward and right of the turret facing the rear, one man to the right of the turret facing the turret, four men to the rear of the turret (two each side facing outwards), and one man on each side of the rear facing inwards.

They enter and leave by the large electrically-operated ramp at the rear, which is hinged at the bottom and has two doors, each with a firing port. Over the top of the troop compartment are two roof hatches which are hinged in the centre and can be locked vertical. Seven periscopes are fitted in the roof of the troop compartment, one at the front on the right, two in either side and two at the rear. The basic AMX-10P is also in service carrying two Euromissile MILAN launchers with ten missiles carried in the hull. If required the MILAN launchers can be mounted on the sides of the hull top, one each side.

The torsion bar suspension consists of five single rubber-tyred road wheels with the drive sprocket at the front, idler at the rear and three track return rollers. The first and fifth road wheel stations are fitted with hydraulic shock absorbers. The tracks have replaceable rubber pads.

The AMX-10P is fully amphibious, being propelled in the water by two water jets at the rear of the hull, one either side of the ramp. Before entering the water the two bilge pumps are switched on (one in the engine compartment and one in

AMX-10P MICV showing amphibious capabilities (GIAT)

Model of AMX-10P 25 MICV showing roof arrangement (GIAT)

AMX-10P Marine as delivered to Indonesian Marines with GIAT CIBI 50 turret (Terry J Gander)

the troop compartment) and the trim vane is erected at the front of the hull. When not in use the trim vane is stowed on the glacis plate. The AMX-10P can be delivered without the amphibious capability.

Standard equipment includes an NBC system in the right side of the hull and a heater. The vehicle can be delivered without the NBC system or the heater and optional equipment includes an NBC detector and decontamination equipment.

In the future it is possible that the present 280 hp engine will be replaced by a more powerful version developing 350 hp, a new transmission fitted and that the turret will be fitted with a stabilisation system. An AMX-10P fitted with a hydrostatic transmission is already being tested.

Variants

AMX-10P 25 MICV
The prototype of the AMX-10P 25 was shown for the first time in June 1983. It is based on the standard AMX-10P hull without the original two-man turret. The commander now sits to the left of the turret and has a single-piece hatch cover that opens to the front, five day periscopes and a day/night periscope.

Mounted in the centre of the hull roof is the new GIAT Dragar one-man turret armed with a 25 mm GIAT dual-feed cannon which has 175 rounds of HE and 45 rounds of armour-piercing ammunition for ready use. A 7.62 mm machine gun is mounted coaxially with the 20 mm cannon on the right side of the turret and has 200 rounds of ready use ammunition. A belt stopping device stops the machine gun firing at the right moment so that ammunition resupply can be carried out without having to reload the weapon.

Turret traverse and weapon elevation are electric at a speed of 45 degrees a second and the weapons can be elevated from −10 to +45 degrees with turret traverse being a full 360 degrees. The gunner has four M336 periscopes for forward observation, two fixed rear vision blocks and a day/night sight for aiming the weapons. This has a night channel with a magnification of ×4.5 and a day channel with a magnification of ×1 and ×6. As an option a thermal camera can be fitted and the turret stabilised.

This model weighs 14 300 kg loaded and 11 700 kg empty and has a crew of three: commander, gunner and driver, and can carry eight fully-equipped troops.

AMX-10P Marine
The AMX-10P has been developed by GIAT to meet the requirements of the Indonesian Marines. The batch of 50 AMX-10P Marine and AMX-10 PAC 90 Marine Fire Support Vehicles delivered from 1982 to Indonesia were fitted with the Baudouin 6 F11 SRX diesel developing 276 hp in place of the standard HS-115 diesel engine.

All of the vehicles were specially modified for naval operations and have 12-inch water jets to give a maximum water speed of 10 km/h, reinforced waterproofing, special protection against salt corrosion, strong transparent wave breaker on the front of the hull, side rings and an emergency pneumatic engine starter.

The original two-man turret of the AMX-10P has been removed and over the rear troop compartment of the AMX-10P Marine is the GIAT CIBI 50 turret armed with an externally-mounted 12.7 mm machine gun with 120 rounds of ready use ammunition. This weapon can be elevated from −10 to +45 degrees and turret traverse is a full 360 degrees. The AMX-10P has a crew of two and can carry a landing party of 13.

AMX-10 Ambulance
This model is unarmed and is fitted with a fixed commander's cupola with three forward-facing vision blocks, and has a crew of three: the driver and two orderlies. The vehicle can carry three stretcher patients or one stretcher and four seated patients. The AMX-10 ambulance has an air-conditioning system, searchlight, washing facilities, oxygen system and blood transfusion equipment.

AMX-10P Driver Training Vehicle
This is the basic vehicle with its turret removed and replaced by an observation position for the instructor and drivers not under instruction.

AMX-10 ECH Repair Vehicle
This has the Toucan I one-man turret and a crew of five which consists of the commander/chief mechanic, three mechanics and the driver. On the right side of the roof at the rear is a crane with a capacity of 6000 kg. When it is being used two jacks are positioned under the rear of the hull between the ground and the floor of the vehicle. The AMX-10 ECH is used to carry out engine changes on other

AMX-10 ECH repair vehicle changing powerpack of AMX-10P
(ECP Armées)

members of the AMX-10P family as well as changing torsion bars on both the AMX-10P and the AMX-30. This model is in production.

AMX-10 HOT (Anti-tank)

This is the basic AMX-10P with the Toucan II turret replaced by a new two-man Lancelot turret based on TH 20 turret with four ready-to-launch HOT missiles and a further 16 to 20 missiles carried in the rear of the hull. The crew of five consists of the commander and gunner in the turret, two missile loaders and the driver. The turret has powered traverse through 360 degrees at a speed of 50 degrees a second and manual traverse at a speed of 10 degrees a second. The missiles can be elevated from −12 to +18 degrees at a speed of 18 degrees a second (powered) and 22 degrees a second (manual). The missiles are launched by the gunner who is seated on the left side of the turret and has an M509 sight with a magnification of ×3 and ×12, while the commander operates the M427 laser rangefinder which has a maximum range of 8000 metres and a magnification of ×8.3. In addition the turret has six periscopes and two vision blocks. The AMX-10 HOT has a combat weight of 14 100 kg and an unloaded weight of 12 400 kg. This model is in production and in service with Saudi Arabia.

AMX-10 PC (Command Vehicle)

This is the command member of the AMX-10P and is identical to the basic vehicle except that it has additional communications equipment and a crew of six (two officers, one NCO, two radio operators and the driver). Mounted on the top of the hull at the rear is a portable generator which is positioned on the ground when the vehicle is being used in the static role. When two AMX-10 PCs are back to back a canopy can be erected between them, and in addition an awning can be erected at the side of the hull. This model is in service with the French Army and several other armies.

AMX-10P with RATAC

This has no turret and is fitted with a roof-mounted RATAC (Radar For Field Artillery Fire) pulse Doppler radar scanner. The vehicle has a crew of five: commander, radar operator, assistant radar operator, radio operator and driver. The radar has four operating modes: ground surveillance, acquisition and identification, angular deviation measure-

ment and automatic tracking. The radar is in the forward part of the vehicle on the right side, with the radar operating console behind it and the plotting table at the rear on the right. Height including radar is 2.84 metres. This model is in production.

AMX-10 RAV

Under development is an ammunition resupply vehicle for use with the 155 mm GCT. This will have a hydraulic crane to handle the pallets of ammunition.

AMX-10RC (Reconnaissance Vehicle)

This 6 × 6 reconnaissance vehicle armed with a turret-mounted 105 mm gun uses many automotive components of the AMX-10P series. A tracked version of the AMX-10RC, called the AMX-10C, was developed to the prototype stage, but has not been placed in production.

AMX-10 SAO (Artillery Observation Vehicle)

The AMX-10 SAO is used for battlefield observation and artillery fire-control and is an AMX-10P with its Toucan II turret replaced by a new two-man turret armed with an externally-mounted 7.62 mm machine gun on the right side. Mounted on the top of the turret are four electrically-operated smoke dischargers firing forwards. Turret traverse is electric, two speed, with a maximum speed of 50 degrees a second. The turret has a laser rangefinder with a maximum range of 8000 metres coupled to a day sight with a magnification of ×8 and a night sight with a magnification of ×4.5. It also has a binocular telescope with a magnification of ×2.5 and ×10, which has adjustable cross-wires, retractable sun filter and can be elevated from −10 to +45 degrees. The crew of five consists of the commander (who normally operates the binocular telescope), second in command (who normally operates the laser rangefinder), two radio operators and a driver. The AMX-10 SAO is fitted with a vehicle attitude corrector which enables it to establish its exact position. The ATILA system message transmitter unit (CMS) can be used in the SAO vehicle and if required the SICLAMEN iff system can be fitted. Production of this model began in 1980.

AMX-10 SAT (Artillery Survey Vehicle)

This is based on the AMX-10 PC command vehicle but internally has been modified to carry gyro-stabilised theodo-

AMX-10P HOT with turret with four Euromissile HOT ATGWs ready-to-launch

45

lite, topographic survey theodolite, distance measuring equipment and a navigation system.

AMX-10 TM (Mortar Tractor)
This model tows a 120 mm Brandt rifled mortar model MO-120-RT-61 as well as carrying 60 rounds of ammunition, of which 56 are stored horizontal and four vertical. The AMX-10 TM has a crew of six and is fitted with a Toucan I turret armed with a 20 mm cannon and a 7.62 mm machine gun, which have elevations of +50 degrees and depressions of −8 degrees, turret traverse being a full 360 degrees. The turret is manually operated: maximum traverse speed is 12 degrees a second and maximum elevation speed 16 degrees a second. This model is in production.

AMX-10 VOA (Artillery Observer Vehicle)
This is based on the AMX-10PC command vehicle chassis and has been designed for use by artillery observers. Its crew of four consists of commander, observer, radio operator and driver. The turret, which is manned by one or two men, is provided with equipment for day and night observation and local defence. The equipment fitted in the turret enables the acquisition of target co-ordinates and the manual or automatic transmission of artillery messages. Armament consists of a 7.62 mm machine gun and four smoke dischargers.

AMX-10Ps used in the ATILA Control System
Two versions of the AMX-10P have been developed to mount parts of the ATILA automatic artillery fire-control system. The AMX-10 VFA is used at regimental and battery level and the AMX-10 VLA, which does not have a computer, is used as an artillery liaison vehicle.

AMX-10 SAF
This is also known as the AMX-10PC SAF and is used with the ATILA artillery fire-control system. It has a crew of five consisting of the radio operator, driver, two warrant officers and one commanding officer, and is fitted with an auxiliary power unit in the forward part of the vehicle, two air- conditioning systems for the electronics and crew, multi-purpose computer, data processing equipment centre, man-machine interface (screen/keyboard) and three radio sets.

AMX-10 TMC-81 Fire Support Vehicle
Shown for the first time at the 1981 Satory Exhibition of Military Equipment was the AMX-10 TMC-81 fire support vehicle which has been developed specifically for the export market. It has a modified AMX-10 PAC 90 turret fitted with a Brandt 81 mm CL 81 smooth-bore gun with a semi-automatic breech and can be used for direct and indirect fire. The weapon has an elevation of +66 degrees, depression of −7 degrees and turret traverse of 360 degrees. Elevation/depression and turret traverse are both manual.

A total of 108 HE projectiles with a muzzle velocity of 400 metres a second and a maximum range of 7200 metres are carried. In addition ten APFSDS projectiles which have a muzzle velocity of 1000 metres a second and will penetrate 50 mm of armour at an incidence of 45 degrees at a range of 1000 metres are carried. If required a 7.62 mm or 12.7 mm machine gun can be mounted on the turret roof for anti-aircraft defence.

The crew of four consists of the commander and gunner in the turret and driver and loader/mechanic in the hull. Mobil-

ity and amphibious characteristics remain the same as the basic AMX-10P.

AMX-10 PAC 90 Fire Support Vehicle

Development
The AMX-10 PAC 90 has been developed primarily for the export market by the Atelier de Construction d'Issy-les Moulineaux and was first announced in 1978. It basically consists of an AMX-10P MICV hull fitted with the TS 90 turret which is also mounted on the Panhard ERC 90 F4 Sagaie (6 × 6) armoured car as well as the Renault VBC 90 (6 × 6) armoured car. The AMX-10 PAC 90 has been evaluated by several countries and is in service with Indonesia. The Indonesian Marine models have automotive characteristics and modifications similar to the AMX-10P Marine's described earlier in this section.

The primary role of the AMX-10 PAC 90 is that of anti-tank and fire support on the battlefield at ranges of between 1000 and 2500 metres, but it can also be used as a reconnaissance vehicle or as an APC as well as transporting MILAN anti-tank or 81 mm mortar teams.

Description
The hull is made of all-welded aluminium and is divided into three compartments: driver's at the front on the left with the engine to his right and the fighting compartment at the rear.

The driver has a single-piece hatch cover that opens to the rear in front of which are three periscopes, the centre one replaceable by an infra-red or image intensification periscope for driving at night.

The all-welded steel turret is at the rear of the hull with the commander seated on the left and the gunner on the right, both with a single-piece hatch cover that opens to the rear. The commander has seven periscopes and the gunner five and the gunner also has an M563 telescopic sight with a magnification of ×5.9.

The GIAT 90 mm gun has a muzzle brake, thermal sleeve, 35-degree oblique wedge type semi-automatic breech-block and a hydro-pneumatic recoil system. It fires canister, high

AMX-10 PAC 90 fire support vehicle fitted with roof-mounted 12.7 mm (0.50) M2 HB anti-aircraft machine gun

explosive, high explosive long range, HEAT, smoke and APFSDS projectiles with the latter capable of penetrating 320 mm of armour at an incidence of 0 degrees.

A total of 20 rounds of ammunition, 12 HEAT and 8 HE, are carried in the turret, 16 in the turret bustle to the rear of the commander, who also loads the gun, and four behind the commander's seat. Another ten rounds are carried in the hull. A 7.62 mm machine gun is mounted coaxially to the left of the main armament, and 2000 rounds of ammunition for it are carried in the turret with an additional 1200 rounds carried in the hull. Two smoke dischargers are mounted either side of the turret towards the rear.

The PAC 90 can be fitted with one of four fire-control systems: (1) Basic as installed in the TS 90 turret. (2) Basic plus TCV 107 laser rangefinder with reading applied manually by the gunner. (3) Basic plus laser plus computer with target information being displayed in gun sight. (4) Fully automatic, full computerisation with laser rangefinder, tachometer and tilt sensor for corrections automatically applied to gunsight aiming point, both day and night.

Optional equipment includes a 7.62 mm or 12.7 mm anti-aircraft machine gun, the replacement of the coaxial 7.62 mm weapon by a 12.7 mm weapon, Canasta LLLTV and a SOPELEM day/night sight. The day sight has a magnification of ×5 and a 10-degree field of view and the night sight a ×7 magnification and a 7-degree field of view. Further developments planned include independent elevation of the coaxial machine gun, a fire-control system for engaging moving targets and an electric traverse system which will allow the turret to be traversed through 180 degrees in seven seconds.

Standard turret equipment includes a turret ventilator, 120-watt searchlight mounted to the left of the main armament, and moving in elevation with it, and an 80-watt searchlight on the turret roof.

The four infantrymen are seated on individual seats at the rear of the hull and enter and leave by the large ramp in the hull rear, which has two doors, each with a firing port. There are four periscopes in the rear of the troop compartment, one in each side and two at the rear.

SPECIFICATIONS
(data in square brackets relates to AMX-10 PAC 90 where different)

CREW	3 + 8 [3 + 4]	FORDING	amphibious	AMMUNITION	
COMBAT WEIGHT	14 200 [14 800] kg	GRADIENT	60%	main	800 [30]
UNLOADED WEIGHT	11 700 [13 800] kg	SIDE SLOPE	30%	coaxial	2000
POWER-TO-WEIGHT		VERTICAL OBSTACLE			[7.62 mm: 3200,
RATIO	19.71 [18.92] hp/tonne	forwards	0.7 m		12.7 mm: 1000]
GROUND PRESSURE	0.53 [0.56] kg/cm²	reverse	0.6 m	FIRE-CONTROL SYSTEM	
LENGTH GUN FORWARD	n/app [7.22 m]	TRENCH	1.6 m	Turret power control	electric [manual]
LENGTH	5.778 [5.87] m	ENGINE	Hispano-Suiza	by commander	yes [no]
WIDTH	2.78 [2.83] m		HS-115 V-8 water-cooled	by gunner	yes
HEIGHT			super-charged diesel	Max rate power traverse	50°/s (10°/s manual)
overall	2.57 [2.73] m		developing 280 hp at		[360°/20 s]
to hull top	1.92 m		3000 rpm (manufactured by	Max rate power elevation	30°/s (26°/s manual)
GROUND CLEARANCE	0.45 m		Renault Véhicles Industriels)	Gun elevation/depression	+50°/−8°
TRACK WIDTH	420 mm	TRANSMISSION	pre-selective with		[+15°/−8°]
LENGTH OF TRACK			4 forward and 1 reverse	Turret traverse	360°
ON GROUND	3 m		gears	commander's override	yes
MAX ROAD SPEED		SUSPENSION	torsion bar		
4th gear	65 km/h	ELECTRICAL SYSTEM	24 V		
3rd gear	34.4 km/h	BATTERIES	6 × 12 V		
2nd gear	15.4 km/h	ARMAMENT			
1st gear	9.4 km/h	main	1 × 20 mm cannon		
MAX WATER SPEED			[1 × 90 mm]		
(water jets)	7 km/h	coaxial	1 × 7.62 mm MG		
FUEL CAPACITY	528 litres	anti-aircraft	n/app [1 × 7.62 mm or 1 ×12.7 mm, optional]		
MAX ROAD RANGE	600 km	SMOKE-LAYING EQUIPMENT	2 × 2 smoke dischargers		

Status: In production. In service with France, Greece, Indonesia (AMX-10 PAC 90 and AMX-10P Marine), Qatar, Mexico, Morocco, Saudi Arabia and the United Arab Emirates.

Manufacturer: Atelier de Construction Roanne (ARE).

Enquiries to Groupement Industriel Des Armements Terrestres (GIAT), 10 place G Clémenceau, 92211 Saint-Cloud, France.

AMX VCI Infantry Combat Vehicle

Development

The AMX VCI (Véhicule de Combat d'Infanterie) was developed in the early 1950s to meet the requirements of the French Army following the cancellation of the Hotchkiss TT 6 and TT 9 APCs. The first prototype was completed in 1955 and the first production vehicles in 1957 at the Atelier de Construction Roanne (ARE). When the ARE started production of the AMX-30 MBT, production of the complete AMX-13 tank family, including the AMX VCI, was transferred to the Creusot-Loire facility at Châlon-sur-Saône where production continues today. So far production of the AMX-13 family of vehicles, including the VCI, has amounted to over 15 000 units, of which some 3000 are VCIs.

When originally introduced into service with the French Army the vehicle was called the Transport de Troupe Chenillé Model 56 (or TT 12 CH Mle 56 for short), which was later changed to the Véhicule Transport de Personnel (or AMX VTP for short) and more recently to the Véhicule de Combat d'Infanterie. It was used in large numbers by the French Army but is now being replaced by the AMX-10P amphibious MICV.

Description

The chassis of the AMX VCI is similar to that of the AMX-13 light tank. The hull of the vehicle is divided into three compartments with the driver and engine compartments at the front and the troop compartment at the rear.

The driver is seated at the front of the vehicle on the left with the engine compartment to his right. The driver has a single-piece hatch cover that opens to the left in front of which are three periscopes. The centre periscope can be replaced by an infra-red or image intensification periscope for night driving.

The petrol engine is mounted facing the rear and can be removed through the roof in 40 minutes. The engine transmits power via the clutch to the gearbox at the front of the hull, to the right of which is the Cleveland type steering differential.

Mounted on the glacis plate is a splash board to prevent water rushing up the front of the vehicle when fording and a spare wheel is normally carried on the glacis plate.

The troop compartment is behind and above the driver with the gunner seated on the left and the vehicle commander to his right. When the VCI was originally introduced into the French Army the gunner had a single-piece hatch cover with eight vision devices which swivelled to open, forward of which was a pintle-mounted 7.5 mm machine gun. This was later replaced by a ring-mounted 12.7 mm machine gun or a Creusot-Loire CAFL 38 turret armed with a 7.5 mm or a 7.62 mm machine gun. The 12.7 mm machine gun has an elevation of +68 degrees and a depression of −10 degrees with the gunner exposing his head above the turret ring, but in addition the weapon can be aimed and fired from inside the vehicle, in which case the weapon has an elevation of +5 degrees and a depression of −10 degrees. Elevation, depression and traverse are all manual. The CAFL 38 turret's machine gun has an elevation of +45 degrees, a depression of −15 degrees and a turret traverse of 360 degrees, all of which are manual. The turret has a two-piece hatch cover that opens front and rear, six periscopes and an optical sight.

The vehicle can be fitted with most other modern turrets such as the Toucan I, Creusot-Loire TLi G (twin 7.62 mm MGs), CB 20 (20 mm cannon) and CB 60 HB (with 60 mm Brandt mortar) to name a few.

The vehicle commander is seated to the right of the gunner and has a single-piece hatch cover that opens forwards, to the front and right side of which are three periscopes.

The troop compartment is at the rear: the ten infantrymen sit back to back down the centre of the hull and enter and leave the vehicle by two doors in the hull rear that open outward. Each door has a single firing port. In each side of the troop compartment are two two-piece hatch covers. The lower part of each has two firing ports and folds forwards into the horizontal and the upper part folds upwards through 180 degrees to rest on the troop compartment roof.

The torsion bar suspension consists of five rubber-tyred road wheels with the drive sprocket at the front, idler at the rear and four (in some cases three) return rollers that support the inside of the track only. The first and last road wheel stations have hydraulic shock absorbers. The steel tracks have 85 links each side when new and can be fitted with rubber pads.

When originally introduced into service the VCI was not fitted with an NBC system but one was subsequently fitted to later production vehicles for the French Army. Infra-red driving lights are standard on most vehicles but they do not have any amphibious capability.

Variants
Listed below are the current variants of the AMX VCI family

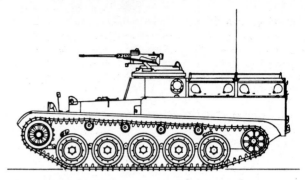

AMX VCI ICV armed with 12.7 mm (0.50) Browning M2 HB machine gun

AMX VCI used by French Gendarmerie with troop compartment hatches open

AMX VCI ICV with rear doors open showing seating arrangements (ECP Armées)

in service or production, excluding trials vehicles such as the Roland or minelayer.

Ambulance (VTT/TB)
The VTT/TB (Transport de Blessés) is the ambulance member of the family, is unarmed and has a crew of four, driver, surgeon and two orderlies/stretcher bearers. The vehicle can transport three stretcher and four sitting patients at once.

Anti-aircraft Vehicle

This private venture vehicle was first shown in 1983 and is essentially an AMX VCI with the machine gun turret removed and commander's roof hatch welded shut. Over this has been fitted an ESD TA 20/RA 20 turret armed with two 20 mm cannon.

Command Post (VTT/PC)

The VTT/PC (Poste de Commandement) is the basic VCI adapted for use as a command vehicle and has a crew of six to eight depending on its use. Internally the vehicle has two map tables and additional communications equipment.

Cargo (VTT/Cargo)

This version can carry up to 3000 kg of cargo.

Combat Engineer Vehicle (VCG)

The VCG (Véhicule de Combat du Génie) is based on the VCI and is designed to carry out engineer work in the forward battle area. Mounted at the front of the hull is a hydraulically-operated dozer blade for clearing obstacles and preparing fire positions. An A-frame is pivoted at the front of the hull. When not in use it is split at its upper end and lies back along either side of the hull. Other equipment includes a hydraulic winch with 63 metres of cable and a maximum capacity of 4500 kg, tools and cutting equipment. The VCG has a crew of ten, commander, gunner, driver and seven men and weighs 17 800 kg.

ENTAC Anti-tank Vehicle

As far as it is known this model, which was used only by the Belgian Army, is no longer in front line service.

MILAN Anti-tank Vehicle

Belgium has converted some of its mortar-carrying vehicles to the anti-tank role. A MILAN ATGW system is fitted on the left or right of the forward superstructure.

Fire-control Vehicle (VTT/LT)

The VTT/LT (Véhicule de commandement du tir) is a development of the basic VTT/PC command vehicle, has a crew of seven and is fitted with additional communications equipment, plotting table, fire computing table, four-channel switchboard for battery communications and an external loudspeaker.

RATAC Radar Vehicle (VTT/RATAC)

This is the basic vehicle fitted with the RATAC (Radar de Tir pour Artillerie de Campagne) radar which detects, identifies, locates and automatically tracks ground targets such as tanks, vehicles, personnel, light aircraft and helicopters or shell bursts. The radar itself is mounted on the roof of the vehicle on the right side.

155 mm Support Vehicle (VTT/VCA)

The VTT/VCA (Véhicule Chenillé d'Accompagnement) is designed to accompany the 155 mm Mk F3 self-propelled gun and carries the remainder of the gun crew and ammunition. The crew of eight consists of the driver, layer, loader, gunner, and four ammunition members. A total of 25 155 mm projectiles is carried plus 25 charges and 49 fuzes. The vehicle can also tow an ARE 2T F2 ammunition trailer containing 30 projectiles plus charges and fuzes. The vehicle is normally fitted with the CAFL 38 turret armed with a 7.5 mm or a 7.62 mm machine gun.

81 mm Mortar Carrier (VTT/PM)

The VTT/PM (Porte Mortier) has an 81 mm mortar firing forward through the roof of the personnel compartment. It has an elevation from +43 to +80 degrees and a total traverse of 40 degrees. A total of 88 long mortar bombs can be carried plus 40 short mortar bombs. The crew of six consists of the driver, commander, observer and three mortarmen. A baseplate is carried enabling the mortar to be deployed away from the vehicle if required.

120 mm Mortar Carrier (VTT/PM)

The VTT/PM (Porte Mortier) has a 120 mm Brandt type MO 120 LT mortar firing forwards through the roof of the personnel compartment. The mortar has a maximum range

Belgian Army AMX VCI ICV fitted with one-man CAFL 38 turret armed with 7.62 mm (0.30) machine gun (C R Zwart)

with PEPA/LT projectile of 8300 metres. When fired away from the vehicle with the aid of the baseplate carried the range is increased to 8950 metres. The mortar has an elevation of from +45 to +77 degrees and a total traverse of 46 degrees. A total of 60 mortar bombs is carried and the crew of six consists of the driver, commander, layer, gunner and two mortarmen.

SPECIFICATIONS

CREW	3 + 10	FUEL CAPACITY	410 litres	BATTERIES	4 × 12 V, 190 Ah
COMBAT WEIGHT	15 000 kg	ROAD RANGE		ARMAMENT	1 × 20 mm cannon,
UNLOADED WEIGHT	12 500 kg	petrol engine	350 km		or 1 × 12.7 mm MG,
POWER-TO-WEIGHT		diesel engine	400–440 km		or 1 × 7.62 mm/7.5 mm
RATIO		FORDING	1 m		MG
petrol engine	16.67 hp/tonne	GRADIENT	60%	SMOKE-LAYING-	
diesel engine	18.67 hp/tonne	VERTICAL OBSTACLE		EQUIPMENT	none
GROUND PRESSURE	0.7 kg/cm²	forwards	0.65 m	ARMOUR	
LENGTH	5.7 m	reverse	0.45 m	Hull front	15 mm at 55°
WIDTH	2.67 m	TRENCH	1.6 m		(corresponding to
HEIGHT		TURNING RADIUS	skid turns		40 mm)
to turret top	2.41 m	ENGINE	SOFAM model 8Gxb	Hull sides	20 mm
to hull top	2.1 m		8-cylinder water-cooled	Troop compartment front	30 mm
GROUND CLEARANCE	0.48 m		petrol developing 250 hp at	Troop compartment sides	20 mm
TRACK	2.159 m		3200 rpm	Troop compartment	
TRACK WIDTH	350 mm	TRANSMISSION	manual with 5 forward and 1	hatches	15 mm
LENGTH OF TRACK			reverse gears	Hull top	15 mm
ON GROUND	3.012 m	STEERING	Cleveland type differential	Hull floor front	20 mm
MAX ROAD SPEED		CLUTCH	Single-disc	Hull floor rear	10 mm
petrol engine	60 km/h	SUSPENSION	torsion bar	Hull rear	15 mm
diesel engine	64 km/h	ELECTRICAL SYSTEM	24 V		

Note: This vehicle is now offered fitted with the American General Motors model 6V-53T, turbo-charged 6-cylinder diesel developing 280 hp at 2800 rpm. The company also offers a kit to enable this engine to be installed in existing vehicles by the user. All members of the AMX-13 family, including the AMX VCI, can also be fitted with the Baudouin 6 F 11 SRY diesel developing 270 hp at 3200 rpm.

Status: In production. In service with Argentina (some of which were assembled there), Belgium, Ecuador, France (including Gendarmerie), Indonesia, Italy, Kuwait (34 vehicles, including command vehicles, fitted with the Detroit Diesel Model 6V-53T were delivered in 1982–83), Morocco, Netherlands (ambulance model designated AMX-gwt, APC model AMX-prs, command vehicle AMX-prco and cargo model AMX-prvr, all were due to be phased out of service by 1984), Venezuela and the United Arab Emirates.

Manufacturer: Creusot-Loire at Châlon sur Saône.

Enquiries to Creusot-Loire, Armament Department, 15 rue Pasquier, 75383 Paris Cedex 08, France.

Renault VAB Armoured Personnel Carrier

Development

In the late 1960s the French Army decided to issue its infantry units with both tracked and wheeled vehicles. The mechanised units would be issued with the tracked AMX-10P MICV, then already under development, and the remaining units with wheeled APCs as the tracked AMX-10P was considered too expensive and sophisticated for many of the roles it was expected to undertake.

In 1970 the French Army issued a requirement for a Front Armoured Vehicle (VAB or Véhicule de l'Avant Blindé) which would meet the requirements of the remaining infantry units and would be capable of undertaking a wide range of roles including use as an APC, cargo carrier and mortar towing vehicle.

To meet this requirement Panhard and Saviem/Renault Group built prototypes of both 4 × 4 and 6 × 6 vehicles between 1972 and 1973. These were tested by the Section Technique de l'Armée de Terre between May 1973 and early 1974 and in May 1974 the 4 × 4 version of the Saviem/Renault Group entry was selected for service.

No pre-production vehicles were built and first production vehicles were delivered to the French Army in 1976. The French Army has a requirement for between 4000 and 5000 VABs. At present the French Army is ordering the 4 × 4 version only but it is expected that the 6 × 6 version, which is already in production for export, will be ordered in the future.

Prime contractor for the VAB is Renault Véhicules Industriels which supplies automotive components to Creusot-Loire at Usine de Saint-Chamond for final assembly.

In June 1981 Renault announced that since production of the VAB had begun late in 1976 over 1500 vehicles had been built for the home and export markets with 4300 ordered for the French Army and 700 for export from at least eight countries. Fifty VABs in both 4 × 4 and 6 × 6 configuration

VAB (6 × 6) Transport de Troupes (APC) for export fitted with Creusot-Loire CB 127 gun ring shield for 12.7 mm M2 HB machine gun

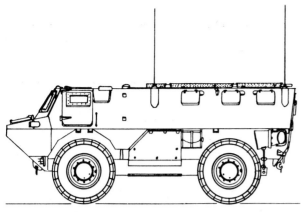

Basic 4 × 4 version of VAB as used by French Army

VCI (4 × 4) fitted with Toucan I turret with 20 mm cannon and coaxial 7.62 mm machine gun

VAB (6 × 6) internal security vehicle with front-mounted obstacle-clearing blade, firing port in side and Creusot-Loire TLi series turret armed with 12.7 mm and 7.62 mm machine guns

are being built a month (30 for French Army and 20 for export). The largest export order so far is for 426 units from Morocco, including APCs, command vehicles and the version with the Euromissile Mephisto HOT anti-tank system. The 1983 French Army Budget was for 225 (4 × 4) VABs. In 1984–85 the French Army ordered 486 VABs with a further 855 to be ordered in 1986–88. A total of 1327 VABs will be delivered between 1984 and 1988 and a further 600 after 1988.

Description

The basic model used by the French Army is the 4 × 4 VAB VTT (Véhicule Transport de Troupe) which has a crew of two (commander/machine gunner and driver) and carries ten fully-equipped infantrymen. The following description relates to this vehicle.

The all-welded steel hull of the VAB provides the crew with protection from small arms fire and shell splinters. The driver sits at the front of the vehicle on the left with the commander/machine gunner to his right. Both crew members have a side door that opens to the front, with a bullet-proof window in its upper part that is hinged at the top and opens outwards and can be covered by a shutter. In front of them is a bullet-proof windscreen that can be covered by a flap hinged at the top. Over the driver's position is a single-piece hatch cover that opens to the front. A similar hatch is mounted over the commander's position but vehicles issued to the French Army have a Creusot-Loire rotating gun mount type CB.52 armed with a 7.62 mm machine gun with an elevation of from −15 to +45 degrees with the shield in the normal position and from −20 to +80 degrees in the anti-aircraft position; in both cases traverse is a full 360 degrees. Other armament installations available include the Creusot-Loire TLi.52A.

The engine compartment, which is fitted with a fire-extinguishing system, is immediately behind the driver with the air-inlet and air-outlet louvres in the roof and the exhaust pipe running along the top of the hull on the right side. Power is transmitted from the engine to the wheels by a hydraulic torque converter and a gearbox with five forward and one reverse gears. Gears are shifted using a small pneumatically-operated lever which also operates the clutch. The axles have differential reduction gears with double reduction and differential locking. The wheels are independently suspended by torsion bars and hydraulic shock absorbers. Steering is hydraulically assisted on the front wheels, or, in the case of the 6 × 6 model, on the front four wheels. The tyres are Michelin radials, the pressure of which can be adjusted to suit the type of ground being crossed.

There is a passageway on the right side of the hull which connects the crew compartment at the front with the personnel compartment at the rear. The infantrymen enter and leave the VAB via two doors in the rear of the hull which open outwards. Each door has a window which can be opened to the outside and which is covered by an armoured shutter.

The infantrymen are seated on bench seats that run along either side of the hull. In each side of the hull are three windows which can be opened to the outside and can be covered by an armoured shutter. They can be locked open on the outside to allow the infantrymen to use their small arms from inside the vehicle.

On the basic VAB there are three hatches over the troop compartment, one in the centre and two at the rear, all of which open towards the front. The troop compartment is 2.46 metres long, 1.375 metres wide and 1.35 metres high and has a total floor area of 3.38 square metres. The seats can be quickly folded up to enable cargo to be carried. The lack of a central pillar at the rear enables cargo, up to 2000 kg, to be quickly loaded with the aid of a fork lift truck.

The VAB is fully amphibious, being propelled in the water by two Dowty water jets at the rear of the hull, each fitted with a deflector for steering and reverse thrust, which is hydraulically controlled by a joystick mounted on the dashboard. Before entering the water the bilge pumps are switched on and the trim vane, which is folded back onto the glacis plate when not required, is erected at the front of the hull. At present the French Army VABs are not fitted with the water jets for financial reasons, although the PC command post version is.

In the French Army, the VAB is used to transport MILAN anti-tank teams. Optional equipment for the VAB includes an air-conditioning system, armoured grenade thrower hood, firing gun port with incorporated observation port, gas dispenser, NBC system (standard for French Army vehicles), infra-red or passive night vision equipment, public address system and a front-mounted winch with a capacity of 7000 kg and supplied with 60 metres of cable.

Variants

VCI (Infantry Combat Vehicle)

The VCI (Véhicule de Combat de l'Infanterie) has a crew of three (commander, driver and gunner) and carries eight fully-equipped infantrymen. Armament consists of a Toucan I turret armed with a 20 mm cannon and a 7·62 mm coaxial machine gun. A total of 700 rounds of 20 mm and 2000 rounds of 7·62 mm ammunition is carried. It was developed for the export market. This model has also been adopted by the French Air Force as the VIB (Vehicule d'Intervention du Base). This is the 4 × 4 model fitted with a GIAT Toucan I turret. The VCI can also be fitted with the new Creusot-Loire TL 20 turret.

VAB Echelon (Repair Vehicle)

This is fitted with welding equipment, work bench and tools for carrying out vehicle repairs in the field. Armament consists of a Creusot-Loire TLi.52A turret over the commander's position. This model has been adopted by the French Army and other foreign armies.

VCAC HOT (Anti-tank) Mephisto

This model is now in service with the French Army in its 4 × 4 configuration and is basically the VAB with the Euromissile Mephisto system with four ready-to-launch HOT missiles. When travelling the launcher is retracted into the hull making the vehicle very difficult to distinguish from the APC version. A further eight missiles are carried in reserve in the hull.

VCAC HOT (Anti-tank) UTM 800

This has been developed for the export market and is a VAB fitted with the Euromissile UTM 800 turret with four ready-to-launch HOT missiles and a further 16 missiles in reserve in the hull. This model is known to be in service with Qatar.

VCAC MILAN (Anti-tank) MCT

For trials purposes a VAB (4 × 4) vehicle has been fitted with the Euromissile MILAN Compact Turret (MCT) with two 2000 metre range MILAN ATGWs in the ready-to-launch position.

VAB PC (Command Vehicle)

This has been developed to meet the requirements of the French Army and is the basic VAB fitted with mapboards and additional communications equipment, with a crew of six. The VAB could be used to mount the RASIT ground surveillance radar, RATAC artillery radar, and be used as a

VCAC HOT with Euromissile UTM 800 turret with four ready-to-launch HOT ATGWs (Christopher F Foss)

VCAC HOT anti-tank vehicle with Euromissile Mephisto launcher in elevated position and missiles ready for launch

fire direction centre (VAB FDC) and forward observation officer vehicle (VAB FOO) acting as part of the ATILA system and to mount parts of the RITA communications system.

VAB Sanitaire (Ambulance)

This is unarmed and can carry four stretcher or ten seated patients, or two stretcher and five seated patients. This version, which has been adopted by the French Army, is fitted with a ventilation system and carries first aid equipment.

VMO (Internal Security Vehicle)

This is called the Vehicule de Sécurité and has been developed for export. It can be fitted with a variety of light armament installations over the commander's position including the Creusot-Loire TLi.52A armed with a 7·62 mm machine gun or the Creusot-Loire TLi 52 G turret. Mounted at the front of the hull is a hydraulically-operated obstacle-clearing blade, and special protection is fitted against petrol bombs. Mounted in each side of the hull and at the rear is a special firing port with a vision block over it, which allows three of the crew members to use their small arms from inside the vehicle in complete safety.

VTM 120 (6 × 6) mortar towing vehicle

VTM 120 (Mortar Towing Vehicle)

This is called the Véhicule Tracteur de Mortier, is already in service with the French Army and tows a Brandt 120 mm mortar. The VTM 120 has a crew of six, a Creusot-Loire TLi.52A turret at the front of the hull and carries 70 mortar bombs. An 81 mm mortar version of the VAB has been developed to the prototype stage. In this model the mortar fires through a two-part opening in the roof.

120 mm Mortar Carrier

The private venture 120 mm mortar carrier version of the VAB was shown for the first time in June 1983. The Brandt MO 120 LT mortar is turntable-mounted, firing through a two-part roof hatch that opens either side. The mortar, which is normally towed behind a tracked or wheeled vehicle, has a maximum range of 6700 metres. The crew of six consists of the driver, commander/machine gun operator and four mortarmen. The prototype was shown at Satory fitted with a Creusot-Loire TLi 52 A turret with a 7·62 mm machine gun, special Barracuda paint, Jaeger fire-extinguishing system and a Crouzet land navigation system.

Anti-aircraft Vehicles

The VAB chassis was to have been the basis for the now cancelled VADAR twin 20 mm self-propelled anti-aircraft gun system for the French Army. It has been fitted with the ESD TA 20/RA 20 twin 20 mm turret, and nine of these have been sold to Oman. The VAB can also be fitted with a six-round MATRA SATCP anti-aircraft missile system.

VBC 90

This is a 6 × 6 armoured car with a TS 90 turret armed with a long-barrelled 90 mm gun that uses automotive parts of the VAB (6 × 6) vehicle.

SPECIFICATIONS

(4 × 4 version; data in square brackets relate to 6 × 6 model where different)

CREW	2 + 10	MAX ROAD SPEED		ENGINE	MAN D. 2356 HM 72
CONFIGURATION	4 × 4 [6 × 6]	5th gear	92 km/h	(see note below)	6-cylinder in-line
COMBAT WEIGHT	13 000 [14 200] kg	4th gear	58 km/h		water-cooled diesel
UNLOADED WEIGHT	11 000 [12 200] kg	3rd gear	34 km/h		developing 235 hp at 2200
POWER-TO-WEIGHT		2nd gear	20 km/h		rpm
RATIO	18.07 [16.54] hp/tonne	1st gear	12 km/h	TRANSMISSION	Transfluid with 5 forward and
LENGTH	5.98 m	reverse	13 km/h		1 reverse gears
WIDTH	2.49 m	MAX WATER SPEED	7 km/h	STEERING	recirculating ball,
HEIGHT (to hull top)	2.06 m	FUEL CAPACITY	300 litres		hydraulically-assisted
GROUND CLEARANCE		MAX ROAD RANGE	1000 km	TYRES	14.00 × 20
axles	0.4 m	FORDING	amphibious	BRAKES	disc
hull	0.5 m	GRADIENT	60%	SUSPENSION	independent (torsion bar and
TRACK	2.035 m	SIDE SLOPE	35%		telescopic shock absorbers)
WHEELBASE	3 [1.5 + 1.5] m	TRENCH	n/app [1 m]	ELECTRICAL SYSTEM	24 V
ANGLE OF APPROACH/		VERTICAL OBSTACLE	0.6 m	BATTERIES	4 × 12 V 6TN
DEPARTURE	45°/45°	TURNING RADIUS	9 m		

Status: In production. In service with Central African Republic, Cyprus (84 ordered in 1984), France, Ivory Coast (13 4 × 4), Lebanon (6 plus a further batch of 30 delivered in 1983–84), Mauritius (11 4 × 4), Morocco (including 11 mortar towing, 86 command vehicles, 20 ECH repair vehicles, 32 Mephisto anti-tank vehicles, remainder being APCs or internal security vehicles), Oman (24 6 × 6), Qatar (160, including 24 UTM-800), United Arab Emirates (20 6 × 6) and other undisclosed countries, including some in the Middle East.

Note: From 1983 the MAN engine was replaced in production vehicles by the Renault VI MIDS 06.20.45, six-cylinder in-line water-cooled turbo-charged diesel developing 230 hp at 2200 rpm.

Manufacturers: Prime contractor is Renault Véhicules Industriels with the collaboration of Creusot-Loire. Marketing by Société des Matériels Spéciaux Renault V.I-Creusot-Loire, 316 Bureaux de la Colline, 92213 Saint-Cloud, Cedex, France.

Berliet VXB-170 Armoured Personnel Carrier

Development

In the mid-1960s, as a private venture, Berliet started the development of a 4 × 4 armoured personnel carrier which would use automotive components from its wide range of tactical military vehicles then in production. The first prototype of this vehicle, called the BL-12, was completed in March 1968 and shown for the first time at the 1969 Satory

Exhibition of Military Equipment. A second vehicle was built for the French Army but it did not place a production order for the BL-12.

The French Gendarmerie placed an order for five slightly modified vehicles which were delivered from 1971. Following successful trials with these vehicles the French Gendarmerie placed an initial order for 50 vehicles for internal security use, the first of which were completed at Berliet's Bourge facility in 1973. The total Gendarmerie requirement was for about

400 vehicles but substantially fewer than this were eventually ordered.

The VXB-170 (Véhicule Blindé à Vocations Multiples, or Multi-Purpose Armoured Vehicle) was one of the three entries in the competition for the VAB vehicle for the French Army. This competition was however won by the Renault (4 × 4 and 6 × 6) range of vehicles. In 1975 Berliet became part of the Renault Group which also controlled Saviem so after completion of the VXB order for the French Gendarmerie, Gabon and Senegal, production stopped.

Description

The hull of the VXB is made of all-welded steel. The driver is seated at the front of the hull on the left side with the commander to his right. In front of the driver and commander is a large windscreen which, when in action, is covered by a two-piece armoured screen hinged at the top. To the left of the driver and right of the commander is a smaller window, covered by a flap hinged at the bottom when in action. Over the top of the driver's position are three observation periscopes for when the windscreen is covered and over the commander's position is a single-piece hatch cover that opens to the right with a swivel-mounted periscope for all-round observation.

The main armament is installed in the centre of the vehicle behind the driver's and commander's position. There is an entry door in each side of the hull and a third door at the rear of the hull on the right side. In addition to the roof hatch on which the main armament is installed there are three other roof hatches: two in line with the doors in the sides of the hull, one of which opens forwards and the other to the rear and a third in the aisle which connects the personnel compartment with the door in the rear of the hull.

In the original model there were seven firing ports, two in the left side (one of which was in the door), four in the right side (of which one was in the door) and one in the door in the rear of the vehicle. Vehicles delivered to the French Gendarmerie have five bullet-proof windows, two in each side of the hull (of which one is in the door) and one in the door in the rear of the vehicle. These can be opened to allow the troops to fire their weapons from inside the vehicle. The Gendarmerie vehicles also have a single-piece hatch cover over the driver's rather than the commander's position and there is no hatch cover over the aisle.

The engine is at the rear of the hull on the left side and access panels are provided in the top and rear of the hull for maintenance.

Power is transmitted from the engine to the gearbox and then by a propeller shaft to the two-speed transfer box in the

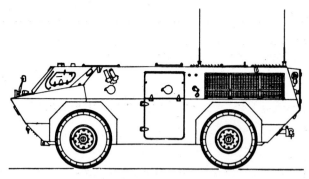

Berliet VXB-170 APC without armament installed

Berliet VXB-170 with Creusot-Loire STB.80 mount and 7.62 mm machine gun

centre of the vehicle under the floor. Power is then taken from the transfer box to the front and rear axles via propeller shafts. The front and rear wheels have planetary reduction gears and the rear axle has a pneumatically-controlled inter-wheel differential lock. The suspension at each wheel station consists of a concentric helical spring and a hydraulic shock absorber.

The basic vehicle is fully amphibious, being propelled in the water by its wheels. Optional equipment includes a heater, hydraulic obstacle-clearing blade at the front of the hull (as fitted to French Gendarmerie vehicles), infra-red or passive night vision equipment, NBC system, winch with a capacity of 3500 to 4500 kg (and 60 metres of cable) and bullet-proof tyres.

The vehicles delivered to the French Gendarmerie were originally fitted with a simple pintle-mounted machine gun but some were subsequently fitted with the SAMM S365.3 (now designated the BTM 103) light turret which is armed with a 7.62 mm machine gun and a 40 mm grenade launcher. Elevation limits of the weapons are from −15 to +60 degrees.

SPECIFICATIONS					
CREW	1 + 11	MAX SPEED		STEERING	hydraulic power-assisted
CONFIGURATION	4 × 4	road	85 km/h		
COMBAT WEIGHT	12 700 kg*	water	4 km/h	SUSPENSION	helical springs and hydraulic shock absorbers
UNLOADED WEIGHT	9800 kg	FUEL CAPACITY	220 litres		
POWER-TO-WEIGHT RATIO	13.38 hp/tonne	MAX RANGE ROAD (at 50 km/h)	750 km	TYRES	14.00 × 20
				ELECTRICAL SYSTEM	24 V
LENGTH	5.99 m	FORDING	amphibious	BATTERIES	4 × 12 V
WIDTH	2.5 m	GRADIENT	60%	ARMAMENT	1 × 7.62 mm MG
HEIGHT (without armament)	2.05 m	SIDE SLOPE	30%	SMOKE-LAYING EQUIPMENT	2 smoke dischargers either side of hull (optional)
		VERTICAL OBSTACLE	0.3 m		
GROUND CLEARANCE (transfer case)	0.45 m	TURNING RADIUS	7.8 m		
		ENGINE	Berliet model V 800 M V-8 diesel developing 170 hp at 3000 rpm	ARMOUR	7 mm
TRACK	2.04 m			* Depending on armament	
WHEELBASE	3 m				
ANGLE OF APPROACH/ DEPARTURE	45°/45°	TRANSMISSION	pre-selective with 6 forward and 1 reverse gears		
		TRANSFER BOX	2-speed		

Status: Production complete. In service with France (Gendarmerie), Gabon and Senegal.

Manufacturer: Berliet, Bourge. Société des Automobiles Berliet, 160 boulevard de Verdun, 92400 Courbevoie, France.

Panhard VCR Armoured Personnel Carrier

Development

The VCR (Véhicule de Combat à Roues) range of armoured personnel carriers was developed by Panhard as a private venture from 1975 and is aimed specifically at the export market. The range was first shown in 1977 at the Satory Exhibition of Military Equipment and entered production at Panhard's new Marolles factory the following year. First production vehicles, equipped with the Euromissile UTM 800 turret, were completed in 1979. The VCR range of armoured personnel carriers uses 95 per cent of the automotive components of the Panhard ERC range of 6 × 6 armoured cars which was also shown for the first time in 1977. Latest production vehicles have a redesigned hull, troop compartment roof 400 mm above the commander's

Panhard VCR/TT (Transport de Troupes) armed with Creusot-Loire STB rotary support shield fitted with 7.62 mm machine gun and winch mounted on hull front. This particular vehicle has been modified to carry electronic warfare equipment

Panhard VCR/TT fitted with front-mounted winch, windscreen cover over driver's position and armed with Creusot-Loire gun-ring model CB 127 with 12.7 mm (0.50) M2 HB machine gun

position, external stowage boxes, more internal hull space, twin doors at the hull rear and fuel tanks repositioned from inside the troop compartment to under the floor.

In June 1983 Panhard issued new specifications for the VCR range of 6 × 6 APCs. These showed that there had been slight changes to the vehicle with the wheelbase increased from 1.425 + 1.425 metres to 1.66 + 1.425 metres. This has made the hull slightly longer and increased the overall weight of the vehicle. The specifications for the VCR/TH anti-tank version remain unchanged except for an increase in loaded and empty weights.

Description

The all-welded steel hull of the VCR/TT (Transport de Troupes) protects the crew against small arms fire and shell splinters. The floor of the hull consists of two plates welded together to form a flat V which helps the vehicle to slide off obstacles and also offers resistance to damage from mines.

The driver sits at the front of the hull in the centre and has a single-piece hatch cover that opens to his right with three integral periscopes for forward observation, the centre one replaceable by an infra-red or image intensification periscope for driving at night.

The commander sits to the rear of the driver on the left side at a higher level and has a single-piece hatch cover that opens forwards and seven periscopes around his position.

The engine is to the rear of the driver on the right side and power is transmitted through the single clutch plate to a transversely-mounted Panhard gearbox (as fitted to the AML armoured car and M3 APC) with six forward and one reverse gears and incorporating a limited slip differential. Drive from the bevel gears to the road wheels is by a train of gears housed within trailing arms which independently locate the wheels.

The front and rear wheels are sprung by single coil springs with telescopic hydraulic dampers. The centre wheels, which are raised off the ground when on roads, are sprung by hydro-pneumatic units. The centre wheels are powered even when raised clear of the road surface. All wheels have disc brakes. Only the front wheels are steered, and steering is hydraulically assisted. The low-pressure tyres are fitted with

Panhard VCR/TT built to latest production standard without armament installed

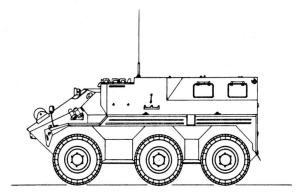

Hutchinson cellular inner tubes which enable the vehicle to travel for at least 100 km at 30 km/h when the tyres have been punctured by bullets.

The ten infantrymen are seated on bench seats: five along each side of the hull facing each other. They enter and leave the vehicle by a large door in the rear of the hull which is hinged on the right side and has a single firing port. Two observation/firing hatches in each side of the troop compartment open upwards and can be locked open. The VCR/TTs built for the United Arab Emirates have a wider hull with double doors at the rear to give increased leg room.

The armament is mounted to the rear of the commander's position in the roof. When armed with a 7.62 mm machine gun the VCR/TT can carry nine men plus its crew of three (commander, driver and gunner, who sits on one of the bench seats when not manning the machine gun) but when heavy armament is installed, eg a 20 mm cannon, only six infantrymen can be carried plus a crew of three. The VCR/TT can be fitted with a variety of armament installations including a Creusot-Loire STB ring mount with a shield (which forms the hatch cover when not in use) and a 7.62 mm machine gun, Creusot-Loire CB rotating gun ring with a 7.62 mm machine gun, Creusot-Loire turret with twin 7.62 mm

Panhard VCR/TH with Euromissile UTM 800 turret with four ready-to-launch HOT ATGWs and Mascot 7.62 mm remote-controlled machine gun mount at rear

Panhard VCR/IS ambulance clearly showing higher hull of this model

machine guns, Creusot-Loire gun-ring model CB 20 with 20 mm cannon, Creusot-Loire gun ring with Brandt 60 mm breech-loaded mortar, Euromissile MCT MILAN turret with two ready-to-launch MILAN ATGWs, Creusot-Loire one-man turret Model TL.20 armed with a 20 mm cannon and a 7.62 mm machine gun, or a GIAT Toucan I turret armed with a 20 mm cannon, 7.62 mm machine gun and four smoke dischargers. There is also a single-piece hatch cover in the roof of the troop compartment at the rear which opens towards the front. A 7.62 mm machine gun on a Creusot-Loire STR rail mount can be mounted behind it. Two smoke dischargers can be mounted on either side of the hull if required.

The VCR is fully amphibious being propelled in the water by its wheels, with steering by turning the front road wheels as for land operations. Optional equipment includes a front-mounted winch with 60 metres of cable and a capacity of 3000 kg, NBC system, air-conditioning system and passive night vision equipment.

Variants

VCR/AT Repair Vehicle
The VCR/AT (Atelier Vehicle) is the latest member of the family and is the basic vehicle modified to undertake repairs in the field. It has no recovery capability although it can tow other vehicles.

Equipment installed includes a generator, tools, work benches, inspection lamp, tow bars and tow cables. A penthouse can be erected at the rear to enable repairs to be carried out in bad weather. A block and tackle can be erected at the rear allowing the VCR/AT to carry out engine and other component changes.

VCR/TH (Tourelle Hot) Anti-tank Vehicle
This is the basic VCR/TT fitted with the Euromissile UTM 800 HOT turret mounted on a raised plinth to the rear of the commander's position. The turret has four ready-to-launch HOT missiles and another ten missiles carried in reserve in the hull are loaded via a hatch in the right rear of the roof, which opens to the right. The turret has an optical sight with a magnification of ×3 (18-degree field of view) and ×12 (5-degree field of view), elevation being +10 degrees, depression −6 degrees and turret traverse 360 degrees.

Mounted on the roof at the rear on the left is a GIAT Mascot remote-controlled 7.62 mm machine gun, which can be elevated from −10 to +50 degrees and traversed through a full 360 degrees. Two hundred rounds of ready-use ammunition are provided for the weapon. Two smoke dischargers are mounted on the front of the hull at either side. Panhard has delivered 100 of these vehicles to Iraq.

VCR/IS (Intervention Sanitaire) Ambulance
The VCR/IS (Véhicule Blindé d'Intervention Sanitaire) is the ambulance member of the family and has much higher hull behind the commander than the basic VCR. The vehicle has a crew of three (commander, driver and orderly) and can carry four stretcher or six sitting and two stretcher patients.

The casualties enter the vehicle through a door at the rear of the hull that opens to the left and has a single vision port. Unlike the basic APC, there are no observation flaps in the sides of the hull.

Equipment carried includes folding stretchers, cupboards and instrument storage lockers, water tank, refrigerator and breathing and blood transfusion equipment. If required a tent, which is stowed in boxes on either side of the hull, can be erected at the rear of the hull.

VCR/PC (Poste de Commandement) Command Vehicle

This is basically the VCR/TT adapted for use as a command vehicle with mapboards, tables and additional communications equipment. It is probable that a command version based on the hull of the VCR/IS ambulance will be developed as this has more headroom than the basic vehicle.

SPECIFICATIONS Model	VCR/TT	VCR/PC	VCR/TH	VCR/AT	VCR/IS
	(APC)	(command)	(anti-tank)	(repair)	(ambulance)
CREW	3 + 9	6	4	4	3 + 4
CONFIGURATION	6 × 6	6 × 6	6 × 6	6 × 6	6 × 6
COMBAT WEIGHT	7900 kg	7900 kg	7800 kg	8200 kg	8100 kg
UNLOADED WEIGHT	6800 kg	7300 kg	7000 kg	7200 kg	7500 kg
POWER-TO-WEIGHT RATIO	19.6 hp/tonne	19.6 hp/tonne	19.8 hp/tonne	18.9 hp/tonne	19.15 hp/tonne
LENGTH	4.875 m	4.875 m	4.565 m	4.875 m	4.875 m
WIDTH	2.478 m	2.478 m	2.478 m	2.478 m	2.478 m
HEIGHT					
including armament	2.56 m (7.62 mm MG)	2.56 m	2.968 m	2.71 m	n/app
to hull top	2.13 m	2.13 m	2.03 m	2.13 m	2.53 m
GROUND CLEARANCE					
4 wheels	0.315 m	0.315 m	0.315 m	0.315 m	0.315 m
6 wheels	0.37 m	0.37 m	0.37 m	0.37 m	0.37 m
TRACK	2.16 m	2.16 m	2.16 m	2.16 m	2.16 m
WHEELBASE	1.66 m + 1.425 m	1.66 m + 1.425 m	1.425 m + 1.425 m	1.66 m + 1.425 m	1.66 m + 1.425 m
ANGLE OF APPROACH/ DEPARTURE	53°/45°	53°/45°	53°/45°	53°/45°	53°/45°
MAX SPEED					
road	100 km/h	100 km/h	100 km/h	100 km/h	100 km/h
water	4 km/h	4 km/h	4 km/h	4 km/h	4 km/h
MAX ROAD RANGE	800 km	800 km	800 km	800 km	800 km
FUEL CAPACITY	242 litres	242 litres	242 litres	242 litres	242 litres
FORDING	amphibious	amphibious	amphibious	amphibious	amphibious
GRADIENT	60%	60%	60%	60%	60%
SIDE SLOPE	30%	30%	30%	30%	30%
VERTICAL OBSTACLE	0.8 m	0.8 m	0.8 m	0.8 m	0.8 m
TRENCH	1.1 m	1.1 m	1.1 m	1.1 m	1.1 m
ENGINE	Peugeot PRV V-6 petrol developing 155 hp at 5500 rpm				
TRANSMISSION	Panhard with 6 forward and 1 reverse gears				
STEERING	power-assisted	power-assisted	power-assisted	power-assisted	power-assisted
CLUTCH	hydraulic control	hydraulic control	hydraulic control	hydraulic control	hydraulic control
TYRES	11.00 × 16	11.00 × 16	11.00 × 16	11.00 × 16	11.00 × 16
ELECTRICAL SYSTEM	24 V	24 V	24 V	24 V	24 V
ARMAMENT	1 × 7.62 mm MG, or 1 × 20 mm cannon (see text)	optional	launcher with 4 HOT ATGWs, plus remote-controlled 7.62 mm MG	optional	none
SMOKE DISCHARGERS	optional	2 × 2	2 × 2	2 × 2	2 × 2
ARMOUR (estimated)	8–12 mm	8–12 mm	8–12 mm	8–12 mm	8–12 mm

Status: In production. In service with Iraq (100 VCR/TH), Mexico (2) and the United Arab Emirates (86).

Manufacturer: Société de Constructions Mécaniques Panhard et Levassor, 18 avenue d'Ivry, 75621 Paris, France.

Panhard VCR (4 × 4) Armoured Personnel Carrier

Development

This vehicle has been developed as a private venture and was announced in June 1979. It is essentially a 4 × 4 version of the Panhard VCR (6 × 6) APC which is already in production and is fully described in the previous entry. It may well be the replacement for the successful Panhard M3 (4 × 4) APC which entered production in 1971. Ninety-five per cent of the automotive components of the 4 × 4 VCR are identical to those of the 6 × 6 VCR (Véhicule de Combat à Roues).

Description

The only major difference from the 6 × 6 model is that the 4 × 4 has a slightly different roof arrangement. The main armament installation is behind the commander's position and a variety of armaments can be mounted there including a Creusot-Loire STB ring mount with a shield (which forms the hatch cover when not in use) and a 7.62 mm machine gun, Creusot-Loire CB rotating gun ring with a 7.62 mm machine gun, Creusot-Loire turret with twin 7.62 mm machine guns, Creusot-Loire gun ring model CB.20 with a 20 mm cannon, Creusot-Loire gun ring with a Brandt 60 mm breech-loaded mortar and the Euromissile MCT MILAN turret with two MILAN ATGWs ready to launch. There is also a single-piece front-opening hatch cover in the roof of the troop compartment at the rear behind which a 7.62 mm machine gun on a Creusot-Loire STR rail mount can be mounted.

The VCR is fully amphibious, being propelled in the water by two waterjets, one either side of the hull, which have deflectors for steering when afloat.

Panhard VCR/TT with trim boards erected at front of hull after amphibious operations

Panhard VCR (4 × 4) with Euromissile Mephisto missile launcher raised and HOT ATGWs ready for launching (Christopher F Foss)

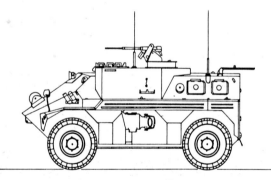

Panhard VCR (4 × 4) APC armed with Creusot-Loire CB rotating gun ring with 7.62 mm machine gun

Variants

In addition to being used as an armoured personnel carrier, the VCR (4 × 4) can be used for other roles such as command, ambulance and cargo carrier. A VCR (4 × 4) with a redesigned hull fitted with a Euromissile Mephisto launcher system with four HOT ATGWs and another eight missiles carried in reserve was shown at the 1979 Paris Air Show. This model weighs 7800 kg and has a crew of three consisting of commander, gunner/loader and driver.

SPECIFICATIONS

CREW	3 + 9
CONFIGURATION	4 × 4
COMBAT WEIGHT	7800 kg
UNLOADED WEIGHT	6800 kg
POWER-TO-WEIGHT	
RATIO	19.87 hp/tonne
LENGTH	4.875 m
WIDTH	2.478 m
HEIGHT	
with 7.62 mm turret	2.694 m
to hull top	2.13 m
GROUND CLEARANCE	
maximum	0.37 m
minimum	0.315 m
TRACK	2.16 m
WHEELBASE	3.085 m
STEERING	hydraulically assisted
MAX SPEED	
road	100 km/h
water	7.2 km/h
FUEL CAPACITY	242 litres
MAX ROAD RANGE	800 km
FORDING	amphibious
GRADIENT	60%
SIDE SLOPE	30%
VERTICAL OBSTACLE	0.4 m
ENGINE	Peugeot V-6 petrol developing 155 hp at 5500 rpm
TRANSMISSION	Panhard manual with 6 forward and 1 reverse gears
TYRES	11.00 × 16
ELECTRICAL SYSTEM	24 V
ARMOUR (estimated)	8–12 mm

Status: Production. In service with Argentina.

Manufacturer: Société de Constructions Mécaniques Panhard et Levassor, 18 avenue d'Ivry, 75621 Paris, France.

Panhard M3 Armoured Personnel Carrier

Development

The M3 armoured personnel carrier was designed as a private venture by Panhard with the first prototype being completed in 1969. This had square-cut sides with a single door in each side of the hull and twin doors in the hull rear. It was intended that each door would have a single circular firing port. Mounted on the top of the hull was a Creusot-Loire CAFL.38 turret armed with a 7.5 mm machine gun.

The first production vehicle, with a redesigned hull incorporating three hatches either side of the troop compartment, was completed in 1971. Since then over 1500 M3's have been built and exported to over 33 countries. Ninety-five per cent of the Panhard M3s automotive components are identical to those of the Panhard AML series of light armoured vehicles of which over 4000 have been built.

Description

The hull of the M3 is made of all-welded steel with the driver seated at the front of the vehicle. He has a single-piece hatch cover that opens to the right in which there are three periscopes, the centre one replaceable by an infra-red or image intensification periscope for night driving.

The engine is immediately behind the driver with the air-inlet louvres above and to the rear of the driver, air-outlet louvres on either side of the roof and the two exhaust pipes running along the top of the hull, one on each side.

The gear casing is crosswise and consists of two gearboxes in one coupled on both sides of the bevel pinion. The low-

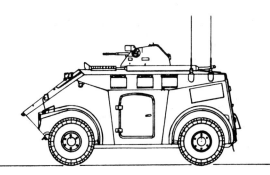

Panhard M3 APC fitted with Creusot-Loire TL.2i series turret armed with twin 7.62 mm machine guns

Panhard M3 APC of 1st Armoured Squadron, Irish Army, fitted with one-man Creusot-Loire TL.2i series turret armed with 7.62 mm MAG GPMGs (Denis McCarthy)

range gearbox comprises two low gears, top and one reverse for use in rough country and the high-range gearbox has three low ranges and one overdrive. When the low-range gearbox is in direct drive, the four ratios of the high-range box command the four upper gears of the range (6th, 5th, 4th and 3rd).

Drive is transmitted from the main gearbox to the two lateral boxes, which transmit power to the front wheels by pinions and to the rear wheels by drive shafts that run along the inside of the hull.

Ball type differentials in the gearbox and in each of the rear lateral transfer boxes prevent wheel slip. The suspension at each wheel station consists of coil springs and hydro-pneumatic shock absorbers acting on suspension arms of the wheel mechanism. The tyres have puncture-proof Hutchinson inner tubes.

There are four doors in the M3, one in each side of the hull and two in the rear. The rear doors both have a firing port. Along the upper part of each side of the hull are three hatches hinged at the top that can be locked open. When being used as an APC a maximum of ten men can be carried in addition to the crew of two, or 1360 kg of cargo.

There are two circular hatches in the roof, one behind the engine compartment and a second one at the rear with a single-piece hatch cover that opens forwards and is normally fitted with a Creusot-Loire STR rail armed with a 7.62 mm machine gun. A wide range of armament installations can be mounted on the forward hatch, brief details of which follow:

Creusot-Loire STB rotary support shield armed with 7.62 mm machine gun, elevation +45 degrees, depression −15 degrees, total traverse 360 degrees:
Creusot-Loire CB rotating gun-ring with 7.62 mm machine gun, elevation +45 degrees, depression −15 degrees, total traverse 360 degrees:
Creusot-Loire CAFL.38 turret with 7.62 mm machine gun, elevation +45 degrees, depression −15 degrees, total traverse 360 degrees:
Creusot-Loire TLi.G turret armed with 7.62 mm machine gun and 40 mm smoke discharger, elevation +55 degrees, depression −13 degrees, total traverse 360 degrees:
Creusot-Loire TL.2i turret armed with twin 7.62 mm machine guns with an elevation of +55 degrees, depression −13 degrees, total traverse 360 degrees:
Creusot-Loire CB.127 gun ring shield armed with 12.7 mm (0.50) machine gun, elevation +65 degrees, depression −15 degrees, traverse 360 degrees:
Creusot-Loire CB.20 gun ring shield armed with 20 mm cannon, elevation +65 degrees, depression −15 degrees, total traverse 360 degrees:
Creusot-Loire gun ring shield with 60 mm Brandt breech-loaded mortar with an elevation of +75 degrees, depression of −15 degrees and a total traverse of 360 degrees:
Euromissile MCT turret with two ready-to-launch MILAN ATGWs:
Toucan I turret armed with a 20 mm cannon and a 7.62 mm machine gun.

The basic Panhard M3 is fully amphibious without preparation, being propelled in the water by its wheels, steering when afloat by turning the front wheels as on land. Optional equipment includes an air-conditioning system and smoke dischargers.

Variants

M3/VDA Anti-aircraft Vehicle
This model is in service with Abu Dhabi and the Ivory Coast and is fitted with a one-man power-operated turret armed with twin 20 mm cannon and a surveillance radar.

M3/VAT Repair Vehicle
This model has a crew of five (commander, driver and three mechanics) and equipment fitted includes a pulley block with

Panhard M3 APC showing obstacle-crossing capabilities

Infantry entering Panhard M3 APC

Panhard M3/VLA engineer vehicle with obstacle-clearing blade raised at front of hull

struts and tackle, cutting equipment, generator, benches, vice, tow bars, tow cables and a complete range of tools.

M3/VPC Command Vehicle

This model has additional communications equipment, two additional batteries, and map tables. Its basic crew consists of commander, assistant commander, driver and two radio operators plus command staff. Armament normally comprises a 7.62 mm machine gun on a Creusot-Loire STB mount.

M3/VLA Engineer Vehicle

This model is essentially the M3 APC fitted with a removable hydraulically-operated dozer blade at the front of the hull and has a crew of six consisting of commander/gunner, driver, pioneer section commander and three pioneers.

M3/VTS Ambulance

This model has a crew of three (driver and two orderlies) and can carry four stretcher patients, or six sitting wounded, or two stretcher patients and three sitting wounded. It is unarmed and has a large single-piece door in the rear of the hull that is hinged on the left. Medical equipment carried includes oxygen, blood transfusion and a complete first aid outfit.

M3/Radar

The Panhard M3 can also be used to carry electronic warfare equipment, this model is called the M3/VSB, as well as being fitted with a variety of radar systems such as the RASIT battlefield surveillance radar or the ESD RA 20S surveillance radar. The latter is used with the Panhard M3/VDA twin 20 mm self-propelled anti-aircraft gun system when this is not equipped with its own individual radar.

SPECIFICATIONS

CREW	2 + 10	4th gear, high range	35 km/h	TRANSMISSION	manual with 6 forward and 1 reverse gears
CONFIGURATION	4 × 4	3rd gear, high range	18.8 km/h		
COMBAT WEIGHT	6100 kg	3rd gear, low range	18.8 km/h	CLUTCH	centrifugal with electro-magnetic automatic control
UNLOADED WEIGHT	5300 kg	2nd gear, low range	9.3 km/h		
POWER-TO-WEIGHT		1st gear, low range	4.5 km/h		
RATIO	14.75 hp/tonne	reverse	5.5 km/h	SUSPENSION	independent, coil spring and hydro-pneumatic shock absorbers acting on suspension trailing arms of wheel mechanism
LENGTH	4.45 m	MAX WATER SPEED	4 km/h		
WIDTH	2.4 m	FUEL CAPACITY	165 litres		
HEIGHT		MAX ROAD RANGE	600 km		
with Creusot-Loire TL.2i		FUEL CONSUMPTION	0.26 litre/km		
turret armed with twin 7.62		FORDING	amphibious	TYRES	11.00 × 16
mm	2.48 m	GRADIENT	60%	BRAKES	
machine guns		SIDE SLOPE	30%	main	hydraulic, dual circuit
to hull top	2 m	VERTICAL OBSTACLE	0.3 m	parking	handbrake operating on gearbox output shaft
GROUND CLEARANCE	0.35 m	TRENCH			
TRACK	2.05 m	1 channel	0.8 m		
WHEELBASE	2.7 m	5 channels	3.1 m	ELECTRICAL SYSTEM	24 V
ANGLE OF APPROACH/		TURNING RADIUS	6.55 m	BATTERIES	2 × 12 V
DEPARTURE	68°/50°	ENGINE	Panhard Model 4 HD	ARMOUR	8–12 mm
MAX ROAD SPEED			4-cylinder air-cooled petrol		
6th gear, high range	90 km/h		developing 90 hp at 4700		
5th gear, high range	61 km/h		rpm		

Status: In production. In service with Algeria (in 1982 ordered 44 APCs with SAMM MG turret, five VPC, two VAT, two VLA, two VTS, all for Gendarmerie use), Angola (left behind when Portugal withdrew), Bahrain, Burundi (9 ordered in 1982), Chad (including some with Toucan 1 turret), Gabon, Iraq, Ireland, Ivory Coast, Kenya, Lebanon, Malaysia, Mauritania, Morocco, Niger, Nigeria (including four with RASIT radars, 4 VTS, 4 VAT and 6 VPC), Portugal, Rwanda, Saudi Arabia, Senegal, Spain (army and marines), Sudan (including some with RASIT surveillance radar and some with ESD RA 20S airspace surveillance radar), Togo, United Arab Emirates, Upper Volta and Zaïre.

Manufacturer: Société de Constructions Mécaniques Panhard et Levassor, 18 avenue d'Ivry, 75621 Paris, France.

ACMAT Armoured Personnel Carrier (TPK 4.20 VSC)

Development
The TPK 4.20 VSC armoured personnel carrier has been developed as a private venture by Ateliers de Construction Mécanique de l'Atlantique (ACMAT) and is essentially the well known VLRA (4 × 4) 2500 kg long-range reconnaissance vehicle fitted with an armoured body. The VLRA is used by some 37 countries in Europe, Africa, the Middle East and the Far East.

Description
The hull of the TPK 4.20 VSC is made of all-welded nickel chrome molybdenum steel 5.8 mm thick and the vehicle has a similar layout to the basic VLRA with the engine at the front, behind which are seats for the commander and driver, and the troop compartment at the rear.

Immediately in front of the driver and commander is a bullet-proof windscreen which is covered when in a combat area by a hatch hinged at the top. The commander and driver enter and leave the vehicle by a side door that opens to the rear. This has a bullet-proof window covered by a flap that opens upwards below which is a circular firing port if required. Above the commander's and driver's positions is a single-piece hatch cover opening to the rear.

The troops are carried on bench seats down either side of the hull. The sides of the rear troop compartment are carried upright to give the maximum possible protection to the occupants. If fire is to be returned or if rapid dismounting is required, these sides can be hinged outward and downwards

ACMAT VSC with sides and rear of body folded down to show 81 mm mortar and troop seating arrangements

ACMAT VBL light armoured car with commander's and driver's armoured shutters raised

61

at their mid-point as shown in the accompanying photographs. The vehicle can also be delivered with a fully-enclosed, removable rear compartment to give improved protection from roof-mounted snipers.

If required an 81 mm Brandt mortar can be mounted in the rear. Various 12.7 mm and 7.62 mm machine guns can be pintle-mounted in the rear troop compartment.

VBL Light Armoured Car

This has the same chassis and hull front as the VSC armoured personnel carrier but has a fully-enclosed troop compartment at the rear. The troops are seated on bench seats down either side of the hull. In each side of the hull are four bullet-proof sliding vision blocks.

In the rear of the VBL are two outward opening doors, in each of which is a bullet-proof vision block covered by an armoured flap.

Mounted in the centre of the roof is the one-man turret armed with a 7.62 mm machine gun which is aimed using a roof-mounted periscope, or a Creusot-Loire one-man turret model TLi armed with a 12.7 mm (0.50) M2 HB machine gun. A Euromissile MILAN ATGW system can also be installed.

The VBL can be fitted with optional equipment including different radios and an air-conditioning system as well as being modified for more specific roles such as ambulance or command post.

SPECIFICATIONS (TPK 4.20 VSC)

CREW	2 + 8/10	TRACK	1.66 m	TRANSFER BOX	2-speed
CONFIGURATION	4 × 4	WHEELBASE	3.6 m	STEERING	worm and nut
COMBAT WEIGHT	7300 kg	ANGLE OF APPROACH/		SUSPENSION	leaf springs and double
UNLOADED WEIGHT	5880 kg	DEPARTURE	45°/35°		action hydraulic shock
WEIGHT ON FRONT AXLE		MAX SPEED	95 km/h		absorbers
empty	3300 kg	FUEL CAPACITY	360 litres	TYRES	12.50 × 20
loaded	3550 kg	MAX RANGE	1600 km	NUMBER OF TYRES	4 + 1 spare (run
WEIGHT ON REAR AXLE		FORDING	0.8 m		flat)
empty	2580 kg	GRADIENT	60%	BRAKES	
loaded	3750 kg	TURNING RADIUS	8.5 m	main	air/hydraulic
LENGTH	5.98 m	ENGINE	Perkins model 6.354.4	parking	mechanical
WIDTH	2.1 m		6-cylinder diesel developing	ELECTRICAL SYSTEM	24 V
HEIGHT (hull top)	2.205 m		125 hp at 2800 rpm	BATTERIES	2 × 6TN AS 188
GROUND CLEARANCE		GEARBOX	Type 435 manual with 4	ARMOUR	5.8 mm
axle	0.273 m		forward and 1 reverse gears		
hull	0.5 m	CLUTCH	single dry plate		

Status: Production. In service with a number of countries including Gabon and Ivory Coast.

Manufacturer: ACMAT, Ateliers de Construction Mécanique de l'Atlantique, Le Point du Jour, 44600 Saint-Nazaire, France.

GERMANY, FEDERAL REPUBLIC

Marder Mechanised Infantry Combat Vehicle

Development

In the late 1950s a chassis was developed which could be used for a number of basic vehicles including the Jagdpanzer Kanone and Jagdpanzer Rakete, reconnaissance tank (developed to the prototype stage but not placed in production), an MICV (which eventually became the Marder) and various other supporting vehicles, most of which did not enter service.

In January 1960 contracts for the design and construction of prototypes of the MICV were awarded to two groups of companies: the Rheinstahl group comprising Rheinstahl-Hanomag, Ruhrstahl, Witten-Annen and Büro Warnecke and the partnership Henschel Werke of Kassel and MOWAG of Kreuzlingen, Switzerland. Three vehicles were built by Hanomag, two by Henschel and two by MOWAG, known as the first series prototypes.

Between 1961 and 1963 the second series of prototypes was built, four by Hanomag, one by Henschel and three by MOWAG. There was then a pause in the development of the

vehicle as priority was given to the Jagdpanzer Kanone (which entered production at the works of both Hanomag and Henschel in 1965) and the Jagdpanzer Rakete (which entered production at the works of both Hanomag and Henschel in 1967 when production of the Kanone had been completed).

In 1966 the military requirements were completed and in 1967 the construction of the third and final series of prototypes began. Ten prototypes were built, three by Hanomag, four by Henschel and three by MOWAG.

Following the takeover of Henschel Werke in 1964 by the Rheinstahl Group most of the final development work was completed by Rheinstahl. The ten pre-production vehicles were completed in 1967/68 and in October 1968 the first vehicles were delivered to the West German Army for troop trials which ran from October 1968 to March 1969. In April 1969 companies were asked to tender for series production of the vehicle which was officially named the Marder in May 1969. In October 1969 Rheinstahl was nominated as prime contractor with MaK of Kiel as a sub-contractor. The first production vehicle was delivered to the Army in December

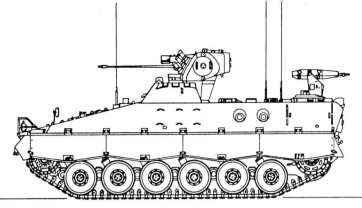

1970 but the first vehicles were not officially handed over until May 1971. Two production lines were established, one at Kassel and one at MaK of Kiel. The original contract covered the construction of 1926 vehicles by Rheinstahl and 875 vehicles by MaK but in 1974 Rheinstahl received a further order for 210 vehicles and total production by MaK (now Krupp MaK) amounted to 975 vehicles. Production of the Marder was finally completed in 1975.

The chassis of the Marder MICV remained in production at Kassel for the Roland 2 surface-to-air missile system until 1983.

Description

The all-welded hull of the Marder provides the crew with protection from small arms fire and shell splinters, with the front of the vehicle giving complete protection from 20 mm projectiles.

The driver sits at the front of the hull on the left side and has a single-piece hatch cover that opens to the right, in front of which are three periscopes, the centre one of which can be replaced by a passive night driving device. One of the infantrymen sits to the rear of the driver and has a single-piece hatch cover that opens to the right, with a periscope that can be traversed through a full 360 degrees.

The engine compartment is to the right of the driver and is coupled to a Renk four-speed HSWL-194 planetary gearbox and a stepless hydrostatic steering unit which transmits

power to the tracks via two final drive assemblies mounted at the front of the hull. The radiators are mounted at the rear of the hull, one either side of the ramp, with cooling air being sucked in through grilles in the top of the hull by an axial cooling fan.

The two-man turret, designed by Keller and Knappich, is mounted in the forward part of the roof with the commander on the right and the gunner on the left. The commander has a single-piece hatch cover that opens to the right while the gunner has a single-piece hatch cover that opens to the rear.

The 20 mm Rheinmetall MK 20 Rh 202 cannon is mounted externally and has an elevation of +65 degrees, depression of −17 degrees and 360-degree turret traverse. It is fed from three different belts which allows the gunner to select one type of ammunition at a time, for example AP when engaging light AFVs and HE when engaging softer targets. The empty cartridge cases are automatically ejected outside the turret.

Both the commander and gunner have a PERI Z 11 sight for use in the ground and anti-aircraft role with a magnification of ×2 and ×6 which can be replaced by an infra-red night periscope. In addition the commander has eight periscopes for all-round observation and the gunner has three.

Mounted coaxially above and to the right of the 20 mm cannon is a 7.62 mm MG 3 machine gun and mounted to the left of the 20 mm cannon are six electrically-operated smoke

Marder MICV with camouflage netting stowed on glacis plate and skirting removed to show suspension detail

dischargers. Mounted externally to the left of the gun mount is an infra-red/white light searchlight that moves in elevation with the main armament.

The six infantrymen are seated in the troop compartment at the rear of the hull, three down each side facing outwards. Their seating unit was designed by MOWAG and can be adjusted so that four men can sleep. Entry and exit is by a power-operated ramp at the rear of the hull that opens downwards. In each side of the troop compartment are two MOWAG-designed spherical firing ports and in the roof either side are two circular roof hatches and three periscopes. The firing ports, used in conjunction with the periscopes, allow four of the infantrymen to use their weapons from inside the vehicle in complete safety. All Marders have an NBC system.

Mounted over the top of the troop compartment at the rear of the hull is a MOWAG-designed remote-controlled 7.62 mm MG 3 machine gun, which has an elevation of +60 degrees, a depression of −15 degrees and a total traverse of 180 degrees.

The torsion bar suspension each side consists of six dual rubber-tyred road wheels with the drive sprocket at the front and the idler at the rear, and three track return rollers. The first, second, fifth and sixth road wheel stations have a hydraulic shock absorber. The Diehl tracks have replaceable rubber pads.

The Marder can ford to a depth of 1.5 metres without preparation or to 2.5 metres with the aid of a kit. An amphibious kit has been developed for the Marder but has not yet been adopted.

All Marders used by the West German Army except command vehicles have been fitted with a Euromissile MILAN ATGW launcher.

Variants

There have been many variants of the Marder MICV, especially in the early days of the project, including an anti-aircraft gun vehicle (called the Flak Zwilling but cancelled in favour of the Gepard), ambulance (2HK 2/2), cargo carrier (RU121), artillery observation vehicle (called the Beobachtungs Panzer Artillerie, but cancelled in favour of a cheaper model based on an M113A1 chassis), 120 mm mortar carrier (245 were ordered in 1969 but subsequently cancelled, instead the mortars were mounted in M113A1 APCs, the conversion work being carried out by Thyssen Henschel), multiple rocket launcher and Rapier SAM vehicle (private venture between the then British Aircraft Corporation and Rheinstahl, consisted of the clear weather Rapier system mounted on the top of the Marder chassis with four ready-to-launch missiles). More recently Thyssen Henschel has suggested that a 160 mm mortar be carried in place of the 120 mm mortar.

Marder with 25 mm cannon

The West German Army has a requirement for a new 25 mm cannon to replace the Rheinmetall 20 mm Rh 202 weapon at present installed in the turret of the Marder MICV and the Luchs reconnaissance vehicle, as well as the twin Rheinmetall anti-aircraft system. The Oerlikon proposal to install the GDD-A turret was rejected primarily on cost grounds.

To meet this requirement Rheinmetall and Mauser have each designed a 25 mm cannon which has been tested in a slightly modified turret of a Marder MICV. The Rheinmetall cannon is designated the Rh 205 and the Mauser cannon the

Marder MICV with Euromissile MILAN mounted on right side of turret

Model E. In addition to firing AP and HE ammunition an APFSDS projectile has been developed which will penetrate the armour of the Soviet BMP MICV. The Mauser E cannon has been selected but will not be introduced until the late 1980s for financial reasons.

Upgraded Marder

From 1982 most Marders were upgraded to one of two new standards, A1 or A1A, at the rate of about 80 vehicles per month.

A1

This is the complete upgrade and 670 vehicles have been brought up to this standard. Main improvements are better firepower due to double belt feed for 20 mm cannon, improved night capabilities with installation of PERI Z 59 night sight with sight head PERI Z 16 which uses image intensification technique with thermal pointer, remaining active infra-red searchlight and sight are retained, holder for commander's NBC mask on upper mounting for MILAN ATGW, new racks for water cans inside, stowage for image intensification equipment, flaps for periscopes, storage for helmets and two five-metre tow ropes. This model weighs 30 000 kg, has a crew of four and carries five instead of six infantrymen.

A1A

As A1 version but without the passive night vision equipment. 1466 Marders have been brought up to this standard.

Marder with Radar System

First prototypes of the Radarpanzer TÜR (Tiefflieger-Überwachungs-Radar) based on the chassis of the Marder MICV were delivered to the West German Army late in 1981. This is an extensively modified Marder hull with turret removed and replaced by a hydraulically-operated arm on top of which is mounted a Siemens radar with a range of some 30 km. This model has a crew of four and a loaded weight of 32 000 kg, length 7.2 metres, width 3.2 metres and height travelling 3.1 metres. Armament consists of two 7.62 mm machine guns and four smoke dischargers mounted on either side of the hull at the rear.

Marder with LWT-3 Turret

This has completed its trials and is a Marder fitted with a new turret armed with a 20 mm cannon which is fully stabilised. LWT-3 stands for Light Weapon Turret with three-axis stabilisation.

Support Tank 35 mm

Thyssen Henschel has proposed that the Marder chassis be fitted with a new two-man turret armed with an externally-mounted 35 mm cannon, 7.62 mm coaxial machine gun and an ATGW launcher. This would be called the 35 mm support tank and have a combat weight of 30 000 kg. The 35 mm cannon is the same as that installed in the Gepard twin 35 mm self-propelled anti-aircraft gun system already used by the German Army and has dual feed. The larger diameter turret would mean that two of the circular roof hatches over the troop compartment would have to be removed.

Marder/Dragon Chassis with FL-15 Turret

In mid-1983, for trials purposes, the chassis of the Marder/Dragon was fitted with the new French Fives-Cail Babcock FL-15 turret armed with a 105 mm gun.

Marder with EMG

Rheinstahl Henschel and Krupp MaK have also used a Marder chassis for testing the Externally Mounted Gun (EMG) concept. A prototype, called the VTS-1, with a 105 mm gun mounted externally on the hull top has been built for trials and also evaluated by Sweden. The companies carried out two studies, study B with the commander and gunner turning with the gun and study D with the commander and gunner remaining stationary in the hull.

Roland Surface-to-air Missile System

The West German Army uses the Marder chassis to mount the Euromissile Roland 2 SAM. By late 1978 Thyssen Henschel had received orders for 140 Marder chassis for the Roland 2 SAM system, which were delivered at the rate of 35 a year with final deliveries made early in 1983.

TAM Medium Tank Family

To meet the requirements of the Argentinian Army Thyssen Henschel has developed the TAM Medium Tank (Tanque Argentino Mediano). To operate with the TAM Thyssen Henschel has developed the VCTP MICV of which 300 are being built in Argentina. The VCTP is similar to the Marder but has a more powerful 720 hp engine, less sophisticated two-man turret armed with a 20 mm cannon and a 7.62 mm anti-aircraft machine gun, three gun ports in each side of the troop compartment and two rectangular roof hatches that are hinged on the outside. A remote-controlled 7.62 mm machine gun is fitted at the rear of the hull. The VCTP can carry twelve men including its crew and has a maximum road speed of 75 km/h. To increase the operating range of the vehicle to 915 km two long-range drum-type fuel tanks are mounted at the rear on the left and right sides.

Using the chassis of the TAM/VCTP Thyssen Henschel

has developed a whole range of vehicles including a 155 mm self-propelled gun (using the turret of the French 155 mm GCT), 57 mm Support Tank, or Begleitpanzer, 57 mm anti-aircraft vehicle and the Dragon twin-30 mm self-propelled anti-aircraft gun system.

Note: The Thyssen Henschel VCTP (previously known as the VCI) designation relates only to vehicles being used by the Argentinian Army. For other markets, the company calls the vehicle the TH 302.

SPECIFICATIONS	
CREW	4 + 6
COMBAT WEIGHT	28 200 kg
POWER-TO-WEIGHT RATIO	21.27 hp/tonne
GROUND PRESSURE	0.8 kg/cm²
LENGTH	6.79 m
WIDTH	3.24 m
HEIGHT	
top of searchlight	2.95 m
turret top	2.86 m
rear MG mount	2.475 m
hull top	1.905 m
FIRING HEIGHT	
20 mm cannon	2.56 m
7.62 mm coaxial MG	2.735 m
GROUND CLEARANCE	0.45 m
TRACK	2.62 m
TRACK WIDTH	450 mm
LENGTH OF TRACK ON GROUND	3.9 m
MAX ROAD SPEED (forward and reverse)	
4th gear	75 km/h
3rd gear	47 km/h
2nd gear	31 km/h
1st gear	16 km/h
FUEL CAPACITY	652 litres
MAX ROAD RANGE	520 km
FORDING	1.5 m
with preparation	2.5 m
GRADIENT	60%
VERTICAL OBSTACLE	1 m
TRENCH	2.5 m
TURNING RADIUS	
4th gear	30 m
3rd gear	20 m
2nd gear	13.5 m
1st gear	6.5 m
ENGINE	MTU MB 833 Ea-500 6-cylinder liquid-cooled diesel developing 600 hp at 2200 rpm
TRANSMISSION	4-speed HSWL-194 planetary
SUSPENSION	torsion bar
ELECTRICAL SYSTEM	24 V
BATTERIES	6 ×12 V
ARMAMENT	
main	1 × 20 mm cannon
coaxial	1 × 7.62 mm MG
other	1 × 7.62 mm MG
SMOKE-LAYING EQUIPMENT	6 smoke dischargers
AMMUNITION	
main	1250
7.62 mm	5000
FIRE-CONTROL SYSTEM (main turret)	
Commander's fire-control override	yes
Turret power control	electro-hydraulic/ manual
by commander	yes
by gunner	yes
Max rate power traverse	60°/s
Max rate power elevation	40°/s
Gun elevation/depression	+65°/–17°
Gun stabiliser	
vertical	no
horizontal	no

Marder MICV from rear showing remote controlled 7.62 mm machine gun over rear troop compartment

Marder deep fording showing snorkel fitted on right side of hull

Status: Production of the Marder has been completed. VCTP is in production in Argentina. Brazil has four Roland SAM systems based on the Marder chassis in service. Production of the Marder can be resumed if further orders are received.

Manufacturers: Production of the Marder was undertaken by Rheinstahl (now Thyssen Henschel) of Kassel and Krupp MaK of Kiel. Thyssen Henschel, Postfach 102969, D 3500 Kassel, Federal Republic of Germany.

Transportpanzer 1 (Fuchs) Armoured Personnel Carrier

Development

In 1964 the West German Ministry of Defence examined its requirements for a new generation of military vehicles for the 1970s. This generation was to have included an 8 × 8 armoured amphibious reconnaissance vehicle, 4 × 4 and 6 × 6 armoured amphibious load carriers and a complete range of 4 × 4, 6 × 6 and 8 × 8 tactical cargo trucks, some of which were to be amphibious. All were to share many common components which would, where possible, be from commercial sources both to reduce costs and simplify procurement of spare parts.

In 1964 a Joint Project Office was formed to undertake development of the complete range of vehicles. Companies in the Joint Project Office were Büssing, Klöckner-Humbolt-Deutz, Friedrich Krupp, MAN and Rheinstahl-Henschel. Daimler-Benz did not join the Joint Project Office but went ahead on its own to develop a similar range of vehicles which were finally chosen.

After severe and extensive trials the 8 × 8 armoured amphibious reconnaissance vehicle became the Spähpanzer Luchs and 408 vehicles were built by Rheinstahl Wehrtechnik between 1975 and 1978. The 4 × 4, 6 × 6 and 8 × 8 tactical trucks were built by MAN and all were delivered to the Federal German Army by 1980. The 4 × 4 armoured amphibious load carrier became the Transportpanzer 2 and the 6 × 6 armoured amphibious load carrier became the Transportpanzer 1. The Transportpanzer 2 was not placed in production but further development was undertaken by EWK and the eventual result was the APE Amphibious Engineer Reconnaissance Vehicle which was developed to the prototype stage but not placed in production.

In 1977 Rheinstahl Wehrtechnik (now Thyssen Henschel), under licence from Daimler-Benz, was awarded a production contract for 996 Transportpanzer 1 vehicles for delivery from 1979 at the rate of 160 vehicles per year. The first production vehicle was handed over to the West German Army, which also calls the vehicle the Fuchs, in December 1979. Major sub-contractors to the company are Daimler-Benz (axles, engine and steering), Jung (hull) and Zahnradfabrik Friedrichshafen (transmission).

The Transportpanzer will be used by the West German Army in the following roles:

RASIT radar

This model is fitted with the RASIT battlefield surveillance radar (radar unit, target tracking and locating unit and radio) manufactured by LMT of France. The radar is mounted in the forward part of the hull and when operating is raised hydraulically to a maximum height of 1.8 metres above the vehicle's roof. A 30-metre cable allows remote operation of the system. This model is known in the West German Army as the Panzeraufklärungsradargerät, or PARA for short, and 110 will be built.

Transportpanzer 1 fitted with Keller and Knappich E-6 ring mount armed with 20 mm Rheinmetall cannon, six smoke dischargers on side of hull and showing two propellers under hull rear

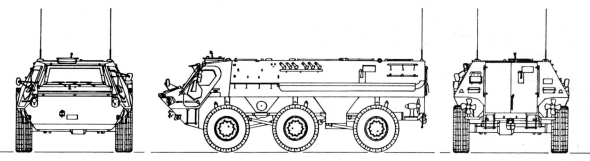

Transportpanzer 1 without armament installed

Command and Communications Vehicle

One hundred and thirty-four of these will be built under the designation of FüFu. This model has a 5 kW generator in the left wing of the rear door, fuel being supplied from the main tank, communications equipment, map board, two folding tables with personnel lamps, three folding seats and a box with a padded seat. Up to four antennas can be fitted, including a very high one at the right rear of the hull.

NBC Reconnaissance Vehicle

One hundred and forty of these are being built. The NBC detection equipment includes radiation and chemical agent detection units, sampling instruments and markers. All operations are carried out inside the vehicle which gives protection against NBC agents. The West German Army designation for this vehicle is the ABC Erkundsgruppe (ABC-ErkdGrp).

Engineer Vehicle

Two hundred and twenty of these will be used by combat engineers and to carry mines, demolition equipment and other specialised equipment.

Electronic Warfare

This model, known as the TPz 1 Eloka, is fitted with the EK 33 jammer kit. Unlike other models of the Transportpanzer it has no amphibious capability, only one roof hatch and a 15 kW generator to provide power for the extensive electronic warfare system installed.

Supply Carrier

Two hundred and twenty vehicles are being issued to supply units for use in the forward area. It can also be used as an ambulance, carrying four stretcher patients or two stretcher and four sitting patients.

Description

The all-welded steel hull of the Transportpanzer 1 protects the crew from small arms fire and shell splinters. The hull has a rhomboid cross section and incorporates spaced armour in certain areas.

The driver sits at the front of the hull on the left with the vehicle commander to his right. A large bullet-proof windscreen to their front can be covered by an armoured shutter hinged at the top when in action. Four periscopes are fitted in the roof of the vehicle to the front of the driver's hatch for use when the windscreen is covered by the armoured shutter, the centre one of which can be replaced by a passive periscope for driving at night. The commander has a circular roof hatch, which opens to the left rear. Both the driver and

commander have a door in the side of the hull with an integral window that can be covered by a shutter in a combat area.

The engine compartment behind the driver and commander is provided with an automatic fire-extinguishing system. There is a small passage on the right side between the front of the vehicle and the passenger/cargo area at the rear. The air-inlet and air-outlet louvres are in the roof of the vehicle with the exhaust pipe running along the left side of the hull.

The powerpack consists of an eight-cylinder Mercedes-Benz OM 402A exhaust turbo-charged diesel developing 320 hp and a six-speed planetary gear torque converter transmission on the side of the engine and connected to it by spur gearing. Above the engine are the air cleaner system and the cooling system, with a hydraulically-driven fan above the transmission. Attached to the powerpack are the vehicle parking brake, 5 kW alternator, brake supply system and hydraulics, including the oil supply reservoir.

The powerpack can be removed in about ten minutes as all disconnecting points on the powerpack for mountings, functionally connected shafts for automotive and amphibious devices, pneumatic, hydraulic and electric supply or control lines are designed as quick-disconnect points. The engine of the Fuchs can be run outside the vehicle for test purposes.

The troop/cargo compartment is at the rear of the vehicle and is 3.2 metres long, 1.25 metres high and 2.5 metres wide at its widest point. In each side of the hull is a small vision port protected by an armoured shutter. There are three hatches in the roof of the troop compartment: a large one-metre circular one in the forward part on which the main armament is normally mounted, a single-piece hatch cover to the rear of the first one on the right side which opens to the

Transportpanzer 1 with armoured shutter over commander's and driver's windscreen open (C R Zwart)

left, and to the rear and left of the second hatch is a the third one which opens to the right.

The ten infantrymen are seated on individual bucket seats, five down each side of the hull. The seats can be folded up to enable cargo to be carried. Normal means of entry for the infantrymen is through two large doors in the rear of the hull. The right door has a vision port covered by an armoured shutter when not in use.

Nominal amphibious payload is 2000 kg but in the non-amphibious mode it can carry up to 4000 kg of cargo.

Steering is hydraulically assisted on the front four wheels. An electrically-driven back-up pump automatically maintains the supply of hydraulic fluid to the steering box and propellers in case of hydraulic failure. The rigid axles incorporate hub-mounted planetary gears and are positioned by guide rods supported by progressively acting coil springs. All axles have differential lock ups and hydraulic shock absorbers. The tyres are of the run-flat type.

The Transportpanzer 1 is fully amphibious, being propelled in the water by two Schottel four-bladed propellers beneath the floor level of the vehicle at the rear of the hull. For steering when afloat the propellers can be traversed through 360 degrees. Before entering the water a trim vane, which is stowed on the glacis plate when travelling, is hydraulically erected at the front of the hull. The three bilge pumps each have a capacity of 180 litres per minute.

An NBC system, fitted as standard, can also be used to ventilate the crew and personnel compartments. Armament varies according to mission requirements but can consist of a 7.62 mm MG 3 machine gun mounted over the commander's position or a 20 mm Rheinmetall cannon mounted on a Keller and Knappich E-6 ring mount over the first circular roof hatch. The 7.62 mm machine gun has an elevation of +40 degrees and a depression of −15 degrees. The 20 mm cannon has an elevation of +75 degrees with depression being determined by a contour limiter, and 150 rounds of ready-use ammunition are provided. All vehicles have six smoke dischargers mounted on the left side of the hull firing forwards.

Variants

Daimler-Benz has transferred a licence for the sale and production of the Transportpanzer 1 outside West Germany to GLS (Gesellschaft für Logistischen Service), a 100 per cent

Transportpanzer 1 as delivered to Venezuela in 1983 armed with 12.7 mm and 7.62 mm machine guns

Transportpanzer 1 with RASIT battlefield surveillance radar raised (C R Zwart)

subsidiary of Krauss-Maffei, Munich. GLS is now undertaking a world-wide marketing campaign for the Transportpanzer which has already been tested in Malaysia, Indonesia, the Philippines, Venezuela, Belgium, Norway and the Netherlands.

In 1983 Venezuela placed an order for ten Transportpanzer 1s which were delivered in September that year. These vehicles did not have the standard NBC system installed but had smoke dischargers, an 8000 kg capacity winch, an air-conditioning system and two roof-mounted weapon systems. To the rear of the engine compartment is a KUKA turret with an externally-mounted 12.7 mm machine gun while behind this and facing the rear is a Wegmann 11/1 mount with a shield and a 7.62 mm machine gun. These vehicles have full amphibious capability.

The Rheinmetall 105 mm Super Low Recoil gun has been successfully tested on the MC 601 chassis, a derivative of the Transportpanzer 1 (6 × 6) vehicle.

Export vehicles will not have the extensive range of equipment fitted as standard to vehicles of the West German Army and GLS is therefore offering the following equipment as options: 12 000 Kcal/h heater, induction warming device, NBC system with an output of three cubic metres a minute, Teldix FNA vehicle navigation system, six electrically-operated launcher cups for smoke or fragmentation grenades on both sides of the hull, 5000 Kcal/h air-conditioning system with two evaporators, automatic fire-extinguishing system, intercom system with external and internal telephones, passive night vision equipment for the driver, trailer coupling, non-skid chains, self-recovery winch and a maximum of six ball mounts to enable the crew to use their small arms from inside the vehicle.

Export Variants

GLS has proposed further variants of the Transportpanzer 1:
Armoured mortar carrier with hull-mounted 81 mm mortar or towing 120 mm mortar
Armoured missile launcher with turret-mounted TOW, HOT or MILAN ATGWs
Armoured support vehicle for use in a variety of roles such as ambulance, cargo, recovery and maintenance
Armoured infantry fighting vehicle with various armament

options including 20 or 25 mm cannon with the option of a 7.62 mm remote-controlled machine gun over the rear part of the troop compartment.

Early in 1981 an 8 × 8 version of the Transportpanzer was designed and built in five weeks to meet the requirements of the Royal Netherlands Army. This has an additional axle and is fitted with an FMC turret armed with a 25 mm Oerlikon cannon, the turret being the same as that fitted to the FMC-designed AIFVs of the Dutch Army. This model weighs 17 200 kg and can carry 13 fully equipped troops in addition to its crew of two. The prototype has the usual two doors at the rear but the company is recommending a ramp at the rear similar to the one fitted to APCs such as the M113.

Other family vehicles, already conceived, have a weight limit of up to 20 000 kg.

Other armament installations under consideration include the Emerson elevating TOW launcher as fitted to the tracked M901 Improved TOW Vehicle which is now in service with the US Army.

Components of the Transportpanzer 1 (6 × 6) vehicle are used as the basis for the Wildcat armoured anti-aircraft truck.

The chassis of the Wildcat can also be fitted with other armament installations. For trials purposes the chassis has already been fitted with a two-man turret fitted with a Cockerill 90 mm Mark III gun and coaxial 7.62 mm machine gun.

SPECIFICATIONS

CREW	2 + 10*	ANGLE OF APPROACH/		STEERING	hydraulic, recirculating ball	
CONFIGURATION	6 × 6	DEPARTURE	45°/45°	TYRES	14.00 × 20	
COMBAT WEIGHT	17 000 kg	MAX SPEED		BRAKES		
UNLOADED WEIGHT	14 200 kg	road	105 km/h	main	air-assisted, dual circuit	
POWER-TO-WEIGHT		water	10.5 km/h	parking	spring-loaded acting on	
RATIO	18.82 hp/tonne	FUEL CAPACITY	390 litres		gearbox output shaft	
LENGTH	6.76 m	MAX ROAD RANGE	800 km	ELECTRICAL SYSTEM	24 V/250 Ah	
WIDTH	2.98 m	FORDING	amphibious	BATTERIES	4 × 12 V, 125 Ah	
HEIGHT		GRADIENT	70%	ARMAMENT	1 × 20 mm cannon	
(to hull top)	2.3 m	TURNING RADIUS	8.5 m		or 1 × 7.62 mm MG	
GROUND CLEARANCE		ENGINE	Mercedes-Benz model OM	SMOKE-LAYING		
axles	0.406 m		402A V-8 liquid-cooled	EQUIPMENT	6 smoke dischargers	
hull	0.506 m		diesel developing 320 hp at	* Maximum is 14 for export vehicles		
TRACK			2500 rpm			
front	2.54 m	TRANSMISSION	ZF model 6 HP 500 6-speed			
rear	2.56 m		automatic with torque			
WHEELBASE	1.75 m + 2.05 m		converter			

Status: In production. In service with the Federal German Army and Venezuela.

Manufacturer: Thyssen Henschel, Postfach 102969, D 3500 Kassel, Federal Republic of Germany.

Marketing: GLS, Postfach 500231, D-8000 Munich 50, Federal Republic of Germany.

HWK 11 Armoured Personnel Carrier

Forty of these vehicles were built by Henschel-Werke between 1964 and 1965 and these remain in service with the Mexican Army.

Condor Armoured Personnel Carrier

Development

The Condor has been developed as a private venture by Thyssen Henschel as a successor to its UR-416 armoured personnel carrier. Main improvements over the earlier vehicle can be summarised as: increased road speed and load carrying capacity, improved ballistic protection and its being fully amphibious. Although designed primarily as an armoured personnel carrier, the vehicle can also be adopted for a wide range of other roles including anti-tank, cargo carrier, command vehicle and reconnaissance vehicle.

The first prototype was completed in 1978 and the vehicle is now in production. Wherever possible, standard automotive components have been used in the design of the Condor, both to reduce costs and to enable spare parts to be obtained from a commercial source.

Late in 1981 Thyssen Henschel was awarded a contract by the Malaysian Government for 459 Condor armoured personnel carriers, the last of these was completed in March 1984. Some of the Malaysian Condors were fitted with a British Helio Mirror FVT 900 one-man turret armed with

an Oerlikon 20 mm cannon and variants included an ambulance and a command post vehicle. Since then a third customer has placed an order for the Condor vehicle.

Thyssen Henschel Condor APC fitted with Rheinmetall 20 mm one-man turret TF 20 15 A and turret-mounted smoke dischargers

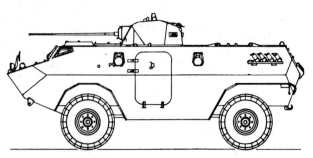

Thyssen Henschel Condor armoured personnel carrier

Thyssen Henschel Condor APC fitted with Rheinmetall twin 7.62 mm machine gun turret TUR-1 (Christopher F Foss)

Description

The hull of the Condor is made of all-welded steel and provides the crew with protection from 7.62 mm small arms fire, shell splinters and anti-personnel mines. The driver sits at the front of the vehicle on the left and has a single-piece hatch cover that opens to the rear. Bullet-proof windows are provided to the front and sides of the driver with the front windscreen being provided with a washer and wiper. When in a combat area the windows are covered by armoured shutters hinged at the bottom. The driver then observes the terrain ahead via a roof-mounted periscope.

The engine, which is the same at that used in the well-known Daimler-Benz Unimog range of cross-country vehicles, is mounted to the right of the driver with the air-inlet and air-outlet louvres in the top of the hull to the right and rear of the driver and the exhaust pipe on the right side of the hull. The engine is mounted on three shock-absorbing suspension points and power is transmitted to the gearbox by a short drive shaft. The gearbox is a Daimler-Benz model UG3/40-8/13.85 GPA and has eight gears which can be used in both directions. Power is transmitted to the front and rear axles by Cardan shafts mounted inside torque tubes.

The two rigid axles are located by Panhard type-bars and torque tubes with axle motion being damped by progressively acting coil springs. Each axle has two double-acting hydraulic shock absorbers and a differential lock. The tyres allow a maximum road speed of 50 km/h to be maintained, even after they have been punctured and deflated, to a maximum range of 30 km. If the vehicle is driven at a lower speed the range is longer.

The commander sits to the rear of the driver facing the centre of the vehicle and has a single-piece hatch cover over his position. The nine infantrymen are seated on individual seats to the rear. In either side of the Condor is a one-piece door that opens on the outside sliding to the rear. At the hull rear is a two-part hatch, the upper part opening upwards, the lower downwards. Various combinations of firing ports and vision blocks can be fitted in the hull sides and rear. Two circular hatches in the roof, one to the left rear of the turret and the other to the right, open to the front and rear respectively.

The Rheinmetall TF 20 15 A one-man turret is mounted on the forward part of the Condor's roof, offset to the right side and fitted with a single-piece hatch cover that opens to the rear. In the forward part of the turret roof is a periscopic sight with a magnification of ×4, the prism head of which moves in elevation with the weapons. Each side of the peris-

SPECIFICATIONS

CREW	3 + 9
CONFIGURATION	4 × 4
COMBAT WEIGHT	12 000 kg
UNLOADED WEIGHT	9500 kg
POWER-TO-WEIGHT	
RATIO	14 hp/tonne
LENGTH	6.05 m
WIDTH	2.47 m
HEIGHT	
to turret top	2.79 m
to hull top	2.1 m
GROUND CLEARANCE	0.475 m
TRACK	1.85 m
WHEELBASE	3.306 m
ANGLE OF APPROACH/	
DEPARTURE	50°/58°
MAX SPEED	
road	100 km/h
water	8 km/h
FUEL CAPACITY	260 litres
MAX ROAD RANGE	900 km
FORDING	amphibious
GRADIENT	60%
SIDE SLOPE	30%
VERTICAL OBSTACLE	0.55 m
ENGINE	Daimler-Benz OM 352A 6-cylinder super-charged water-cooled diesel developing 168 hp
TRANSMISSION	manual giving 8 speeds in both directions
CLUTCH	single dry plate
SUSPENSION	coil springs with double-acting hydraulic shock absorbers
TYRES	14.50 × 20
BRAKES	dual circuit hydraulic disc brakes
ELECTRICAL SYSTEM	24 V
ARMAMENT	
main	1 × 20 mm cannon
coaxial	1 × 7.62 mm MG
SMOKE-LAYING	
EQUIPMENT	2 × 3 smoke dischargers
AMMUNITION (in turret)	
20 mm	220 rounds
7.62 mm	500 rounds
FIRE-CONTROL SYSTEM	
Turret power control	manual
by commander	no
by gunner	yes
Gun elevation/depression	+60°/−7°
Turret traverse	360°

Status: In production. In service with Malaysia and Uruguay.

Manufacturer: Thyssen Henschel, Postfach 102969, D-3500 Kassel, Federal Republic of Germany.

copic sight is an observation periscope. For forward observation a broad unity periscope is installed. Lateral and rear areas can be observed through five vision blocks.

The turret is armed with a Rheinmetall 20 mm automatic cannon MK 20, Rh 202 and a coaxial 7.62 mm machine gun which have an elevation of +60 degrees and a depression of −7 degrees, turret traverse being a full 360 degrees. Turret traverse and gun elevation are manual. Fitted on both sides of the turret are three electrically-operated smoke dischargers.

The Condor is fully amphibious, being propelled in the water by a propeller mounted under the hull rear. This can be traversed through a full 360 degrees by the driver who has an indicator to show the propeller's position. Before entering the water a trim vane is erected at the front of the vehicle. When not required this is stowed under the nose of the Condor. Optional equipment includes an air-conditioning system, intercom, night vision equipment, NBC system, radios, propeller kit, supplementary heating equipment and a winch with 50 metres of cable that can be used to the front or rear of the vehicle.

Variants
Other armament installations can be fitted including a Rheinmetall turret armed with twin 7.62 mm machine guns and a turret armed with ATGWs such as HOT.

TM 170 Armoured Personnel Carrier

Development
The TM 170 armoured personnel carrier is the largest member of the Thyssen Maschinenbau range of wheeled armoured vehicles which also includes the TM 90 and TM 125. It is based on the chassis of a Daimler-Benz cross-country vehicle and spare parts are therefore easily obtainable world-wide.

The TM 170 was announced for the first time in 1978 and entered production in 1979. It has been designed primarily for use as an armoured personnel carrier or an internal security vehicle, but can be adapted for a wide range of other roles such as an ambulance, anti-tank vehicle, command post or reconnaissance vehicle.

The TM 170 has been selected by the West German Border Guard and State police to replace the old MOWAG MR 8 series of APCs, designated the SW1 and SW2. The TM 170

TM 170 armoured personnel carrier with remote controlled 20 mm cannon

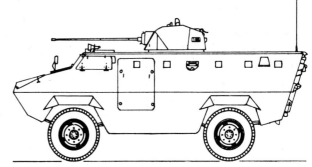

TM 170 APC fitted with turret-mounted 20 mm cannon

will be designated the SW4, the SW3 being the armoured version of Mercedes-Benz (4 × 4) light vehicle. The first order for 87 vehicles was placed in July 1982 with deliveries to run from 1983–85. The total requirement is for about 250 vehicles.

Description
The hull of the TM 170 is all welded which provides protection from small arms fire and shell splinters. The engine is at the front of the hull, commander and driver immediately behind the engine and the troop compartment at the rear. The body is attached to the chassis at four points by gimbal mounts and can quickly be removed for repair or maintenance. The engine is coupled to a manual gearbox and the driver can select either 4 × 4 drive for cross-country use or 4 × 2 drive for roads. All vehicles have run-flat tyres as standard.

The driver sits on the left with the commander to his right. Both have a windscreen to their front which can be covered in action by an armoured shutter hinged at the bottom which folds forwards onto the bonnet when not in use. The commander and driver each have three roof-mounted periscopes for observation to the front and side of the vehicle when the armoured windscreen shutters are raised. To their side is a window which is covered in action by a shutter hinged at the bottom, while over each of their positions is a single-piece hatch cover that opens to the rear of the vehicle.

A maximum of ten fully-equipped troops can be carried seated on individual seats down each side of the hull. There is a door in each side of the hull immediately behind the commander and driver, with a single firing port in each. There is also an entrance hatch at the rear of the hull which folds downwards on the outside. In the centre of it is a vision block with a spherical firing port underneath and a small firing port either side. In each side of the hull, to the rear of the side entrance door, are four firing ports and one vision block with a spherical firing port underneath. The spherical firing ports enable the crew to use their small arms from within the vehicle in complete safety. A rifle or SMG fitted in one of the spherical firing ports has a traverse of 16 degrees left and right, an elevation of +23 degrees and a depression of −8 degrees.

In the centre of the roof is a large circular single-piece hatch cover that opens to the rear, where a variety of armament installations can be mounted.

The TM 170 is fully amphibious, being propelled in the water by its wheels or by two water jets, which give it a maximum speed of 9 km/h. Before entering the water a trim vane, which folds back onto the bonnet when not required, is erected at the front of the hull.

The vehicle can be fitted with the following optional equipment: auxiliary heater, fire warning and extinguishing system, hydraulically-operated 5000 kg capacity winch with 40 metres of 12 mm diameter cable, flashing lights, loudspeaker, NBC system, radios and smoke dischargers.

The following armament installations are available for the TM 170: pintle- or ring-mounted 7.62 mm machine gun, turret armed with twin 7.62 mm machine guns, turret armed with Rheinmetall 20 mm cannon, surveillance cupola with an obstacle-clearing blade mounted at the front of the hull, turret armed with two HOT ATGWs ready to launch, Hughes TOW ATGW launcher, cupola with 20 mm cannon which can be aimed and fired from within the vehicle.

Variants

There are no variants of the TM 170 at present apart from the different armament installations mentioned above.

Police version of TM 170 showing obstacle-clearing blade at front of hull lowered and armoured shutters for windows lowered

SPECIFICATIONS

CREW	2 + 10	GROUND CLEARANCE	0.48 m	FORDING	amphibious
CONFIGURATION	4 × 4	TRACK	1.84 m	GRADIENT	80%
COMBAT WEIGHT	11 200 kg	WHEELBASE	3.25 m	ENGINE	Daimler-Benz OM 352
UNLOADED WEIGHT	8800 kg	ANGLE OF APPROACH/			super-charged diesel
POWER-TO-WEIGHT		DEPARTURE	45°/48°		developing 168 hp at
RATIO	15 hp/tonne	MAX SPEED			2800 rpm
LENGTH	6.12 m	road	100 km/h	ELECTRICAL SYSTEM	24 V
WIDTH	2.45 m	water	9 km/h	BATTERIES	2 × 12 V
HEIGHT		FUEL CAPACITY	175 litres	ARMAMENT	optional
(without armament)	2.32 m	MAX ROAD RANGE	700 km		

Status: In production. In service with the West German Border Guard and State police.

Manufacturer: Thyssen Maschinenbau, Stockumerstrasse 28, 5810 Witten-Annen, Federal Republic of Germany.

TM 125 Armoured Personnel Carrier

Development

The TM 125 armoured personnel carrier is a member of the Thyssen Maschinenbau range of wheeled armoured vehicles which also includes the TM 90 and the TM 170. It is based on the chassis of a Daimler-Benz cross-country vehicle and spare parts are therefore easily available world-wide.

The TM 125 was announced for the first time in 1978 and entered production the following year. Although designed primarily for use as an armoured personnel carrier, it can also be used for other roles such as ambulance, cargo/ammunition carrier, command and radio vehicle, internal security vehicle and as a reconnaissance vehicle.

Description

The hull of the TM 125 is made of all-welded steel which provides protection from both small arms fire and shell splinters. The engine is at the front of the hull, driver and commander immediately behind the engine and the troop compartment at the rear. The body is attached to the chassis at four points by gimbal mounts and can quickly be removed for repair or maintenance. The engine is coupled to a manual gearbox and the driver can select either 4 × 4 drive for cross-country use or 4 × 2 drive for roads. All vehicles have run-flat tyres as standard, enabling the vehicle to travel up to 80 km at a speed of up to 40 km/h with the tyres deflated.

The driver sits on the left with the commander to his right. Both have a windscreen to their front which can be covered in action by an armoured shutter hinged at the bottom. When not in use it folds forwards onto the bonnet. The commander

and driver are each provided with three roof-mounted periscopes for observation to the front and sides of the vehicle when the armoured windscreen shutters are raised. To their side is a window which is covered by a shutter hinged at the bottom when in action, and over the top of their positions is a single-piece hatch cover that opens to the rear.

A maximum of ten fully-equipped troops can be carried on seats down each side of the hull. There is a door with a single

TM 125 with trim vane erected for amphibious operations

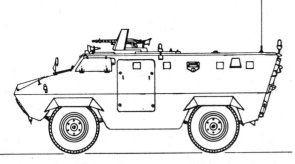

TM 125 armed with 7.62 mm machine gun protected by shield

firing port in each side of the hull immediately behind the commander's and driver's positions. There is also a hatch at the rear of the hull which folds downwards on the outside. In the centre of it is a vision block with a spherical firing port beneath, and a small firing port either side. In each side of the hull, to the rear of the side door are three firing ports and one vision block with a spherical firing port underneath. The spherical firing ports enable three members of the crew to use their small arms from inside the vehicle in complete safety. A rifle or SMG fitted in one of the spherical firing ports has a traverse of 16 degrees left and right, an elevation of +23 degrees and a depression of −8 degrees.

In the centre of the roof is a large circular hatch cover that opens to the rear, where a variety of armament installations can be mounted.

The TM 125 is fully amphibious, being driven in the water by two propellers at a speed of 8 km/h. Steering in the water is by turning the front wheels, as on land. Before entering the water a trim vane, which is folded back onto the bonnet when not required, is erected at the front of the hull.

The vehicle can be fitted with the following optional equipment: auxiliary heater, fire warning and extinguishing system, hydraulically-operated winch with a capacity of 5000 kg and provided with 40 metres of 12 mm diameter cable, night vision equipment, flashing lights, loudspeaker, NBC system, radios and smoke dischargers.

The following armament installations are available for the TM 125: pintle- or ring-mounted 7.62 mm machine gun, turret armed with twin 7.62 mm machine guns, turret armed with Rheinmetall 20 mm cannon, surveillance cupola with an obstacle-clearing blade mounted on the front of the hull, turret with two HOT ATGWs ready to launch, Hughes TOW ATGW launcher, cupola armed with Rheinmetall 20 mm cannon which can be aimed and fired from within the vehicle.

Variants

There are no variants of the TM 125 at present apart from the different armament installations mentioned above.

SPECIFICATIONS

CREW	2 + 10	WHEELBASE	2.9 m	ENGINE	Daimler-Benz OM 352
CONFIGURATION	4 × 4	ANGLE OF APPROACH/			4-cylinder super-charged
COMBAT WEIGHT	7600 kg	DEPARTURE	46°/43°		diesel developing 125 hp
UNLOADED WEIGHT	5410 kg	MAX SPEED		TRANSMISSION	manual with 4 forward and 1
POWER-TO-WEIGHT		road	85 km/h		reverse gears
RATIO	16.44 hp/tonne	water	8 km/h	TRANSFER CASE	2-speed
LENGTH	5.54 m	FUEL CAPACITY	175 litres	ELECTRICAL SYSTEM	24 V
WIDTH	2.46 m	MAX ROAD RANGE	700 km	BATTERIES	2 × 12 V
HEIGHT		FORDING	amphibious	ARMAMENT	optional, see text
(without armament)	2.015 m	GRADIENT	80%		
GROUND CLEARANCE	0.46 m	SIDE SLOPE	40%		
TRACK	1.78 m	VERTICAL OBSTACLE	0.55 m		

Status: Production.

Manufacturer: Thyssen Maschinenbau, Stockumerstrasse 28, 5810 Witten-Annen, Federal Republic of Germany.

UR-416 Armoured Personnel Carrier

Development

The UR-416 was developed by Rheinstahl Maschinenbau (now Thyssen Maschinenbau) as a private venture, the first prototype being completed in 1965. Production began in 1969 since when over 750 vehicles have been built the vast majority of which have been exported, mainly to South America and Africa.

The vehicle has been designed primarily for internal security operations but can also be used for a wide variety of other roles such as command and communications, reconnaissance and field workshop. The UR-416 is essentially the chassis of a Daimler-Benz cross-country vehicle fitted with an armoured body: spare automotive parts are identical to those used in the truck and are therefore available from commercial sources.

Description

The hull of the UR-416 is all welded which provides the crew with protection from small arms fire, shell splinters and anti-personnel mines. The driver sits at the front of the vehicle, just behind the engine, with the commander to his

UR-416 without armament installed and four smoke dischargers mounted either side of hull at rear

right. Both have a windscreen to their front with a wiper and a washer, which is covered in action by an armoured shutter hinged at its upper part when forward observation is maintained by a single periscope in the forward part of the roof.

The engine is coupled to a manual gearbox which has eight forward and two reverse gears. For normal road use only the rear axle is engaged but when travelling across country the front axle is also engaged and when travelling across very rough country the front and rear axle differential locks are engaged.

The eight fully-equipped men are seated to the rear of the commander and driver, three down each side of the hull facing outwards and two at the back facing the rear. Each man has an individual seat which can be folded upwards. There are three doors, one in each side of the hull and one at the rear. The side doors are in two parts: the lower part folds downwards to form a step and the upper part is hinged on one side and folds flat onto the side of the hull. The rear door is similar to the side doors, but is much wider. The spare wheel is mounted on the upper part of the rear door.

There are five firing ports in each side of the hull: one in the side door and a further two in the hull rear, both in the upper part of the door.

In the roof of the UR-416, behind the commander and driver, is a circular single-piece hatch that opens to the rear. The basic model is normally armed with a 7.62 mm machine gun with a shield, which has an elevation of +75 degrees, a depression of −10 degrees and a total traverse of 360 degrees. It can also be delivered with a horseshoe-shaped rail on which a 7.62 mm machine gun and shield can be mounted with a traverse of 230 degrees. To the rear of this armament installation is a forward-opening single-piece hatch cover, normally with a single firing port which can be used when the hatch is locked vertical.

Forward of the commander's and driver's position are two ventilators which draw in fresh air from the outside and pipe it to two channels which run down either side of the crew compartment. Each channel has six controlled air-outlets which can be adjusted by the crew. The crew compartment also has handrails, lights and mountings for personnel equipment.

A feature of the UR-416 is that the armour body can be removed from the chassis for repair or maintenance. The lifting equipment consists of three jacks, one of which is fitted under each side of the hull and the third at the rear acting as a pivot. Before lifting begins four Cardan joints and the two main electric sockets are disconnected and once the body is clear of the chassis it can be driven away.

Optional equipment includes an air-conditioning system, fire-extinguishing system, heater, night vision equipment, run-flat tyres, smoke dischargers (turret or hull mounted) and a rear-mounted 5000 kg capacity winch with 40 metres of 12 mm diameter cable.

Variants

Ambulance
Carrying eight sitting or four sitting and two lying patients plus a crew of two.

Anti-tank
Armed with a Bofors 90 mm recoilless-rifle model PV 1110, or ATGWs such as the West German MBB Mamba or American Hughes TOW.

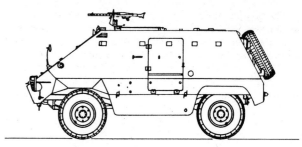
UR-416 fitted with pintle-mounted 7.62 mm machine gun

UR-416 fitted with Rheinmetall TF 20 15 turret with Rheinmetall MK 20 Rh 202 20 mm cannon

Command and Communications
Fitted with additional communications equipment and mapboards.

Internal Security
The internal security model can be fitted with an obstacle-clearing blade at the front of the hull. The lower half of the blade is made of welded steel with web stiffening, and the upper half consists of a pipe framework with a robust wire-grille which gives the driver and commander forward observation. The height of the blade can be adjusted hydraulically from the driver's seat and it can also be removed for transport when it is usually stowed at the rear of the hull.

The vehicle can be fitted with the same turrets as the reconnaissance model but two cupolas have been specifically developed for internal security operations. The first of these has a single-piece hatch cover that opens to the rear and eight vision blocks. Under the vision block in the forward part of the cupola is a firing port which will accept a rifle or similar weapon with an elevation of +25 degrees, a depression of −5 degrees and a traverse of 15 degrees left and right.

The second model has a cupola with 16 vision blocks arranged in two tiers of eight. Under the lower vision block in the forward part of the cupola is a spherical firing port which will accept a rifle, which then has an elevation of +25 degrees and a depression of −5 degrees, traverse being 15 degrees left and right. Under the upper vision block in the forward part of the cupola is another spherical firing port which will also accept a rifle, which then has an elevation of up to 65 degrees and enables fire to be brought to bear on snipers. Traverse of the weapon is 15 degrees left and right.

Reconnaissance

This can be fitted with most types of turret on the market today including the West German Rheinmetall turret models TF 20 15 and TUR 1.

Workshop

This has a full range of tools, workbenches, vice and cutting equipment, and an A-frame can be erected at the front of the hull to enable the vehicle to change engines and other components. When the A-frame is in use two stabilisers are lowered at the front of the hull.

SPECIFICATIONS

CREW	2 + 8	ANGLE OF APPROACH/		TRANSMISSION	manual, 8 forward and 2
CONFIGURATION	4 × 4	DEPARTURE	47°/51°		reverse gears
COMBAT WEIGHT	7600 kg	MAX ROAD SPEED	85 km/h	STEERING	hydraulic, power assisted
UNLOADED WEIGHT	5700 kg	FUEL CAPACITY	150 litres	CLUTCH	single dry plate
POWER-TO-WEIGHT		MAX ROAD RANGE	600–700 km	TYRES	12.50 × 20
RATIO	15.78 hp/tonne	FUEL CONSUMPTION		BRAKES	
LENGTH		(road)	0.25 litre/km	main	hydraulic, air assisted
without spare wheel	4.99 m	FORDING	1.4 m	parking	mechanical on rear wheels
WIDTH	2.3 m	GRADIENT	70%	ELECTRICAL SYSTEM	24 V
HEIGHT		VERTICAL OBSTACLE	0.55 m	BATTERIES	2 × 12 V
with turret	2.52 m	TURNING RADIUS	6.45 m	ARMAMENT	
to hull top	2.225 m	ENGINE	Daimler-Benz OM 352	basic model	1 × 7.62 mm MG
GROUND CLEARANCE	0.44 m		6-cylinder water-cooled	SMOKE-LAYING	
TRACK	1.78 m		diesel developing 120 hp at	EQUIPMENT	optional
WHEELBASE	2.9 m		2800 rpm	ARMOUR	9 mm

Status: In production. Known users of the UR-416 include Ecuador, El Salvador, Ethiopia, West Germany, Greece, Kenya, Morocco, Netherlands, Peru, Spain (National Police), Togo, Turkey, Venezuela and Zimbabwe. (In many of these countries the vehicle is used by the police rather than by the army.)

Manufacturer: Thyssen Maschinenbau, Stockumerstrasse 28, 5810 Witten-Annen, Federal Republic of Germany.

GREECE

Leonidas Armoured Personnel Carrier

This is essentially the Austrian Steyr 4K 7FA APC manufactured under licence in Greece for the Greek Army. As far as it is known its physical characteristics are identical to the original Austrian version. The first Greek Leonidas armoured personnel carrier was completed in 1982. Initially about ten per cent of the vehicle was made in Greece increasing by 1983 to 30 per cent, including the hull. It is expected that the Leonidas will be fitted with a new Greek-designed

Chassis of Leonidas armoured personnel carrier fitted with Brazilian ENGESA ET-90 turret armed with EC-90 90 mm gun

Leonidas armoured personnel carrier without 12.7 mm M2 HB machine gun

turret armed with a 12.7 mm machine gun or a 20 mm cannon. It is possible that an armoured reconnaissance vehicle armed with a 90 mm or 105 mm gun will be developed. The chassis of the basic Austrian APC has already been fitted with the Brazilian ENGESA ET-90 turret armed with the EC-90 90 mm gun and the French GIAT TS 90 turret armed with a long-barrelled 90 mm gun. At a later date a self-propelled anti-aircraft system based on this chassis will also be developed using the Greek-designed Artemis twin 30 mm towed anti-aircraft gun system.

Status: Production. In service with the Greek Army.

Manufacturer: Steyr Hellas SA, Industrial Area, Sindos Thessaloniki, POB 239, Greece.

HUNGARY

PSZH-IV Armoured Personnel Carrier

Development
After developing and producing the FUG amphibious scout car the Hungarian defence industry went on to produce a wheeled APC which is used in the Hungarian Army in place of the Soviet or Czechoslovak/Polish models, in spite of the fact that it carries a smaller landing party and has less cross-country capability.

The PSZH-IV has also been acquired by East Germany for use with border troops in place of older Soviet equipment.

A certain amount of confusion has arisen over this vehicle and its predecessors. The original Hungarian scout car was officially known as the FUG, and because of the small size and 4 × 4 configuration observers in the West promptly dubbed the 1966 prototype and the PSZH-IV as FUG-66 and FUG-70 as well. The so-called FUG-66, which mounted an egg-shaped turret and dummy automatic cannon, appeared only on a single manoeuvre parade in Bratislava. The so-called FUG-70 turned out to be an armoured personnel carrier designated the PSZH-IV.

Description
The all-welded hull of the PSZH-IV has the driver and commander seated at the front of the vehicle, both with a hatch cover in front of them hinged at the top and opening forwards, and a windscreen with a wiper blade. The hatch cover is equipped with an integral vision block for observation when the hatch is closed.

A door, four vision blocks and two firing ports are provided in each side of the hull. The ports are positioned one either side of the hull door, next to a vision block. The six infantrymen are seated around the sides and rear of the fighting compartment in what must be very cramped positions.

The turret is in the centre of the vehicle and is a different shape from the one on the BRDM-2, with a stepped top with the forward-facing periscopes in the top part. Like the turret fitted to the BRDM-2 it has no roof hatch. The sight for aiming the armament is in the roof of the turret, just in front of the periscope. A ventilator fan is provided in the left side of the turret.

The engine is behind the turret and is much more powerful than that installed in the earlier FUG. The PSZH-IV is fully amphibious, propelled in the water by two waterjets at the rear of the hull. Before entering the water a trim board, which is stowed folded on the glacis plate when not in use, is erected at the front of the hull. Standard equipment includes infra-red driving lights, an NBC system and a central tyre-pressure system that allows the driver to adjust the tyre pressure to suit the type of ground being crossed.

PSZH-IV armoured personnel carriers of the Hungarian Army on parade

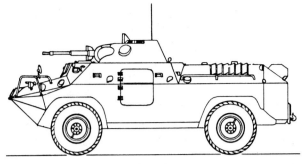

PSZH-IV armoured personnel carrier

Main armament comprises a Soviet 14.5 mm KPVT machine gun and there is a 7.62 mm PKT machine gun mounted coaxially to its left. An infra-red searchlight is mounted coaxially to the right of the main armament.

Variants

A turretless version of the PSZH-IV is used as a command vehicle and other variants of the vehicle exist such as an ambulance and a radiological-chemical reconnaissance vehicle. There is also a turreted command vehicle which does not carry the landing party of six but is armed with a 14.5 mm machine gun.

SPECIFICATIONS

CREW	3 + 6	FUEL CAPACITY	200 litres	AMMUNITION	
CONFIGURATION	4 × 4	MAX CRUISING RANGE		main	500
COMBAT WEIGHT	7500 kg	(road)	500 km	coaxial	2000
POWER-TO-WEIGHT		FORDING	amphibious	GUN ELEVATION/	
RATIO	13.3 hp/tonne	GRADIENT	60%	DEPRESSION	+30°/−5°
LENGTH	5.7 m	VERTICAL OBSTACLE	0.4 m	ARMOUR (max)	14 mm
WIDTH	2.5 m	TRENCH (with channels)	0.6 m		
HEIGHT	2.3 m	ENGINE	Csepel D.414.44 4-cylinder		
FIRING HEIGHT	2.05 m		in-line water-cooled diesel		
GROUND CLEARANCE	0.42 m		developing 100 hp at		
TRACK	1.9 m		2300 rpm		
WHEELBASE	3.3 m	TYRES	30.00 × 18		
MAX SPEED		ARMAMENT			
road	80 km/h	main	1 × 14.5 mm MG		
water	9 km/h	coaxial	1 × 7.62 mm MG		

Status: Production complete. In service with Bulgaria, Czechoslovakia (OT-66), East Germany, Hungary and Iraq.

Manufacturer: Hungarian state arsenals.

INDIA

Indian Armoured Personnel Carrier Development

The Indian Army APC fleet consists of some 700 to 800 BTR-50, BTR-60 (8 × 8), BTR-152 (6 × 6), OT-62, OT-64 (8 × 8) APCs, plus a small number of recently introduced BMPs. The Combat Vehicle Research and Development Establishment is known to be developing a new APC or IFV, but progress has been slow as main emphasis has been on the development of the new Indian MBT to succeed the Vijayanta in production.

In mid-1983 it was announced that India was to manufacture the Soviet BMP MICV under licence at a new factory in the Medak District of Andhra Pradesh State. It is probable that the more recent BMP, armed with a 30 mm cannon, 7.62 mm coaxial machine gun and a Spandrel ATGW system is the model selected. The 7.62 mm machine gun will be of local manufacture to ensure commonality with other Indian armoured vehicles.

IRELAND

Timoney Armoured Personnel Carrier

Development

In January 1972 Technology Investments Limited began design work on a 4 × 4 armoured personnel carrier which would meet the requirements of the Irish Army for a vehicle capable of world-wide deployment when operating under United Nations control.

The first prototype, called the Mk 1, was completed in mid-1973 and was followed by a further two prototypes called the Mk 3. In 1976 the Engineering Division of Beherman Demoen of Belgium negotiated a licence with Technology Investments to undertake production of the Timoney APC. The first Belgian vehicles were completed in 1978 and Beherman Domoen was awarded a contract from the Belgian Government for 123 vehicles (43 for the Air Force and 80 for the Gendarmerie) and from the Argentine Government for five vehicles all of which were delivered by early 1981.

In September 1981 Beherman Demoen and Vickers Defence Systems of the United Kingdom signed a ten-year agreement for Vickers to develop and build an improved version of the BDX in the UK. This was subsequently called the Valkyr and full details are given under the United Kingdom.

Technology Investments built five pre-production Mk 4 vehicles for the Irish Army which has a requirement for up to 100 vehicles of this type. They have been produced at the company's new manufacturing facility at Gibbstown which has the capacity to produce 40 vehicles a year.

There are only minor differences between the Timoney and BDX vehicles, mainly concerned with internal seating arrangements and the position of the firing ports and/or vision blocks. The Irish vehicles have a twin 7.62 mm machine gun turret designed by Technology Investments. The weapons have an elevation of +55 degrees, a depression of −11 degrees and 360-degree turret traverse. Gun elevation and depression and turret traverse are manual. The all-welded turret has a two-piece hatch cover that opens to the front and rear, periscopic sight for aiming the weapons, vision blocks, two smoke dischargers either side and a search-light that moves in elevation with the main armament.

Description

A full description of the Timoney/BDX armoured personnel carrier together with full technical specifications will be found in the BDX armoured personnel carrier entry under Belgium.

Variants

Technology Investments has also suggested that the Timoney APC could be extended into a 6 × 6 APC which would be able to carry 17 men including its crew of two. Other projected variants include the Mk 2 amphibious armoured reconnaissance vehicle with a crew of three and six infantrymen which would have a maximum loaded weight of 6803 kg, maximum road speed of 98 km/h and would be fully amphibious. The powered turret could be fitted with a wide range of armament installations up to a 90 mm gun or a 106 mm recoilless rifle. An amphibious load carrier with a capacity of 5080 kg is also projected.

Mark 6 APC

Further development of the Mk 5 APC, which was the model produced under licence in Belgium, has resulted in the Mk 6, of which five pre-production vehicles were delivered to the Irish Army early in 1982.

The Mk 6 has many improvements over the Mk 5 including redesign of the glacis plate and of the driver's vision ports which are lower, more horizontal and slightly forward of the slope of the glacis plate. The vision ports have a pronounced reveal on the top and sides as have the three firing ports which are arranged symmetrically along each side. The sides of the vehicle are continued up vertically for some 75 per cent of the height before being angled inwards. The air intakes, which are located over the driver's compartment are also lower than in the earlier models.

The wheelbase has been increased from 2.87 metres to 3 metres while the track has been widened from 1.93 to 2.2 metres; these and other changes to the hull have increased weight to around 8000 kg unladen.

Timoney Mk 6 APC fitted with Creusot-Loire TLi 127 turret armed with 12.7mm M2 HB and coaxial 7.62 mm machine guns and smoke dischargers

Irish Army Timoney Mk IV APC from rear with all doors closed (Denis McCarthy)

The original Chrysler petrol engine has been replaced by a four-cylinder Detroit Diesel 4-53T, this together with the increased fuel capacity has increased the vehicle's operating range to around 1000 km. The Allison AT-540 automatic transmission has been retained.

This, like the earlier Timoney vehicles, has the patent Timoney two-speed transfer case and reduction hubs. The former takes the drive from the shaft at the rear of the engine to the rear axles and, when engaged, via a secondary shaft to the front steering axle. The reduction hubs contain single stage epicyclic reduction gears which supply the additional reduction ratios required. The main differential incorporates no-spin locking units to minimise loss of traction in off-road operations.

The suspension system has also been designed and patented by Timoney. Each of the four wheels is an independent unit suspended by two unequal transverse wishbones and sprung by a single helical spring with a concentric telescopic damper. The drive from the axle units is transmitted by means of splined shafts with universal joints at each end in the case of both the permanently driven rear axles and of the front axles which are normally only powered when operating over rough terrain.

The vehicle can be fitted with a wide range of armament installations including the Creusot-Loire TLi 127 turret armed with a 12.7 mm M2 HB machine gun.

Mark 6 Fire Support Vehicle

In March 1982 Technology Investments unveiled the Mk 6 fire support vehicle which is essentially the Mk 6 APC with the French Hispano-Suiza Lynx 90 turret armed with a 90 mm gun, 7.62 mm coaxial and 7.62 mm anti-aircraft machine guns. In addition to the crew of three, which consists of the commander, gunner and driver, the vehicle can carry nine fully-equipped infantrymen.

SPECIFICATIONS (Mk 6)

CREW	3 + 9	CLUTCH	hydraulic, torque converter	TYRES	12.00 × 20 or
CONFIGURATION	4 × 4	MAX ROAD SPEED	95 km/h		14.00 × 20
COMBAT WEIGHT	9980 kg	RANGE	1000 km	ARMAMENT	
UNLOADED WEIGHT	8000 kg	FUEL CAPACITY	300 litres	main	1 × 90 mm gun
LENGTH	4.95 m	FORDING	amphibious	coaxial	1 × 7.62 mm MG
WIDTH	2.5 m	GRADIENT	70%	anti-aircraft	1 × 7.62 mm MG
HEIGHT OVERALL	2.746 m	SIDE SLOPE	50%	SMOKE LAYING	
GROUND CLEARANCE	0.4 m	VERTICAL OBSTACLE	0.4 m	EQUIPMENT	2 × 2 smoke
WHEELBASE	3 m	STEERING	hydraulically assisted,		dischargers
TRACK	2.2 m		manual in case of hydraulic	ARMOUR	
ENGINE	Detroit Diesel Model 4-53T		failure	Floor	10 mm
TRANSMISSION	Allison AT-540	SUSPENSION	independent wishbones with	Roof	12 mm
	fully-automatic, 4 forward		helical springs and	Hull front, back	
	and 1 reverse gears		telescopic dampers	and sides	14 mm
		BRAKES	disc, dual hydraulic circuit		

Status: Ten vehicles have been delivered to the Irish Army.

Manufacturer: Technology Investments Limited, Gibbstown, Navan, Co Meath, Ireland.

ISRAEL

NIMDA Shoet II Armoured Personnel Carrier

Development

The Shoet II (6 × 6) armoured personnel carrier has been developed as a private venture by NIMDA for the export market. When announced in mid-1981 it was stated that the Shoet II had passed all official Israeli Defence Force trials and that it had been approved for military service. Wherever possible standard and proven commercial automotive components have been used in the Shoet.

NIMDA Shoet II APC with two machine guns forward, one 7.62 mm MAG machine gun and one grenade launcher at rear

Description

The Shoet II APC is very similar in appearance to the Soviet BTR-152 (6 × 6) APC and has a hull of all-welded steel which provides complete protection from small arms fire up to 7.62 mm in calibre and shell splinters.

The engine is at the front, driver and commander in the centre, and the open-topped troop compartment, provided with external stowage racks along either side, is at the rear.

The commander and driver have adjustable seats and are each provided with a forward opening side door, the upper part, which has a sliding vision port, folds down externally.

Entry to the troop compartment is via two doors in the hull rear. Up to four 7.62 mm or 12.7 mm machine guns can be mounted around the top of the hull. Standard equipment includes night vision equipment, armoured fuel tanks and a central tyre pressure regulation system which allows the driver to adjust the tyre pressure to suit the type of ground being crossed (70 psi road, 35 psi sand and 15 psi mud).

Variants

The Shoet can be used for a wide range of roles including ambulance, anti-aircraft (gun or missile), anti-tank (106 mm recoilless rifle or ATGW), cargo, command, forward air control, fire suppression (81 mm mortar plus machine guns), reconnaissance, and recovery.

The reconnaissance model can be armed with twin 12.7 mm (0.50) M2 HB machine guns, twin 7.62 mm (0.30) machine guns, single 7.62 mm machine gun at rear, 52 mm light mortar, smoke launchers and grenade launchers.

SPECIFICATIONS

CREW	2 + 10	ENGINE	Detroit Diesel General	STEERING	integral hydraulic
CONFIGURATION	6 × 6		Motors 6V-53 6-cylinder	TURNING RADIUS	18 m
COMBAT WEIGHT	9700 kg		water-cooled diesel	SUSPENSION	semi-elliptical springs and
UNLOADED WEIGHT	8000 kg		developing 172 hp at		rubber AAOM springs
POWER-TO-WEIGHT			2800 rpm	BRAKES	
RATIO	18 hp/tonne	TRANSMISSION	Allison MT-643 automatic,	main	air
LENGTH	6.64 m		hydro-mechanical, 4 forward	parking	mechanical
WIDTH	2.2 m		and 1 reverse gears (torque	ELECTRICAL SYSTEM	24 V
HEIGHT	2.08 m		converter lockup above	ARMOUR	
RANGE	350 to 400 km		42 km/h for maximum fuel	Hull front	10 mm
FUEL CAPACITY	170 litres		saving)	Hull sides	8 mm
MAX ROAD SPEED	90 km/h	TRANSFER CASE	2-speed	Hull floor	14 mm
GRADIENT	60%	TYRES	11.00 × 20		
SIDE SLOPE	30%	NUMBER OF TYRES	6		

Status: Development complete. Ready for production.

Manufacturer: NIMDA Company Limited, PO Box 33319, Tel Aviv 61332, Israel.

ITALY

VCC-80 Infantry Fighting Vehicle

Development

Following feasibility studies the project definition phase has been completed and prototypes are now under construction for technical and operational trials. The 60-month development contract was awarded in February 1982 and covers the construction of four prototypes, the first of which should be completed in 1985. The company has already built a full scale mock-up of the VCC-80.

The VCC-80 is being developed by a consortium of companies including FIAT and OTO Melara.

The VCC-80 will weigh about 19 tonnes and have a high power-to-weight ratio and good cross-country mobility, it will have superior cross-country mobility to the Leopard 1 and will be able to operate with MBTs expected to enter service at the end of this century.

Description

The all-welded hull of the VCC-80 gives the crew more protection than the current IFV which is a further development of the FMC M113. The low overall height of the VCC-80, only 2.25 metres, also increases the vehicle's survivability on the battlefield.

The driver sits at the front left side of the vehicle and has a single-piece hatch cover that opens to his right. Forward and either side of this are three periscopes, the centre one of which can be replaced by an image intensification periscope for driving at night.

The powerpack is to the right of the driver with the air-inlet and air-outlet louvres being in the top of the hull and the exhaust outlet on the right side of the hull. The engine will develop about 500 bhp giving the VCC-80 a power-to-weight ratio of about 25 bhp/tonne. It will have a maximum road speed of 70 km/h, road range of 600 km, and be able to accelerate from 0 to 40 km/h in 15 seconds. Mobility characteristics include a 60 per cent gradient, 40 per cent side slope, vertical obstacle of 0.85 metre and trench crossing of 2.5 metres.

The power-operated turret is in the centre of the hull with the commander on the left and the gunner on the right, each having individual hatch covers. The commander is also the squad leader when the infantry squad is dismounted from the vehicle.

Full-scale mock-up of VCC-80 showing roof-mounted sights for commander and gunner

Full-scale mock-up of VCC-80 with ramp lowered at rear of vehicle

The commander has periscopes for all-round observation and in front of his hatch is a periscope that can be traversed through a full 360 degrees. In front of the gunner's hatch is a sight for aiming the 25 mm cannon and 7.62 mm machine gun.

Main armament consists of an Oerlikon 25 mm KBA-B02 cannon. A very advanced fire-control system is fitted which includes a laser rangefinder and thermal image night vision equipment.

A 7.62 mm MG 42/59 is mounted coaxially to the left of the main armament. The armament has an elevation of +60 degrees and a depression of −10 degrees, the former allows it to engage slow flying aircraft and helicopters.

Mounted either side of the turret are three electrically-operated smoke dischargers.

The seven infantrymen sit at the rear of the VCC-80 and two firing ports, each with a vision block above, allow some of the infantry to fire their small arms from within the vehicle in safety.

The infantry enter and leave the vehicle via a power-operated ramp at the rear of the hull, which has an integral door for emergency use should the ramp fail to open. Over the top of the troop compartment are two oblong hatches that are hinged in the centre and can be locked vertical if required.

The suspension, which will be either torsion bar or hydro-pneumatic, will consist of six road wheels with the drive sprocket at the front, idler at the rear and three track return rollers. The upper part of the track is covered by a skirt to reduce dust.

Standard equipment includes a full range of passive night vision equipment and complete NBC system which allows the vehicle to operate continuously for eight hours in a contaminated area.

Status: Under development.

Manufacturer: OTO Melara and FIAT, via Valdilocchi 15, 19100 La Spezia, Italy.

OTO Melara OTO C13 Armoured Personnel Carrier

Development
The OTO C13 armoured personnel carrier has been designed by OTO Melara specifically for the export market and compared with earlier armoured personnel carriers has superior armour protection, greater mobility and a lower profile.

The C13 was announced in 1982. The first prototype, with no firing ports, was completed early in 1983 and the second prototype, which has firing ports, completed later the same year.

Description
The hull of the C13 is of all-welded aluminium construction with sloped front and upper hull sides to give maximum possible protection within the weight limits of the vehicle. Armour protection is increased by a steel armour plate system which bolts to the hull front and sides. This gives the C13 protection against armour-piercing machine gun projectiles (12.7 mm calibre at a range of less than 100 metres), artillery and shell fragments.

Second prototype of OTO Melara C13 APC showing firing ports/ vision blocks in side of troop compartment

Second prototype of OTO Melara C13 APC fitted with OTO Melara T 90 CKL turret armed with 90 mm gun

OTO Melara has a new concept of additional armoured structures with light weight and very high effectiveness under advanced development.

The driver sits at the front of the vehicle on the left side and has a single-piece circular hatch cover over his position which lifts and swings to his left rear to open. To his front and left side are four periscopes, one of which can be replaced by an infra-red or passive periscope for night driving.

The powerpack and all mechanical components are to the right of the driver with a large access hatch opening both from the outside and from the crew compartment. The air-inlet and air-outlet louvres are in the hull top and left side. The engine cooling radiator and fan is mounted above the engine with the latter being coupled to the engine and the steering control differential which is at the very front of the hull.

The machine gunner/commander is seated in the centre of the hull and has a cupola with five periscopes for frontal and side observation which can be manually traversed through 360 degrees. Mounted on the forward part of the cupola is a 12.7 mm M2 HB machine gun. Either side of the cupola is a bank of four electrically-operated smoke dischargers firing forwards. The machine gunner/commander is provided with lateral and rear armour protection.

The troop compartment is at the rear of the hull and the troops enter via a large power-operated ramp at the rear which is larger than that of the M113 and has a door in the left side. Over the top of the troop compartment are three roof hatches, one oblong hatch each side that opens upwards towards the centre of the vehicle and a circular one at the rear which has a single-piece hatch cover that opens forwards and can be locked on top of the hull. Mounted in the roof of the troop compartment, one either side at the rear is an electric fan to remove fumes from the vehicle when the weapons are fired. The troops have individual bucket-type seats that can be folded upwards.

Five vision blocks each with a firing port underneath allow most of the troops to fire their weapons from within the vehicle, three of these are in the right side of the hull and two in the left.

There is ample stowage space for personnel equipment for the 12 men and the five short-barrelled 5.56 mm firing port weapons.

The suspension is of the torsion bar type and consists of six dual rubber-tyred road wheels with the drive sprocket at the front, idler at the rear and three track return rollers. Hydraulic shock absorbers are fitted at the first, second, third and sixth road wheel stations. The upper part of the track is covered by a ballistic shroud which can be lifted to give access to the upper part of the suspension.

Standard equipment includes two bilge pumps (one front and one rear) and an automatic fire-extinguishing system in both crew and engine compartments. Optional equipment includes an air-conditioning system and an amphibious kit.

OTO Melara has suggested that the C13 armoured personnel carrier could be fitted with the following armament installations:

T 90 CKL Turret

This two-man power-operated turret is armed with a 90 mm Cockerill Mk III gun, 7.62 mm machine gun mounted coaxially with the main armament and a similar weapon mounted on the turret roof for anti-aircraft defence. Mounted either side of the turret are three electrically-operated smoke dischargers.

T 60 Turret

This two-man turret is armed with a hyper-velocity 60 mm gun which has anti-tank and anti-helicopter capabilities, the automatic loading system enables a high rate of fire to be achieved.

T 25 Turret

This two-man turret is armed with a 25 mm KBA cannon.

T 20 Turret

This two-man turret is armed with a 20 mm cannon and indentical to that installed on the FIAT/OTO Melara Type 6616 (4 × 4) armoured car.

Variants

OTO Melara has also proposed that the chassis be used for a coastal defence version of the OTOMAT missile. A typical coastal battery would consist of four launch vehicles each armed with two OTOMAT missiles, two transport vehicles, one fire-control vehicle and one support vehicle.

Other variants under development are a recovery vehicle, an ambulance which would have the same hull configuration as the C13 APC and a cargo vehicle with a different hull shape.

SPECIFICATIONS						
CREW	2 + 10	MAX ROAD SPEED	70 km/h	STEERING	hydrostatic with indirect
COMBAT WEIGHT	13 800 kg	FUEL CAPACITY	450 litres		power-assisted control
POWER-TO-WEIGHT		CRUISING RANGE	480 km		operated by steering wheel
RATIO	24.2 hp/tonne	GRADIENT	60%	BRAKES	service brakes
GROUND PRESSURE	0.53 kg/cm²	SIDE SLOPE	30%		hydraulically-actuated,
LENGTH	5.65 m	VERTICAL OBSTACLE	0.7 m		ventilated disc brakes.
WIDTH	2.6 m	TRENCH	2 m		Parking brake mechanically
over tracks	2.54 m	ENGINE	Isotta Fraschini model ID 38		actuated
HEIGHT			SS V6 90° V-6 supercharged	SUSPENSION	torsion bar
hull top	1.72 m		diesel developing 334 hp at	ELECTRICAL SYSTEM	24 V
inc MG	2.475 m		2800 rpm	ARMAMENT	1 × 12.7 mm MG
GROUND CLEARANCE	0.4 m	TRANSMISSION	automatic, 5 forward and 1	ARMOUR	
LENGTH OF TRACK ON			reverse gears with	aluminium	50 mm max
GROUND	3.334 m		hydrodynamic torque	steel appliqué	6 mm or 8 mm
			converter		

Status: Development complete. Ready for production.

Manufacturer: OTO Melara, via Valdilocchi 15, 19100 La Spezia, Italy.

Infantry Armoured Fighting Vehicle

Development

The Infantry Armoured Fighting Vehicle (IAFV) is the result of a development programme by the Automotive Technical Service (Servizio Tecnico della Motorizzazione) of the Italian Army to increase the combat effectiveness of the M113A1 APC. The Infantry Armoured Fighting Vehicle is based on the M113A1 APC which OTO Melara has been manufacturing under licence from the FMC Corporation of the USA since the 1960s. Main improvements over the M113A1 can be summarised as increased firepower, improved armour protection, the infantry's ability to aim and fire their weapons from inside the hull and improved seating arrangements. The IAFV is called the VCC-1, or Camillino, by the Italian Army. Final deliveries were made to the Italian Army in 1982 when production of the TOW version of the VCC-1 for Saudi Arabia began.

IAFV with all hatches closed and armed with 12.7 mm M2 HB MG

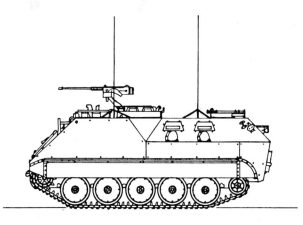

Description

The hull of the IAFV is made of all-welded aluminium with an additional layer of steel armour on the front and sides of the hull to improve ballistic protection.

The driver sits at the front of the hull on the left and has a single-piece hatch cover that opens to the right. There are four M17 periscopes to the front and left of his position and a single M19 periscope, which can be traversed through a full 360 degrees, mounted in the hatch cover. The M19 can be replaced by an infra-red periscope for night driving.

The engine is mounted to the right of the driver with the air-inlet and air-outlet louvres in the roof of the vehicle. The engine compartment is fitted with a fire warning and extinguishing system and the engine is coupled to an Allison TX-100 transmission which consists of a three-speed gearbox and a two-stage torque converter which gives six forward and two reverse gears. Access to the engine for maintenance is by a panel in the glacis plate and panels inside the crew compartment.

The vehicle commander sits immediately behind the driver and has a single-piece hatch cover that opens to the rear and five M17 periscopes. The gunner sits to the right of the commander and has a three-piece hatch cover that provides protection to his sides and rear when raised, and five M17 periscopes.

The six infantrymen sit at the rear of the vehicle, three down each side of the hull on individual seats. The first four face outwards and the last two inwards. The upper part of the hull sides of the personnel compartment are sloped to improve ballistic protection and in each side of the hull are two firing ports each with a rectangular vision block over it. The infantry enter and leave the vehicle by a power-operated ramp in the rear of the hull. There is a firing port in the right side of the ramp and an emergency door in the left side should the ramp fail to open. In the roof of the personnel compartment, at the rear, is a rotating hatch which is covered by a three-part triangular hatch cover when not in action. The

IAFV with firing ports open and armour protection for 12.7 mm machine gun raised

IAFV with all roof hatches closed and armour plates for 12.7 mm M2 machine gun lowered

SPECIFICATIONS	
CREW	2 + 7
COMBAT WEIGHT	11 600 kg
POWER-TO-WEIGHT	
RATIO	18.53 bhp/tonne
GROUND PRESSURE	0.57 kg/cm²
LENGTH	5.041 m
WIDTH	2.686 m
over tracks	2.54 m
HEIGHT	
over MG	2.552 m
over commander's cover	2.032 m
to hull top	1.828 m
GROUND CLEARANCE	0.406 m
TRACK	2.159 m
TRACK WIDTH	381 mm
LENGTH OF TRACK	
ON GROUND	2.667 m
MAX SPEED	
road	64.4 km/h
water	5 km/h
FUEL CAPACITY	360 litres
RANGE	550 km
FORDING	amphibious
GRADIENT	60%
SIDE SLOPE	30%
VERTICAL OBSTACLE	0.61 m
TRENCH	1.68 m
ENGINE	GMC model 6V-53 6-cylinder water-cooled diesel developing 215 bhp at 2800 rpm
TRANSMISSION	Allison TX-100 with 3 forward and 1 reverse gears coupled to 2-stage torque converter which gives 6 forward and 2 reverse gears
SUSPENSION	torsion bar
ELECTRICAL SYSTEM	24 V
ARMAMENT	
main	1 × 12.7 mm MG
secondary	1 × 7.62 mm MG
SMOKE-LAYING	
EQUIPMENT	none
AMMUNITION	
main	1050
secondary	1000

SPAAG System

The chassis of the VCC-1 is being used as the basis for the quad-25 mm SPAAG system being developed for the Italian Army by OTO Melara.

VCC-1 with TOW

Saudi Arabia has placed an order worth 350 000 million Lire with OTO Melara for 200 VCC-1 vehicles fitted with the

Saudi Arabian VCC-1 with Emerson Improved TOW System installed on roof (Christopher F Foss)

forward part of the cover folds forwards and is locked vertical and the two side covers open to the outside of the vehicle and are also locked vertical to provide protection for the machine gunner. A 7.62 mm machine gun can be mounted at this position to provide covering fire to the rear of the vehicle.

Two fans in the top of the hull, one either side of the rear gunner's position, expel fumes from the personnel compartment. There are two aluminium fuel tanks each side of the ramp at the rear.

The torsion bar suspension consists of five dual rubber-tyred road wheels with the drive sprocket at the front and the idler at the rear. There are no track return rollers. The first and last road wheel stations are provided with a hydraulic shock absorber.

The basic model of the IAFV is called the Mk 1 and is armed with a pintle-mounted 12.7 mm M2 HB machine gun. The Mk 2 version, which is not in service with the Italian Army, has a remote-controlled 12.7 mm machine gun. The Mk 3 version, still at the prototype stage, has an externally-mounted 20 mm cannon.

The IAFV is fully amphibious, being propelled in the water by its tracks. Before entering the water a trim board is erected at the front of the hull and the two electric bilge pumps are switched on. The vehicle is fitted with infra-red driving lights but has no NBC system.

same Emerson TOW ATGW system as the M901 Improved TOW Vehicle. The first ten production vehicles were delivered early in 1983 and final deliveries were made in 1984.

VCC-2

This is the Italian-built M113 with appliqué armour fitted to the front and sides. There are two firing ports with a bullet-proof vision block above in either side of the rear troop compartment. Some of these vehicles were deployed in Lebanon with Italian Army units operating as part of the United Nations peacekeeping forces.

Status: Production complete but can be resumed if further orders are received. In service with Italy and Saudi Arabia (TOW version only).

Manufacturer: OTO Melara, via Valdilocchi 15,19100 La Spezia, Italy.

New FIAT Wheeled Armoured Personnel Carriers

Development

Early in 1984 FIAT announced that it was developing, as a private venture, a new family of wheeled armoured vehicles. The lightest model in the range is the FIAT 6634G Armoured Vehicle Light (AVL), the heaviest model is the 6 × 6 FIAT 6636G Armoured Vehicle Heavy (AVH). Both of these use proven commercial automotive components and the 6 × 6 model has hydro-pneumatic suspension.

Description

The FIAT 6634G has an all-welded hull giving protection from small arms fire and shell splinters. The driver sits at the front of the hull on the left side and has a single-piece hatch cover that opens to the right. To his front and sides is a bullet-proof observation block and in the roof to the front of the hatch cover is a single forward-facing periscope which can be replaced by a passive periscope for night driving. The engine compartment is to the right of the driver. In either side of the hull is a door that opens to the front of the vehicle; in the upper part of each is a vision block with a firing port underneath. In the rear of the hull is an upward-opening hatch, also with a vision block with a firing port underneath.

FIAT 6634G Armoured Vehicle Light (AVL) with side and rear hatches open. Cupola not fitted wth 12.7 mm M2 HB machine gun

Model of FIAT 6636G Armoured Vehicle Heavy (AVH) with two-man power-operated turret

The troop compartment is at the rear of the hull and in the centre of the roof is an M113 type cupola with periscopes, single-piece hatch cover that opens to the rear and a pintle-mounted 12.7 mm M2 HB machine gun. There are five individual seats in the rear, including the one under the cupola. Mounted either side of the hull rear firing forwards is a bank of three electrically-operated smoke dischargers. A larger 4 × 4 vehicle is called the FIAT Type 6633H; this is fully amphibious being propelled in the water by two water jets mounted under the hull at the rear.

The FIAT 6636G has a similar layout but is longer, wider and heavier. Two individual seats are provided to the rear of the driver, the first one for the commander and the second for the machine gunner who has a similar cupola to the FIAT 6634G's. The troops sit on bench seats down either side the troop compartment facing the centre. Over the top of the troop compartment at the rear are two rectangular roof hatches that open to the outside and a single circular roof hatch that opens to the right. The troops enter the vehicle via a forward-opening door (with a vision block) between the second and third axle. Additional firing ports and vision blocks are provided in the hull and there is also a hatch in the hull rear. On either side of the hull at the rear is a bank of three fixed smoke dischargers firing forwards.

The FIAT 3336G is fully amphibious, being propelled in the water by two water jets mounted at the hull rear, one either side. Various armament installations can be fitted up to a 105 mm turret mounted gun.

SPECIFICATIONS (provisional)

Model	6634G	6633H	6636G
CONFIGURATION	4 × 4	4 × 4	6 × 6
LENGTH	4.75 m	6.098 m	6.7 m
WIDTH	2 m	n/a	2.85 m
HEIGHT (without armament)	1.6 m	1.9 m	2 m
GROUND CLEARANCE	0.34 m	0.43 m	0.4 m
WHEELBASE	2.5 m	3 m	1.6 m + 2 m
ANGLE OF APPROACH/ DEPARTURE	45°/45°	40°/45°	45°/45°
TYRES	11.00 × 16	14.00 × 20	14.00 × 20

Status: Development. Prototypes of all three vehicles have been completed.

Manufacturer: INVECO Defence Vehicle Division, Corso Lombardio 20, 10099 S Mauro Torinese (TO), Italy.

FIAT-OTO Melara Type 6614 APC. Commander's cupola not fitted with 12.7 mm machine gun (Paul Handel)

FIAT-OTO Melara Type 6614 APC from rear with ramp lowered

FIAT-OTO Melara Type 6614 Armoured Personnel Carrier

Development
The Type 6614 APC is a joint development between FIAT and OTO Melara, the former responsible for the hull and the automotive components and the latter for the armament installation. The vehicle shares many common components with the FIAT-OTO Melara Type 6616 armoured car.

The Type 6614 is currently being manufactured under licence in South Korea (qv).

Description
The hull of the Type 6614 is all welded which provides the crew with protection from small arms fire and shell splinters.

The driver sits at the front of the hull on the left side and has a single-piece domed hatch cover that opens to the right. To the front and side of the driver are five vision blocks which cover an arc of 200 degrees, the centre three with wiper blades.

The engine is mounted at the front of the vehicle to the right of the driver and is separated from the personnel compartment by a fireproof bulkhead. The engine is coupled to a manual five-speed transmission from which power is transmitted to the two-speed transfer case and then to the front and rear axles by propeller shafts. Both front and rear differ-

entials are mechanically lockable. The planetary final drives, front and rear, consist of epicyclic gear trains in the wheel hubs.

Entry doors in each side of the hull both open forward and have a vision block and a firing port. There are another three vision blocks and firing ports in each side of the hull. At the rear of the hull is a large ramp hinged at the bottom, either side of which is a single vision block and firing port. The ten infantrymen, one of whom acts as gunner, have individual seats which can be folded up. In the centre of the roof is mounted the main armament installation. On the basic vehicle this consists of an M113 type cupola which has five periscopes and a single-piece hatch cover that opens to the rear. Mounted on the forward part of this is a 12.7 mm (0.50) M2 HB machine gun. Other types of armament can be mounted if required, for example a fully-enclosed turret armed with single or twin 7.62 mm machine guns. Two roof hatches over the top of the troop compartment open either side of the vehicle. A ventilator is mounted in the roof at the rear.

The suspension, front and rear, is of the independent strut and link type with a helical spring and coaxial rubber bump stop. Each wheel station has two hydraulic shock absorbers, and anti-roll bars are fitted as standard. The tyres are of the run-flat type.

The vehicle is fully amphibious, being propelled in the water by its wheels. Standard equipment includes four electrically-operated bilge pumps with a capacity of 180 litres per minute each. Optional equipment includes passive or active night vision equipment, air-conditioning system (by Normalair-Garrett Limited), fire-extinguishing system in the wheel arches, spare wheel and holder, two three-barrelled

FIAT-OTO Melara Type 6614 APC with 12.7 mm machine gun

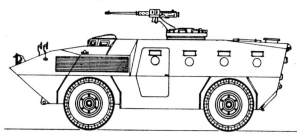

FIAT-OTO Melara Type 6614 armoured personnel carrier used in ambulance role without armament

76 mm smoke dischargers and a front-mounted 4500 kg capacity winch with 40 metres of 12 mm diameter cable.

Variants

Although designed primarily for use as an APC the Type 6614 can also be used for other roles such as reconnaissance and internal security. Projected variants include an ambulance, cargo, command and mortar carrier (in production). For trials purposes a Type 6614 APC has been fitted with an SNIA BPD FIROS 6 multiple rocket system.

SPECIFICATIONS

CREW	1 + 10
CONFIGURATION	4 × 4
COMBAT WEIGHT	8500 kg
WEIGHT ON FRONT AXLE	
LOADED	4500 kg
WEIGHT ON REAR AXLE	
LOADED	4000 kg
POWER-TO-WEIGHT	
RATIO	18.82 hp/tonne
LENGTH HULL	5.86 m
WIDTH	2.5 m
HEIGHT	
to hull top	1.78 m
inc MG mount	2.18 m
GROUND CLEARANCE	
axles	0.37 m
hull front	0.485 m
hull centre	0.385 m
hull rear	0.385 m
TRACK	1.96 m
WHEELBASE	2.9 m
ANGLE OF APPROACH/	
DEPARTURE	40°/45°
MAX SPEED	
road	100 km/h
water	4.5 km/h
FUEL CAPACITY	142 litres
MAX ROAD RANGE	700 km
FUEL CONSUMPTION	
(road)	0.2 litre/km
FORDING	amphibious
GRADIENT	60%
SIDE SLOPE	30%
VERTICAL OBSTACLE	0.4 m
TURNING RADIUS	7.9 m
ENGINE	Model 8062.24 super-charged liquid-cooled in-line diesel develop-ing 160 hp at 3200 rpm
TRANSMISSION	manual with 5 forward and 1 reverse gears
TRANSFER CASE	2-speed
STEERING	hydraulic
CLUTCH	single dry plate, hydraulically-operated
SUSPENSION	independent
TYRES	14.50 × 20 (run-flat)
BRAKES	
main	drum, air-over-hydraulic (dual circuit)
parking	drum, hand-operated, on transfer front output shaft
ELECTRICAL SYSTEM	24 V
BATTERIES	2 × 12 V, 100 Ah
ARMAMENT	1 × 12.7 mm MG
ARMOUR	6–8 mm

Status: In production in Italy and South Korea. In service with Italy, South Korea, Libya, Peru (including 10 in mortar carrying model), Somalia (270 ordered in 1977 and delivered by 1979) and Tunisia (120 ordered in 1979).

Manufacturer

INVECO Defence Vehicle Division, Corso Lombardio 20, 10099 S Mauro Torinese (To), Italy.

ASA Guardian Armoured Security Vehicle

Development

The Guardian armoured security vehicle has been developed as a private venture by Advanced Security Agency (ASA) and was announced for the first time in 1982. The company built three prototypes of the Guardian Mk 1 armoured security vehicle. The Mk 1 was followed by the Mk 2 which has been tested, approved and purchased by the Italian Army for use with the Italian contingent of the MLF in the Lebanon which has since been withdrawn. By December 1983 a total of 11 Mk 2s had been built.

Both the Mk 1 and Mk 2 are based on the chassis of the FIAT Campagnola (4 × 4) light vehicle as used by the Italian and other armed forces, although the manufacturer can build similar vehicles on other chassis. In mid-1984 the company announced that prototypes of the Guardian had also been built on the chassis of the Land-Rover One Ten (4 × 4) and Mercedes-Benz 280 GE (4 × 4) chassis.

Description

The layout of the Guardian is conventional with the engine at the front, driver and commander in the centre and the four troops seated at the rear, two each side facing inwards.

The body is made of ASALOY which is hard and tough and provides protection against small arms up to 7.62 mm NATO fired from a range of 20 metres and shell splinters. The glass used in the windows is also armoured.

The commander and driver are each provided with a windscreen which has a wiper with a firing port between them. In each side of the Guardian is a door that opens to the front, this has an armoured glass window in its upper part and a firing port below.

ASA Guardian Mk 2 armoured security vehicle

ASA Guardian Mk 2 armoured security vehicle

In each side of the troop compartment at the rear is a bullet-proof window with a firing port underneath. The four troops enter via a door in the rear that is hinged on the left and has a bullet-proof window with a firing port below. An opening ventilation hatch is provided in the roof.

Engagement of front wheel drive while the vehicle is in motion is possible with both high and low gears. Front and rear limited slip differentials operate by means of friction discs. Steering is of the power, worm and roller type with the articulating steering column having two universal joints.

Standard equipment includes an armoured radiator, air-conditioning system, roof-mounted flashing lights and special bumpers front and rear.

Optional equipment includes a diesel engine in place of the petrol engine, armoured floor, compressor to inflate tyres, additional fuel tank, protective grilles for windscreen, bullet-proof tyres, winches, fire warning and extinguishing system, heavy duty alternator, public address system, siren, spotlamps, smoke grenade launchers and radios.

ASA Guardian Mk 2 armoured security vehicle from rear

Variants

These include an armoured ambulance and a specialised command vehicle.

SPECIFICATIONS

CREW	2 + 4	WHEELBASE	2.3 m	SUSPENSION	independent on all four wheels. Double acting hydraulic dampers, trailing, longitudinal torsion bars
CONFIGURATION	4 × 4	ANGLE OF APPROACH/			
COMBAT WEIGHT	2730 kg	DEPARTURE	44°/44°		
UNLOADED WEIGHT	2180 kg	ROAD SPEED			
POWER-TO-WEIGHT		max	120 km/h	TYRES	9.50 × 15C
RATIO	29.3 bhp/tonne	min	3 km/h	BRAKES	power-assisted drum brakes on all four wheels with floating shoes. Independent front and rear hydraulic circuits. Circuit warning lights. Mechanical parking brakes on rear wheels
TOWED LOAD		FORDING	0.7 m		
road	1740 kg	GRADIENT	100%		
cross-country	900 kg	TURNING RADIUS	5.4 m		
LENGTH	3.68 m	STEERING	power, worm and nut		
WIDTH	1.75 m	ENGINE	4-cylinder petrol developing		
HEIGHT OVERALL	2.12 m		80 bhp at 2800 rpm		
GROUND CLEARANCE	0.245 m	TRANSMISSION	manual, 5 forward and 1	ELECTRICAL SYSTEM	24 V
TRACK			reverse gears	BATTERIES	2 × 12 V, 45 Ah
front	1.395 m	TRANSFER CASE	2-speed		
rear	1.435 m				

Status: Production. In service with the Italian Army.

Manufacturer: Advanced Security Agency SpA, 5 Via Besana, 20122 Milano, Italy.

JAPAN

Type 88 Mechanised Infantry Combat Vehicle

Development

The 1984 Japanese defence budget included a 600 million yen request for the construction of four prototypes of a new Mechanised Infantry Combat Vehicle. In fiscal year 1981 funding was provided for prototypes of the turret and hull. If trials with the four prototypes are successful it is expected this vehicle will be standardised as the Type 88 MICV in 1988.

Description

The hull of the Type 88 will be of all-welded aluminium construction with the engine compartment at the front of the hull on the left side and the driver on the right. The driver will have a single-piece hatch cover and periscopes for forward observation, one of which will be replaceable by a passive periscope for night driving.

The two-man power-operated turret will be in the centre of the hull with the gunner on the left and the commander on the right, both with individual hatch covers. Forward of the gunner's hatch will be a periscopic sight for aiming the 35 mm cannon with two periscopes giving observation to the left side. The commander has a periscopic sight forward of his hatch and at least six periscopes for all-round observation.

Main armament will be an Oerlikon-Bührle 35 mm KDE cannon which has a cyclic rate of fire of 200 rounds a minute. First weapons will be supplied direct from Switzerland with licenced production eventually being undertaken in Japan.

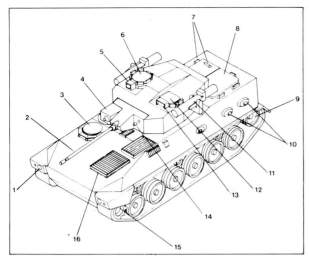

Japanese Type 88 MICV (1) driving lights (2) Oerlikon-Bührle 35 mm KDE automatic cannon (3) driver's hatch (4) night vision system (thermal imaging sight and laser designator) (5) commander's periscopic sight (6) commander's hatch (7) infantry's observation periscope (8) infantry's hatch (9) idler wheel (10) firing ports (11) medium range laser-guided anti-tank missile (Chyu-MAT) launcher (12) gunner's hatch (13) gunner's periscopic sight (14) Type 74 7.62 mm coaxial machine gun (15) driving wheel (16) engine louvre (Kensuke Ebata)

Mounted either side of the turret will be a Chyu-MAT medium range laser-guided anti-tank missile developed by Kawasaki Heavy Industries. The first prototype of the basic infantry version was completed early in 1984. Once the missiles have been launched new missiles have to be reloaded manually.

The troop compartment is at the rear of the hull with three spherical firing ports in each side of the hull, twin hatches in the roof and periscopes for observation and weapon aiming.

Suspension will probably be of the torsion bar type with six dual rubber-tyred road wheels, drive sprocket at the front, idler at the rear and three track return rollers.

The vehicle will not have any amphibious capability, but will be fitted with an NBC system and a full range of passive night vision equipment.

Status: Development. Many enter service in late 1980s.

Type 73 Armoured Personnel Carrier

Development

The development of a new armoured personnel carrier to supplement the SU 60 began in fiscal year 1967 under the direction of the Technical Research and Development Institution of the Japanese Defence Agency although before this, in 1964, Mitsubishi Heavy Industries had built as a private venture an amphibious all-welded aluminium APC under the designation XU.

In January 1967 the following requirements were issued for the new APC: a maximum speed of over 60 km/h, ability to carry 12 men including the crew, to be fully amphibious, have all-welded aluminium armour, have provision for the infantry to use their small arms from inside the vehicle and be armed with a 20 mm cannon, 12.7 mm machine gun and one 7.62 mm machine gun.

In 1967 the following manufacturers started on the manufacture of specific components: Hitachi Manufacturing Company (differential), Kobe Iron Works (aluminium alloy), Komatsu Manufacturing Company (tracks), Mitsubishi Heavy Industries (engine, steering and suspension), and Nihon Electric Corporation (night vision equipment).

In 1968 an automotive test rig, called the SUT, was completed and tested. The following year Mitsubishi Heavy Industries and the Komatsu Manufacturing Company each built two prototype vehicles, one steel and one aluminium.

Type 73 APC from rear showing position of two banks of three electrically-operated smoke dischargers (Kensuke Ebata)

Type 73 APCs clearly showing position of armament, side skirts and buoyancy aids attached to outside of road wheels (Ryuta Watanabe)

The Mitsubishi models were designated the SUB-I-1 (armed with a 12.7 mm machine gun in an open mount) and SUB-I-2 with the same armament. The Komatsu models were designated SUB-II-1 and SUB-II-2, both armed with a 12.7 mm turret-mounted machine gun. A turret-mounted Rheinmetall 20 mm cannon was installed on one prototype but did not progress beyond the prototype stage. The Mitsubishi SUB-I-2 had a hydro-pneumatic suspension system similar to that fitted to the Type 73 MBT.

After trials, in December 1972, the second prototype of the Mitsubishi model, with aluminium armour, was selected for use by the Japanese Ground Self-Defence Force and after minor modifications and improvements was standardised as the Type 73 APC. Due to budgetary restrictions, production has been very slow, 34 being ordered in fiscal year 1973, 18 in 1974, 17 in 1975, 7 in 1976, 6 in 1977, 6 in 1978, 6 in 1979 and 9 in 1980. By the end of the fiscal year 81 Mid Term Defence Programme 105 Type 73 APCs had been procured. It is expected that 225 Type 73 APCs will be in service by the end of 1988.

Description

The hull of the Type 73 APC is made of all-welded aluminium armour with the bow machine gunner seated at the front of the hull on the left side. The bow machine gun has an elevation, depression and traverse of 30 degrees. The gunner has a single-piece hatch cover that opens to the left and has a single periscope which can be traversed through 360 degrees.

The driver sits at the front of the hull on the right side and has a single-piece hatch cover that lifts and swings horizontally to the rear to open, and has an integral periscope. To the front of the driver's position are three periscopes.

The commander sits slightly behind the bow machine-gunner and driver and has a single-piece hatch cover that opens to the rear. Six vision blocks give the commander all-round observation.

The engine is mounted to the rear of the bow machine gunner on the left side of the hull with the air-inlet, air-outlet and exhaust pipe in the roof. The engine and transmission are mounted as a powerpack and can be removed from the vehicle as a complete unit in half an hour. The machine gunner sits behind the driver and has a cupola that can be traversed through a full 360 degrees. The cupola has a

single-piece hatch cover that opens to the rear and six periscopes for all-round observation. The 12.7 mm (0.50) M2 HB machine gun is not provided with a shield as it can be aimed and fired from inside the cupola. The 12.7 mm machine gun has an elevation of +60 degrees, depression of −10 degrees and can be traversed through 360 degrees.

The Type 73 carries nine infantrymen of whom one normally mans the 12.7 mm (0.50) machine gun position. The eight infantrymen sit in the troop compartment at the rear of the hull down either side on seats that can be folded up, and enter the vehicle via two doors at the rear of the hull that open outwards. There is a T-shaped firing port in each door and two in each side of the troop compartment. Over the top of the troop compartment are two single-piece hatch covers that open either side of the hull top. Mounted at the very rear of the hull top, one either side, is a three-barrelled smoke discharger that fires forwards over the front of the vehicle.

The torsion bar suspension consists of five dual rubber-tyred road wheels with the drive sprocket at the front and the idler at the rear. There are no track return rollers. A hydraulic shock absorber is provided for the first road wheel station.

The basic model of the Type 73 APC is not amphibious. An amphibious kit has been developed and fitted to some vehicles. The kit consists of buoyancy aids attached to the outside of each of the road wheels, skirts fitted to cover the upper part of the tracks to improve water flow, box type structures fitted on top of the hull over the air-inlet, air-outlet and exhaust to stop water entering when afloat and a trim vane fitted on the front of the hull. The trim vane is in two parts and is hinged horizontally. A transparent panel in the right side provides forward vision for the driver. When afloat the vehicle is propelled in the water by its tracks.

The Type 73 is fitted with passive infra-red night vision equipment and an NBC system.

Variants

The only variant is the Type 75 self-propelled ground-wind measuring unit. This is used in conjunction with the Type 75 self-propelled 130 mm multiple rocket launcher which also uses some components of the Type 73. The measuring unit has a mast which when extended is 12.5 metres high and can measure wind velocity in two directions up to a maximum of 30 km/h. The wind velocity measuring equipment was developed by Meisei Electric.

In 1978 some Type 73 APCs were fitted with three firing ports and three periscopes in either side of the hull for trials by the 7th Division. Once these trials had been completed the

Type 73 armoured personnel carrier

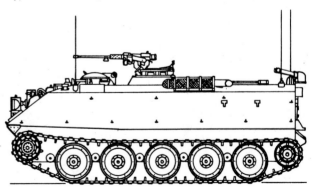

vehicles were converted back to their original configuration. The Type 74 105 mm self-propelled howitzer and Type 75 multiple rocket launcher both use the same engine as the Type 73.

SPECIFICATIONS

CREW	3 + 9
COMBAT WEIGHT	13 300 kg
POWER-TO-WEIGHT	
RATIO	22.6 hp/tonne
LENGTH	5.8 m
WIDTH	2.8 m
HEIGHT	
including MG	2.2 m
to hull top	1.7 m
GROUND CLEARANCE	0.4 m
TRACK	2.56 m
TRACK WIDTH	380 mm
LENGTH OF TRACK	
ON GROUND	3.67 m
MAX SPEED	
road	70 km/h
water	7 km/h
MAX RANGE	300 km
FUEL	450 litres
FORDING (with kit)	amphibious
GRADIENT	60%
VERTICAL OBSTACLE	0.7 m
TRENCH	2 m
TURNING RADIUS	7 m
ENGINE	Mitsubishi 4ZF air-cooled 2-stroke V4 diesel developing 300 hp at 2200 rpm
SUSPENSION	torsion bar
ELECTRICAL SYSTEM	24 V
ARMAMENT	
main	1 × 12.7 mm MG
bow	1 × 7.62 mm MG
SMOKE-LAYING	
EQUIPMENT	2 × 3 smoke dischargers

Status: In production. In service only with the Japanese Ground Self-Defence Force.

Manufacturer: Mitsubishi Heavy Industries, Sagamihara. Mitsubishi Heavy Industries, 5-1, Marunouchi 2-chome, Chiyoda-ku, Tokyo, Japan.

Type SU 60 Armoured Personnel Carrier

Development

In the mid-1950s the Japanese Ground Self-Defence Force issued a requirement for a full tracked armoured personnel carrier. Development began in 1956 with overall control of the project managed by the Technical Research and Development Headquarters of the Japanese Self-Defence Agency. In 1957 prototypes of the APC were completed by Komatsu and Mitsubishi. The Komatsu prototype was called the SU-I and the Mitsubishi model the SU-II.

Both prototypes weighed 10.6 tonnes, carried nine men and had a maximum road speed of 45 km/h. Between 1957 and 1958 the SU-I and SU-II were tested alongside an American-supplied M59 APC. Eleven second series prototypes were manufactured by Mitsubishi Heavy Industries and the Komatsu Manufacturing Corporation. Mitsubishi built 5 SU-II (Kai) Ms, one SV (Kai) M and one SX (Kai) M, M standing for Mitsubishi and Kai for modified. Komatsu built two SU-II (Kai) Ks, one SV (Kai) K and one SX (Kai) K, K standing for Komatsu. The SV was the 81 mm mortar carrier and the SX was the 107 mm (4.2 inch) mortar carrier.

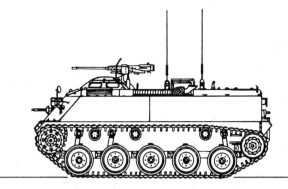

Type SU 60 armoured personnel carrier

Type SU 60 APC showing bow-mounted 7.62 mm machine gun (Keiichi Nogi)

In both the mortar was mounted in the rear compartment but on the SX the top of the hull was sloped to the rear to avoid muzzle blast from the 107 mm mortar, but this also decreased the weight of the vehicle.

In July 1959 four prototypes of the SU-II (Kai) were completed and tested through to October 1959 and in 1960 the vehicle was standardised as the Type 60 APC with the mortar carriers being standardised as the Type 60 self-propelled 81 mm mortar and the Type 60 107 mm (4.2 inch) mortar.

The first production contract for 24 vehicles was provided for in the 1959 budget and production was undertaken by Komatsu and Mitsubishi and final orders were placed with funding from the 1972 budget. The vehicle is expected to remain in service until the late 1980s as the more recent Type 73 APC is still being built only in relatively small numbers.

Description

The hull of the SU 60 is made of all-welded steel with the driver seated at the front of the hull on the right. The driver has a single-piece hatch cover over his position that opens to the right, in front of which are three M17 periscopes. The bow machine gunner sits at the front of the hull on the left and has a single-piece hatch cover that opens to the left rear, with an integral M6 periscope for aiming the 7.62 mm (0.30) M1919A4 bow machine gun.

The commander sits immediately behind the driver's and bow machine gunner's position and has a single-piece hatch cover that opens to the left rear. Eight vision blocks provide all-round observation for the commander.

Type SU 60 APC showing arrangement of roof hatches. This particular vehicle is not fitted with 12.7 mm and 7.62 mm machine guns (Kensuke Ebata)

Type SX 4.2-inch (107 mm) mortar carrier with roof hatches open and ramp down to show position of mortar (Panzer Magazine)

The engine is on the left side of the hull to the rear of the bow-machine gunner and power is transmitted to the differential at the front of the hull by a short propeller shaft.

The gunner sits to the rear of the commander on the right side of the hull and has a two-piece hatch cover that opens either side of his position. The 12.7 mm (0.50) M2 HB machine gun can be traversed through a full 360 degrees and is provided with a shield.

The troop compartment is at the rear of the hull with the six infantrymen seated on individual seats three down each side of the hull. They enter and leave the vehicle by two doors in the rear of the hull that open outwards. The right door has a small observation slit. Over the top of the troop compartment is a single-piece hatch cover that opens forwards. To the rear of this is a two-part hatch cover that opens either side of the hull. Each of the latter is in two parts hinged in the centre. There is no provision for the infantry to use their small arms from inside the vehicle.

The torsion bar suspension consists of five dual rubber-tyred road wheels with the drive sprocket at the front, idler at the rear and three track return rollers. The first, second and fifth road wheel stations are provided with a hydraulic shock absorber. The SU 60 APC has no NBC system, no night vision equipment and no amphibious capability.

SPECIFICATIONS

CREW	4 + 6
COMBAT WEIGHT	11 800 kg
UNLOADED WEIGHT	10 600 kg
POWER-TO-WEIGHT	
RATIO	18.64 hp/tonne
GROUND PRESSURE	0.57 kg/cm²
LENGTH	4.85 m
WIDTH	2.4 m
HEIGHT	
including MG	2.31 m
to hull top	1.7 m
GROUND CLEARANCE	0.4 m
TRACK	2.05 m
TRACK WIDTH	350 mm
LENGTH OF TRACK	
ON GROUND	3.18 m
MAX ROAD SPEED	45 km/h
MAX RANGE	230 km
FORDING	1 m
GRADIENT	60%
VERTICAL OBSTACLE	0.6 m
TRENCH	1.82 m
TURNING RADIUS	7 m
ENGINE	Mitsubishi model 8 HA 21 WT, V-8 air-cooled 4-cycle turbo-charged diesel developing 220 hp at 2400 rpm
TRANSMISSION	manual with 3 forward and 1 reverse gears and torque converter
STEERING	controlled differential
SUSPENSION	torsion bar
ELECTRICAL SYSTEM	24 V
BATTERIES	2 × 12 V
ARMAMENT	
main	1 × 12.7 mm MG
bow	1 × 7.62 mm MG
SMOKE-LAYING	
EQUIPMENT	none

Variants

Type SV 60 81 mm Mortar Carrier

This is essentially a Type 60 APC with an 81 mm mortar mounted in the back of the hull firing to the rear with two doors in the rear of the hull. A bipod and baseplate are carried on the glacis plate to enable the mortar to be deployed away from the vehicle. The mortar has an elevation from +40 degrees to +85 degrees, traverse of 40 degrees left and right and a maximum range of 3000 metres. Twenty-four mortar bombs are carried. The SV 60 has a crew of five and weighs 12 100 kg fully loaded. Armament consists of one roof-mounted 12.7 mm (0.50) anti-aircraft machine gun. Only 18 of these vehicles were built.

Type SX 60 4.2-inch (107 mm) Mortar Carrier

This has a 4.2-inch (107 mm) mortar mounted in the rear of the hull firing to the rear. A baseplate and stand are carried on the glacis plate enabling the mortar to be deployed away from the vehicle. The mortar has an elevation from +37 degrees to +65 degrees, traverse of 40 degrees left and right and a maximum range of 4000 metres. Eight mortar bombs are carried. The SX 60 has a crew of five, weighs 12 900 kg fully loaded but is fitted with the 12.7 mm anti-aircraft machine gun only. It can be distinguished from the 81 mm mortar carrier by the lack of a bow machine gun and the distinct chamfer to the rear of the top of the hull of the Type SX 60. The SX 60 has a single-piece ramp at the rear of the hull hinged at its lower part. Only 18 of these vehicles were built.

Other variants

There are at least three other variants of the Type SU 60 APC, an NBC detection vehicle, a dozer and a model modified to resemble the Soviet BMD airborne combat vehicle used by the Japanese Ground Self-Defence Force for training purposes. Only two dozers are in service, used by the 7th Division for clearing snow. A prototype of a 105 mm self-propelled howitzer was built under the designation SY 60 but was never placed in production.

Status: Production complete. In service only with Japanese Ground Self-Defence Force.

Manufacturers: Mitsubishi Heavy Industries, Maruko, Tokyo. Komatsu Manufacturing Corporation. Mitsubishi Heavy Industries, 5-1, Marunouchi 2-chome, Chiyoda-ku, Tokyo, Japan.

KOREA, REPUBLIC

KM900 Armoured Personnel Carrier

This is essentially the Italian FIAT-OTO Melara Type 6614 armoured personnel carrier manufactured under licence in South Korea. The basic model is designated the KM900 while more specialised models are designated the KM901. It is assumed that the latter include ambulance, command and mortar carriers. As far as it is known the specifications of the South Korean model are identical to those vehicles built in Italy.

Status: In production. In service with the South Korean Army.

Manufacturer: Asia Motors Co, Inc, 1-60, Yoido-Dong, Yungdeugpo-Ku, Seoul, Korea, CPO Box 5022.

NETHERLANDS

YP-408 Armoured Personnel Carrier

Development

The YP-408 was developed by DAF (Van Doorne Automobielfabrieken) from 1956 to meet the requirements of the Dutch Army. The first mock-up was completed in 1957 and the first prototypes in 1958 powered by an American Hercules JXLD petrol engine which developed 133 hp, had individual hatch covers for both the driver and machine gunner and a different roof hatch arrangement over the personnel compartment from production vehicles.

After trials and modifications, a production order was placed for 750 vehicles, the first of which were delivered in 1964 with final deliveries in 1968.

As of January 1984 the Netherlands Army had eight battalions of YP-408 vehicles and all of these will have been phased out of service by 1988. They are being replaced by FMC AIFVs, called the YPR 765 by the Netherlands Army.

Description

The hull of the YP-408 is all welded with the engine at the front, driver and gunner behind the engine and the personnel compartment at the rear of the hull.

The engine is provided with a device which enables the driver to close off the crankcase ventilation without leaving his seat. This is done whenever there is a risk of water entering the engine, for example when fording. Closing off the crankcase ventilation system creates an overpressure in the crankcase. The engine-driven air compressor supplies air to the brake system and can also be used to inflate the tyres.

Power from the main gearbox is transmitted to an auxiliary gearbox through a short propeller shaft. A central differential is incorporated in the auxiliary box. To the left and right of the latter are the transfer boxes from which power is transmitted to the final drive boxes at the front and rear wheels.

The driver sits to the rear of the engine on the left with the machine gunner to his right. The driver has a one-piece hatch cover over his position that opens to the left with a single periscope that can be traversed through 360 degrees. A periscope is also provided to the front of the driver's position and a second to his left in the side of the hull. The driver's seat can be adjusted vertically and when he is driving with his head out a canvas cover with a window and wiper can be fitted. The gunner is provided with a periscope to his front and another to his right in the side of the hull. The DAF-designed gun mount for the 12.7 mm (0.50) M2 HB machine gun can be traversed through 360 degrees by handwheel or by the gunner's shoulder. The weapon can be elevated to +70 degrees and depressed to −8 degrees, and has a traverse of eight degrees left and right in its mounting. The gunner has two hatch covers, each of which opens vertically to his side to give him a measure of protection when using the machine gun.

There are six hatches over the troop compartment which open three each side of the vehicle. The infantrymen are seated on bench seats, five down each side of the hull facing each other. They enter and leave the vehicle by two doors in the rear of the hull, each of which has a single firing port.

Basic PWI-S(GR) APC without armament installed (Dutch Army)

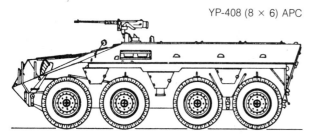

YP-408 (8 × 6) APC

Many of the automotive components of the YP-408 are identical to those of the DAF YA 328 (6 × 6) tactical truck which is also used by the Dutch Army. Although the YP-408 has eight wheels, the second axle is not driven. Steering, which is power assisted, is on the front four wheels.

The first road wheels are independently suspended on two trailing arms with transverse torsion bars. The second pair of wheels is also independent but the torsion bars are mounted longitudinally for reasons of space. The rear axle consists of a centre axle with equalising beams and leaf springs. The vertical movement of the equalising beams is restricted by steel cables between the beams and the hull of the vehicle.

In an emergency, when one of the tyres of the first axle or rear tandem axle has a puncture, a wheel from the second front axle can be used as a spare. The wheel with the puncture is then fitted on the second axle and suspended from the hull with a special chain to keep it clear of the ground. The tyres have reinforced side walls which enable the vehicle to be driven for 50 km at a reduced speed if they are punctured.

The YP-408 is not amphibious and has no NBC system but does have a heater. The following infra-red night vision equipment can be fitted if required: headlamps, driver's periscope with a 46-degree field of view, a sight for the machine gun with a magnification of ×3.2 and a 14-degree field of view, and a searchlight for the machine gun.

Variants

PWI-S(GR)
This is the basic APC and its designation stands, in Dutch, for Pantser Wagen Infanterie-Standaard (Groep).

PWI-S(PC) (Command Vehicle)
This is a platoon commander's vehicle and is similar to the PWI-S(GR) but is fitted with additional communications equipment and an additional periscope mounted in the roof at the rear of the vehicle which has a magnification of ×3, a field of view of 15 degrees, an elevation range of between −10 degrees and +10 degrees and can be traversed through 360 degrees. This periscope is also fitted in the PWCO model. The PWI-S(PC) has a crew of nine: platoon commander, gunner, driver and six infantrymen.

PWCO (Command Vehicle)
This is a company or battalion commander's vehicle and has a crew of six: commander, three staff men, driver and gunner. The seats on the right side of the vehicle have been retained but those on the left have been removed and replaced by a folding table, mapboard and additional communications equipment. To increase working space a tent can be erected at the rear of the vehicle. The heater on this model works independently of the main engine and a flexible exhaust pipe is provided to prevent exhaust gases entering the vehicle when it is stationary. The electrical system includes a 3 kVA alternator and two additional batteries. The PWCO is recognisable externally by its three radio antennas.

PWI-S (PC) command vehicle showing two radio aerials at rear and fitted with 12.7 mm M2 HB machine gun

PW-MT (Mortar Tractor) with rear doors locked open towing 120 mm Brandt mortar

PW-GWT (Ambulance)

This model is unarmed and has a crew of three, driver and two medical orderlies. It can carry two stretcher patients (left side of hull) and four seated patients (right side of hull) and spare stretchers are carried on the outside of the vehicle.

PW-V (Freight)

This model has been designed to carry 1500 kg of cargo and has a crew of two, driver and gunner. It is the only member of the family not fitted with a radio as standard. The freight compartment has a floor consisting of five pivoted removable sections which form a flat load surface. The crew compartment is separated from the freight compartment by a grille to protect the crew from sliding loads. The internal equipment of the PW-V is identical to that of the PW-GWT ambulance and the vehicle can therefore be converted into an ambulance.

PW-MT (Mortar Tractor)

This tows a French 120 mm Brandt mortar as well as carrying the seven-man mortar team (mortar group commander, four mortarmen, driver and gunner) and mortar bombs. A special rack in the crew compartment for the 50 mortar bombs keeps them in position in the event of emergency braking. The rear doors on this model are slightly different as they have been shortened at the bottom to allow them to open when the mortar is being towed.

PWAT (Anti-tank Vehicle)

This is the basic vehicle fitted with the Hughes TOW ATGW system.

PWRDR (Radar)

This is the basic vehicle fitted with the British ZB 298 ground surveillance radar.

SPECIFICATIONS

CREW	2 + 10	SIDE SLOPE	70%
CONFIGURATION	8 × 6	VERTICAL OBSTACLE	0.7 m
COMBAT WEIGHT	12 000 kg	TRENCH	1.2 m
UNLOADED WEIGHT	9500 kg		(2.9 m diagonally)
WEIGHT ON FIRST AXLE		TURNING RADIUS	9 m
LOADED	3500 kg	ENGINE	DAF model DS 575 6-cylinder
WEIGHT ON SECOND			in-line water-cooled direct
AXLE LOADED	2500 kg		injection turbo-charged
WEIGHT ON REAR BOGIE			diesel developing 165 hp
AXLE LOADED	6000 kg		(SAE) at 2400 rpm
POWER-TO-WEIGHT		TRANSMISSION	manual with 5 forward and 1
RATIO	13.75 hp/tonne		reverse gears
LENGTH	6.23 m	TRANSFER CASE	2-speed
WIDTH	2.4 m	STEERING	hydraulic
HEIGHT		TYRES	11.00 × 20
to top of MG	2.37 m	BRAKES	
to hull top	1.8 m	main	air/hydraulic
GROUND CLEARANCE	0.518 m		(dual circuit)
TRACK		parking	handbrake acts on brake
front	2.054 m		drums fitted on propeller
rear	2.08 m		shaft to rear wheels.
WHEELBASE	1.275 m + 2.145 m (centre of		Air-actuated parking brake
	first axle to centre of second		also provided
	axle and centre of second	ELECTRICAL SYSTEM	24 V
	axle to centre of rear bogie)	BATTERIES	2 × 12 V, 100 Ah
ANGLE OF APPROACH/		ARMAMENT	1 × 12.7 mm MG
DEPARTURE	42°/70°	SMOKE-LAYING	
MAX ROAD SPEED	80 km/h	EQUIPMENT	3 smoke dischargers either
FUEL CAPACITY	200 litres		side of hull front
MAX RANGE		FIRE-CONTROL SYSTEM	
road	500 km	Turret power control	manual
cross-country	400 km	Gun elevation/depression	+70°/−8°
FUEL CONSUMPTION	0.4 litre/km	ARMOUR	8–15 mm
FORDING	1.2 m		
GRADIENT	60%		

Status: Production complete. In service with the Netherlands. Five YP-408s were handed over to the South American state of Suriname when it became independent in 1975.

Manufacturer: DAF Trucks, Geldropseweg 303, 5645 TK Eindhoven, Netherlands.

NIGERIA

Steyr 4K 7FA Armoured Personnel Carrier

In 1981 Nigeria took delivery of 25 Steyr-Daimler-Puch 4K 7FA series of tracked vehicles, including 17 of the basic 4K 7FA G 127 APCs armed with a 12.7 mm M2 HB machine gun. Nigeria subsequently ordered an additional 70 vehicles, including 47 4K 7FA G 127 APCs, four Greif ARVs and 19

81 mm mortar carriers, armoured ambulances and mobile command posts. Unconfirmed reports have stated that some of the second order will be made under licence in the Steyr factory in north Nigeria in Boshni state. This factory is already building Steyr-Daimler-Puch trucks for both civil and military applications.

PORTUGAL

BRAVIA Mk II Armoured Personnel Carrier

Development
In 1983 BRAVIA announced that it had built a prototype of a new 6 × 6 armoured personnel carrier called the BRAVIA Mk II and that it was developing an 8 × 8 model, the BRAVIA Mk III.

Description
The hull of the BRAVIA is of all-welded construction with the driver sitting at the front left with vision blocks for forward observation. There is a vision block in either side of the hull at the front with a firing port underneath. A variety of armament installations can be mounted at the rear of the driver's position including a turret with a 76 mm, 90 mm or 105 mm gun with a 7.62 mm coaxial machine gun and a 7.62 mm or 12.7 mm anti-aircraft machine gun. Other weapon systems include a 20 mm anti-aircraft gun. In either side of the hull is a two-part entry hatch, the lower part opens

downwards to form a step, the upper part opens to the rear and has a vision block with a firing port underneath.

The engine compartment is at the rear of the hull on the right side with an aisle connecting the crew compartment with a door in the rear of the hull on the left side, hatches are provided in the roof. In the left side of the hull are three vision blocks, each with a firing port underneath.

The BRAVIA Mk II is fully amphibious and propelled in the water by its wheels, steering on the front wheels when afloat, as on land. Mounted in the nose of the vehicle is a winch and optional equipment includes night vision equipment for the commander, gunner and driver.

Artist's impression of BRAVIA Mk II armoured personnel carrier with two-man turret armed with 90 mm Mecar gun, 7.62 mm co-axial machine gun and bank of four electrically-operated smoke dischargers either side

SPECIFICATIONS (provisional)	
CREW	2 + 10
COMBAT WEIGHT	12 200 kg
UNLOADED WEIGHT	9100 kg
POWER-TO-WEIGHT	
RATIO	24.59 hp/tonne
LENGTH	6 m
WIDTH	2.5 m
HEIGHT WITH TURRET	2.9 m
GROUND CLEARANCE	
max	0.54 m
min	0.36 m
TRACK	2.1 m
WHEELBASE	3.7 m
MAX ROAD SPEED	115 km/h
FUEL CAPACITY	300 litres
MAX RANGE ROAD	750 km
FORDING	amphibious
GRADIENT	65%
VERTICAL OBSTACLE	0.9 m
ENGINE	Detroit Diesel 6V-53T, 6-cylinder diesel developing 300 hp at 2800 rpm
TRANSMISSION	Allison MT-653-TR
TRANSFER CASE	2-speed
SUSPENSION	semi-elliptical springs
ELECTRICAL SYSTEM	24 V
ARMAMENT	see text

Status: Prototype.

Manufacturer: BRAVIA SARL, Av Eng Duarte Pacheco 21, 5°,-A, Lisbon, Portugal.

Chaimite Armoured Personnel Carrier

Development
The Chaimite range of 4 × 4 armoured vehicles was developed by BRAVIA (Sociedade Luso – Brasileira de Via-

Chaimite V-200 with turret-mounted 7.62 mm and 12.7 mm machine guns

turas Equipamentos SARL) in the 1960s to meet the requirements of the Portuguese armed forces. The first prototype of the Chaimite was completed in 1966 and by early 1981 production had amounted to over 400 vehicles. It is reported that the Portuguese Army has 79 Chaimate armoured personnel carriers. In appearance the Chaimite is very similar to the American Cadillac Gage Commando range of 4 × 4 multi-mission vehicles which entered production in 1964, and for this reason there is often confusion about the original source of these vehicles. The basic APC is called the V-200, but BRAVIA has now developed a whole range of vehicles which use the same basic hull.

Description (V-200)

The hull of the Chaimite APC is made of all-welded steel. The driver sits towards the front of the vehicle with the second crew member, normally the commander, to his right. Over their positions is a two-piece hatch cover that opens either side of the vehicle. The driver and commander each have a vision block to their front between which is a single firing port. To the left of the driver and the right of the commander are a vision block and firing port.

There is a two-part door in each side of the hull, the upper part opening to the rear and the lower part folding downwards to form a step. There are two vision blocks and two firing ports in each side of the hull between the front of the vehicle and the side door.

The main armament is installed immediately behind the driver's and commander's position.

The engine is at the rear of the vehicle on the left side and is separated from the personnel compartment by a fireproof bulkhead. Access to the engine for maintenance is through two hatches in the roof and a single hatch in the left side of the hull. The engine compartment is equipped with a fire extinguisher operated by the driver.

A door at the rear of the hull on the right side opens left and has a single vision block and a single firing There is an additional forward-opening hatch in th the vehicle to the right of the engine compartment is also a firing port and vision block below it in the right of the hull.

Power is transferred from the engine to the transmission then to the transfer case and then to the front and rear axles. The axles are of the fully floating double reduction type with locking differentials. The tyres are of the run-flat type.

Mounted in the front of the Chaimite is a hydraulic winch with a maximum capacity of 4530 kg, provided with 38.1 metres of 11 mm diameter cable with a maximum breaking strength of 8090 kg. Optional equipment includes infra-red night vision equipment.

The Chaimite is fully amphibious and propelled in the water by its wheels.

The V-200 is fitted with a BRAVIA-designed turret armed with twin 7.62 mm (0.30) machine guns, twin 5.56 mm machine guns or one 7.62 mm (0.30) and one 12.7 mm (0.50) machine gun. The weapons can be elevated manually from −15 to +50 degrees, traverse is manual through a full 360 degrees. The turret with twin 7.62 mm (0.30) machine guns is provided with 500 rounds of ready-use ammunition (250 rounds per gun) plus a further 9000 rounds carried in the vehicle in reserve. The turret has a single-piece hatch cover that opens to the rear, vision blocks and an M28C periscopic sight mounted in the left side of the turret for aiming the machine guns. If required the turret can be fitted with a device for launching five 60 mm anti-personnel, anti-tank,

Chaimite V-200 with one-man turret armed with twin 7.62 mm machine guns

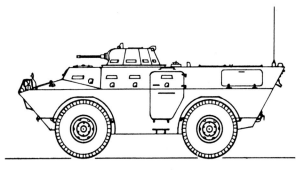

Chaimite V-400 with turret armed with Mecar 90 mm gun, 7.62 mm coaxial machine gun and 7.62 mm anti-aircraft machine gun

smoke, illuminating or incendiary grenades. The turret can also be fitted with four 3.5-inch rocket launchers either side of the turret, which can be fired from inside the vehicle but are reloaded from outside.

Variants

V-300

This model has a crew of four or five and can be fitted with a one- or two-man turret. The former is the Oerlikon GAD-AOA turret armed with a 20 mm KAA-001 cannon, which has an elevation from −12 to +70 degrees.

The following two-man turrets can be fitted to the V-300; BRAVIA turret armed with a 20 mm cannon (with 100 ready rounds and 300 rounds in reserve), 7.62 mm coaxial machine gun (500 ready rounds) and a 7.62 mm anti-aircraft machine gun (500 ready rounds) and 3000 rounds of 7.62 mm ammunition in reserve; French SAMM S 530 (new version is designated TAB 220) turret armed with twin 20 mm M621 cannon with an elevation of +75 degrees and a depression of −10 degrees, or ESD TA-20 turret armed with twin 20 mm cannon.

V-400

The following two-man turrets can be fitted to the V-400: turret armed with Mecar 90 mm gun with an elevation of +25 degrees, depression of −8 degrees and 360-degree turret traverse, a 7.62 mm machine gun mounted coaxially with the main armament and a 7.62 mm machine gun mounted on the turret roof for anti-aircraft use. Can also be fitted with 60 mm grenade launchers as fitted to the V-200. Ammunition capacity is 61 rounds of 90 mm (of which 21 are for ready use) and 3500 rounds of 7.62 mm (of which 500 are for ready use). In April 1983 a BRAVIA Chaimite V-400 fitted with a French Hispano-Suiza Lynx 90 turret was successfully tested in Portugal. The turret was armed with the GIAT 90 mm F1 gun with a maximum elevation of +35 degrees and had a SOPELEM day/night fire-control system. During trials all shots hit the target with a grouping (height plus width) of 1.5 metres. The gun was also fired with the turret traversed 90 degrees left and right with the vehicle on a negative slope. Turret armed with Bofors 90 mm gun with a 7.62 mm machine gun mounted coaxially with the main armament and a 7.62 mm anti-aircraft machine gun.

V-500

This is a command and communications vehicle.

V-600

This is a mortar carrier and has an 81 mm or 120 mm mortar.

V-700

ATGW vehicle armed with HOT or Swingfire ATGW. The latter model would have the same turret as fitted to the British Ferret Mk 5 vehicle.

V-800

This is the ambulance version and is unarmed.

V-900

Crash rescue vehicle.

V-1000

This is a riot control vehicle and can be fitted with various armament installations including a water cannon.

SPECIFICATIONS (V-200)			
CREW	11	GRADIENT	65%
CONFIGURATION	4 × 4	SIDE SLOPE	40%
COMBAT WEIGHT	7300 kg	VERTICAL OBSTACLE	0.9 m
POWER-TO-WEIGHT		ENGINE	Model M75 V-8 water-cooled
RATIO	28.76 hp/tonne		petrol developing 210 hp at
LENGTH HULL	5.606 m		4000 rpm (or V-6 diesel)
WIDTH	2.26 m	TRANSMISSION	manual with 5 forward and 1
HEIGHT			reverse gears
including turret	2.26 m	TRANSFER CASE	single speed
hull top	1.84 m	STEERING	power-assisted
GROUND CLEARANCE		CLUTCH	single dry plate,
hull	0.61 m		hydraulically-operated
differential	0.41 m	SUSPENSION	semi-elliptical springs and
WHEELBASE	2.667 m		hydraulic single-action
ANGLE OF APPROACH/			shock absorbers
DEPARTURE	52°/46°	TYRES	14.00 × 20
MAX ROAD SPEED		BRAKES	
1st gear	13.7 km/h	main	hydraulic
2nd gear	22.6 km/h	parking	on output shaft of
3rd gear	37.9 km/h		transmission
4th gear	62 km/h	ELECTRICAL SYSTEM	24 V
5th gear	99 km/h	ARMAMENT	see text
reverse	13.7 km/h	ARMOUR	
water	7 km/h	Hull front upper	6.35 mm at 75°
FUEL CAPACITY	300 litres	Hull front lower	7.94 mm at 40°
MAX ROAD RANGE		Hull sides upper	6.35 mm at 30°
petrol engine	804–965 km	Hull sides lower	7.94 mm at 10°
diesel engine	1367–1529 km	Hull top	6.35 mm
MAX CROSS-COUNTRY		Hull floor	9.35 mm
RANGE		Hull rear	6.35 mm at 30°
petrol engine	563–724 km	Turret front	7.94 mm
diesel engine	1046–1207 km	Turret sides	6.35 mm
FORDING	amphibious	Turret top	6.35 mm

Status: In production. The Chaimite is known to be in service with Lebanon, Libya, Peru, Philippines and Portugal (Army and Navy).

Manufacturer: BRAVIA SARL, Av Eng Duarte Pacheco 21, 5°,-A, Lisbon, Portugal.

Commando Mk III Armoured Personnel Carrier

Development

The Commando Mk III APC was developed by BRAVIA in 1977 to meet the requirements of the Portuguese National Guard and has since been exported to at least two countries for internal security use. The first prototype of the Commando Mk III APC was completed in 1977 with production vehicles following the same year. The vehicle is basically a short wheelbase version of the BRAVIA Gazela (4 × 4) one-ton truck chassis fitted with an armoured body.

In appearance the Commando Mk III is very similar to the British Shorland armoured patrol car, but the Portuguese vehicle has a longer wheelbase, is much heavier and can also be used as an APC.

Description

The engine is at the front of the vehicle, driver and commander in the centre and the personnel compartment at the rear. The driver sits on the left of the vehicle with the commander to his right. They each have a windscreen to their front which can be covered quickly by an internally-controlled drop-down armoured visor containing a laminated glass observation block. The commander and the driver have a side door, the top part of which folds down on the outside for improved visibility and has a laminated glass observation block.

The five troops sit to the rear of the driver's and commander's position and are provided with four firing ports with a laminated observation window over each, one in each side of the hull and two in the rear. The interior of the vehicle is lined

Commando Mk III APC with driver's and commander's hatches open

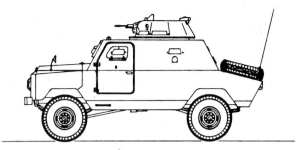

Commando Mk III armoured personnel carrier

SPECIFICATIONS

CREW	3 + 5
CONFIGURATION	4 × 4
COMBAT WEIGHT	4855 kg
UNLOADED WEIGHT	4330 kg
WEIGHT ON FRONT AXLE LOADED	2236 kg
WEIGHT ON REAR AXLE LOADED	2619 kg
POWER-TO-WEIGHT RATIO	
with 81 hp engine	16.68 hp/tonne
with 150 hp engine	30.89 hp/tonne
LENGTH	4.975 m
WIDTH	1.93 m
HEIGHT	
to turret top	2.42 m
to hull top	2.05 m
GROUND CLEARANCE	0.21 m
TRACK	
front	1.72 m
rear	1.665 m
WHEELBASE	3.03 m
ANGLE OF APPROACH/ DEPARTURE	49°/47°
MAX ROAD SPEED	
diesel engine	90 km/h
petrol engine	110 km/h
FUEL CAPACITY	160 litres
MAX ROAD RANGE	
diesel engine	800 km
petrol engine	600 km
GRADIENT	70%
TURNING RADIUS	7.65 m
ENGINE	Perkins 4-cylinder in-line diesel developing 81 hp at 2800 rpm or Dodge H225 6-cylinder in-line petrol developing 150 hp at 4000 rpm
TRANSFER CASE	2-speed
STEERING SYSTEM	recirculating ball, worm and nut
CLUTCH	single dry plate
SUSPENSION	heavy duty semi-elliptical springs and telescopic shock absorbers at each wheel station
TYRES	9.00 × 16 or 10.50 × 16
BRAKES	
main	hydraulic on all wheels
parking	mechanical operating on rear wheels
ELECTRICAL SYSTEM	24 V
BATTERIES	2 × 12 V, 105 Ah
ARMAMENT	see text
ARMOUR	
Hull	6.35–7.94 mm
Turret front	7.94 mm
Turret sides	6.35 mm
Turret top	6.35 mm

Status: In production. In service with Portuguese National Guard and at least two other countries.

Manufacturer: BRAVIA SARL, Av Eng Duarte Pacheco 21, 5°,–A, Lisbon, Portugal.

with non-inflammable pvc foam and ventilation is provided by a fresh air system with electric fan boost.

The BRAVIA-designed turret is mounted in the centre of the roof and is armed with twin 7.62 mm machine guns or one 7.62 mm and one 12.7 mm machine gun. The weapons can be elevated from −15 to +60 degrees manually and traverse is manual through a full 360 degrees. The turret has a single-piece hatch cover that opens to the rear, vision blocks and a periscopic sight in its forward part for aiming the machine guns. The turret can be fitted with a device for launching five 60 mm anti-personnel, anti-tank, smoke, illuminating or incendiary grenades.

Optional equipment includes sand tyres, run-flat tyres and an air-conditioning system.

Variants

The Commando Mk III is also available without the turret.

ROMANIA

TAB-77 Armoured Personnel Carrier

Development/Description

It is believed that Romania is now making the Soviet BTR-70 (8 × 8) armoured personnel carrier under licence. The Romanian vehicle is however powered by a single diesel engine rather than the two petrol engines fitted to the BTR-70 and has the same turret as the TAB-72 armoured personnel carrier.

Status: Production. In service with the Romanian Army.

Manufacturer: Romanian state arsenals.

TAB-72 Armoured Personnel Carrier

Development

The TAB-72 (8 × 8) APC was first seen in public during a parade in Bucharest in August 1972. It is very similar to the Soviet BTR-60PB (8 × 8) APC but has two 140 hp instead of two 90 hp petrol engines as installed in the Soviet vehicle, the turret-mounted machine guns are capable of high elevation to enable them to engage aerial targets and additional vision devices are provided in the troop compartment. The TAB-72 has a central tyre-pressure regulation system, NBC system and infra-red night vision equipment for the driver only.

TAB-72 mortar carrier with mortar raised and roof hatches open

Description

Identical to the Soviet BTR-60PB with the exception of the turret.

Variants

The only known variant is the TAB-72 82 mm mortar carrier. This is the TAB-72 with its turret removed and modifications made to the troop compartment to allow an 82 mm mortar to be raised when the roof hatches are swung open through 180 degrees either side. Between 50 and 100 mortar bombs are carried.

Provisional drawing of TAB-72 (8 × 8) APC

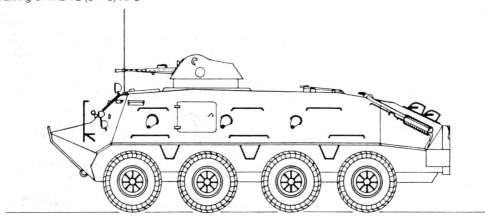

SPECIFICATIONS					
CREW	3 + 8	FUEL CAPACITY	290 litres	AMMUNITION	
CONFIGURATION	8 × 8	MAX ROAD RANGE	500 km	main	500 rounds
COMBAT WEIGHT	11 000 kg	FORDING	amphibious	coaxial	2000 rounds
POWER-TO-WEIGHT		GRADIENT	60%	FIRE-CONTROL SYSTEM	
RATIO	25.4 hp/tonne	VERTICAL OBSTACLE	0.4 m	Turret power control	manual
LENGTH	7.22 m	TRENCH	2 m	Gun elevation/depression	+85°/−5°
WIDTH	2.83 m	ENGINES	2 × V-6 liquid-cooled petrol	Turret traverse	360°
HEIGHT (overall)	2.7 m		developing 140 hp each	ARMOUR	
GROUND CLEARANCE	0.47 m	TRANSMISSION	manual, 5 forward and 1	Hull (max)	9 mm
WHEELBASE	4.21 m		reverse gears	Turret (max)	7 mm
MAX SPEED		TYRES	13.00 × 18		
road	95 km/h	ARMAMENT			
water	10 km/h	main	1 × 14.5 mm MG		
		coaxial	1 × 7.62 mm MG		

Status: Production complete. In service with the Romanian army.

Manufacturer: Romanian state arsenals.

SOUTH AFRICA

Ratel Infantry Fighting Vehicle

Development

In the 1950s the United Kingdom supplied South Africa with 250 Alvis Saracen (6 × 6) armoured personnel carriers, many of which remain in service. In 1968 Sandock-Austral, which was then building an improved version of the French Panhard AML (4 × 4) armoured car called the Eland, started design work on a new infantry fighting vehicle, the Ratel, to meet the requirements of the South African Infantry Corps and, at a later date, the South African Armoured Corps.

The user required a vehicle with good armoured protection, high road speed, large operational range with little maintenance, good firepower and high cross-country mobility. Wherever possible proven commercial components have been used.

Ratel FSV 90 with 7.62 mm anti-aircraft machine gun on commander's cupola and armoured visors over driver's windows lowered

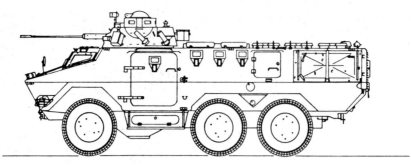

Ratel 20 IFV with two-man turret armed with 20 mm cannon and 7.62 mm machine gun

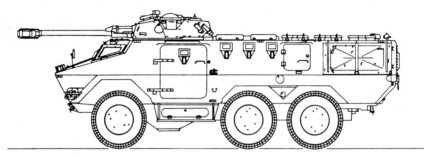

Ratel FSV 90 with two-man turret armed with 90 mm gun and 7.62 mm machine gun

The first prototype was completed in July 1974, followed by four pre-production vehicles, the first completed in 1976. The first production models were designated the Mark 1 and were followed in 1979 by the Mark 2, the current production model being the Mark 3. The differences are mainly the result of operational experience in Namibia and long-range penetration raids into Angola. Most of the modifications have subsequently been retrofitted to earlier vehicles when they return to Sandock-Austral for overhaul.

Description (FSV 90)

The hull of the Ratel is made of all-welded steel that provides complete protection from 7.62 mm small arms fire and shell splinters, with protection over the frontal arc against 12.7 mm armour-piercing rounds. Emphasis has also been placed on providing protection against mines.

The driver sits at the front of the vehicle with excellent forward visibility through three large bullet-proof windows to his front and sides. In combat areas they can be quickly covered by armoured shutters hinged at the bottom and activated by the driver with a single handle from within the vehicle. With the shutters in position the driver observes the terrain through three periscopes, one to the front and one either side. Over the driver's position is a single-piece hatch cover that opens to the left. The driver's seat and steering wheel are adjustable and he can also enter his compartment from the rear so enabling drivers to be changed without one of them leaving the vehicle.

Mounted on the roof of the vehicle immediately behind the driver's position is the two-man all-welded turret, identical to the Eland (4 × 4) armoured car's. The commander sits on the left and the gunner on the right. The commander's cupola has vision blocks for all-round observation and a single-piece hatch cover opening to the rear, plus an orientation vane sight. The gunner has four periscopes for observation plus an

M494 optical sight for aiming the main and secondary armament, and a single-piece hatch cover that opens to the rear.

The main armament is a 90 mm semi-automatic quick-firing gun which is a further development of the weapon fitted in the 90 mm version of the Eland (4 × 4) armoured car. This has an elevation of +15 degrees and a depression of −8 degrees with turret traverse being a full 360 degrees. Depression can be obtained through 285 degrees only because of the troop compartment to the turret rear. Gun elevation and turret traverse are manual, operated by the gunner. When travelling the turret is often traversed to the rear. The 90 mm

Ratel 60 with troop compartment hatches closed and 7.62 mm machine gun on forward part of two-man turret (Christopher F Foss)

gun fires the following types of ammunition which are manufacturered by ARMSCOR:

Type	HEAT	HE	Practice
MUZZLE VELOCITY	750 m/s	640 m/s	750 m/s
WEIGHT	7.1 kg	8.8 kg	7.1 kg
EFFECTIVE RANGE	1200 m	2200 m	1200 m

Twenty-nine rounds of 90 mm ammunition are carried in the turret and 40 rounds in the hull. A 12.7 mm M2 HB machine gun can be mounted over the 90 mm gun for training.

Mounted to the left of the 90 mm gun is a 7.62 mm coaxial machine gun for which 2000 rounds of 7.62 mm ammunition are carried in the turret with a further 4000 rounds on the hull. Both the main and coaxial weapons are fired electrically and above the coaxial machine gun is an extractor fan to remove fumes from the turret.

Mounted either side of the turret towards the rear is a bank of two 81 mm electrically-operated smoke dischargers which can be operated by the commander or gunner. A 7.62 mm anti-aircraft machine gun is mounted externally at the gunner's station and on top of the turret is a hand-operated searchlight. In the left side of the turret there is an ammunition resupply hatch.

The Ratel 90 carries a crew of ten, one fewer than the Ratel IFV, to enable the 40 rounds of ammunition to be carried inside the hull. The crew consists of the vehicle commander, driver, main gunner (90 mm), rear anti-aircraft gunner, section commander and five infantrymen.

In either side of the hull behind the driver's position is a large door opened pneumatically by the driver. It opens forwards and has a vision block with a firing port underneath.

The section commander sits near the left door and the five infantrymen on bench seats down the middle of the vehicle behind the turret, two on the left and three on the right. In both sides of the troop compartment there are three bullet-proof vision blocks with a firing port underneath and over the top of the troop compartment are four roof hatches that are hinged on the outside and can be locked vertical. There is a passageway from the troop compartment to the rear of the vehicle on the right side, above which are two roof hatches that open outwards and a circular mount with a single-piece hatch cover on which the 7.62 mm machine gun can be mounted. In the rear of the hull on the right side is a door. Its lower part folds down to form a step and the upper part opens to the left.

The engine compartment is at the rear of the Ratel on the left side with access panels in the roof for maintenance.

The six-cylinder direct injection turbo-charged diesel is coupled to a fully automatic powershift gearbox with a hydro-dynamic torque converter. The gearbox can also be operated manually and has a mechanical emergency gearshift. Power is transmitted to the three axles in two stages with final reduction by means of planetary gearing housed in the wheel hubs. The three axles are each provided with their own lockable differential and longitudinal differential locks. Suspension consists of progressively acting coil springs and large hydraulic shock absorbers. The hydro-pneumatic braking system can be assisted by an exhaust brake provided through the engine.

Ratel 20 IFV at speed on South African Defence Force test track (Christopher F Foss)

The powerpack can be removed from the vehicle by two men with a crane in less than 30 minutes, quick disconnect couplings and connectors are provided in all power, hydraulic, electric and pneumatic circuits.

Standard equipment includes a complete set of tools, spades, picks, shovels and axes, tow bar and towing cables, first aid kit, two petrol stoves, fire extinguishers, emergency spares, two 50-litre drinking water tanks, two external stowage boxes, radios, intercom and remote handset with 1000 metres of cable.

Optional equipment includes night vision equipment, air-conditioning and ventilation system and the replacement of the standard D3256 BTXF 6-cylinder diesel developing 282 hp by an ADE 407 TI diesel developing 315 hp.

Variants

Ratel 60 IFV

This model has a crew of 11 consisting of a vehicle commander, driver, main gunner, anti-aircraft gunner, section commander and six infantrymen. It is fitted with a two-man turret armed with a 60 mm mortar, 7.62 mm coaxial and 7.62 mm anti-aircraft machine gun with an additional 7.62 mm anti-aircraft machine gun at the rear of the vehicle on the right side. The 60 mm mortar is breech loaded and is capable of firing HE, smoke and illuminating bombs to a maximum range of 1500 metres. The muzzle velocity varies with the charge.

A typical ammunition load would consist of 38 to 45 HE bombs, three smoke and three illuminating bombs.

Ratel 20 IFV

This model has the same crew as the Ratel 60 IFV but is fitted with a two-man turret armed with a 20 mm F2 cannon (M693) with a 7.62 mm machine gun mounted coaxially to the left and a similar weapon mounted on the turret roof for anti-aircraft defence. There is also a 7.62 mm anti-aircraft machine gun at the rear on the right side. Turret traverse and weapon elevation are manual. The weapons have an elevation of +38 degrees and a depression of −8 degrees. The

SPECIFICATIONS

Model	Ratel 20	Ratel 90	Ratel command	Ratel logistic
CREW	11	10	9	3
CONFIGURATION	6 × 6	6 × 6	6 × 6	8 × 8
COMBAT WEIGHT	18 500 kg	19 000 kg	18 000 kg	29 000 kg
UNLOADED WEIGHT	16 500 kg	17 000 kg	16 000 kg	19 000 kg
POWER-TO-WEIGHT RATIO	15.24 hp/tonne	14.84 hp/tonne	15.67 hp/tonne	14.83 hp/tonne
LENGTH (hull)	7.212 m	7.212 m	7.212 m	8.739 m
WIDTH (hull)	2.516 m	2.516 m	2.516 m	2.516 m
HEIGHT				
overall	2.915 m	2.915 m	2.755 m	2.84 m
to hull top	2.105 m	2.105 m	2.105 m	n/app
GROUND CLEARANCE	0.34 m	0.34 m	0.34 m	0.415 m
TRACK	2.08 m	2.08 m	2.08 m	2.08 m
WHEELBASE	2.809 + 1.4 m	2.809 + 1.4 m	2.809 + 1.4 m	5.91 m
ANGLE OF APPROACH/ DEPARTURE	44°/45°	44°/45°	44°/45°	40°/42°
MAX ROAD SPEED	105 km/h	105 km/h	105 km/h	86 km/h
FUEL CAPACITY	430 litres	430 litres	430 litres	560 litres
MAX RANGE				
road	1000 km	1000 km	1000 km	700 km
cross-country	14 h	14 h	14 h	14 h
FUEL CONSUMPTION				
road	0.4 litre/km	0.4 litre/km	0.4 litre/km	0.4 litre/km
cross-country	1 litre/km	1 litre/km	1 litre/km	1 litre/km
FORDING	1.2 m	1.2 m	1.2 m	1.2 m
GRADIENT	60%	60%	60%	60%
SIDE SLOPE	30%	30%	30%	30%
VERTICAL OBSTACLE	0.35 m	0.35 m	0.35 m	0.6 m
TRENCH	1.15 m	1.15 m	1.15 m	2.1 m
TURNING RADIUS	7.95 m	7.95 m	7.95 m	10.5 m
ENGINE	D 3256 BTXF 6-cylinder in-line turbo-charged diesel developing 282 hp at 2200 rpm			ADE 423 T turbo-charged V 10-cylinder in-line diesel developing 430 hp at 2300 rpm
TRANSMISSION	automatic, 6 forward and 2 reverse gears with hydro-dynamic torque converter			automatic, 6 forward and 1 reverse gears with hydro-dynamic torque converter
STEERING	mechanical, recirculating ball with hydraulic assistance			mechanical, recirculating ball with hydraulic assistance
TYRES	14.00 × 20	14.00 × 20	14.00 × 20	14.00 × 20
BRAKES				
main	hydro-pneumatic on front wheels and air/mechanical on rear 4 wheels			hydro-pneumatic on front wheels and air/mechanical on rear 4 wheels
crawl	pneumatic/mechanical on rear 4 wheels			pneumatic/mechanical on rear 4 wheels or on all wheels
parking	mechanical on rear 4 wheels			mechanical on rear 4 wheels
AXLES				
front	steering axle with steering damper and intermediate steering arm, lockable differential			steering axle with steering damper and intermediate steering arm, lockable differential. 2nd front steering axle with transfer train, lockable differential (transverse and longitudinal). 3rd rear,
middle	non-steering with transfer train, lockable differential (transfer and longitudinal)			non-steering with transfer train, lockable differential (transverse and longitudinal).
rear	non-steering and lockable differential			4th rear, non-steering with lockable differential
SUSPENSION	solid axle with single coil springs and double acting hydraulic shock absorbers supported by wishbones and longitudinal arms			
ELECTRICAL SYSTEM	24 V	24 V	24 V	24 V
BATTERIES	2 × 12 V, 100 Ah	2 × 12 V, 100 Ah	2 × 12 V, 100 Ah	2 × 12 V, 100 Ah
ARMAMENT				
main	1 × 20 mm cannon	1 × 90 mm gun	1 × 12.7 mm MG	n/app
coaxial	1 × 7.62 mm MG	1 × 7.62 mm MG	none	n/app
anti-aircraft, turret	1 × 7.62 mm MG	1 × 7.62 mm MG	1 × 7.62 mm MG	1 × 12.7 mm (front) MG
anti-aircraft, rear	1 × 7.62 mm MG	1 × 7.62 mm MG	1 × 7.62 mm MG	none
AMMUNITION				
90 mm	none	69	none	none
20 mm	1200	none	none	none
7.62 mm	6000	6000	3600	none
12.7 mm	none	none	300	600
FIRE-CONTROL SYSTEM				
Turret power control	manual, 360°	manual, 360°	manual, 360°	n/app
by commander	yes	yes	yes	yes
Gun elevation/depression (main)	+38°/−8°	+15°/−8°	+38°/−8°	n/app
ARMOUR				
Hull front	20 mm at 60°	20 mm at 60°	20 mm at 60°	20 mm at 60°
Hull sides upper	8 mm at 65°	8 mm at 65°	8 mm at 65°	8 mm at 65°
Hull sides lower	10 mm at 90°	10 mm at 90°	10 mm at 90°	10 mm at 90°
Hull top	6 mm	6 mm	6 mm	6 mm
Hull floor	8 mm and 10 mm	8 mm and 10 mm	8 mm and 10 mm	8 mm and 10 mm
Hull rear	10 mm	10 mm	10 mm	10 mm

20 mm cannon fires armour-piercing, high explosive and practice rounds produced by ARMSCOR.

Ratel 12.7 mm Command

This command vehicle has a crew of nine: the vehicle commander, driver, main gunner and six command post personnel. The two-man turret is armed with a 12.7 mm M2 HB machine gun, a 7.62 mm machine gun mounted on the turret roof for anti-aircraft defence and a similar weapon at the hull rear as on other members of the Ratel family. This command vehicle is fitted with three radios, tape recorder with time injection, civilian type combined receiver and cassette recorder in the hull, intercom for all key personnel, internal loudspeakers, public address system, pneumatic mast and map boards.

Ratel 8 × 8 Logistic Support Vehicle

The vehicle is at the prototype stage and has been designed to support the Ratel IFV and FSV on extended operations away from its main base. The crew of three consists of the commander, gunner and driver, all seated in the fighting compartment at the front of the hull. The driver has the same layout as in the basic Ratel and in each side of the hull is a forward-opening door provided with a vision block with a firing port underneath.

The logistic support vehicle can carry nine containers to ISO specifications, each 1 × 1.2 × 1.2 metres. The following types of containers are already available: armoured ammunition, equipment with five-man tents, toilets, showers and rations, 800-litre water, refrigerator/freezer on 220-volt 50 Hz AC supply. The containers are unloaded with the aid of a 4.6-tonne hydraulic crane. Integral field tanks in the hull carry 2000 litres of fuel and a hydraulically-driven pump and

Ratel command vehicle armed with 12.7 mm and 7.62 mm machine guns in two-man turret with raised cupolas for commander and gunner (Christopher F Foss)

system provides for pressure filling of own bunker tanks from an external supply, filling two vehicles simultaneously on both sides of the vehicle bunker, pumping from one external bunker to another and pressure filling by an external pump; hand pumps are provided in case of power failure. A 12.7 mm anti-aircraft machine gun is fitted as standard.

Standard equipment includes tanks for 500 litres of fresh water, generator set, three spare wheels, spare parts and tools.

Future variants

Other versions under development include an anti-tank or missile carrier, ambulance and an 81 mm mortar carrier.

Status: In production. In service with Morocco and South Africa.

Manufacturer: Sandock-Austral Beperk Limited, PO Box 6390, West Street Industrial Sites, Boksburg, Transvaal, South Africa.

SPAIN

BMR-600 Infantry Fighting Vehicle

Development

In 1972 the Comisión de Desarrollo de Vehículos Blindados of the Dirección de Investigación of the Spanish Army Ministry and the Dirección de Proyectos of ENASA started development work on a wheeled IFV to meet the requirements of the Spanish Army. ENASA, in which Pegaso is integrated, was responsible for the automotive side of the vehicle while the Army concentrated on the armour and the armament installation. Between 1975 and 1976 the prototype, called the Pegaso 3.500, was tested under a wide range of operational conditions. It was powered by a Pegaso 9156/8 diesel which developed 353 hp at 2200 rpm and gave the vehicle a maximum road speed of 110 km/h. The engine

was behind the driver on the left side of the hull and the armament installation to the right of the engine compartment. Redesigned prototypes had the engine on the right side of the hull and the armament installation to the rear of the driver. The company designation for this vehicle is the BMR 3560, the specific variants are designated:

Pegaso 3560/1 APC
Pegaso 3560/3 81 mm mortar carrier
Pegaso 3560/4 120 mm mortar towing
Pegaso 3560/5 battalion command
Pegaso 3564 fire support with TS-90 90 mm turret
Pegaso 3562 VEC cavalry vehicle

After comparative trials between the BMR-600 (Blindado Medio de Ruedas), the French VAB and the Swiss MOWAG Piranha vehicles, the BMR-600 was selected for the Spanish

Production BMR-600 IFV with driver's hatches open and fitted with cupola armed with remote-controlled 12.7 mm machine gun. This vehicle is not fitted with water jets for amphibious operations

Army and an initial production order for 15 vehicles was placed in 1979. The Spanish Army has a requirement for 500 vehicles of this type. First production vehicles were handed over to the Spanish Army in 1979.

In 1982 Egypt signed a contract for a large number of vehicles, believed to be 600 of which 100 will be in the fire support configuration, with finance from Saudi Arabia. Deliveries will run from 1983–86.

Description
The hull of the BMR-600 is made of all-welded aluminium armour supplied by the British company Alcan Plate Limited. The hull incorporates spaced armour at the front giving protection against 7.62 mm armour-piercing rounds. Protection is provided over the remainder of the vehicle against 7.62 mm ball attack.

The BMR-600 has a crew of two consisting of the machine gunner/radio operator and driver and can carry ten fully-equipped infantrymen and a commander who dismounts with them. The driver sits at the front of the vehicle on the left side and has a bullet-proof windscreen in front of him and a smaller bullet-proof windscreen either side (or a periscope). In action his front windscreen can be covered by a flap and forward vision is then through a periscope mounted in the roof. There is a single-piece hatch cover over his position that lifts and swings to the right. The engine is to the right of the

driver with the air-inlet and air-outlet louvres in the roof and the exhaust pipe on the right side of the hull. There is an engine access plate in the front of the hull. The engine compartment has a semi-automatic fire-detection and suppression system.

Non-amphibious version of BMR-600 used in mortar role with baseplate and bipod on right side of hull

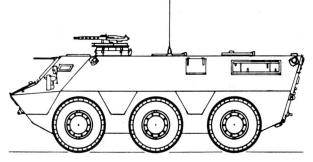

BMR-600 IFV

BMR-600 towing Esperanza 120 mm mortar

SPECIFICATIONS

CREW	2 + 11
CONFIGURATION	6 × 6
COMBAT WEIGHT	13 750 kg
LOADED WEIGHT	
front axle	5000 kg
middle axle	4450 kg
rear axle	4300 kg
POWER-TO-WEIGHT	
RATIO	23 hp/tonne
LENGTH	6.15 m
WIDTH	2.5 m
HEIGHT	
including armament	2.36 m
to hull top	2 m
GROUND CLEARANCE	
(adjustable)	0.4 m
TRACK	2.08 m
WHEELBASE	1.65 m + 1.65 m
ANGLE OF APPROACH/	
DEPARTURE	50°/45°
MAX SPEED	
1st gear	17 km/h
2nd gear	56 km/h
3rd gear	69 km/h
4th gear	100 km/h
reverse	12 km/h
water	10 km/h
FUEL CAPACITY	300 litres
MAX RANGE	700 km
FORDING	amphibious
GRADIENT	68%
SIDE SLOPE	30%
VERTICAL OBSTACLE	0.8 m
TRENCH	1.2 m
TURNING RADIUS	7.5 m
ENGINE	Pegaso 9157/8 6-cylinder in-line diesel developing 306 hp at 2200 rpm
TRANSMISSION	ZF 6 HP 500 automatic with 6 forward and 1 reverse gears Torque converter and hydraulic retarder
STEERING	hydraulic
SUSPENSION	ZF hydro-pneumatic independent each wheel, MacPhearson type
TYRES	13.00 × 20
BRAKES	
main	disc hydraulic, dual circuit, air-assisted on all wheels
parking	disc operating on propeller transmission
emergency	hydraulic, air-operated
ELECTRICAL SYSTEM	24 V
BATTERIES	2 × 12 V, 150 Ah
ARMAMENT (main)	1 × 12.7 mm MG
AMMUNITION	2500 rounds
GUN ELEVATION/	
DEPRESSION	+60°/−15°
TURRET TRAVERSE	360°

The machine gunner/radio operator sits behind the driver and has a CETME cupola that can be traversed through a full 360 degrees and is provided with a single-piece hatch cover that opens to the rear and eight periscopes. A 12.7 mm machine gun is mounted externally.

Over the top of the troop compartment are two roof hatches that open to the rear. The infantrymen enter and leave the vehicle by a ramp in the rear of the hull that opens downwards and has a door in the left side in case the ramp fails to open. Depending on the model, six firing ports with a vision block can be fitted to the sides and rear of the vehicle.

The BMR-600 has an independent suspension system for each wheel station that is a combination of the hydro-pneumatic and MacPhearson type. This allows each wheel station to be raised or lowered through 275 mm, according to the terrain being crossed. Steering is power-assisted on both the front and rear axles. All three Pegaso designed and built axles are of the double reduction type with self-locking differentials. The tyres are of the run-flat type.

The vehicle is fully amphibious, being propelled in the water by water jets either side of the hull at the rear, which have deflectors for steering when afloat. When propelled in the water by the two water jets the BMR-600 has a maximum speed of 10 km/h. It is also available without the water jets when it is powered in the water by its wheels at a speed of 4.5 km/h. Before entering the water a trim vane, which is folded back onto the glacis plate when not in use, is erected at the front of the hull and the bilge pumps are switched on. Mounted at the rear of the BMR-600 is a winch with a capacity of 4500 kg. Optional equipment includes various radio systems, 14.00 × 20 tyres, run-flat tyres, and air-conditioning system. It can also be delivered without the amphibious capability.

Variants

The vehicle has already been fitted with other armament installations such as the French Toucan I turret and the MOWAG 7.62 mm remote-controlled machine gun mounting. It can also be fitted with an 81 mm mortar in the rear of the vehicle with a baseplate and tripod carried externally so the mortar can be deployed outside the vehicle. It can also tow the Spanish Esperanza 120 mm mortar with the crew and ammunition carried inside the vehicle.

The BMR-600 is suitable for a wide range of other roles

including an ambulance carrying four stretcher patients and two attendants, battalion, brigade or division command vehicle, fire support vehicle (for trials purposes it has already been fitted with the French GIAT TS 90 turret armed with a 90 mm gun), section or company command vehicle, radio vehicle, anti-tank vehicle (it has already been successfully tested fitted with the Euromissile HCT turret with four HOT ATGWs ready-to-launch), and anti-aircraft vehicle with 20 mm Meroka or similar system.

Status: Production. In service with Egypt and Spain.

Manufacturer: Empresa Nacional de Autocamiones S.A., Military Division, Avda de Aragón, 402 Madrid-22, Spain. Production is undertaken at the company's facilities at Valladolid.

BLR Armoured Personnel Carrier

Development

The BLR (Blindado Ligero de Ruedas) APC has been designed by Empresa Nacional de Autocamiones to meet the requirements of the Spanish Army and police for an APC with good cross-country mobility, provision for the crew to observe the terrain and capable of being used for a wide range of operational roles such as airport security, border patrol and IS operations. Its company designation is BLR 3545.

Description

The all-welded steel hull of the BLR gives the crew complete protection against small arms fire (up to 7.62 mm × 51 armour-piercing ammunition) over its frontal arc and against 7.62 mm × 51 ball ammunition over the remainder of the vehicle. The glass vision blocks give the same degree of

BLR (4 × 4) APC showing engine compartment in centre of vehicle at rear and all side doors open

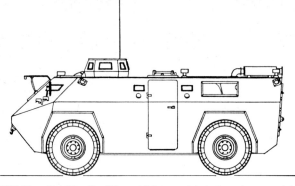

BLR (4 × 4) APC with different firing ports/windows from model shown in photographs

protection as the vehicle's frontal arc. The driver sits at the front of the hull on the left with the vehicle commander to his right. In front of each is a large bullet-proof windscreen which in action is covered by a steel shutter hinged at the top with an integral vision slit. The windscreens have a double wiper facility, one the conventional type and the other using a solvent to deal with paints and spray. To the left of the driver and to the commander's right is a smaller bullet-proof window and above each of their positions is a single hatch cover that opens to the rear. In front of the commander and below the windscreen are two firing ports to give covering fire over the frontal arc.

There are four doors in the BLR, one in each side of the vehicle opening forwards and two at the rear, one either side of the engine compartment. The rear two open outwards and both have a vision block.

In each side of the hull there are five bullet-proof windows. In the centre of the hull roof, behind the commander's and driver's positions, is a cupola with eight vision blocks and a single-piece hatch cover. This cupola can be traversed through a full 360 degrees and has a 7.62 mm machine gun and shield for the gunner.

In the roof, over each of the side doors is a single-piece hatch cover that opens to the centre of the vehicle and similar hatches are provided in the roof either side of the engine compartment.

The personnel compartment has a volume of 14 cubic metres and all personnel can enter the vehicle in 16 seconds and leave in ten. The BLR is smoke- and gas-proof, ventilated by two rear suction units and an interior intake equipped with a filter.

The engine compartment is at the rear of the vehicle in the centre with the air inlet and air outlet in the top and rear of the vehicle. It can be delivered with a 170 hp engine coupled to a manual transmission or a 224 hp engine coupled to an automatic transmission.

An unusual feature of the BLR is that in addition to the engine compartment being fitted with a semi-automatic fire-extinguishing system, each of four road wheels has outlets for extinguishing fires. The tyres of the BLR are fitted with puncture-proof Hutchinson O-rings.

Mounted at the front of the vehicle is a winch with a capacity of 4500 kg and optional equipment includes smoke or CS gas dischargers which can be activated by the vehicle commander. It can also be fitted with various types of communications equipment as well as a siren and loudspeakers. Optional equipment includes PTO, run-flat tyres, radios, specialised anti-riot equipment and the more powerful engine and automatic transmission already mentioned.

BLR (4 × 4) APC with 7.62 mm machine gun and all hatches and doors open. Note ditch crossing channels at rear of hull on right

According to the manufacturer the BLR can be fitted with a wide range of other armament systems including 12.7 mm machine guns, 20 and 25 mm cannon and up to 90 mm guns.

Variants

There are no variants of the BLR but it can be adopted for other roles such as command/communications vehicle or an ambulance.

SPECIFICATIONS

CREW	3 + 12	ENGINE	Pegaso 9220 6-cylinder water-cooled developing 220 hp or Pegaso 9100/41 6-cylinder water-cooled developing 170 hp
CONFIGURATION	4 × 4		
COMBAT WEIGHT	11 600 kg		
WEIGHT UNLOADED	9600 kg		
POWER-TO-WEIGHT		TRANSMISSION	
RATIO (170 hp engine)	14.66 hp/tonne	Pegaso 9220	automatic with 6 forward and 1 reverse gears with torque converter and transfer case
LENGTH	5.65 m		
WIDTH	2.5 m		
HEIGHT (hull top)	1.99 m	Pegaso 9100	manual with 6 forward and 1 reverse gears
GROUND CLEARANCE	0.32 m		
TRACK		CLUTCH	single dry plate
front	1.96 m	STEERING	hydraulic, power-assisted
rear	2.135 m		
WHEELBASE	3.15 m	TRANSFER CASE	2-speed
ANGLE OF APPROACH/		SUSPENSION	semi-elliptical springs and double-action hydraulic shock absorbers at each wheel station
DEPARTURE	42°/35°		
MAX SPEED	86 km/h		
FUEL CAPACITY	250 litres	TYRES	13.00 × 20
RANGE	800 km	BRAKES	
FORDING	1.1 m	main	dual circuit, air
GRADIENT	75%	parking	mechanical
SIDE SLOPE	30%	ELECTRICAL SYSTEM	24 V
TURNING RADIUS	7.625 m	BATTERIES	2 × 12 V, 85 Ah

Status: Production. In service with Spanish Marines and Guardia Civil (rural para-military police).

Manufacturer: Empresa Nacional de Autocamiones SA, Military Division, Avda de Aragón, 402 Madrid – 22, Spain.

BMU-2 Armoured Personnel Carrier

Development
The BMU-2 armoured personnel carrier has been developed
by Land-Rover Santana, Empresa Nacional Santa Barbara
de Industrias Militares SA and Macosa mainly for use in
internal security. It is a long wheelbase Land-Rover chassis
with a fully armoured body that gives the crew complete
protection from small arms fire and shell splinters.

Description
The layout of the BMU-2 is similar to the Land-Rover's with
the fully-protected radiator and engine at the front, commander and driver in the centre and the troop compartment
at the rear.

The commander and driver have a bullet-proof window to
their front and sides. In the centre of the vehicle is a one-piece
door that opens forwards with a bullet-proof window in its
upper part. The four troops sit on individual seats in the
troop compartment but there is no provision for them to aim
and fire their small arms. There is a door in the back of the
BMU-2 and a single-piece hatch cover opening to the rear in
the roof. The spare wheel and tyre are carried on the roof.

Standard equipment includes an air-conditioning and ventilation system, convoy lights, external adjustable rear-view
mirrors, battery disconnect switch, tool box, jack and wedges
and an electrical socket.

BMU-2 armoured personnel carrier with roof hatch open

Variants
The manufacturer has suggested that the BMU-2 can be
modified to carry out other roles such as reconnaissance
(armed with single or twin 7.62 mm MG3 machine guns),
anti-tank (with 106 mm recoilless rifle type M40) and
casualty evacuation (carrying two to five wounded).

SPECIFICATIONS

CREW	1 + 5	MAX RANGE	550 km	SUSPENSION	semi-elliptical springs front and rear with hydraulic double acting shock absorbers
CONFIGURATION	4 × 4	FUEL CONSUMPTION			
COMBAT WEIGHT	3300 kg	road	0.156 litre/km		
MAX TOWED LOAD		cross-country	0.2 litre/km		
(braked)	2000 kg	GRADIENT	45%	BRAKES	
LENGTH	4.74 m	SIDE SLOPE	33%	main	hydraulic, tandem parking system, servo assisted
WIDTH	1.99 m	TURNING RADIUS	8 m		
HEIGHT	2.315 m	ENGINE	6-cylinder in-line diesel	parking	drum, mechanical on transmission
GROUND CLEARANCE	0.26 m		developing 94 bhp at		
TRACK	1.3 m		4000 rpm	TYRES	9.00 × 16 or
WHEELBASE	2.768 m	TRANSMISSION	manual, 4 forward and 1		6.50 × 16
ANGLE OF APPROACH/			reverse gears	ELECTRICAL SYSTEM	12 V
DEPARTURE	40°/31°	TRANSFER CASE	2-speed	ARMOUR	5 mm
MAX ROAD SPEED	90 km/h	CLUTCH	single dry plate		
FUEL CAPACITY	100 litres	STEERING	recirculating ball		

Status: Prototype.

Manufacturer: Empresa Nacional Santa Barbara de Industrias Militares SA, Dirección Comercial c/ Manual Cortina,
2 Madrid-10, Spain.

SWEDEN

Fighting Vehicle 90 (Stridsfordon 90)

According to the guidelines set by the Swedish Government
in the 1982 defence plan, the proportion of mechanised units
in the Swedish Army is to be increased. The anti-tank and
anti-aircraft capability of these units, especially in the North
of Sweden, is to be improved and all units will have an
increased level of protection against artillery splinters and
attack from small arms fire.

After studying various ways of integrating this mechanisa-
tion into the unit organisation, the most promising seems to

be an additional number of mechanised battalions. These
would be equipped with retrofitted versions of today's
armoured vehicles and a number of new vehicles. The new
vehicles would enter service at the beginning of the 1990s
and they have been given the name Fighting Vehicle 90
(Stridsfordon 90).

According to the Swedish Army, the tactical demands on
the vehicle to have adequate effect against various targets
and good mobility in Swedish terrain cannot be fulfilled at a
reasonable cost by a single type of new vehicle. Instead a
complete family of new vehicles is planned and will include

Full scale mock-up of Fighting Vehicle 90 proposed by Hägglund and Söner showing long-barrelled 40 mm multi-purpose gun

Frontal view of Fighting Vehicle 90 proposed by Hägglund and Söner with two-man turret armed with 40 mm gun. Multi-purpose gun is only one of weapon stations under consideration

HEIGHT (overall)	2.5 m
MAX ROAD SPEED	70 km/h
MAIN ARMAMENT	1 × 40 mm automatic gun
ENGINE	Swedish truck diesel
TRANSMISSION	automatic
STEERING	clutch and brake

Status: Study.

Manufacturer: Not selected. Above specifications relate to vehicle proposed by Hägglund and Söner, Box 600, S-89101 Örnsköldsvik, Sweden.

Pansarbandvagn 302 Armoured Personnel Carrier

Development
Early in 1961 the Swedish Army issued a requirement for a new full tracked amphibious APC to replace the interim Pbv 301 which was developed from 1958 by Hägglund and Söner and was essentially the old Strv m/41 light tank rebuilt for use as an APC.

Pbv 302 APC showing roof arrangement

an armoured personnel carrier, self-propelled anti-aircraft gun, mortar carrier and a recovery vehicle. The vehicles are intended to have a high development potential for future improvements, mainly in the area of armour protection and armament. They are also designed to have the lowest possible total cost cover the lifetime of the vehicle.

Vehicle families from Sweden and abroad have been studied and in 1984 a British Alvis Stormer APC and a CVR(T) were tested in Sweden. The Swedish alternatives make use of domestic standard components as far as possible, for example diesel engines and gearboxes from commercial vehicle manufacturers.

PROVISIONAL SPECIFICATIONS (Hägglunds Fighting Vehicle 90)
CREW	3 + 8
COMBAT WEIGHT	20 000 kg
LENGTH (chassis)	6.4 m
WIDTH	3.1 m

Pbv 302 Mk 2 with Lyran launcher on right side of roof at rear

Late in 1961 Hägglund and Söner was awarded a contract to develop a new full tracked amphibious APC. The first of two prototypes was completed in December 1962 and in October the following year the company was awarded an initial production contract for 700 Pansarbandvagn 302 APCs (or Pbv 302 for short). The first production Pbv 302s were completed in February 1966 and production continued until December 1971.

Since developing the Pbv 302, Hägglund and Söner has developed a complete family of light full tracked armoured vehicles which now includes the Ikv-91 light tank/tank destroyer, Brobv 941 bridgelayer and the Bgbv 82 armoured recovery vehicle.

Description

The hull of the Pbv 302 is made of all-welded rolled steel with the front of the hull providing complete protection against projectiles up to 20 mm in calibre. Above the tracks the hull sides are double skinned which gives both increased buoyancy and a measure of protection against attack from HEAT projectiles.

The driver sits at the front of the vehicle in the centre and has a single-piece hatch cover that opens to the rear, in front of which are three periscopes.

The Hägglunds-designed turret to the left and slightly to the rear of the driver is armed with a 20 mm Hispano Suiza cannon with an elevation of +50 degrees and a depression of −10 degrees, turret traverse being a full 360 degrees. The 20 mm cannon has a cyclic rate of fire of 500 rounds per minute and fires both HE and AP projectiles. Three belts

each holding 135 rounds of HE ammunition are carried plus ten magazines of AP ammunition, each magazine holding ten rounds. The gunner has a monocular sight with a magnification of ×8 for use against ground targets. For aerial targets the turret hatch is opened to the rear and the gunner uses the open sights mounted on the weapon itself. There are three periscopes for forward and one for rear observation.

The commander sits to the right, and slightly to the rear, of the driver and has a single-piece hatch cover that opens to the rear, plus five periscopes for all-round observation.

The powerpack, which consists of the engine, clutch and transmission, is mounted under the floor of the vehicle. From the transmission power is taken forward to a cross shaft with clutches and disc brakes at either end which provide a clutch

Pbv 302 amphibious APC

Bplpbv 3023 armoured fire direction post vehicle in travelling configuration showing access panels in glacis

and brake steering system. The air inlet, air outlet and exhaust pipe are immediately behind the driver.

The nine infantrymen sit at the rear of the vehicle, three on each side facing inwards, one at the front facing forwards and two at the rear back to back. The personnel enter and leave the Pbv 302 by two large doors in the rear of the hull.

Over the top of each side of the troop compartment is a hydraulically-operated hatch which, when opened, allows the infantry to use their small arms from inside the vehicle. The hatches are operated by the commander of the vehicle and can be opened half way if required. A pressure-sensitive bar is fitted along the top of the hull under the hatch and if a weapon or hand is in contact with the strip the hatch remains open.

The torsion bar suspension consists of five dual rubber-tyred road wheels with the drive sprocket at the front and the idler at the rear. Hydraulic shock absorbers are fitted at the first and last road wheel stations. The tracks are the Hägglunds M70 type which have a life of over 10 000 km with one recondition, and have 20 per cent better traction on soft soil than earlier tracks.

The Pbv 302 is fully amphibious, being propelled in the water by its tracks. Before entering the water a trim vane is erected at the front of the hull and the bilge pumps switched on. The Pbv 302 has no NBC system, although one could be fitted.

The basic Pbv 302 can be used, with minor modifications, as a cargo carrier (carrying 2000 kg of cargo) and ambulance (carrying four stretchers in its basic form and up to six with a special kit).

Variants

Pbv 302 Mk 2 APC
This model was announced in 1978 and is a further development of the Mk 1. Three pre-production vehicles have been completed. Main differences are that the rifle-squad commander at the rear has a separate cupola which enables him to observe forward of the vehicle and still be the first man out.

The cupola has a single-piece hatch cover that opens to the rear and three periscopes. The turret retains the 20 mm cannon, although it could be replaced by a 25 mm cannon if required, and has been fitted with three smoke dischargers on either side. Mounted on the right side of the hull at the rear are two Bofors Lyran launchers for which eight illuminating shells are carried. There have also been minor improvements to the turret, and to the commander's and driver's vision equipment. An additional layer of spaced armour has been provided on the front of the vehicle and the two trim vanes at the front of the hull have added buoyancy aids. The left rear door has been fitted with a vision block.

Product-improved Pbv 302 APC
Hägglunds has proposed that the Pbv 302 could be easily developed into a full MICV with the following modifications, which could be incorporated into existing Swedish Army vehicles, or new vehicles could be built to the new standard. The MICV version would carry fewer infantryman who would sit back to back down the centre of the troop compartment. The sides of the troop compartment would be sloped (in a similar manner to those of the American M2 Bradley Infantry Fighting Vehicle) and each side would have three spherical firing ports with a vision block over each. The current engine would be replaced by the Volvo THD 100C diesel which develops 310 hp and would be coupled to an Allison HT 740 gearbox. A Hägglunds hydrostatic steering system would be fitted and the current 20 mm cannon would be replaced by an Oerlikon 25 mm KBA cannon. If required, the armament could be stabilised and have powered elevation and traverse. One prototype of the product-improved Pbv 302 APC has been completed.

Armoured Command Vehicle
This is designated the Stripbv 3021 and can be distinguished from the Pbv 302 by its four rather than two radio antennas. The radios are mounted on the right side of the troop compartment and four radio operators are normally carried plus command staff who are provided with mapboards.

Armoured Observation Post Vehicle
This is designated the Epbv 3022 and is issued on the scale of ten per armoured brigade. The major difference is that the commander's hatch has been replaced by a new cupola manned by the fire-control officer. The cupola has a combined binocular and optical rangefinder which can be changed between ×4 binocular and ×10 coincidence rangefinder using the same eyepieces. The cupola is hand-cranked in traverse and the line of sight is manually elevated, an azimuth sensor driven by the turret ring gives the accurate azimuth to the target. In the personnel compartment are three radios, two wire links and a navigation system which displays information at one of the operator's positions. Externally the Epbv 3022 is recognisable by its three radio antennas, additional cupola and additional buoyancy aids on the two trim vanes at the front of the hull.

Armoured Fire Direction Post Vehicle
This is designated the Bplpbv 3023 and has a crew of three (commander, gunner and driver) and also carries a ranging section of seven. Externally it is recognised by its four radio antennas and additional equipment carried on the roof of the troop compartment. Internally it has four radios and a fire direction computer.

SPECIFICATIONS

CREW	2 + 10	FUEL CAPACITY	285 litres	CLUTCH	double-disc clutch plate
COMBAT WEIGHT	13 500 kg	MAX ROAD RANGE	300 km		
POWER-TO-WEIGHT		FORDING	amphibious	SUSPENSION	torsion bar
RATIO	20.74 hp/tonne	GRADIENT	60%	ELECTRICAL SYSTEM	24 V
GROUND PRESSURE	0.6 kg/cm²	VERTICAL OBSTACLE	0.61 m	BATTERIES	2 × 12 V
LENGTH	5.35 m	TRENCH	1.8 m	ARMAMENT (main)	1 × 20 mm cannon
WIDTH	2.86 m	ENGINE	Volvo-Penta model	SMOKE-LAYING	
HEIGHT			THD 100B hori-	EQUIPMENT	1 × 6 smoke
to turret top	2.5 m		zontal 4-stroke turbo-		dischargers
to hull top	1.9 m		charged 6-cylinder	AMMUNITION (main)	405 HE plus 100 AP
GROUND CLEARANCE	0.4 m		in-line diesel	FIRE-CONTROL SYSTEM	
TRACK	2.42 m		developing 280 hp at	Turret power control	manual
TRACK WIDTH	380 mm		2200 rpm	Gun elevation/depression	+50°/−10°
LENGTH OF TRACK		TRANSMISSION	Volvo-Penta T60	Turret traverse	360°
ON GROUND	2.98 m		manual with 8		
MAX SPEED			forward and 2		
road	66 km/h		reverse gears		
water	8 km/h	STEERING	clutch and brake		

Status: Production complete. In service only with the Swedish Army.

Manufacturer: AB Hägglund and Söner, AFV Division, S-891 01, Örnsköldsvik, Sweden.

SWITZERLAND

MOWAG Improved Tornado Mechanised Infantry Combat Vehicle

Development

The Improved Tornado MICV has been developed as a private venture by MOWAG with the first prototype completed in the spring of 1980.

In addition to being employed as an MICV with a one- or two-man main weapon station, the basic vehicle can be adapted to a variety of other uses including ambulance, ATGW carrier, command vehicle, fire support combat vehicle, maintenance and recovery vehicle, mortar carrier, multiple rocket launcher carrier and a reconnaissance vehicle.

MOWAG Improved Tornado MICV fitted with one-man Oerlikon-Bührle GBD-COA turret armed with 25 mm cannon, 7.62 mm machine gun and electrically-operated smoke dischargers and remote-controlled 7.62 mm machine gun mount above either side of troop compartment

MOWAG Improved Tornado MICV fitted with Oerlikon-Bührle two-man turret GBD-BOB armed with 25 mm cannon, 7.62 mm machine gun and twin TOW launcher

Description

The hull of the MOWAG Tornado is made of all-welded steel and provides the crew with complete protection from small arms fire and shell splinters. To give increased protection against larger calibre weapons spaced armour is provided over the frontal arc of the vehicle.

The driver sits at the front of the hull on the left and has a single-piece hatch cover that opens to the right in front of which are three periscopes, the centre one of which can be replaced by a passive one for night driving. The driver steers the Tornado with a steering wheel. The commander sits behind the driver and has a single-piece hatch cover that opens to the right and five periscopes, three to his front and two to his left. When the Tornado is fitted with a two-man turret, the commander sits in the turret, not to the rear of the driver.

The engine compartment is to the immediate right of the driver and separated from the remainder of the vehicle by an NBC-proof bulkhead. The engine compartment has an automatic fire-extinguishing system which can also be operated manually. The air-inlet and air-outlet louvres are in the roof with the exhaust outlet in the right side of the hull. The engine, steer-shift transmission, air intake and exhaust system is rubber-mounted as a complete unit and can easily be removed from the vehicle for field replacement or maintenance.

The electric/hydraulically-operated four-speed transmission with torque converter reduces driver fatigue. The four speeds can be used in either direction and high speed reverse capability is provided. The torque converter has an automatic lock-up clutch and a retarder integrated in the transmission relieves the vehicle brakes during prolonged downhill driving. The hydrostatic steering transmission allows infinitely variable steering up to a fixed radius, turning about either track or pivot steer about vertical axis in both directions.

The torsion bar suspension consists of six dual rubber-tyred road wheels with the drive sprocket at the front, idler at the rear and three track return rollers. The first, second and sixth road wheel stations are fitted with heavy duty hydraulic shock absorbers. The tracks are fitted with quickly replaceable rubber pads which can be replaced by rubber pads with spikes for driving on icy surfaces. The upper part of the track is covered by a skirt which is hinged at its upper part to allow access to the track and suspension for maintenance.

The armament station, such as an Oerlikon two-man 35 mm GDD-AOE turret, Oerlikon 25 mm two-man turret GBD-BOB, or an Oerlikon 25 mm GBD-COA one-man turret, is mounted in the roof of the vehicle.

On the top of the personnel compartment, one either side, is a remote-controlled machine gun mount designed by MOWAG, armed with a 7.62 mm machine gun with an elevation of +60 degrees, a depression of −15 degrees and a total traverse of 230 degrees. The mounts are each provided with one periscope for aiming the machine gun and two vision blocks.

In each side of the hull are two spherical firing ports which enable the crew to fire an SMG from inside the hull in complete safety.

The six infantrymen are seated three down each side of the hull facing outward and enter and leave the vehicle by the large power-operated ramp in the rear of the hull which opens downwards. In an emergency this can be opened manually. There is an emergency escape hatch in the floor of the personnel compartment.

The Tornado can ford to a depth of 1.3 metres without preparation. An over-pressure ventilation system is fitted as standard and has an air flow of four cubic metres a minute when being used for ventilation and three cubic metres a minute when used for NBC protection.

Variants

See development.

SPECIFICATIONS

CREW	3 + 7
COMBAT WEIGHT	22 300 kg
UNLOADED WEIGHT	18 800 kg
POWER-TO-WEIGHT RATIO	17.7 hp/tonne
GROUND PRESSURE	0.63 kg/cm²
LENGTH	6.7 m
WIDTH	3.15 m
HEIGHT (hull top)	1.75 m
GROUND CLEARANCE	0.45 m
TRACK	2.7 m
TRACK WIDTH	450 mm
LENGTH OF TRACK ON GROUND	3.786 m
MAX SPEED	66.1 km/h
FUEL CAPACITY	500 litres
MAX ROAD RANGE	400 km
FORDING	1.3 m
with preparation	1.7 m
GRADIENT	60%
SIDE SLOPE	40%
VERTICAL OBSTACLE	0.85 m
TRENCH	2.2 m
ENGINE	Detroit Diesel 8V-71T, V-8 2-cycle turbo-charged diesel developing 390 hp at 2500 rpm
TRANSMISSION	Renk HSWL 194 automatic hydro-mechanical steer/shift, 4 speeds in both directions
SUSPENSION	torsion bar
ELECTRICAL SYSTEM	24 V
BATTERIES	6 × 12 V, 300 Ah
ARMAMENT	see text

Status: Trials.

Manufacturer: MOWAG Motorwagenfabrik AG, 8280 Kreuzlingen, Switzerland.

WAG Piranha Armoured Personnel ~ier

Development

The Piranha range of 4 × 4, 6 × 6 and 8 × 8 armoured vehicles was developed by MOWAG as a private venture in the early 1970s and is designed for the home and export markets. The first prototype was completed in 1972 with first production vehicles following in 1976. In February 1977 Canada placed an initial order for 350 6 × 6 Piranhas (subsequently increased to 491) which were built under licence in Canada by the Diesel Division of General Motors Canada. Additional information on the Canadian vehicles will be found under Canada. General Motors Canada has also delivered 8 × 8 models of the Piranha to meet the United States Marine Corps requirements for a Light Armored Vehicle (LAV); details of these vehicles are given under Canada. In September 1982 General Motors of Canada was awarded a contract for the supply of 969 LAVs which are being manufactured under licence from MOWAG.

The MOWAG Piranha in the 4 × 4 and 6 × 6 model is also manufactured under licence in Chile by Cardoen Industries for which there is a separate entry.

The Piranha range has been designed to undertake a wide range of roles such as ambulance, anti-tank (armed with ATGWs), cargo, command, internal security, mortar carrier, recovery and reconnaissance. Many components of the vehicle are identical to all members of the family such as the front and rear hull sections, doors, hatches, wheel drives, wheels, differentials, suspension, steering and propellers.

Description

The all-welded steel hull of the Piranha protects the crew from small arms fire and shell splinters. The driver sits at the front of the vehicle on the left side and has a single-piece hatch cover that opens to the rear. In front of his hatch cover are three periscopes, the centre one of which can be replaced

by a night vision periscope. The engine is to the right of the driver with the air-inlet and air-outlet louvres in the top of the hull and the exhaust outlet on the right side of the hull.

The main armament is normally installed in the centre of the hull. The troop compartment is at the rear and the troops enter and leave the vehicle by two doors in the rear of the hull that open outwards. There are two hatch covers over the roof of the troop compartment, which open outwards. MOWAG-designed spherical firing ports, with a vision block over each, can be fitted into each of the rear doors and two in either side of the hull to enable the crew to fire their weapons from inside the vehicle.

The automatic locking differentials are flexibly mounted within the hull. The suspension is of the independent type with coil springs on the front axle and torsion bars on the rear. All wheel stations have hydraulic shock absorbers. On the 6 × 6 vehicle the first axle has coil springs and the rear two axles have torsion bars and on the 8 × 8 vehicle the front two axles have coil springs and the rear two axles have torsion bars. The suspension allows the roadwheel a maximum travel of 0.32 metre. The tyres are of the run-flat type.

All members of the family are fully amphibious, being propelled in the water by two propellers mounted at the rear of the hull. Before entering the water a trim vane, which is stowed under the nose of the vehicle when not in use, is erected at the front of the hull. Standard equipment includes an NBC and air-conditioning system and optional equipment includes night vision devices of the infra-red or passive type.

Variants

Piranha (4 × 4)

A variety of armament installations can be mounted up to and including a 20 mm turret-mounted cannon, for example one or two 7.62 mm remote controlled machine guns, turret armed with an externally-mounted 12.7 mm (0.50) M2 HB machine gun or an Oerlikon 20 mm GAD-AOA turret.

MOWAG Piranha (8 × 8) APC fitted with two-man Belgium CM 90 turret armed with Cockerill 90 mm Mk III gun, 7.62 mm coaxial machine gun and electrically-operated smoke dischargers to give coverage to front, sides and rear of vehicle

MOWAG Piranha (4 × 4) APC with two MOWAG-designed remote-controlled 7.62 mm machine gun installations

Piranha (6 × 6)

A variety of armament installations can be fitted including a 12.7 mm MG turret, 20 mm GAD-AOA Oerlikon turret, 25 mm GBD series Oerlikon turret, 30 mm turret, 35 mm GDD-AOE or GDD-BOE Oerlikon turret, turret as fitted to the Alvis Scorpion armed with 76 mm gun, turret armed with a 90 mm Cockerill gun, 81 mm mortar mounted in the rear. More specialised versions include an unarmed ambulance, fitted with a roof-mounted air-conditioning system, and a radar carrier. This has a RASIT battlefield surveillance radar mounted on the roof which can be lowered inside the vehicle under armoured protection.

Piranha (6 × 6) Anti-tank Vehicle

The Swiss Army requires 400 MOWAG Piranha (6 × 6) armoured personnel carriers for use in the anti-tank role to replace the 106 mm M40 recoilless rifles used at present. It is expected that Swfr 500 million will be included in the 1985 Swiss defence budget for the procurement of production vehicles. Each Swiss infantry regiment will have a tank destroyer company with three sections, each with three MOWAG Piranha (6 × 6) vehicles fitted with the Hughes TOW missile system.

Six MOWAG Piranha (6 × 6) armoured personnel carriers fitted with two different TOW systems are being considered by the Swiss Army. The first is the Norwegian Thune-Eureka one-man power-operated turret which has two TOW missiles ready-to-launch with additional missiles carried in the hull.

The second model, which has been developed by MOWAG, has a raised cupola over the centre of the vehicle with a TOW 2 ATGW system inside. This is pedestal mounted and raised above the roof of the vehicle when required; when retracted it is covered by two armoured hatches. This model also has two banks of three electrically-operated smoke dischargers, a 7.62 mm machine gun for local protection and a Bofors Lyran launcher for illuminating targets at night.

Piranha (8 × 8)

A variety of armament installations can be fitted including all those of the 6 × 6 model plus twin 20 or 30 mm anti-aircraft guns, multiple rocket launcher with two banks of 15 81 mm launcher tubes, and mortar tractor towing a 120 mm mortar. Late in 1980 an 8 × 8 Piranha was shown in the United

Second version of MOWAG Piranha (6 × 6) vehicle as used in anti-tank role with Hughes TOW 2 ATGW launcher raised

States fitted with an AAI developed turret armed with a 75 mm ARES cannon to meet the US Mobile Protected Weapon System requirement.

MOWAG Piranha (6 × 6) APC with RASIT battlefied surveillance radar and remote-controlled 7.62 mm machine gun

SPECIFICATIONS

Model	4 × 4	6 × 6	8 × 8
CREW (max)	10	14	15
COMBAT WEIGHT*	7800 kg	10 500 kg	12 300 kg
UNLOADED WEIGHT	6700 kg	8000 kg	8800 kg
POWER-TO-WEIGHT RATIO (diesel engine)	27.7 hp/tonne	28.6 hp/tonne	24.4 hp/tonne
LENGTH	5.32 m	5.97 m	6.365 m
WIDTH	2.5 m	2.5 m	2.5 m
HEIGHT (without armament)	1.85 m	1.85 m	1.85 m
GROUND CLEARANCE	0.5 m	0.5 m	0.5 m
TRACK			
front	2.18 m	2.18 m	2.18 m
rear	2.2 m	2.2 m	2.2 m
WHEELBASE	2.42 m	2.04 m + 1.04 m	1.1 m + 1.135 m + 1.04 m
ANGLE OF APPROACH/ DEPARTURE	40°/45°	40°/45°	40°/45°
MAX SPEED			
road	100 km/h	100 km/h	100 km/h
water	9.5 km/h	10.5 km/h	10.5 km/h
FUEL CAPACITY	200 litres	200 litres	300 litres
MAX ROAD RANGE	700 km	600 km	780 km
FORDING	amphibious	amphibious	amphibious
GRADIENT	70%	70%	70%
SIDE SLOPE	35%	35%	35%
VERTICAL OBSTACLE	0.5 m	0.5 m	0.5 m
TURNING RADIUS	6.3 m	7.3 m	7.7 m
ENGINE (Detroit Diesel model)	6V-53 developing 216 hp at 2800 rpm	6V-53T developing 300 hp at 2800 rpm	6V-53T developing 300 hp at 2800 rpm
TRANSMISSION (Allison model)	MT-653 automatic, 5 forward/ 1 reverse gears	MT-653 automatic, 5 forward/ 1 reverse gears	MT-653 automatic, 5 forward/ 1 reverse gears
SUSPENSION	independent	independent	independent
TYRES	11.00 × 16	11.00 × 16	11.00 × 16
BRAKES (main)	air hydraulic (dual circuit) on all vehicles		
ELECTRICAL SYSTEM	24 V	24 V	24 V
ARMAMENT	depends on role	depends on role	depends on role

* Dependent on role.

Status: In production. In service with Canadian Armed Forces, Chile, Ghana (4 × 4), Liberia (4 × 4), Nigeria (6 × 6), Sierra Leone and United States Marine Corps. In 1984 it was reported that Taiwan had placed an order for 50 MOWAG Piranha (6 × 6) vehicles.

Manufacturer: MOWAG Motorwagenfabrik AG, 8280 Kreuzlingen, Switzerland.

MOWAG MR 8 Series of Armoured Personnel Carriers

Development
In the 1950s the MOWAG Company designed a series of 4 × 4 armoured vehicles as a private venture under the designation of the MR 8 series. The armoured personnel carrier version, called the MR 8-01, was subsequently tested by the Federal German Border Police (the Bundesgrenzschutz, or BGS for short). The BGS placed an order with MOWAG for 20 production vehicles which were delivered to West Germany in 1959/60 and production was then undertaken in Germany by Büssing and Henschel who together built some 600 vehicles, some of which have since been transferred from the BGS to the West German Police.

The BGS uses two basic models, the SW1 and the SW2. The SW1, or Geschützter Sonderwagen 1 (Kfz 91) is unarmed and used as an armoured personnel carrier, but some vehicles have been fitted with an obstacle-clearing blade at the front of the hull. The SW2 is fitted with a turret-mounted 20 mm cannon.

Description (SW1)
The all-welded hull of the MR 8-01 protects the crew from small arms fire and shell splinters. The driver sits at the front of the hull on the left with the commander to his right, both with a windscreen to their front which is covered in action by a steel shutter hinged at the top. Each shutter has a vision block for observation when it is lowered. Over the top of the driver's position is a single-piece hatch cover that opens to the right and when the driver is driving with his head out a windscreen and wiper can be erected in front of him. A vision block is fitted in each side of the hull to the left of the driver and the right of the commander.

The hull top immediately behind the commander and driver has a distinct step upwards with a vision block fitted in

SW1 with all doors and hatches open and two parts of cupola locked vertical

the face of the personnel compartment for forward observation. In the roof of the vehicle, to the rear of the driver, is a six-sided cupola which is split down its centre line to open either side. Each half of the cupola has three vision blocks and can be locked vertical. In the left side of the hull is a two-part door, the left part with a firing port and the right part with a vision block. There is a similar door in the right side of the hull and a door in the rear of the hull on the right side, which has two parts with a vision block in the right side. There are also two hatches in the roof of the MR 8-01.

The engine, air-inlet and air-outlet louvres are in the left side of the hull and the exhaust outlet at the rear. Panels to allow easy access to the engine for maintenance are provided in hull side, rear and roof.

The MR 8-01 has no amphibious capability, no NBC system and no night vision equipment, although the last two could have been fitted if specified.

Variants

The SW2 has a different shaped hull top with no step and is fitted with a turret armed with a 20 mm Hispano-Suiza cannon with four smoke dischargers mounted either side of the turret. The SW2 normally has a crew of four and has a single door in each side of the hull, each with a firing port.

Other variants developed by MOWAG to the prototype stage included the MR 8-09 with a turret-mounted 20 mm cannon, MR 8-23 armed with a turret-mounted 90 mm Mecar gun, MR 8-30 fitted with an 81 mm multiple rocket system and the MR 9-32 with a 120 mm mortar.

SPECIFICATIONS	
CREW	2 + 5
CONFIGURATION	4 × 4
COMBAT WEIGHT	8200 kg
UNLOADED WEIGHT	7000 kg
POWER-TO-WEIGHT RATIO	19.63 hp/tonne
LENGTH	5.31 m
WIDTH	2.2 m
HEIGHT	
to turret top	2.2 m
to hull top	1.88 m
GROUND CLEARANCE	
hull	0.5 m
axles	0.3 m
TRACK	1.95 m
WHEELBASE	2.6 m
ANGLE OF APPROACH/ DEPARTURE	45°/44°
MAX ROAD SPEED	80 km/h
RANGE	400 km
FORDING	1.1 m
GRADIENT	60%
SIDE SLOPE	40%
ENGINE	Chrysler type R 361 6-cylinder petrol developing 161 hp
TRANSMISSION	manual with 5 forward and 1 reverse gears
TRANSFER CASE	2-speed
TYRES	10.00 × 20
ELECTRICAL SYSTEM	24 V
ARMAMENT	see text

Status: Production complete. In service only with the Federal German Border Police and Federal German Police.

Manufacturer: MOWAG Motorwagenfabrik AG, 8280 Kreuzlingen, Switzerland.

MOWAG Grenadier from rear showing MOWAG-designed spherical firing ports and propeller at hull rear

MOWAG Grenadier Armoured Personnel Carrier

Development

The Grenadier was developed as a private venture by MOWAG and is suitable for a wide range of roles including use as an ambulance, armoured personnel carrier, cargo/ ammunition carrier, command and radio vehicle, internal security vehicle and as a reconnaissance vehicle. The first prototype of the Grenadier was completed in 1966 with the first production vehicle following in 1967.

Description

The hull of the Grenadier is all welded and provides the crew with protection from 7.62 mm small arms fire.

The driver sits at the front of the hull on the left side and has a single-piece hatch cover that opens to the right, to the front of which are three periscopes. A windscreen and wiper can be fitted in front of the driver's position in wet weather.

The engine compartment to the right of the driver is separated from the crew compartment by a fireproof bulkhead and the air-outlet and air-inlet louvres are in the roof of the vehicle.

The turret is to the rear of the driver, offset to the left, and has a single-piece hatch cover that opens forwards. There is also a circular hatch cover in the roof of the troop compartment on the right side. The infantry enter and leave the vehicle by two doors in the rear of the hull. On the basic Grenadier there is no provision for the crew to use their small arms from inside the vehicle but if required the vehicle could have been delivered with MOWAG-designed firing ports and vision blocks in each side of the hull and in each of the

MOWAG Grenadier with turret-mounted 20 mm cannon

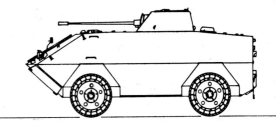

MOWAG Grenadier fitted with remote-controlled 7.62 mm machine gun on turret roof

SPECIFICATIONS

CREW	1 + 8
CONFIGURATION	4 × 4
COMBAT WEIGHT	6100 kg
UNLOADED WEIGHT	4400 kg
POWER-TO-WEIGHT RATIO	33 hp/tonne
LENGTH	4.84 m
WIDTH	2.3 m
HEIGHT	
to turret top	2.12 m
to hull top	1.7 m
FIRING HEIGHT	1.868 m
GROUND CLEARANCE	
hull	0.4 m
axles	0.25 m
TRACK	
front	1.99 m
rear	2 m
WHEELBASE	2.5 m
ANGLE OF APPROACH/DEPARTURE	41°/36°
MAX SPEED	
road	100 km/h
water	9–10 km/h
FUEL CAPACITY	180 litres
MAX ROAD RANGE	550 km
FORDING	amphibious
GRADIENT	60%
SIDE SLOPE	30%
VERTICAL OBSTACLE	0.4 m
TURNING RADIUS	6.45 m
ENGINE	V-8 4-stroke water-cooled petrol developing 202 hp at 3900 rpm
TRANSMISSION	manual with 4 forward and 1 reverse gears
TRANSFER CASE	2-speed
CLUTCH	single dry plate
SUSPENSION	semi-elliptical springs and hydraulic shock absorbers
BRAKES	
main	hydraulic on all wheels
parking	mechanical operating on rear wheels
ELECTRICAL SYSTEM	24 V
BATTERIES	2 × 12 V
ARMAMENT	1 × 20 mm cannon
GUN STABILISER	
vertical	no
horizontal	no

Status: Production complete. No longer available. In service with undisclosed countries.

Manufacturer: MOWAG Motorwagenfabrik AG, 8280 Kreuzlingen, Switzerland.

rear doors, enabling the infantry to use their small arms from within the vehicle in complete safety.

The suspension system, front and rear, consists of semi-elliptical springs and hydraulic shock absorbers. The rigid axles have hypoid gears and self-locking differentials.

The Grenadier is fully amphibious, being propelled in the water by a single three-bladed propeller at the rear of the hull which is engaged when the driver shifts into second gear. The two parallel rudders to the immediate rear of the propeller are connected to the steering wheel. An electric bilge pump is fitted as standard. Before entering the water a trim vane is erected at the front of the hull; when not in use it folds back under the nose of the vehicle.

Optional equipment includes an air-conditioning system, infra-red or passive night vision equipment, electric ventilator and MOWAG-designed bullet-proof cross-country wheels which also provide additional cross-country capability and assist the vehicle in overcoming sandbanks and other natural obstacles when afloat as the wheels rotate simultaneously with the propeller.

The basic vehicle could be fitted with a wide range of armament installations including a turret-mounted 20 mm or 25 mm cannon, an ATGW system, 8 cm multiple rocket launchers or a MOWAG-designed remote-controlled 7.62 mm machine gun mount on the top of a low turret with the gunner being provided with a sight with a magnification of ×4 for aiming the weapon. Smoke dischargers can be fitted on either side of the turret if required.

Variants

There are no variants of the Grenadier apart from the various roles that the vehicle has been designed to undertake.

MOWAG Roland Armoured Personnel Carrier

Development

The Roland was developed as a private venture by MOWAG in the early 1960s and is suitable for a wide range of roles including use as an ambulance, armoured personnel carrier, cargo/ammunition carrier, command and radio vehicle, internal security vehicle and as a reconnaissance vehicle. The prototypes of the Roland were completed in 1963 with series production following in 1964. It is most widely used as an internal security and reconnaissance vehicle, especially in

MOWAG Roland fitted with obstacle-clearing blade at front of hull

MOWAG Roland armed with remote-controlled 7.62 mm GPMG on turret roof

Africa and South America, and its crew normally consists of commander, gunner, driver and three or four infantry.

Description

The hull of the Roland is all welded and protects the crew from 7.62 mm small arms fire. The driver sits at the front of the hull on the left side and has a single-piece hatch cover that opens to the right, in front of which are three periscopes. A windscreen and wiper can be fitted in front of the driver's position in wet weather. To the left of the driver is a vision block protected by a grille.

In either side of the hull, to the rear of the driver's position, is an entry hatch hinged at the top. The left hatch has a vision block protected by a grille beneath which is a firing port. A vision block and firing port are provided to the immediate rear of the right side hatch. The gunner sits on an adjustable seat in the centre of the vehicle with one man to his left facing the front and another to his right facing the rear. Over the gunner's position is a turret which can be manually traversed through a full 360 degrees, and has a single-piece hatch cover

that opens to the rear and a vision block, to the right of which is a small circular hatch that opens to the right.

To the rear of the turret, on the right side, is a circular hatch cover that opens to the rear, to the left of which is the ventilator.

Another door at the rear of the vehicle on the right side opens to the right and has a vision block and a firing port. Two men are seated in the passageway that connects the main crew compartment and the rear door, one facing forward and one facing the rear.

The engine is at the rear of the hull on the left side and is separated from the crew compartment by a fireproof bulkhead. The suspension system, front and rear, consists of semi-elliptical springs and hydraulic shock absorbers. The rigid axles have hypoid gears and self-locking differentials.

The latest model of the MOWAG Roland has a slightly longer wheelbase and is fitted with an automatic instead of a manual transmission.

Standard equipment for the internal security version includes blue flashing lights, electric roof fan, heater, two-tone intermittent siren and wire mesh protection for the headlamps.

The basic vehicle can be fitted with a number of different types of light armament installation including a MOWAG-designed remote-controlled 7.62 mm machine gun mount mounted on top of the low turret with the gunner being provided with a sight with a magnification of ×4 for aiming the weapon. Smoke dischargers can be fitted on either side of the turret if required.

Optional equipment includes an air-conditioning system, infra-red or passive night vision equipment, obstacle-clearing blade mounted at the front of the hull, searchlights, MOWAG-designed firing ports which allow the infantrymen

MOWAG Roland APC armed with pintle-mounted 12.7 mm M2 HB machine gun

to aim and fire their weapons from within the vehicle in safety, and MOWAG bullet-proof cross-country wheels consisting of metal discs either side of the tyre which support the tyre when it has been punctured and also provide additional traction when crossing rough country.

Variants

There are no variants of the Roland apart from the various roles that the vehicle has been designed to undertake.

SPECIFICATIONS (vehicle armed with remote-controlled 7.62 mm MG). Specifications in brackets relate to the model with automatic transmission where it differs from the manual version

CREW	3 + 3	MAX SPEED		TRANSFER CASE	2-speed
CONFIGURATION	4 × 4	road	110 km/h	CLUTCH	single dry plate
COMBAT WEIGHT	4700 [4900] kg	with bullet-proof wheels	80 km/h	SUSPENSION	semi-elliptical springs
UNLOADED WEIGHT	3900 [4000] kg	FUEL CAPACITY	154 [170] litres		and hydraulic shock
POWER-TO-WEIGHT		MAX RANGE (road)	550 [570] km		absorbers
RATIO.	42.9 [33] hp/tonne	FUEL CONSUMPTION	0.28 [0.3] litre/km	TYRES	9.00 × 16
LENGTH	4.44 [4.73] m	FORDING	1 m	BRAKES	
WIDTH	2.01 [2.05] m	GRADIENT	60%	main	hydraulic on all wheels
HEIGHT		SIDE SLOPE	30%	parking	mechanical on rear
to turret top,		VERTICAL OBSTACLE	0.4 m		wheels
without armament	2.03 [2.1] m	TURNING RADIUS	6.45 [6.85] m	ELECTRICAL SYSTEM	12 V
to hull top	1.62 [1.67] m	ENGINE	V-8 4-stroke water-	BATTERY	1 × 12 V, 125 Ah
GROUND CLEARANCE			cooled petrol	ARMAMENT	1 × 7.62 mm MG
(hull)	0.4 [0.42] m		developing 202 hp	GUN STABILISER	
TRACK			at 3900 rpm	vertical	no
front	1.71 [1.66] m	TRANSMISSION	manual with 4 forward	horizontal	no
rear	1.655 [1.66] m		and 1 reverse gears		
WHEELBASE	2.5 [2.65] m		[automatic with		
ANGLE OF APPROACH/			3 forward and		
DEPARTURE	40°/36° [46°/40°]		1 reverse gears]		

Status: In production. In service with Argentina, Bolivia, Chile, Greece, Iraq, Mexico, Peru and other countries.

Manufacturer: MOWAG Motorwagenfabrik AG, 8280 Kreuzlingen, Switzerland.

TAIWAN

Armoured Infantry Fighting Vehicle

Development

The Armoured Infantry Fighting Vehicle (AIFV) was developed by the Republic of China Armoured Fighting Vehicle Development Centre in the 1970s and completed in 1979. It is manufactured by the Republic of China Fighting Machines Command which is responsible for final assembly and testing. About 40 firms are involved in supplying major components for the AIFV including the Taiwan Machinery Manufacturing Corporation (chassis, suspension and power plant) and the Taiwan Aluminium Corporation (hull and tracks).

Description

The AIFV is based on the American M113 APC which has been in service in Taiwan for some years but incorporates features of the M113A2, M113A3 and the FMC AIFV.

The layout of the AIFV is similar to the M113 series with the driver at the front left, engine compartment to his right and the troop compartment at the hull rear.

The hull is of all-welded aluminium armour construction with an additional layer of laminate steel armour bolted to the hull front, sides and rear. Closed cell polyurethane foam is used to fill the space between the two layers of armour and this gives increased buoyancy for amphibious operations.

The driver has a single-piece hatch cover that opens to the rear and periscopes for observation. The engine compartment has a fire fighting system. The vehicle is powered by a British Perkins V8-640 diesel developing about 215 bhp and

Armoured Infantry Fighting Vehicle showing laminate armour kit, shield for 12.7 mm M2 HB machine gun and smoke dischargers

coupled to a transmission developed by the Institute of Industrial Technology in Taiwan and is similar to the M113A1. The air-inlet, air-outlet louvres and exhaust pipe outlet are in the roof of the vehicle.

The commander sits to the rear of the driver who has a cupola that can be traversed through a full 360 degrees. This is provided with a single-piece hatch cover, periscopes for all-round observation, 12.7 mm M2 HB machine gun and a shield that gives front and side protection against small arms fire. Either side of the shield is a bank of three electrically-operated smoke dischargers firing forwards.

The troop compartment is at the rear of the vehicle and the infantry enter and leave via a power-operated ramp in the hull rear. This has an emergency door in the left side. Five firing ports, each with a periscope or a vision block are provided, two in each side of the hull and one at the rear. These allow the infantry to use their 5.56 mm weapons from within the vehicle in safety. It is believed that between six and eight infantrymen are carried plus the crew of two (commander/gunner and driver). In addition there is a hatch in the troop compartment roof.

The suspension is of the torsion bar type and consists of five rubber-tyred road wheels with the drive sprocket at the front and idler at the rear, there are no track return rollers.

The electrical system is similar to that of the M113. Standard equipment includes bilge pumps and infra-red night vision equipment. The AIFV is fully amphibious, being propelled in the water by its tracks, before entering the water the bilge pumps are switched on and the trim vane erected at the front of the hull. An NBC system is not installed at present.

If required an armoured fuel tank, similar to that offered by FMC for the M113A2, can be fitted either side of the hull ramp at the rear.

Physical and performance characteristics of the AIFV are similar those of the M113A2.

Variants
The following variants are believed to be under development:
Mortar carrier (81 mm, 107 mm and 120 mm)
Command posts (command, communications and fire direction)
AIFV with 20 mm or 30 mm cannon
AIFV with Kung Feng IV 126 mm multiple rocket system
AIFV with Hughes TOW ATGW system
AIFV with Kueb Wu ATGW
Others could include fire support vehicle, reconnaissance vehicle, flamethrower, cargo carrier and ambulance.

Status: Production. In service with the Taiwanese Army.

Manufacturer: Fighting Machines Command, ROC Army, Taichung, Taiwan 400.

UNION OF SOVIET SOCIALIST REPUBLICS

BMP-2 Mechanised Infantry Combat Vehicle

Development
The BMP-2 was first seen during the November 1982 Moscow parade although it had been in service with the Soviet Army some years before and had already been deployed by the Group of Soviet Forces Germany and in Afghanistan. The STANAG designation for this vehicle is BMP-M1981.

Description
The chassis of the BMP-2 is almost identical to that of the earlier BMP-1, but it may have increased armour protection. The driver sits at the front of the vehicle on the left side with a single-piece hatch cover that opens to the right. In front of his position are three periscopes, the centre one (TNPO-170) of which can be replaced by a vertically-extensible one (TNPO-350B) which allows the driver to see ahead when the trim vane is erected for amphibious operations. On the BMP-1 the commander sits to the rear of the driver, but on the BMP-2 is moved to the turret so this position is occupied by an infantryman. He has a single-piece hatch cover that hinges forward to open. In front of this and to the left side is a periscope facing towards the front of the vehicle. In the left side of the hull, forward of the infantryman's hatch is a single firing port.

The engine and transmission are to the right of the driver's compartment with the air-inlet and air-outlet louvres on top of the hull. The engine is believed to be a turbo-charged version of the 5D20 installed in the BMP-1 and is believed to have an output of 350 to 400 hp.

The one-man turret of the BMP-1 has been replaced by a new two-man turret with the commander on the right and the

BMP-2 from above with driver's, commander's and troop compartment hatches open

123

gunner on the left. In action the commander would dismount from the vehicle with his squad. The gunner has a single rectangular hatch cover that opens to the front with an integral rear-facing periscope and three fixed periscopes, two to the front and one to the left side. The commander has a cupola with a single-piece hatch cover that opens forward, in the forward part of this are three fixed periscopes for observation to the front. Both the commander and gunner have a day/night sight in front of their hatch covers and the commander also has an infra-red searchlight.

Main armament consists of a 30 mm cannon which has an elevation from about −5 to +50 degrees, with a 7.62 mm machine gun mounted coaxially to the left of the main armament. An infra-red/white seachlight is mounted to the right of the main armament and moves in elevation with it. Mounted either side of the turret is a bank of three electrically-operated smoke dischargers firing forwards.

Mounted on the turret roof between the gunner's and commander's hatches is a Spandrel AT-5 ATGW as on the latest model of the BRDM-2 (4 × 4) amphibious reconnaissance/anti-tank vehicle. The Spandrel is a second generation type and has a maximum range of 4000 metres. All the gunner has to do to ensure a hit is to keep the cross-hairs of his sight on the target. It is possible that a AT-4 Spigot ATGW could be fitted in place of the Spandrel, this has a 2000-metre range.

To the turret rear is the infantry compartment which has only two roof hatches compared to the BMP-1's four. It

BMP-2 with commander's hatch open and Spandrel AT-5 ATGW mounted on turret roof

carries six infantrymen, compared to eight in the BMP-1, who sit down either side of the vehicle back-to-back. Each infantryman has a single firing port and a roof-mounted periscope. The infantry enter and leave the vehicle via two doors in the hull rear, the left one containing a firing port.

The torsion bar suspension either side consists of six road wheels with the drive sprocket at the front, idler at the rear

BMP-2 with all hatches closed and Spandrel AT-5 ATGW mounted on turret roof (Steven Zaloga)

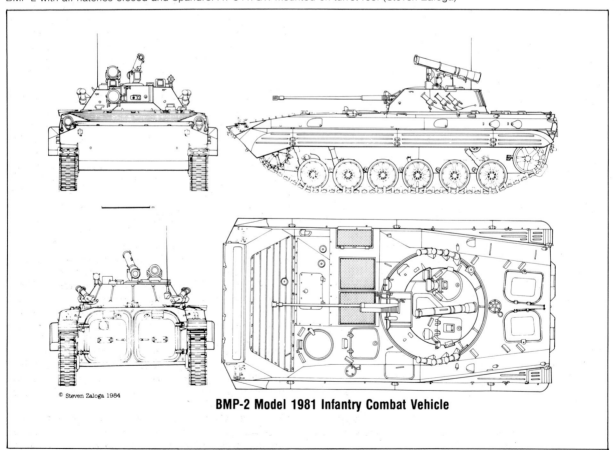

© Steven Zaloga 1984

BMP-2 Model 1981 Infantry Combat Vehicle

and track return rollers. The first, second and sixth road wheel stations have hydraulic shock absorbers. The upper part of the track has a sheet metal cover deeper than that of the BMP-1.

Like the BMP-1, the BMP-2 is fully amphibious. Before entering the water the trim vane stowed on top of the glacis plate is erected, the bilge pumps switched on and the driver's centre periscope replaced by the TNPO-350B.

BMP-2 has an NBC system and, in addition to the infrared searchlight for the commander and infra-red searchlight mounted coaxially with the 30 mm cannon, also has infra-red driving lights.

Variants
There are no known variants of the BMP-2.

SPECIFICATIONS (provisional)	
CREW	3 + 7
COMBAT WEIGHT	14 600 kg
LENGTH	6.71 m
WIDTH	3.09 m
HEIGHT	2.06 m
MAX SPEED	
road	60 km/h
water	6–7 km/h
MAX RANGE	500 km
GRADIENT	60%
VERTICAL OBSTACLE	0.7 m
TRENCH	2 m
ARMAMENT	
main	1 × 30 mm cannon
coaxial	1 × 7.62 mm MG
other	1 × launcher for Spandrel ATGW
SMOKE LAYING EQUIPMENT	2 × 3 smoke dischargers and diesel fuel injected into exhaust

Status: In production. In service with Soviet Union.

Manufacturer: Soviet state arsenals.

BMP-1 Mechanised Infantry Combat Vehicle

Development
The BMP-1 (Boevaya Mashina Pekhota) was developed in the early 1960s as the replacement for the BTR-50P series of tracked APCs and was seen in public for the first time during the 1967 November parade in Red Square, Moscow. For a short period it was called the M-1967 and then the BMP-76PB in the west. Its correct Soviet designation is now known to be the BMP-1. The vehicle uses some suspension components of the PT-76 light amphibious tank. In 1979 production of the BMP was running at some 2000 vehicles a year. Production of the BMP-1 may have been completed in favour of the more recent BMP-2, although it could still be produced for export.

Description
The hull of the BMP-1 is made of all-welded steel which provides the crew with protection from small arms fire and shell splinters. According to American reports the armour provides complete protection from 12.7 mm AP/API rounds over its frontal arc. The well-sloped glacis plate is ribbed, with an infra-red driving light at the front on the right and a white light on the left.

The driver sits at the front of the hull on the left side and has a single-piece hatch cover that opens to the right. In front of his position are three periscopes, the centre one (TNPO-170) of which can be replaced by a vertically extensible one (TNPO-350B) which allows the driver to see ahead when the trim vane is erected for amphibious operations.

The commander is seated behind the driver and has a cupola that can be traversed through a full 360 degrees. In the forward part of the cupola are three periscopes, the centre one of which can be replaced by a TKH-3 binocular sight or a sight with a variable magnification. An infra-red searchlight is mounted on the commander's cupola and controlled from inside the vehicle.

The engine and transmission are to the right of the driver's and commander's positions with the steering system at the front of the hull. The air-inlet and outlet louvres are in the top of the hull. A pneumatic system is provided for air starting of the engine, compressed air and liquid clearing of the driver's and commander's periscopes, actuation of the control linkage operating the valve guard, air intake pipe and dust removal valve, the duplicating pneumatic stopping brake linkage and for disengaging the master clutch.

The one-man turret of the BMP-1 is identical to that installed on the BMD Airborne Combat Vehicle. The gunner has a single-piece hatch cover that opens forwards, in front of which on the left side is a dual-mode 1PN22M1 monocular periscopic sight. In the day mode it has a magnification of ×6 and a 15-degree field of view and in the image intensification mode it has a magnification of ×6.7 and a 6-degree field of view. Its maximum range at night is between 400 and 900 metres. Graticule lines coincide with the different ranges in the gunner's sight and the gunner also has a stadiametric rangefinder to determine range to the target based on a target height of 2.7 metres. The sight is heated and provided with a wiper arm. The gunner has an additional four observation periscopes and a white light or infra-red searchlight is mounted on the right side of the turret.

Main armament of the BMP-1 is a 73 mm model 2A28 smooth-bore, low-pressure, short-recoil gun which weighs 115 kg. This is fed from a 40-round magazine to the right rear of the gunner. After each round is fired the gun is returned to an elevation of +3 degrees 30 minutes for reloading. The weapon fires a fixed fin-stabilised HEAT or HE-FRAG round with an initial velocity of 440 metres a second which increases to 700 metres a second once the projectile has left the barrel and a rocket motor cuts in. The projectile is the same as that used in the SPG-9 infantry weapon and has a maximum effective range of 1300 metres. The HEAT projectile will penetrate 300 mm of armour at an incidence of 0 degrees. Firing from the halt, the BMP-1 has a 50 per cent chance of a first-round hit on a stationary M60A1 MBT at a range of 800 metres falling to 28 per cent at a range of 1300 metres. According to American reports the weapon is not effective in high winds. Maximum rate of fire is eight rounds a minute. The gun elevation and turret traverse mechanism is electric with mechanical controls for emergency use.

Mounted coaxially to the right of the main armament is a 7.62 mm PKT machine gun which is fed from a continuous belt of 2000 rounds honeycombed in an ammunition box mounted below the weapon. There is a turret ventilator system for extracting fumes.

Mounted over the main armament is a launcher for a Sagger wire-guided ATGW. One missile is carried in the ready to launch position with a further two missiles in the turret which are loaded via a loading rail through a hatch in the forward part of the turret roof. A further two missiles are carried in the hull. The controls for the Sagger are normally kept under the gunner's seat and when required are released by pulling a handle. The controls are then locked in position between the legs of the gunner who controls the missile by using the joystick in the conventional manner. The Sagger has a minimum range of 500 metres and a maximum range of 3000 metres. The Sagger can be used only in daylight and once launched a new missile cannot be loaded until the missile has hit the target. Missile loading time is about 50 seconds. It is possible on some vehicles to have a pintle-mounted Spigot AT-4 ATGW on the turret roof in place of the Sagger AT-3.

The troop compartment is at the rear with the eight infantrymen seated back-to-back four down each side of hull. They enter and leave by two doors in the rear of the hull, which have integral fuel tanks (60 litres in the left door and 70 litres in the right) and are hinged on the outside. Each door has a vision device and the left door has a firing port. More recently it has been reported that some vehicles have a power-operated ramp in the hull instead of two doors. Over the top of the hull are four roof hatches, two each side, which are hinged in the centre and can be locked vertical. There are four firing ports in each side of the hull and four heated periscopes in the roof each side for aiming. Each weapon station has a vacuum exhaust system attached to the weapon to remove fumes.

The forward firing port on each side is usually used for the 7.62 mm PKM machine gun and the remaining three either side for the AKMS 7.62 mm assault rifle. Each PKM weapon is provided with 950 rounds of ammunition and each AKMS with 120 rounds. In addition five rounds are carried for the single RPG-7 anti-tank grenade launcher carried in the vehicle and one BMP-1 in each platoon carries an SA-7 Grail

SAM, which is launched by one of the infantrymen standing up in the troop compartment with one hatch open.

The torsion bar suspension either side consists of six rubber-tyred road wheels with the drive sprocket at the front, idler at the rear and three track return rollers. The first and last road wheel stations have a hydraulic shock absorber and the top of the track has a light sheet steel cover, which is normally removed when operating in snow. The track links are of the double pin type with water scoops between the housings.

The BMP-1 is fully amphibious, being propelled in the water by its tracks. Before entering the water the trim vane, which is stowed on the glacis plate of the vehicle when not in use, is erected at the front of the hull, bilge pumps switched on and driver's centre periscope replaced by an extensible one to enable him to see ahead over the trim vane. When afloat and fully loaded, the vehicle is driven in third gear but when empty second gear is used.

If a nuclear explosion takes place, the protection system ensures automatic shutdown of the engine, closing of the engine louvres, stopping the ejector and valves of the turret and troop compartment fans, stopping the fans and supercharger, turning off the electric drive of the turret, and switching on the absorbent filter air delivery system. When the shock wave has passed the driver/mechanic turns on the supercharger, which provides decontaminated air at overpressure for the inhabited compartment of the BMP.

The overpressure system of the BMP consists of the NBC filter element and the blower/dust separator which is mounted in the roof to the rear of the commander's position. There is also a related scavenger system which removes gases from inside the vehicle when weapons are fired.

The blower/dust separator is similar to that used in the T-62 MBT and BTR-60PB/BTR-60PK APCs except that an extra set of fan blades has been added to force the air through

BMP-1 from rear with doors open (Michael Ledford)

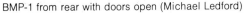

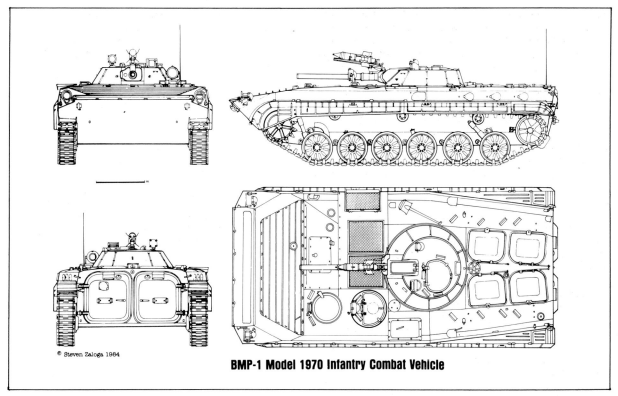

BMP-1 Model 1970 Infantry Combat Vehicle

© Steven Zaloga 1984

BMP-1 Model 1970 Infantry Combat Vehicle (Steven Zaloga)

the NBC filter. When the hatches are closed the blower/dust separator draws contaminated air into the system through an air intake immediately behind the turret. The contaminated air is then drawn through ducts around the turret ring to the blower/dust separator where fallout is separated from the air by the turning action of the propeller.

The air is then forced into a heating chamber (in cold weather) or, if necessary, directed through the NBC filter where the chemical and biological contaminants are removed. The air is then forced through the heating chamber and into the troop and driver's compartments through 11 outlet vents.

The forced air creates a build-up of air pressure inside the vehicle and so prevents NBC agents from leaking into the BMP through areas such as the firing ports which do not have air-tight seals. But if the scavenger system is used when the NBC system is in operation, the effectiveness of the overpressure is reduced.

Variants

Differences between production vehicles
The BMP first shown in Moscow in 1967 is referred to as the BMP Model 1966 and is believed to have been the pre-production vehicle; it was soon followed by the improved version, the BMP Model 1966, initial production batch. This had a curved shock absorber behind the first road wheel and the rear fender and swim vanes were modified by cutting down the number of swimming vanes from seven to four and raising the angle of the fender profile nearer to the horizontal. The fume extraction ports on the hull roof to the rear of the turret were moved outwards and were re-oriented to expel

toward the rear of the BMP. The single torsion bar used to spring the rear roof troop hatches was dropped in favour of a twin torsion bar system.

This was followed by the BMP Model 1966 standard production vehicle on which the two fender tool stowage boxes were removed. The BMP Model 1966 final production type had a modified port for the PKM section machine gun on the centre of the hull side.

In 1970 the BMP-1 Model 1970 was introduced, this was probably the main production variant and has a 200 mm extended nose to improve its amphibious characteristics. The triangular air intake to the turret rear was replaced by a circular telescopic snorkel which is raised when the vehicle is afloat. The roof hatches were also slightly rearranged, the air intake located to the front left of the driver was removed and the NBC sensor cover moved inwards closer to the turret. To the left of the turret is a new prominent NBC filter cover and the PKM port has been redesigned.

Some sources have also mentioned an improved BMP which could have a stabilised 73 mm gun, semi-automatic guidance for the Sagger ATGW, improved NBC system, more powerful engine, improved automatic loader and improved night vision devices.

Egyptian BMP-1s
It has been confirmed that from 1979 between 140 and 150 Egyptian Army BMP-1s were refitted with a French Poyaud 520 6L CS2 diesel engine developing 310 hp at 2800 rpm.

Modified BMP-1s
There have been consistent reports of a version of the BMP-1 with seven road wheels and a ramp at the hull rear in place of

Hungarian Army BMP-1 with Sagger AT-3 ATGW mounted over 73 mm gun

the two doors. It is also said that this model was supplied to Iran and Romania, Romania receiving its vehicles as early as 1977.

Some BMP-1s have been observed fitted with a bank of six smoke dischargers on the turret rear and enlarged side skirts. For use in Afghanistan a number of BMP-1s have had the 73 mm gun replaced by a 30 mm cannon as fitted to the new BMP-2, but these vehicles do not appear to have the AT-5 Spandrel ATGW system.

Also for use in Afghanistan some BMP-1s have been fitted with a 30 mm AGS-17 automatic grenade launcher on their turrets, as far as is known this is not aimed and loaded from within the turret.

Some BMPs used by the Soviet Army in Afghanistan have been fitted with appliqué 6 mm thick steel armour on the upper side of the hull and covering the upper track and return rollers. It is believed that this modification has been incorporated for protection against 12.7 mm rounds fired by DShKM heavy machine guns used by the guerrillas which can penetrate the 16/18 mm side armour of the BMP-1. The vehicle has an additional stowage box on the hull roof towards the rear. There is also a spike-type mount on the right side of the roof which is believed to be for the AT-4 Spigot ATGW man-portable missile launcher.

BMP-1 (Command)

A command version of the BMP-1 is known to exist. It has additional communications equipment, an additional radio aerial on the right rear of the hull, a redesigned troop compartment to incorporate tables and a mapboard and the firing ports on the right side of the hull have been either eliminated or welded up. This model is also known in the US Army as the BMP M1974 Command Vehicle. Other command vehicles include the BMP-1KSh (command and staff vehicle), previously called the BMP M1978 which mounts a larger telescopic antenna and more radio equipment than the BMP M1974 but is unarmed.

BMP-1 (Reconnaissance)

This is known as the BMP-R or the BMP M1976 Reconnais-

sance Vehicle and has the same hull as the BMP but is fitted with a larger two-man turret armed with a 73 mm gun to the rear of which are two roof hatches instead of four rectangular ones as in the case of the BMP. An improved version has also been fielded under the designation of BMP M1976/2 which has a parabolic antenna on the top rear of the turret.

BMP (Radar)

This model appeared in 1975 and has been observed attached to 152 mm M-1973 and 122 mm M-1974 self-propelled units and is believed to be used as an artillery fire adjustment and/or artillery/mortar locating vehicle, as these battalions already use the ACRV-2 Model 2 for the command post/ observation role. The front of the vehicle is identical to the BMP-1 but the vehicle has a new two-man turret which has two single-piece hatch covers that open forwards. They both have periscopes for observation plus a large optical device in front of the hatch. Armament consists of a 7.62 mm machine gun. Mounted on the rear of the turret is a radar with a flat antenna that folds forwards when not operating. To the rear of the turret on the left side is a further circular hatch cover and a telescopic antenna. The Small Fred radar operates in the J-band, with a detection range of 20 km and a tracking range of 7 km. This version is believed to have a crew of five. This model is known as the PRP-3 in the USSR or the BMP M1975 surveillance vehicle, by the US Army.

BMP-PPO Mobile Training Centre

The BMP-PPO (Podvizhniiy Punkt Obucheniya) mobile training centre is essentially a BMP with its turret removed and fitted with eight roof-mounted cupolas for trainees under instruction, plus seats for the vehicle commander and driver. The commander and driver sit at the front left of the vehicle with the eight trainees at the rear, three down either side and two down the centre. Each trainee has two TNPO-170 and one Type MK-4 observation devices mounted in the forward part of the cupola and an A-2 unit of the R-124 intercom set (used via the two-way radio). The instructor has a console with three cassette recorders, AGU-10-3 amplifier, three switches, external loudspeakers and a microphone. There is

BMP-1s with appliqué side armour with Hip-C tactical transport helicopters flying overhead

also an R-123m two-way radio, A-1 and A-2 units from the tank intercom R-124 and ten chest-mounted switches with cables.

For training each platoon would have two standard BMP-1s and one BMP-PPO, with the former being manned as normal practice. The instructor and one trainee take turns to send information while the remainder hear via loudspeakers.

Czechoslovak BMP-1 Armoured Recovery Vehicle

The Czechoslovak Army has fielded an armoured recovery version of the BMP-1 which has had its turret removed and a 1500 kg capacity hydraulically-driven rotating crane mounted on its rear deck. This is capable of changing the weapons and engines of the BMP and similar vehicles.

PRP-3 radar vehicle showing folded Small Fred radar at rear of turret and 7.62 mm PKT machine gun at front (US Army)

SPECIFICATIONS

CREW	3 + 8	TRANSMISSION	manual, 5 forward and 1	ARMOUR	
COMBAT WEIGHT	13 500 kg		reverse gears	Hull front upper	7 mm at 80°*
UNLOADED WEIGHT	12 500 kg	STEERING	clutch and brake	Hull front lower	19 mm at 57°
POWER-TO-WEIGHT		SUSPENSION	torsion bar	Hull side upper	16 mm at 14°
RATIO	22.22 hp/tonne	ELECTRICAL SYSTEM	24 V	Hull side lower	18 mm at 0°
GROUND PRESSURE	0.6 km/cm²	ARMAMENT		Hull rear upper	16 mm at 19°†
LENGTH	6.74 m	main	1 × 73 mm gun	Hull rear lower	16 mm at 19°†
WIDTH	2.94 m	coaxial	1 × 7.62 mm MG	Hull top	6 mm
HEIGHT		other	1 launcher rail for	Hull belly front	5 mm
(over searchlight)	2.15 m		Sagger ATGW	Hull belly rear	7 mm
GROUND CLEARANCE	0.39 m	SMOKE-LAYING		Turret front	23 mm at 42°
TRACK	2.75 m	EQUIPMENT	diesel fuel injected	Turret sides	19 mm at 36°
TRACK WIDTH	300 mm		into exhaust	Turret rear	13 mm at 30°
LENGTH OF TRACK		AMMUNITION		Turret top	6 mm
ON GROUND	3.53 m	main	40	Turret mantlet	26–33 mm
MAX SPEED		coaxial	2000		
road	80 km/h	other	4 + 1 Sagger		
water	6–8 km/h	FIRE-CONTROL SYSTEM			
FUEL CAPACITY	460 litres	Turret power control	electric/manual		
MAX RANGE	500 km	by commander	no		
FUEL CONSUMPTION	1 litre/km	by gunner	yes		
FORDING	amphibious	Gun elevation/depression	+33°/−4°		
GRADIENT	60%	Gun stabiliser		* Does not include wave deflector, does not represent	
SIDE SLOPE	30%	vertical	no	aluminium engine cover	
VERTICAL OBSTACLE	0.8 m	horizontal	no	† Does not include fuel or inner armour of door	
TRENCH	2.2 m				
ENGINE	Type 5D20 6-cylinder in-line water-cooled diesel developing 300 hp at 2000 rpm				

Status: In production. In service with Afghanistan, Algeria, Cuba, Czechoslovakia, Egypt, Ethiopia, Finland, East Germany, Hungary, India (possible licenced production), Iraq, Iran, Korea Democratic People's Republic (North), Libya, Mongolia, Poland, Syria, USSR and Yugoslavia.

Manufacturer: Czechoslovak and Soviet state arsenals.

Note: The Chinese build a similar version of the BMP-1 called the WZ 501, brief details of which are given under China.

BMD Airborne Combat Vehicle

Development

The BMD (Boevaya Mashina Desantnaya, or Airborne Combat Vehicle) entered service with Soviet airborne units in 1970 and was first seen in public during a parade held in Moscow in November 1973. The vehicle was called the M1970 before its Soviet designation became known. It spearheaded the Soviet invasion of Afghanistan in December 1979. It is issued to Soviet Airborne Rifle Divisions on the scale of 330 per division, three command versions at divisional headquarters and three airborne regiments with 109 BMDs each: 10 command vehicles, nine BMDs without turrets and 90 basic BMDs. It is airportable and can be dropped by parachute.

Description

The hull of the BMD is welded. The driver sits at the front of the vehicle in the centre just forward of the turret and has a single-piece hatch cover that opens to the right. Three periscopes are mounted forward of his hatch and the centre one can be replaced by an infra-red periscope for night driving. The vehicle commander sits to the left of the driver/mechanic and alongside the commander's seat is the radio and gyrocompass. The bow machine gunner sits to the driver's right and aims the two bow-mounted 7.62 mm PKT machine guns using a TNPP-220 periscopic sight to which the machine guns are connected by parallelogram drives. The two machine guns are mounted one either side of the vehicle's front firing forwards. A single semi-circular hatch cover is positioned either side of the forward part of the turret. There

BMD without Sagger AT-3 ATGW over 73 mm barrel but with AT-4 Spigot ATGW on right ride of turret, this can be dismounted for use in ground role

suspension combines a hydraulic system for altering the ground clearance and maintaining track tension with pneumatic springs, which enables the ground clearance to be altered from 100 to 450 mm.

The BMD is fully amphibious, being propelled in the water by two water jets at the rear of the hull. Before entering the water a trim vane which is stowed on the glacis plate when not in use is erected at the front of the hull. The vehicle has electric and manual bilge pumps, a gyro-compass, engine pre-heater, smoke-generating equipment, NBC system and a centralised ethylene-bromide fire-extinguishing system as fitted to other Soviet armoured vehicles.

The gunner is provided with a dual mode 1PN22M1 monocular periscopic sight mounted on the left side of the turret roof. In the day mode it has a magnification of ×6 and a 15-degree field of view while in the image intensification night mode it has a magnification of ×6.7 and a 6-degree field of view. Its maximum range at night is between 400 and 900 metres. Graticule lines coincide with the different ranges in the gunner's sight and he also has a stadiametric rangefinder to determine range to the target, based on a target height of 2.7 metres. The sight is heated and has a wiper arm. A white light searchlight is mounted on the right side of the turret although some vehicles have been observed with an infra-red searchlight at this position.

Main armament of the BMD is a 73 mm model 2A28 smooth-bore, low-pressure, short-recoil gun which weighs 115 kg. This is fed from an automatic 40-round magazine to the right rear of the gunner. After each round is fired the gun is returned to an elevation of 3 degrees 30 minutes for reloading. The weapon fires a fixed fin-stabilised HEAT or HE-FRAG round (some reports have said that only one of these rounds is used in BMD) with an initial muzzle velocity of 400 metres per second, which increases to 665 metres per second once the projectile has left the barrel and a rocket motor cuts in. The projectile is the same as that used in the SPG-9

is a single fixed forward-looking periscope to the left and slightly to the rear of the left turntable-mounted periscope.

The turret is similar to the one fitted to the BMP MICV and has a single-piece forward-opening hatch cover to the left of the turret. The gunner has four periscopes, one mounted to each side and two forward of the hatch.

The personnel compartment at the rear of the vehicle has a concertina type cover that opens towards the front. The only means of entry and exit to this compartment is via this hatch. In here are seated the senior gunner, grenade launcher and his assistant, with a roof-mounted TNPO-170 periscope for observation.

The independent suspension consists of five small road wheels with the idler at the front and the drive sprocket at the rear. There are four track return rollers. The independent

BMD airborne combat vehicle with Sagger ATGW over 73 mm gun

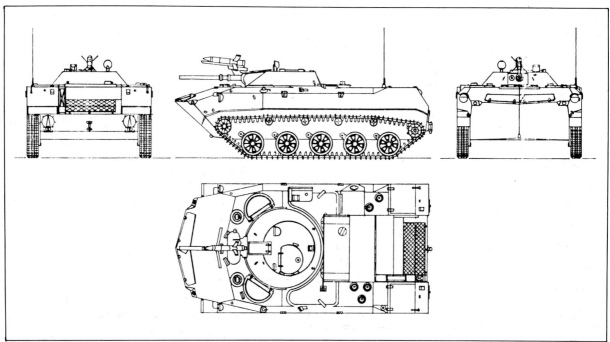

Late production BMD airborne combat vehicles on parade in Red Square Moscow (TASS)

infantry weapon and has a maximum effective range of 1300 metres. According to a number of reports the weapon is not accurate in high wind.

The gun elevation and traverse mechanism is electric with mechanical controls for emergency use.

A 7.62 mm PKT machine gun is mounted coaxially to the right of the main armament and is fed from a continuous belt of 2000 rounds honeycombed in an ammunition box mounted below the weapon. A cartridge case and link collector are mounted in the turret basket. A ventilator system is provided in the turret to extract fumes.

Mounted over the main armament is a launcher rail for a Sagger ATGW. Two missiles are carried inside the turret and are loaded via a loading rail through a hatch in the forward part of the turret roof. The controls for the Sagger are normally kept under the gunner's seat and when required for the Sagger are released by pulling a handle. The controls are then locked in position between the legs of the gunner who controls the missile by using the joystick in the conventional manner. The Sagger has a minimum range of 500 metres and a maximum range of 3000 metres.

Soviet BMD airborne infantry combat vehicles are reported to be equipped with a radio 'beeper' device that allows its crew, who are equipped with direction-finding equipment, to locate their own individual BMD when they are parachuted onto the drop zone.

Variants

Late production BMDs

More recent production versions of the BMD have a ribbed glacis plate, different road wheels with small holes, the earlier versions being spoked, and slightly different vehicle lighting equipment. During the 1983 Moscow parade a BMD was seen without the Sagger ATGW over the 73 mm gun, although the launcher mount was retained, with a man-portable AT-4 Spigot ATGW mounted on the right side of the turret roof.

The BMD M1981/1 is armed with the same 30 mm cannon as the BMP-2, with nine of these issued to each airborne regiment.

SPECIFICATIONS	
CREW	7
COMBAT WEIGHT	6700 kg
POWER-TO-WEIGHT	
RATIO	35.82 hp/tonne
GROUND PRESSURE	0.61 kg/cm²
LENGTH	5.4 m
WIDTH	2.63 m
HEIGHT	1.62–1.97 m
GROUND CLEARANCE	0.1–0.45 m
TRACK WIDTH	230 mm
LENGTH OF TRACK	
ON GROUND	2.84 m
MAX SPEED	
road	70 km/h
water	10 km/h
FUEL CAPACITY	300 litres
RANGE	320 km
FORDING	amphibious
GRADIENT	60%
VERTICAL OBSTACLE	0.8 m
TRENCH	1.6 m
ENGINE	Type 5D-20 V-6 liquid-cooled diesel developing 240 hp
TRANSMISSION	manual, 5 forward and 1 reverse gears
SUSPENSION	hydro-pneumatic
ELECTRICAL SYSTEM	24 V
ARMAMENT	
main	1 × 73 mm gun
coaxial	1 × 7.62 mm MG
forward firing	2 single 7.62 mm MGs
other	1 launcher rail for Sagger ATGW (or roof-mounted AT-4 Spigot on turret)
AMMUNITION	
main	40
coaxial	2000
Sagger	3
FIRE-CONTROL SYSTEM	
Turret power control	electrical and mechanical
by gunner	yes
Gun elevation/depression	+33°/−4°
Gun stabiliser	
vertical	no
horizontal	no
ARMOUR	
Hull (max)	15 mm
Turret (max)	23 mm

82 mm Mortar Carrier

According to some sources the Soviets have fitted an 82 mm mortar in the rear troop compartment of the BMD for use in Afghanistan. It would be more logical to remove the existing turret and mount the 82 mm mortar in this position rather than in the very small troop compartment at the hull rear.

BMD M1979 Series
This has a longer chassis with six instead of five road wheels, five return rollers and no turret. The BMD M1979/1 is an armoured personnel carrier with firing ports and two bow-mounted 7.62 mm PKT machine guns and is usually used to carry two AGS-17 automatic 30 mm grenade launchers with their crews. The BMD M1979/3 command vehicle has a similar hull but no provision for bow-mounted machine guns and no turret. It carries a collapsible Cloths Rail HR antenna and other communications equipment. During the Soviet invasion of Afghanistan some BMDs were used to tow artillery such as the 23 mm ZU-23 anti-aircraft gun.

Status: In production. In service only with Soviet Union.

Manufacturer: Soviet state arsenals.

BTR-50P Armoured Personnel Carrier

Development
The BTR-50P was seen in public for the first time during the 1957 November parade in Moscow. For many years the BTR-50P was the standard APC of the Motor Rifle Regiments of Soviet Tank Divisions and was issued on the scale of 91 (one at headquarters and three battalions each with 30 vehicles) per regiment, but the BTR-50P has now been replaced in most front-line units by the BMP-1 MICV.

The Czechoslovaks have developed a much improved version of the BTR-50P under the designation OT-62, which has its own entry.

Description
The BTR-50P is based on the chassis of the PT-76 light amphibious tank with a new superstructure added to the front of the vehicle. The hull of the BTR-50P is made of all-welded steel with the crew compartment at the front, open-topped troop compartment in the centre and the engine compartment at the rear.

The commander sits in a projecting bay at the front of the hull on the left side, which has three vision devices and a single-piece hatch cover that opens to the front. The driver sits to the right of the commander in the centre and has a single-piece hatch cover immediately in front of him which opens upwards on the outside and has a single vision device. A further three vision devices are mounted in the front of the hull below his hatch cover. There is a vision block mounted in the front of the hull to the right of the driver, over the top of which is a white light or infra-red searchlight which can be operated from inside the vehicle. A single infra-red driving light is normally mounted on the glacis plate.

The 20 infantrymen sit on bench seats which run across the full width of the vehicle and enter and leave by climbing over the side of the hull. Armament consists of a pintle-mounted 7.62 mm SGMB machine gun which has an elevation of +23.5 degrees, a depression of −6 degrees and a total traverse of 90 degrees.

When the BTR-50P was originally introduced there were ramps at the rear of the hull to enable a 57 mm anti-tank gun M1943 (ZIS-2), 76 mm divisional gun M1943 (ZIS-3) or an 85 mm division gun D-44 to be carried and fired from the rear decking. The weapon could also be fired when the vehicle was afloat, but only when the water jets were in operation.

The engine used in the BTR-50P is one half of that fitted to the T-54 MBT. As the vehicle operates in a very cold climate an engine pre-heater is fitted as standard. The power train consists of the engine, master clutch, transmission, steering clutch, inner reduction gear, final drives, water jet propeller and mechanical water drainage pump drive. Power is transmitted through the transmission to the left and right inner reduction gears to the final drives which are connected directly to the track drive sprockets. The vehicle has three fuel tanks, two in the right forward side of the engine compartment and one at the rear. A centralised fire-extinguishing system is provided for the engine compartment: once the sensors have detected a fire, the bottle operates, the engine is switched off, forced blowers are switched on, and, if required, the second extinguisher also operates.

The torsion bar suspension consists of six rubber-tyred road wheels with the drive sprocket at the rear and the idler at

BTR-50PK from rear fitted with additional fuel tanks on rear decking (Egyptian Army)

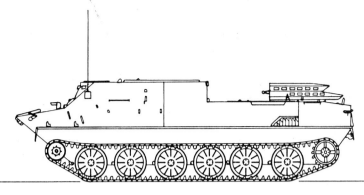

BTR-50P APC complete with ramps on rear decking

the front. There are no track return rollers. The first and last road wheel stations have a hydraulic shock absorber and the steel tracks each have 96 links when new.

The BTR-50P is fully amphibious and propelled in the water by two water jets at the rear of the hull. The only preparation required before entering the water is to erect the trim vane at the front of the hull and switch on the two electric bilge pumps. There is a manual bilge pump for emergency use. Steering is accomplished by opening and closing the two doors over the rear water jets: to go left the left water jet is covered and to turn through 180 degrees the left water jet sucks in water and the right water jet pushes it out. The basic BTR-50P has no NBC system.

During exercises held in Egypt in 1981/82, United States Army troops used BTR-50PK APCs in extensive swimming operations, but found that the vehicle had a number of drawbacks. The engine could only be run at full power while swimming for eight minutes, due to cooling limitations. The use of reverse thrust steering with the BTR-50PK's water jet propulsion system meant that although it had a high water speed it was uncontrollable in a current faster than around 8 km/h. The engine had to be reduced to idle when track drive was engaged or disengaged, making entering or leaving water difficult, especially in a current. In conclusion, the US Army felt that the BTR-50PK was only slightly superior in its amphibious capabilities to the M113A1. In addition the Soviet vehicle was noisy and threw up large clouds of dust when it moved.

Variants

BTR-50PA

This model is almost identical to the BTR-50P but does not have the loading ramps at the rear of the hull and is sometimes armed with a 14.5 mm KPVT heavy machine gun mounted over the commander's position.

BTR-50PK

This model has full overhead armour protection and NBC system with the troops entering and leaving the vehicle by two rectangular roof hatches that open either side. In each side of the hull there are two firing ports and in the roof at the front of the hull a single-piece hatch cover that opens forwards. Two ventilators are fitted, one at the front of the troop compartment on the right side and one at the rear of the troop compartment on the right side. The BTR-50PK is normally armed with a 7.62 mm SGMB machine gun in an unprotected mount.

BTR-50PU (Command)

There are at least two models of the BTR-50PU (Command), designated the models 1 and 2. The model 1 (early model very rarely seen today) has one projecting bay whereas the model 2 has two and is similar in appearance to the Czechoslovak OT-62A APC but the Soviet vehicles have a distinct chamfer between the top and the sides of their hulls. The right bay on the model 2 has three vision devices and no cover.

Behind the driver is a single-piece hatch cover fitted with a periscope, to the rear of which are two oval roof hatches that are hinged in the centre and can be locked vertical.

The BTR-50PU (command) has additional communications equipment, mapboards, table and a navigation system that includes a co-ordinate indicator and a map course plot-

BTR-50PK with trim vane erected and roof hatches open. This model has two circular firing ports in troop compartment (Israeli Ministry of Defence)

Finnish Army BTR-50PK with driver's hatch open and fitted with windscreen and wiper (Finnish Army)

MTP technical support vehicle with its higher roof

SPECIFICATIONS (BTR-50PK)	
CREW	2 + 20
COMBAT WEIGHT	14 200 kg
POWER-TO-WEIGHT	
RATIO	16.9 hp/tonne
GROUND PRESSURE	0.51 kg/cm²
LENGTH	7.08 m
WIDTH	3.14 m
HEIGHT (to hull top)	1.97 m
GROUND CLEARANCE	0.37 m
TRACK	2.74 m
TRACK WIDTH	360 mm
LENGTH OF TRACK	
ON GROUND	4.08 m
MAX SPEED	
road	44 km/h
water	11 km/h
FUEL CAPACITY	400 litres
MAX RANGE	400 km
FUEL CONSUMPTION	1 litre/km
FORDING	amphibious
GRADIENT	70%
SIDE SLOPE	40%
VERTICAL OBSTACLE	1.1 m
TRENCH	2.8 m
ENGINE	model V-6 6-cylinder in-line water-cooled diesel developing 240 hp at 1800 rpm
TRANSMISSION	manual with 5 forward and 1 reverse gears
STEERING	clutch and brake
SUSPENSION	torsion bar
ELECTRICAL SYSTEM	24 V
ARMAMENT	1 × 7.62 mm MG
AMMUNITION	1250
FIRE-CONTROL SYSTEM	
Gun traverse	manual
Gun elevation/depression	+23.5°/−6°
Gun traverse (total)	90°
ARMOUR	
Hull front upper	8 mm at 83°
Hull front lower	10 mm at 53°
Hull sides upper	10 mm at 0°
Hull sides lower	9 mm at 0°
Hull rear upper	7 mm at 0°
Hull rear lower	6 mm at 42°
Hull top	7 mm at 86°
Hull belly front	6 mm
Hull belly rear	6 mm

ter. Externally the vehicle has four or five radio aerials, additional stowage boxes and an auxiliary generator mounted on the rear decking.

MTP Technical Support Vehicle

This is based on a BTR-50PK APC and is used for recovery and repair of armoured personnel carriers and the BMP MICV. In addition it is used to deliver POL supplies to forward units which are difficult to reach with normal truck-mounted bowsers. A distinctive feature of the MTP is the raised workshop compartment which is high enough to allow the crew to work while standing as well as providing sleeping room for the crew of three.

MTK Mine-clearing Vehicle

This is a BTR-50PK APC with a special launcher mounted on top of the hull to the rear of the troop compartment. It fires rockets to which are attached flexible tubes containing high explosives which fall to the ground on to the minefield and are then detonated from the vehicle.

Status: Production complete. In service with Afghanistan, Albania, Algeria, Angola (and OT-62), Bulgaria (and OT-62), Congo, Cyprus, Czechoslovakia (OT-62 only), Egypt (and OT-62), Finland, East Germany, India (and OT-62), Iran, Iraq (and OT-62), Israel (and OT-62), Korea, Democratic People's Republic (North), Libya (and OT-62), Morocco (OT-62 only), Poland (OT-62 only), Romania, Somalia, Sudan (and OT-62), Syria, USSR, Viet-Nam and Yugoslavia.

Manufacturer: Soviet state arsenals.

Note: The Chinese build a similar version of the BTR-50PK called the Type 77; details are give under China.

MT-LB Multi-purpose Tracked Vehicle

Development

The MT-LB was developed in the late 1960s as the replacement for the older AT-P armoured tracked artillery tractor and was initially known as the M-1970 multi-purpose tracked vehicle until its correct Soviet designation became known. It is based on the MT-L unarmoured tracked amphibious carrier.

Typical roles of the MT-LB include use as an artillery prime mover towing 100 mm anti-tank guns and 122 mm howitzers, command and radio vehicle (which usually has at least two whip antennas on the roof), artillery fire-control vehicle and cargo carrier. It is also widely used as an armoured personnel carrier, especially in difficult terrain such as snow or swamp.

Description

The hull of the MT-LB is all-welded steel with the crew compartment at the front, engine immediately behind the crew compartment on the left side and the troop compartment at the rear of the hull.

The driver sits at the front of the hull on the left side and has a single-piece hatch cover, in front of which are three periscopes. The commander sits to the right of the driver in the centre and has a single-piece rear-opening hatch cover and two periscopes. In action, the commander also mans the turret. The machine gun turret is mounted to the right of the commander's position and is armed with a 7.62 mm PKT machine gun. Like the turrets fitted to the BRDM-2 (4 × 4) and BTR-60PB (8 × 8) vehicle, it does not have a hatch cover.

Both the driver and machine gunner have a windscreen in

Yugoslav Army MT-LB with Big Fred artillery/mortar-locating radar mounted at rear. When travelling antenna is folded forward on top of vehicle

front of their positions which when in action is covered by a flap hinged at the top. There is a vision block in each side of the hull, to the left of the driver's and the right of the machine gunner's position.

An aisle provides access from the crew compartment at the front of the vehicle to the personnel compartment at the rear which has inward-facing folding canvas seats for the 11 infantrymen. Two hatches over the top of the troop compartment open forwards. The infantry enter and leave the vehicle by two doors in the rear of the hull, both of which are provided with a firing port. There is an additional firing port and vision block in each side of the troop compartment. An unditching beam is often carried on the roof or side of the vehicle.

The torsion bar suspension consists of six road wheels with the drive sprocket at the front and the idler at the rear with hydraulic shock absorbers on swing arms on the first and last road wheel stations. There are no track return rollers as the top of the track rests on the top of the road wheels. The first and last road wheel stations either side have a hydraulic shock absorber.

The MT-LB is fully amphibious being propelled in the water by its tracks. Before entering the water a trim vane is erected at the front of the vehicle and the bilge pumps, which have a capacity of 450 litres a minute, switched on. Standard equipment on all vehicles includes an NBC system. The MT-LB has air-actuated brakes which can be connected to a trailer. Night vision equipment includes an OU-3GK white/infra-red searchlight with a range of 400 metres for the commander and a TVN-2 infra-red periscope for the driver with a range of 40 metres.

Variants

MT-LBV
The MT-LB can also be fitted with 565 mm wide tracks for operation in snow and swampy ground; it is then called the MT-LBV.

MT-LBU (Command)
This is the command version of the MT-LB and has additional radios, generator, land navigation system and a canvas cover that can be extended to the rear when the vehicle is being used in the static role.

MT-SON
This is the MT-LB fitted with the Pork Trough fire-control radar system mounted on the roof.

MT-LB with Big Fred Radar
In 1981 it was revealed that the Yugoslav Army had acquired a number of MT-LBs from the Soviet Union fitted with a new artillery/mortar-locating radar which has been allocated the NATO reporting name of Big Fred. It is not known if the Big Fred radar was originally thought to be the older Pork Trough radar and it is possible that the MT-LB with Big Fred and MT-SON are the same vehicle.

When travelling the antenna folds forward onto the top of the large turret which is to the rear of the vehicle. The forward turret-mounted 7.62 mm machine gun is retained. The radar is believed to be of a similar type to the British EMI Cymbeline in that the radar measures the slant range and bearing of two points in the mortar bomb/artillery shell trajectory. The time taken for the bomb/projectile to travel between the two points is also measured and the on-board computer uses this information together with the pre-set elevation angles to determine the position of the enemy mortar or artillery piece. This information is then relayed to the field artillery units and the target is engaged. Unconfirmed reports have indicated that the Soviet designation for this vehicle is the TT-LB. The radar has a range of about 20 km. Specifications of the MT-LB with Big Fred are similar to those of the basic MT-LB except for a weight of 11 500 kg, height with antenna down of 2.9 metres and a crew of four to six.

MTP-LB Repair Vehicle
The MTP-LB is designed for field maintenance, repair, and recovery of tanks and other AFVs and is recognisable by its lack of a machine gun turret.

MT-LB multi-purpose tracked vehicle

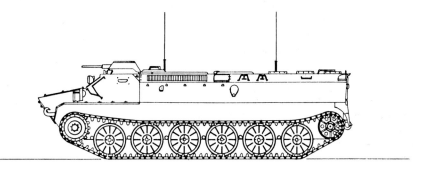

MT-LB used by US Army for training. Turret is traversed right but not fitted with 7.62 mm machine gun (Donald C Spaulding)

Mounted at the front of the vehicle is an A-frame which can lift a maximum load of 1500 kg. Standard equipment includes tools, gas welding and cutting equipment, cable winch with 85 metres of cable and a capacity of 6700 kg, jacking device, towing attachment hooks and a crane.

MT-LB (Ambulance)

This is an MT-LB used as an armoured evacuation vehicle (armoured ambulance) with stretchers fitted in the rear compartment.

MT-LB Engineer Vehicle

This is similar in appearance to the basic MT-LB but mod-ified to mount a plough blade on the roof. Hydraulic devices at the rear of the vehicle allow manual mounting of the plough blade to the rear only. The United States has a number of these vehicles at Fort Irwin, California. East Germany also has its own engineer vehicle. This is the basic MT-LB with a rectangular box on the rear deck for carrying engineer equipment. The vehicle retains its cupola-mounted 7.62 mm machine gun.

SA-13 SAM system

The SA-13 surface-to-air missile system is based on the chassis of the MT-LB multi-purpose tracked vehicle.

SPECIFICATIONS

CREW	2 + 11	VERTICAL OBSTACLE	0.7 m
COMBAT WEIGHT	11 900 kg	TRENCH	2.7 m
UNLOADED WEIGHT	9700 kg	ENGINE	YaMZ 238 V,
MAX PAYLOAD	2000 kg		V-8 cylinder diesel
MAX TOWED LOAD	6500 kg		developing 240 hp
POWER-TO-WEIGHT			at 2100 rpm
RATIO	20.16 hp/tonne	TRANSMISSION	manual with 6 forward
GROUND PRESSURE	0.46 kg/cm²*		and 1 reverse gears
LENGTH	6.454 m	STEERING	clutch and brake
WIDTH	2.85 m	SUSPENSION	torsion bar
HEIGHT (to turret top)	1.865 m	ELECTRICAL SYSTEM	24 V
GROUND CLEARANCE	0.4 m	ARMAMENT	1 × 7.62 mm MG
TRACK WIDTH	350 mm*	AMMUNITION	2500
LENGTH OF TRACK ON		TURRET TRAVERSE	manual, 360°
GROUND	3.8 m	GUN ELEVATION/	
MAX SPEED		DEPRESSION	+30°/−5°
road	61.5 km/h	ARMOUR	7–14 mm
water	5–6 km/h		(estimated)
FUEL CAPACITY	450 litres		
MAX RANGE	500 km		
FUEL CONSUMPTION	0.9–1.2 litres/km		
FORDING	amphibious		
GRADIENT	60%	*The MT-LB can also be fitted with 565 mm wide tracks	
SIDE SLOPE	30%	which reduce ground pressure to 0.27 or 0.28 km/cm²	

Status: In production. In service with Bulgaria, East Germany, Hungary, Poland, USSR and Yugoslavia.

Manufacturer: Soviet state arsenals.

BTR-80 Armoured Personnel Carrier

It is believed that the Soviets have built prototypes of a new 6 × 6 armoured vehicle which has been called the BTR-80 by the US Army, although the Soviet designations are believed to be BTR-72 and BTR-74. One of these may be a replacement for the BRDM-2 and has a turret armed with the same 30 mm cannon as the BMP-2 while the other version may be the armoured personnel carrier and be armed with at least a 14.5 mm KPV machine gun, or a slightly heavier weapon.

Status: In production. In service with USSR.

Manufacturer: Soviet state arsenals, probably same as BTR-70.

BTR-70 (8 × 8) APC from rear showing external stowage and water jet outlet covered by flap

BTR-70 Armoured Personnel Carrier

Development

The BTR-70 (8 × 8) amphibious armoured personnel carrier was shown in public for the first time during the November 1980 parade in Moscow. The East Germans call the BTR-70 the SPW-70, the US Army called it the BTR M1978 for a short period.

It is believed to have been designed by the Dedkov design bureau at Gorki which also developed the BRDM-1, BRDM-2 and BTR-60 wheeled armoured vehicles.

According to the 1984 edition of *Soviet Military Power*, the earlier BTR-60P series remained in production for export while production of the BTR-70 was completed in 1982.

Description

The hull of the BTR-70 is of all-welded steel construction

with improved protection over its frontal arc compared to the original BTR-60 series, the nose is also wider and the front of the vehicle provides added protection to the front wheels.

The commander sits at the front of the hull on the right with the driver to his left. The commander has a single-piece hatch cover that opens to the front, the driver has a single-piece hatch cover that opens at a 45-degree angle towards the centre of the vehicle. Both the commander and driver have a window to their front which is covered in combat by an armoured hatch cover hinged at the top. Each also has three forward and one side-facing periscopes, with a single firing port under the last. To the rear of the commander and driver are two infantry facing the front.

Over the second axle is the turret, with a 14.5 mm and a 7.62 mm machine gun, this turret is identical to that fitted to the BTR-60PB (8 × 8) armoured personnel carrier and the BRDM-2 (4 × 4) armoured car.

The troop compartment is to the rear of the turret with three firing ports and one vision block in each side of the hull.

Standard production version of BTR-70 (8 × 8) armoured personnel carrier (Steven Zaloga)

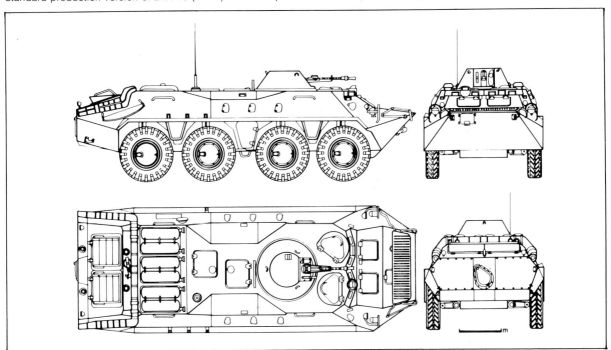

BTR-70 (8 × 8) APC from front with trim van folded back onto glacis plate

Over the top of the troop compartment are two square roof hatches each with a circular firing port, opening to the front and rear respectively. Between the second and third axles is a small door. The six infantrymen sit on a bench seat down the centre, back to back, so enabling them to use the firing ports.

The engine compartment is at the rear of the hull and is fitted with a fire-extinguishing system. The air inlets are in the top of the engine compartment and the air outlets at the rear. The exhaust pipes run from the top of the engine compartment down either side towards the rear. The original two GAZ-49B six-cylinder in-line water-cooled petrol engines have been replaced by two ZMZ-4905 petrol engines developing 115 hp each compared to the 90 hp each of the BTR-60.

Steering is power-assisted on the front two axles, early models of the BTR-70 had the same wheels and tyres as the BTR-60 series. Standard equipment includes an NBC system, central tyre-pressure regulation system and a front-mounted winch.

The BTR-70 is fully amphibious and propelled in the water by a single water jet at the rear of the hull. On the BTR-60 this had a two-part cover but on the BTR-70 a one-part cover is fitted, hinged at the top left. Before entering the water the trim vane is erected at the front of the hull. When travelling this is stowed on top of the hull front whereas on the BTR-60 series it is under the nose of the vehicle.

Variants

BTR-70 with AGS-17
A number of BTR-70s have been seen in Afghanistan fitted with the 30 mm AGS-17 automatic grenade launcher on the roof to the rear of the driver and commander. These vehicles retain the machine gun turret.

BTR-70MS
This is a turretless communications vehicle with the MS standing for Mashina Svyazi (signals vehicle).

SPECIFICATIONS	
CREW	2 + 9
CONFIGURATION	8 × 8
COMBAT WEIGHT	11 500 kg
POWER-TO-WEIGHT	
RATIO	20 hp/tonne
LENGTH	7.85 m
WIDTH	2.8 m
HEIGHT	2.45 m
WHEELBASE	4.8 m
MAX SPEED	
road	80 km/h
water	10 km/h
FUEL CAPACITY	350 litres
	(estimated)
MAX RANGE	600 km
FORDING	amphibious
GRADIENT	60%
VERTICAL OBSTACLE	0.5 m
TRENCH	2 m
ENGINES	2 × ZMZ-4905 6-cylinder
	petrol developing 115 hp
	each
TRANSMISSION	manual with 4 forward and 1
	reverse gears
TRANSFER CASE	2-speed
STEERING	power-assisted
SUSPENSION	torsion bar with hydraulic
	shock absorbers
ELECTRICAL SYSTEM	12 V
ARMAMENT	
main	1 × 14.5 mm MG
coaxial	1 × 7.62 mm MG
AMMUNITION	
main	500
coaxial	2000
FIRE-CONTROL SYSTEM	
Turret power control	manual
Gun elevation/depression	+30°/−5°
Turret traverse	360°

BTR-70KShM
This is a command/staff vehicle with the KShM standing for Komandno-Shtabnaya Maschina.

BREM
This is a turretless BTR-70 fitted with a bow-mounted jib crane and other equipment, BREM stands for Bronirovan-naya Remontno – Evakuatsionannaya Maschina – armoured repair and recovery vehicle.

Status: Production probably complete. Known to be in service with East Germany and the USSR. Possible licenced production in Romania as the TAB-77.

Manufacturer: Gorki Automobile Plant, Gorki, USSR.

BTR-60P Armoured Personnel Carrier

Development

The BTR-60P (8 × 8) amphibious APC was developed in the late 1950s as the replacement for the older and non-amphibious BTR-152 (6 × 6) APC. The vehicle was seen in public for the first time during the 1961 November parade in Moscow. The BTR-60P and its variants are normally used by the Motorised Rifle Divisions, whereas the Tank Divisions have the tracked BMP-1 MICV. In recent years a number of Motorised Rifle Divisions have had their BTR-60Ps replaced by the better armed BMP-1 MICVs. It is also used by Soviet Naval Infantry as its standard APC.

The BTR-60P APC is not used by Czechoslovakia or Poland as both use the Czechoslovak OT-64 (8 × 8) amphibious APC which has a number of advantages over the Soviet vehicle.

A small number of BTR-60PB (8 × 8) armoured personnel carriers were encountered by the US forces during the invasion of Grenada in 1983.

Description

The hull of the BTR-60P is all welded with the driver and commander seated at the front of the hull, open-topped personnel compartment behind them and the engine compartment at the very rear of the hull. The interior of the BTR-60P is open from the driver's and commander's position right through to the engine compartment at the rear.

The driver sits on the left with the vehicle commander to his right. Both have a windscreen to their front which, when in action, is covered by a flap hinged at the top. This has an integral vision device which can be replaced by an infra-red periscope for night vision. To the left of the driver and the right of the commander is a vision block. Mounted above the flap in front of the commander is an infra-red searchlight which can be operated from inside the vehicle.

The infantrymen are seated on bench seats that run across the full width of the hull. In each side of the hull are two half doors and three firing ports. If required bows and a tarpaulin cover can be fitted over the top of the troop compartment.

Main armament comprises a 7.62 mm SGMB or PKB machine gun which is pintle-mounted on the forward part of the hull. Some vehicles have been seen with the heavier 12.7 mm DShKM machine gun at this position. Mounts are also provided for 7.62 mm machine guns on either side of the hull.

The two engines are mounted at the rear of the hull: the first and third axles are powered through the transmission of the right engine and the second and fourth axles through the transmission of the left engine. Torque is transmitted from each engine to the wheels through a single-plate clutch with hydraulic control, a four-speed gear box with synchromesh in third and fourth gears, a two-speed transfer case, the final drives of the two driving axles with gearless differentials and four wheel reducers. Torque from the final drives to the wheel reducers is transmitted through half-axles and gimbal drive gears.

All eight wheels are powered and the first four, which are used for steering, are power assisted. The vehicle can be driven with one wheel missing from the second axle. The suspension is of the torsion bar type with the first and second road wheels on each side being provided with two hydraulic

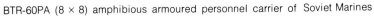

BTR-60PA (8 × 8) amphibious armoured personnel carrier of Soviet Marines

BTR-60PB (8 × 8) APC with driver's windscreen cover open and trim vane folded back under nose of vehicle

BTR-60PB (8 × 8) APC from rear with side door open and covers over water jet closed (via David Isby)

shock absorbers and the third and fourth road wheels with a single hydraulic shock absorber. A central tyre-pressure regulation system fitted as standard on all BTR-60 series APCs enables the driver to adjust the tyre pressure to suit the ground being crossed.

The BTR-60P is fully amphibious, being propelled in the water by a single water jet mounted at the rear of the hull. When not in use the exit at the rear of the hull is covered by a two-part circular plate. Before entering the water a trim vane is erected at the front of the hull, and the bilge pump is switched on. When not in use the trim vane is stowed flat

under the nose of the vehicle. Power is transmitted to the water jet via a PTO and water jet reducer. Direction is changed when afloat by using a hydrodynamic rudder in the hull of the water jet propeller and by turning the front four road wheels. To reverse direction, the shutters of the water jets are closed and water is ejected through side ducts in the rear part of the vehicle that face forwards.

The basic BTR-60P has no NBC system as it has an open top. All vehicles are fitted with infra-red night vision equipment and a front-mounted winch with a maximum capacity of 4500 kg.

Variants

BTR-60PA

This model, which entered service in 1961, has complete overhead armour protection for the troop compartment and is fitted with an NBC system. The commander's and driver's positions are identical to those on the original BTR-60P except that the driver has a roof-mounted periscope and both have a single-piece hatch cover that opens to the rear.

Behind the commander's and driver's hatches is a single rear-opening rectangular hatch, in front of which is a single pintle-mounted 7.62 mm SGMB or PKB machine gun. Many vehicles also have a 7.62 mm machine gun mounted either side of this hatch cover. There is another hatch cover in the roof of the personnel compartment towards the rear on the right side, which opens to the right.

Three firing ports are provided in each side of the hull but no entry doors. The infantrymen are seated on bench seats along the side and rear of the troop compartment.

BTR-60PB

The BTR-60PB is essentially the BTR-60PA fitted with a machine gun turret and other modifications. In place of the vision blocks in the hatches immediately in front of the commander and driver, there are a number of roof-mounted periscopes that give observation to the front and sides of the vehicle.

The turret, which is identical to that fitted to the Soviet BRDM-2 (4 × 4) reconnaissance vehicle and the Czechoslovak OT-64 (8 × 8) model C APC, is armed with a 14.5 mm KPV machine gun and a 7.62 mm PKT machine gun mounted coaxially to the right with the telescopic sight mounted coaxially to the left. The weapons have an elevation of +30 degrees, a depression of −5 degrees and the turret can be traversed through a full 360 degrees. Gun elevation and depression and turret traverse are all manual.

To the rear of the turret on the right side is a single-piece

BTR-60PB (8 × 8) amphibious armoured personnel carrier

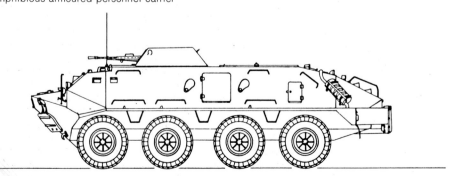

hatch cover that opens to the left and to the left rear of this is a single-piece hatch cover that opens to the right.

In either side of the hull are a single door that opens forwards, two or three firing ports and vision blocks.

There is also a version of the BTR-60PB used as an artillery command and observation post vehicle by the East German Army.

BTR-60PU Command Vehicle
This is essentially the BTR-60P fitted with bows and a tarpaulin cover and internally with seats for the command staff, mapboards and additional communications equipment. A command version of the BTR-60PA is also in service with a roof-mounted generator, ten-metre high radio antenna, which is used in the static role and a rail antenna running along the front, left side and rear of the hull. A similar model is also in service based on the BTR-60PA.

BTR-60PB Forward Air Control Vehicle
This is essentially the BTR-60PB with the armament removed from the turret and the resulting port covered by a plexiglass observation window. To provide power for the additional communications equipment carried a generator is mounted externally on the top of the hull at the rear.

SPECIFICATIONS (Data in square brackets relates to BTR-60PB where this differs from the basic BTR-60PA)

CREW	2 + 16* [2 + 14†]	SIDE SLOPE	40%	FIRE-CONTROL SYSTEM	
CONFIGURATION	8 × 8	VERTICAL OBSTACLE	0.4 m	Turret power control	n/app [manual]
COMBAT WEIGHT	9980 [10 300] kg	TRENCH	2 m	Gun elevation/depression	+23.5°/−6° [+30°/−5°]
POWER-TO-WEIGHT		ENGINES	2 GAZ-49B 6-cylinder in-line	Gun traverse	90° [360° (turret)]
RATIO	18.03 [17.47] hp/tonne		water-cooled petrol	ARMOUR	
LENGTH	7.56 m		developing 90 hp at	Hull front upper	7 mm at 86°
WIDTH	2.825 m		3400 rpm (each)	Hull front lower	9 mm at 47°
HEIGHT		TRANSMISSION	manual with 4 forward and 1	Hull side upper	7 mm at 35°
to turret top	n/app [2.31 m]		reverse gears	Hull side lower	7 mm at 0°
to hull top	2.055 m	TRANSFER CASE	2-speed	Hull rear upper	5 mm at 65°
FIRING HEIGHT	n/app [2.13 m]	STEERING	power-assisted	Hull rear lower	7 mm at 0°
GROUND CLEARANCE	0.475 m	TYRES	13.00 × 18	Hull top	7 mm at 86°
TRACK	2.37 m	SUSPENSION	torsion bar with hydraulic	Hull belly front	5 mm
WHEELBASE	1.35 m + 1.525 m		shock absorbers	Hull belly rear	5 mm
	+ 1.35 m	ELECTRICAL SYSTEM	12 V	Turret front	n/app [7 mm at 43°]
MAX SPEED		ARMAMENT		Turret sides	n/app [7 mm at 36°]
road	80 km/h	main	1 × 7.62 mm MG	Turret rear	n/app [7 mm at 36°]
water	10 km/h		[1 × 14.5 mm MG]	Turret top	n/app [7 mm]
FUEL CAPACITY	290 litres	coaxial	n/app [1 × 7.62 mm MG]		
MAX ROAD RANGE	500 km	SMOKE-LAYING			
FUEL CONSUMPTION	0.58 litre/km	EQUIPMENT	none		
FORDING	amphibious	AMMUNITION		* Max is 16, 12 are normally carried	
GRADIENT	60%	main	2000 [500]	† Max is 14, 8 are normally carried	
		coaxial	n/app [2000]		

Status: Production complete. In service with Afghanistan, Algeria, Angola, Bulgaria, Chad, Congo, Cuba, Ethiopia, Finland, East Germany, India, Iran, Iraq, Israel (unconfirmed), Jibouti, Korea, Democratic People's Republic (North), Libya, Mali, Mongolia, Mozambique, Nicaragua, Romania (built in Romania as the TAB-72, for which there is a separate entry), Somalia, Syria, USSR, Viet-Nam, Yemen Arab Republic (North), Yemen, People's Democratic Republic (South), Yugoslavia and Zambia.

Manufacturer: Soviet state arsenals.

BTR-152 Armoured Personnel Carrier

Development
The BTR-152 was the first Soviet APC to enter production after the Second World War and was first seen in public during a parade in Moscow in 1951.

The first production models were based on the chassis of the ZIL-151 (6 × 6) truck but later vehicles (from and including the BTR-152V1) were based on the chassis of the improved ZIL-157 (6 × 6) truck. The BTR-152 has been replaced in most front-line Soviet Motorised Rifle Divisions by the BTR-60P (8 × 8) amphibious APC, but large numbers remain in reserve and it is still widely used in North Africa and the Middle East. It is used by all members of the Warsaw Pact except Czechoslovakia. In addition to being used as an APC it is also used for towing artillery (eg 57 mm Ch-26), carrying cargo and mortar teams and for minelaying.

Description
The hull of the BTR-152 is made of all-welded steel with the engine at the front, commander and driver immediately behind the engine and the troop compartment at the rear.

Armoured shutters, controlled from inside the driver's compartment, protect the radiator from damage by small arms fire. Power is transmitted from the engine to the transmission and then by a propeller shaft to the transfer box in the centre of the vehicle. Power is then transmitted by a propeller shaft to the front axle and each of the rear axles.

The driver sits on the left of the vehicle with the commander to his right, both with a windscreen which can be covered by an armoured shutter hinged at its upper part. This shutter has a vision block for observation when the shutter is closed. Both the commander and driver have a door in the side of the hull and the upper part, which has a small vision slit, folds down on the outside for increased visibility. The roof over the commander's and driver's position is armoured.

The 17 infantrymen are seated in the open-topped troop compartment at the back of the vehicle, the top of which can be covered by a tarpaulin cover which is normally carried in the vehicle. The seating arrangements depend on the model: in some there are bench seats across the vehicle and others have them down either side. The infantrymen enter and leave

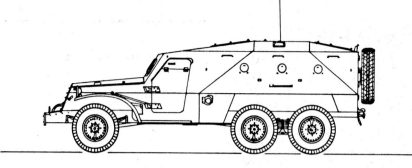

the vehicle by twin doors in the rear of the hull which open outwards, with the left door carrying the spare wheel. There are three firing ports in each side of the hull and another two in the rear, one each side of the doors.

The BTR-152 has no NBC system, no night vision equipment and no amphibious capability. A saw is carried externally on the left side of the hull. The winch, if fitted, is mounted at the very front of the vehicle and has a maximum capacity of 5000 kg and 70 metres of cable. The winch is also equipped with a special block which can be used as a pulley block to increase pulling capacity, or as a conventional block to change the direction of pull. The winch incorporates a three-speed PTO unit (low, high and reverse) controlled by a lever in the driver's compartment.

Some models (see variants) have a central tyre-pressure regulation system which allows the driver to adjust the tyre pressures to suit the type of ground being crossed.

There are three sockets for mounting machine guns, one on the top of the armour cover over the commander's and driver's position and the other two on either side of the troop compartment. The forward mounting normally has a 7.62 mm SGMB machine gun, which can be elevated from −6 to +23.5 degrees and has a traverse of 45 degrees left and right, or a 12.7 mm DShKM heavy machine gun. The side mountings normally have 7.62 mm SGMB machine guns.

Variants

BTR-152
This was the first model to enter service and is also known in the West as the Model A. It has an open top, no winch and no central tyre-pressure regulation system.

BTR-152V1
This was the second model to enter service and is known in the West as the Model B. It has an open top, front-mounted winch and a central tyre-pressure regulation system with external air lines.

BTR-152V2
Basic BTR-152 fitted with central tyre-pressure regulation system but no winch.

BTR-152V3
This is also known as the Model C in the West and has an open roof, front-mounted winch, central tyre-pressure regulation system with internal air lines and infra-red driving lights.

BTR-152K
This model, which is also known as the Model D (or 1961) in the West, has all the modifications of the BTR-152V3 plus

BTR-152K APC with overhead protection

full overhead armour protection. Over the top of the troop compartment are two roof hatches that open to the right, one with a single firing port and one with two.

BTR-152U Command Vehicle
The command vehicle is usually based on the BTR-152V1 or BTR-152V3 APC but has a much higher superstructure to allow the command staff to work upright. There are four windows in the upper part of the superstructure, two on the left, one on the right and one at the back. Access to stowage racks on the roof is by a ladder forward of the roof. The BTR-152U normally tows a trailer carrying additional equipment such as a generator.

BTR-152A Anti-aircraft Vehicle
This is armed with twin 14.5 mm KPV heavy machine guns in a manually-operated turret (ZTPU-2) with a traverse of 360 degrees. The guns have an elevation of +80 degrees and a depression of −5 degrees. The weapons have a maximum horizontal range of 8000 metres and a maximum vertical range of 5000 metres. Effective anti-aircraft range however is 1400 metres and effective range when being used in the ground role is 2000 metres. The KPV machine gun has a cyclic rate of fire of 600 rounds per minute per barrel but its practical rate of fire is 150 rounds per minute per barrel. These weapons and mount are also used on the BTR-40A (4 × 4) anti-aircraft vehicle (which has the same turret as the BTR-152A), towed models of the KPV are called the ZPU-1

BTR-152V2 APC with central tyre-pressure regulation system with internal air lines

BTR-152V2 APC with doors and hatches open (Michael Ledford)

(single barrel), ZPU-2 (twin barrel) and ZPU-4 (quad barrel). KPV machine guns are also mounted in armoured vehicles.

BTR-152 with Quad 12.7 mm M53 MGs

The Egyptians have fitted a number of their vehicles with the Czechoslovak Quad 12.7 mm M53 anti-aircraft system. The M53 consists of four Soviet-designed 12.7 mm DShKM machine guns on a Czechoslovak-designed two-wheeled mount. These weapons have a cyclic rate of fire of 550/600 rounds per minute per barrel but practical rate of fire is 80 rpm per barrel, and each barrel is fed from a drum which holds 50 rounds. The weapons can be elevated from −7 to +90 degrees and traversed through 360 degrees, elevation and traverse being manual. Maximum vertical range is 5600 metres but maximum effective anti-aircraft range is 1000 metres.

BTR-152 with 23 mm ZU-23 AAG

During the fighting in the Lebanon in the summer of 1982 the Israeli Army captured a number of BTR-152 APCs from the PLO which were fitted with the towed twin 23 mm automatic anti-aircraft gun ZU-23 in the rear of the troop compartment. The 23 mm ZU-23 has a maximum vertical effective anti-aircraft range of 2500 metres.

Status: Production complete. In service with Afghanistan, Albania, Algeria, Angola, Bulgaria (reserve), Central African Republic, Chad, China (Type 56), Congo, Cuba, Egypt, Ethiopia, East Germany, Guinea, Guinea-Bissau, Hungary (reserve), India, Indonesia, Iran, Iraq, Israel, Korea, Democratic People's Republic (North), Laos, Mali, Mongolia, Mozambique, Poland (reserve), Romania (reserve), Somalia, Sri Lanka, Sudan, Syria, Tanzania, Uganda, USSR, Yemen Arab Republic (North), Yemen, People's Democratic Republic (South), Yugoslavia, Viet-Nam and Zimbabwe.

Manufacturer: Soviet state arsenals.

BTR-40 Armoured Personnel Carrier

Development

The BTR-40 was the second armoured personnel carrier to enter production in the Soviet Union after the Second World War, the first being the BTR-152 (6 × 6) which entered service in 1950. The BTR-40 (4 × 4) entered production in 1951 and is basically a short wheelbase version of the GAZ-63 truck chassis fitted with an armoured body. The vehicle was originally used both as an armoured personnel carrier and as a command and reconnaissance vehicle, and performed a similar function to the US M3A1 scout car which was supplied to the Soviet Union by the USA during the Second World War.

The BTR-40 was replaced as a command and reconnaissance vehicle in the late 1950s by the BRDM-1 vehicle and now is found only in second-line units in the Warsaw Pact, such as road traffic units, but is still widely used by many other countries that have received Soviet aid.

Description

The hull of the BTR-40 is made of all-welded steel with the

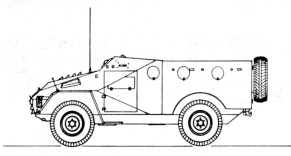

BTR-40 (4 × 4) armoured personnel carrier without armament

BTR-40B APC with overhead armour protection

equipment, no amphibious capability and, unlike most other Soviet wheeled vehicles, has no central tyre-pressure regulation system.

Variants

BTR-40A Anti-aircraft Vehicle

This is armed with twin 14.5 mm KPV heavy machine guns in a turret (ZTPU-2) with a traverse of 360 degrees. The guns have an elevation of +80 degrees and a depression of −5 degrees, both elevation and traverse being manual. The BTR-40A has a crew of five and carries 2400 rounds of 14.5 mm ammunition. The guns have a maximum horizontal range of 8000 metres and a maximum vertical range of 5000 metres but effective anti-aircraft range is 1400 metres, and effective ground range is 2000 metres.

BTR-40B Armoured Personnel Carrier

This is similar to the basic model but has overhead armour protection and four roof hatches, two per side, that open to the outside of the vehicle, with a circular firing port.

engine at the front, commander and driver in the centre and the personnel compartment at the rear.

The driver sits on the left of the vehicle with the vehicle commander to his right, with a windscreen which can be covered by an armoured shutter hinged at its upper part. The shutter has a vision block for observation when it is lowered. Both the commander and driver have a door in the side of the hull, in the upper part of which is a vision flap that hinges open on the outside and has a vision slit.

The eight infantrymen sit in the back of the vehicle, three on a bench seat at the very rear of the hull and the other five on individual seats. The troops enter and leave the vehicle by twin doors in the rear of the hull. The troop compartment has an open top which can be covered by a tarpaulin cover which is normally carried in the vehicle.

There are three pintle mounts for machine guns, one on the rail that runs across the top of the troop compartment immediately behind the commander's and driver's position, and the other two one either side of the troop compartment. The basic vehicle is armed with a single 7.62 mm SGMB machine gun which is normally mounted on the front pintle. This weapon has an elevation of +23.5 degrees, a depression of −6 degrees and a traverse of 45 degrees left and right of the vehicle's centre line.

Early production vehicles had no firing ports but later production vehicles have two or three in each side of the hull and two at the rear of the hull, one either side of the twin doors.

A spare wheel is carried on the rear of the hull in the centre and a saw is carried on the left side of the hull. Some vehicles have a winch with a capacity of 4500 kg mounted at the front of the hull. The BTR-40 has no NBC system, no night vision

SPECIFICATIONS	
CREW	2 + 8
CONFIGURATION	4 × 4
COMBAT WEIGHT	5300 kg
POWER-TO-WEIGHT	
RATIO	15 hp/tonne
LENGTH	5 m
WIDTH	1.9 m
HEIGHT	
without armament	1.75 m
(BTR-40A)	2.5 m
FIRING HEIGHT	
BTR-40A	2.05 m
GROUND CLEARANCE	0.275 m
TRACK	
front	1.588 m
rear	1.6 m
WHEELBASE	2.7 m
MAX ROAD SPEED	80 km/h
FUEL CAPACITY	120 litres
MAX ROAD RANGE	285 km
FUEL CONSUMPTION	0.42 litre/km
FORDING	0.8 m
GRADIENT	60%
SIDE SLOPE	30%
VERTICAL OBSTACLE	0.47 m
TRENCH (with channels)	0.7 m
TURNING RADIUS	7 m
ENGINE	GAZ-40 6-cylinder water-cooled in-line petrol developing 80 hp at 3400 rpm
TRANSMISSION	manual with 4 forward and 1 reverse gears
TRANSFER BOX	2-speed
STEERING	cone worm and dual ridge roller
CLUTCH	single dry plate
TYRES	9.75 × 18
BRAKES	hydraulic drum on all wheels
SUSPENSION	
front	longitudinal semi-elliptical springs with hydraulic shock absorbers
rear	longitudinal semi-elliptical springs with check springs
ELECTRICAL SYSTEM	12 V
MAIN ARMAMENT	1 × 7.62 mm MG
AMMUNITION	1250
ARMOUR	8 mm max

BTR-40Kh Chemical Reconnaissance Vehicle

This is fitted with equipment at the rear of the hull which enables the crew to set marking pennants into the ground while the vehicle is crossing contaminated ground.

BTR-40 Sagger

East Germany has mounted a triple Sagger launcher, with overhead armour protection, on a BTR-40 as a training device. Externally this is recognisable by its lower overall height and its modified hull rear.

Status: Production complete. In service with Afghanistan, Albania, Algeria, Angola, Bulgaria, China (Type 55), Cuba, Egypt, Ethiopia, East Germany, Guinea, Guinea-Bissau, Indonesia, Iran, Israel, Korea, Democratic People's Republic (North), Laos, Libya, Mali, Mozambique, Somalia, Sudan, Syria, Tanzania, Uganda, USSR, Viet-Nam, Yemen Arab Republic (North), Yemen People's Democratic Republic (South) and Yugoslavia.

Manufacturer: Soviet state arsenals.

BTR-40 (4 × 4) APC with spare wheel on left side of hull (Israeli Army)

UNITED KINGDOM

MCV-80 Infantry Combat Vehicle

Development

The initial proposal to consider future armoured personnel carrier requirements for the British Army in 1967 was followed between 1968 and 1971 by in-house Ministry of Defence feasibility studies. Initial industrial work (Project Definition 1) and Ministry of Defence option studies to define an affordable programme took place between 1972 and 1976. Full project definition (Project Definition 2) was undertaken in 1977–78 by GKN Sankey after its competitive selection as prime contractor for the MCV-80.

In 1978 a parallel evaluation of the American XM2 (now known as the Bradley Infantry Fighting Vehicle) took place. The following year full development of the MCV-80 started in parallel with continued study of the XM2.

In June 1980 the following Parliamentary Statement was made on the British Army's APC replacement:

'The Army's present armoured personnel carrier, the FV432 series of vehicles, has been in service since the 1960s and will need to be replaced from the mid-1980s. Two vehicles have been considered for this requirement, the Mechanised Combat Vehicle (MCV-80), designed by the British firm GKN Sankey, and the American Infantry Fighting Vehicle, which would be manufactured under licence in this country.

'After careful assessment of the relevant operational, financial and industrial factors I have decided to select MCV-80 to meet this requirement. The total estimated cost of the replacement programme is about £1000 million and full development will be launched shortly.'

Detailed design work commenced in 1977 and by 1980 three prototypes of the MCV-80 were running and the company was also using test rigs, for example cooling, damper and suspension, to study specific characteristics of components for MCV-80.

In January 1984 the British Ministry of Defence announced that negotiations with GKN Sankey for an initial production order were well advanced but that future orders will be open to competitive tendering by both GKN Sankey and other qualified manufacturers. At the same time it was announced that the MoD would be contracting with GKN Sankey for full development of variants and derivative vehicles, subject to satisfactory completion of preliminary studies. MCV-80 was accepted for service with the British Army in November 1984 and production is expected to commence at Telford in 1986 with first production vehicles being delivered in 1987. The first production order for about 250 vehicles was placed with GKN early in 1985 with the second production batch for 200 vehicles being open to competitive bidding by GKN, Royal Ordnance Leeds, Alvis and Vickers Defence Systems. The third production contract, expected to be ordered later this decade, will be for 550 vehicles. At one time it was expected that between 1800 and 2000 MCV-80s would be procured.

By 1984 ten prototypes had been built; one of these had a highly successful demonstration in the Middle East in 1983. The three versions in the early development stage are the infantry command, artillery observation, repair and recovery vehicle.

Description

The hull of the MCV-80 is of all-welded aluminium construction which provides a significant increase in protection over that of the current FV432 APC. The driver sits at the front of the vehicle on the left side and has a single-piece hatch cover

One of the MCV-80 prototypes from rear (Terry J Gander)

hinged at the rear with a single wide-angle periscope that can be replaced by an image intensification periscope for driving at night.

The powerpack is to the right of the driver and drives, through spur final drive units, the front sprockets. The engine is a Rolls-Royce Motors Condor CV8 TCA diesel developing 550 hp which is coupled to an American Detroit Diesel Allison X-300-4B transmission which will be manufactured under licence in the UK by Rolls-Royce Motors. The X-300 was chosen after trials between it and the General Electric HMPT-500 which is installed in the American FMC M2 IFV and M3 CFV. The automatic transmission has four forward and two reverse gears, and steering is through a hydrostatically-controlled differential steer assembly.

The power assisted vehicle brakes are integral with the transmission. The cooling system covers the engine, generator, transmission and vehicle brakes. The Lucas oil spray cooled 300 Amp generator is also driven from the gearbox by a PTO which also drives the hydraulic pump for the Airscrew-Howden fan.

The two-man steel turret is in the centre of the vehicle, offset slightly to the left of the vehicle's centre line. The turret, which has been designed by Vickers Defence Systems of Newcastle, has seats for the commander on the right, who dismounts with the troops, and the gunner on the left, with both crew members having individual hatch covers that open to the rear. The turret has power traverse with manual controls for emergency use. Both the commander and gunner have day and passive night vision equipment with the commander's system having additional traverse. Additional periscopes give vision to the sides and rear of the turret.

After evaluating the British Rarden 30 mm cannon and the American Hughes Helicopters 25 mm M242 Chain Gun, the former was selected for the MCV-80. Mounted coaxially with the main armament is a Hughes Helicopters 7.62 mm EX-34 Chain Gun with the expended cartridge cases being ejected outside of the turret. This is manufactured under licence at the Royal Small Arms Factory Enfield. Mounted either side of the turret are four electrically-operated smoke dischargers.

The troop compartment is at the rear of the MCV-80 with the troops entering and leaving via twin doors in the rear of the hull, each of which is provided with a vision block. In the roof of the troop compartment are four rotating periscopes, two either side, for use by the infantry. The sides of the troop compartment are sloped inward but there is no provision for the infantry to fire their small arms from within the vehicle. Over the top of the troop compartment are double roof hatches. The MCV-80 carries eight infantrymen, one of whom also commands the vehicle and therefore dismounts with the infantry. The remaining seven sit in the troop compartment, four on the right and three on the left, in separate seats with seat belts. Personal kit can be stowed under the seats or in the sponsons which have interior grilles to hold the kit in position. MCV-80 carries all of the equipment required to fight on the battlefield for a period of 48 hours.

The suspension is of the torsion bar type and consists of six rubber-tyred aluminium road wheels with the drive sprocket at the front, idler at the rear and three track return rollers which support the inside of the track only. Dampers, built into the suspension pivot housing, are fitted on the first, second and sixth road wheel stations. The tracks are conventional rubber-bushed cast steel with rubber pads.

Standard equipment includes an NBC system which is mounted in the side of the hull to the left rear of the driver and

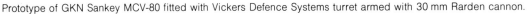
Prototype of GKN Sankey MCV-80 fitted with Vickers Defence Systems turret armed with 30 mm Rarden cannon.

a full range of passive night vision equipment. Either side of the rear troop doors is a stowage box. The MCV-80 has no amphibious capability as this was not required by the British Army.

Variants

The following variants are required by the British Army:
Platoon vehicle and command vehicle fitted with turret armed with 7.62 mm GPMG
Mechanised recovery vehicle with hydraulically-operated blade at the front of the hull, winch and cupola-mounted 7.62 mm GPMG
Mortar carrier with rear-mounted 81 mm mortar and cupola-mounted 7.62 mm GPMG
Mechanised engineer combat vehicle with cupola-mounted 7.62 mm GPMG and EMI Ranger anti-personnel mine laying system on hull roof at rear
Mechanised observation command post vehicle
Mechanised combat repair vehicle with hydraulic crane with extendable jib mounted on roof of hull at rear, fitted with cupola-mounted 7.62 mm GPMG.

In addition to the variants under development or required by the British Army GKN Sankey has proposed the following models for export:
MCV 105 30-tonne battle tank armed with turret-mounted 105 mm gun on a redesigned and lower profile hull with turret at rear
MCV/reconnaissance, same hull as above but with 76 mm or 90 mm gun
MCV/ATGW, with various ATGW systems, for example TOW, HOT or MILAN
MCV/AA, with two-man Thomson-CSF SABRE turret armed with twin 30 mm cannon
MCV/SAML, with eight British Aerospace Rapier SAMs in ready-to-launch position
MCV/MLRS, carrying Vought MLRS at rear (longer chassis)
MCV/MLC, modular load carrier (longer chassis).

An MCV-80 fitted with the same two-man Cockerill CM 90 turret as installed on the SIBMAS (6 × 6) armoured personnel carriers delivered to Malaysia was successfully tested in 1984.

HOT ATGW MCV-80

An MCV-80 chassis with its normal turret replaced by a Euromissile HOT HCT turret with four 4000-metre range HOT ATGWs in the ready-to-launch position with a further 14 missiles carried in reserve in the hull was shown for the first time in September 1982. The one-man turret has powered traverse of 30 degrees left and right and the launcher has powered elevation from −18 to +23 degrees. The missile operator has a sight with a magnification of ×3 and ×12. The company intends to provide a two-man (gunner and commander) version, with a power-operated turret with a traverse of 360 degrees and the commander having all-round surveillance with a panoramic telescopic sight and an override facility.

APC90

This is the MCV-80 with the two-man turret replaced by a simple cupola armed with a 7.62 mm machine gun and one less road wheel either side. The vehicle costs about 25 per cent less than the MCV-80.

SPECIFICATIONS
CREW	2 + 8
COMBAT WEIGHT	24 000 kg
POWER-TO-WEIGHT	
RATIO	22.93 bhp/tonne
GROUND PRESSURE	0.65 kg/cm²
LENGTH	6.34 m
WIDTH	3.034 m
HEIGHT	
hull roof	1.93 m
overall	2.735 m
GROUND CLEARANCE	0.49 m
TRACK	2.54 m
TRACK WIDTH	460 mm
LENGTH OF TRACK ON	
GROUND	3.816 m
MAX ROAD SPEED	
forwards	75 km/h
reverse	48 km/h
ACCELERATION	
(0 to 48 km/h)	18 seconds
FUEL CAPACITY	772 litres
MAX ROAD RANGE	500 km
FORDING	1.3 m
GRADIENT	60%
SIDE SLOPE	40%
VERTICAL OBSTACLE	0.75 m
TRENCH	2.5 m
ENGINE	Rolls-Royce CV8 TCA V-8 diesel developing 550 hp at 2300 rpm
TRANSMISSION	Detroit Diesel Allison X-300-4B fully automatic with torque converter and lock-up clutch, 4 forward and 2 reverse gears
STEERING SYSTEM	differential steering system based on a variable hydrostatic drive
SUSPENSION	torsion bar
ELECTRICAL SYSTEM	24 V
ARMAMENT	
main	1 × 30 mm Rarden cannon
coaxial	1 × 7.62 mm Chain Gun
smoke laying equipment	2 × 4 smoke dischargers
ARMOUR	
Hull	aluminium
Turret	steel

Status: Development of the MCV-80 was completed in late 1984. It is expected that first production vehicles will be completed in 1987.

Manufacturer: GKN Sankey Limited, Defence Vehicles Operations, PO Box 20, Hadley Castle Works, Telford, Shropshire TF1 4RE, England.

FV432 Armoured Personnel Carrier

Development

In the 1950s the Fighting Vehicles Research and Development Establishment (now the Military Vehicles and Engineering Establishment) designed the FV420 series of armoured vehicles. Members of this family included the FV421 load carrier, FV422 armoured personnel carrier, FV423 command vehicle, FV424 Royal Engineers vehicle, FV425 recovery vehicle and the FV426 ATGW vehicle. They never entered production but further development resulted in the FV430 series. The FV431 was an armoured load carrier which never entered production. The APC member of the family was called the FV432 and the first prototype was completed in 1961. For a short period the FV432 was known as the Trojan, but this name was subsequently dropped to avoid confusion with the car company of the same name.

Infantry dismounting from FV432 APC (Ministry of Defence)

In 1962 GKN Sankey was awarded a production contract for the FV432 APC and first production vehicles were completed in 1963. Production continued until 1971 by which time about 3000 FV432s had been built. The first production models were the Mk 1 and were followed by the Mk 2 and finally the Mk 2/1. Late production vehicles are distinguishable by the NBC pack in the right side of the hull which is almost flush against the hull rather than protruding as on earlier vehicles.

The FV432 has now replaced the Alvis Saracen (6 × 6) APC in the British Army of the Rhine and will itself be supplemented in the late-1980s by the MCV-80. The FV433 Abbot 105 mm self-propelled gun, manufactured by Vickers Limited at its Elswick facility, uses many automotive components of the FV432 APC.

Description
The all-welded steel hull of the FV432 provides complete protection against small arms fire and shell splinters. The driver sits at the front of the vehicle on the right side and has a single-piece hatch cover that opens to the left. This has an AFV No 33 Mk 1 wide-angle periscope which can be replaced for night driving by an MEL L5A1 passive periscope.

The commander sits behind the driver and has a cupola that can be traversed manually through 360 degrees. This cupola has a single-piece hatch cover and three AFV No 32 Mk 1 periscopes. Mounted on the forward part of the commander's cupola is a 7.62 mm GPMG, although vehicles used in the command role and other rear area roles are normally fitted with a 7.62 mm Bren LMG. At one time it was proposed to issue many infantry units with FV432s fitted with the turret of the Fox armoured car armed with the 30 mm Rarden cannon; this project was cancelled although a few vehicles were issued to the Berlin Brigade. Many FV432s have been fitted with a Peak Engineering lightweight turret armed with a 7.62 mm GPMG with an elevation of +50 degrees, depression of −15 degrees and 360-degree turret traverse. The turret has a single-piece hatch cover that opens to the rear, three periscopes and eight smoke dischargers mounted four either side of the turret. This turret is mounted over the forward part of the circular troop compartment

hatch. The original four-part hatch has been removed and replaced by a circular steel piece which contains the turret, with a hatch to the immediate rear of the turret.

The engine compartment is to the left of the driver with the air-inlet (forward) and air-outlet (rear) louvres in the roof and the exhaust pipe running along the left side of the hull. The complete engine with its oil tanks and filters is mounted on a common sub-frame which can be removed from the vehicle as a complete unit and reconnected on the ground by extended cables and fuel lines and pre-run for testing. The engine compartment is fitted with a fire wire-detection system. The engine is coupled to the General Motors Allison Division TX-200-4A semi-automatic transmission, which was built under licence in the United Kingdom by Rolls-Royce, which in turn supplies power to the steering unit at the front of the hull via a universally jointed propeller shaft. Access to the steering system for maintenance is via a forward-opening hatch in the glacis plate, behind the trim vane.

The troop compartment is at the rear of the FV432 with the ten (five a side) infantrymen seated on bench seats that run down either side of the hull. The seats are hinged to the lower side plates on either side of the compartment and fold upwards, enabling the vehicle to carry up to 3670 kg of cargo. The infantrymen enter and leave the vehicle via a large door in the rear of the hull which opens to the right and is provided with a vision block. Over the top of the troop compartment is a circular hatch cover that opens to the left and right of the vehicle, each part being hinged in the middle concertina fashion.

The torsion bar suspension consists of five dual rubber-tyred road wheels with the drive sprocket at the front, idler at the rear and two track return rollers. The first and last road wheel stations have a friction shock absorber and the upper part of the track is covered by a light sheet metal covering. The steel tracks are rubber bushed and fitted with removable rubber pads.

There is an NBC system mounted in the right side of the hull which provides fresh air via ducts to both the driver's and troop compartment. Unlike the similar M113, the FV432 is not amphibious without preparation. Before entering the water a flotation screen is erected around the top of the hull, where it is held in position by ten stays, the trim vane erected at the front of the hull and an extension piece fitted to the exhaust pipe. When afloat the vehicle is propelled in the water by its tracks. Most FV432s have now had their amphibious capability removed.

FV432 APC fitted with Peak Engineering lightweight turret armed with 7.62 mm GPMG

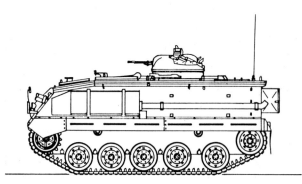

FV432 with Fox turret armed with 30 mm Rarden cannon (Ministry of Defence)

FV432 APC fitted with Peak engineering turret armed with 7.62 mm GPMG (Ministry of Defence)

Variants
(excluding trials variants)

Ambulance
This model is unarmed and carries four stretcher patients or two stretcher and five seated patients, plus a crew of two. The stretchers are easily loaded and unloaded from the vehicle by means of sliding swivel racks.

Carl Gustaf
This is simply the standard FV432 with a bar fitted across the top of the troop compartment on which the Swedish 84 mm Carl Gustaf anti-tank weapon is mounted. The FV432 is also used to carry the Euromissile MILAN ATGW which is deployed away from the vehicle. This has replaced the 120 mm Wombat RR in the British Army.

Command
This model is fitted internally with two mapboards and additional communications equipment. To increase the available working area a penthouse measuring 3.66 × 2.74 × 1.98 metres can be quickly erected at the rear of the hull. The command model has a crew of seven and weighs 15 500 kg.

81 mm Mortar Carrier
This is the basic vehicle fitted with an 81 mm L16 mortar on a turntable in the rear of the hull which can be traversed through a full 360 degrees. The mortar has a maximum range

of 5660 metres and 160 mortar bombs are carried. The vehicle has a crew of six, weighs 16 400 kg and is issued on the scale of six per mechanised infantry battalion.

Maintenance Carrier
This model is designated the FV434 and is operated by the Royal Electrical and Mechanical Engineers. Its primary role is to change major components in the field such as the complete powerpack of the Chieftain MBT. On the right side of the vehicle is an HIAB crane which has a lifting capacity of 1250 kg at 3.96 metres radius to 3050 kg at 2.26 metres radius. The suspension on the FV434 can be locked when the crane is being used. The FV434 has a crew of four and weighs 17 750 kg fully loaded.

Minelayer
The FV432 is used by the Royal Engineers to tow the Bar minelayer which can lay mines at a rate of 600 an hour. In addition an EMI Ranger anti-personnel minelaying system can be mounted on the top of the FV432 to enable a combined anti-tank and anti-personnel minefield to be laid.

Radar
The FV432 is used to mount the Marconi Avionics ZB 298 short-range radar (maximum range 10 000 metres) and the EMI Cymbeline mortar-locating radar (range 20 000 metres). The FV436 fitted with the earlier EMI Green Archer mortar-locating radar is no longer in service with the British Army.

Recovery
This is the basic FV432 with a winch installed in the rear troop compartment. The conversion kits were supplied by the British Rail Derby Locomotive Works from 1972. The winch is driven from the PTO on the engine transfer case and has both high- and low-speed gears. The winch has a maximum pull, using a three-part tackle, of 18 299 kg and maximum winching speeds are 18.34 metres a minute at 6608 kg and 122.4 metres a minute at 3050 kg.

Royal Artillery Vehicles
In addition to using the FV432 with the EMI Cymbeline mortar-locating radar the Royal Artillery uses the FV432 in the battery command role fitted with the Marconi Command

FV432 with 81 mm mortar (Ministry of Defence)

and Control Systems Field Artillery Computer Equipment, and fitted with the Plessey sound ranging system.

Royal Engineers Vehicles
In addition to using the FV432 fitted with the EMI Ranger anti-personnel minelaying system and towing the Bar minelayer the Royal Engineers use it to tow the Giant Viper mine-clearance trailer.

Royal Signals Vehicles
The Royal Signals use a number of specialised communication versions of the FV432 under the designation FV439, most of which have extensive antenna arrays on the roof. It is also used to house parts of the Wavell and Ptarmigan systems.

Swingfire Anti-tank Vehicle
The vehicle, which is designated the FV438, has two launcher bins on the top of the hull rear for the British Aerospace Dynamics Swingfire ATGW with a further 14 missiles carried in the hull. New missiles are loaded from inside the vehicle. The FV438 has a crew of three, a loaded weight of 16 200 kg and is also fitted with a 7.62 mm GPMG. The FV438 is operated by the Royal Armoured Corps.

Status: Production complete. In service only with the British Army.

Manufacturer: GKN Sankey Limited, Defence Vehicles Operations, PO Box 20, Hadley Castle Works, Telford, Shropshire TF1 4RE, England.

Alvis Stormer Armoured Personnel Carrier

Development
In 1980 Alvis Limited purchased the manufacturing and marketing rights of the FV4333 from the British Ministry of Defence. The vehicle was originally designed by the Military Vehicles and Engineering Establishment and the first prototype made a brief appearance at the mobility demonstration at Bovington during the 1978 British Army Equipment Exhibition. In June 1981 Alvis announced that its development of the FV4333 had been designated Stormer.

The Stormer has taken advantage of the existing technology of the Alvis Scorpion CVR(T) family and many of the proven components have been used. The transmission is the same as the CVR(T) but with a modified input gear train (with the designation changed from TN15 to T300) and the suspension uses CVR(T) components with wheel stations increased to six per side. The hull of the Stormer is wider than the CVR(T) and its original petrol engine has been replaced by a Perkins T6/3544 turbo-charged diesel which can also be installed in the Scorpion.

In addition to being used as an APC a wide range of roles are envisaged for this vehicle and it is anticipated that the chassis will be developed for a number of other applications.

In 1981 Alvis was one of three manufacturers to be awarded contracts for vehicles to meet the US Army/Marine Corps requirement for a Light Armored Vehicle (LAV). Alvis was awarded a contract for one Scorpion 90, powered by a Perkins diesel and armed with a Cockerill Mark III 90 mm gun, and three Stormer APCs, each fitted with a two-man Arrowpointe turret armed with a Hughes 25mm M242 Chain Gun and a coaxial 7.62 mm M240 machine gun.

Alvis has also been awarded contracts from the US Army for the hybrid and conceptual designs for the Mobile Protected Weapons System (or Mobile Protected Gun System), which will be based on automotive components of the Stormer APC.

Late in 1981 Malaysia placed an order with Alvis for 26 Scorpion 90 vehicles and 25 Stormer APCs, production of

Alvis Stormer APC fitted with unarmed No 16 cupola, with rear hull door open and showing hatch in hull side for NBC pack

SPECIFICATIONS	
CREW	2 + 10
COMBAT WEIGHT	15 280 kg
UNLOADED WEIGHT	13 740 kg
POWER-TO-WEIGHT RATIO	15.7 bhp/tonne
GROUND PRESSURE	0.78 kg/cm²
LENGTH	5.251 m
WIDTH	2.8 m
over tracks	2.527 m
HEIGHT	
including machine gun	2.286 m
to hull top	1.879 m
GROUND CLEARANCE	0.406 m
TRACK	2.184 m
TRACK WIDTH	343 mm
LENGTH OF TRACK ON GROUND	2.819 m
MAX ROAD SPEED	52.2 km/h
MAX WATER SPEED	6.6 km/h
FUEL CAPACITY	454 litres
MAX ROAD RANGE	
diesel	480 km
petrol	424 km
FORDING	1.066 m
with preparation	amphibious
GRADIENT	60%
VERTICAL OBSTACLE	0.609 m
TRENCH	2.05 m
ENGINE	Rolls-Royce K60 No 4 Mk 4F 2-stroke, 6-cylinder multi-fuel developing 240 bhp at 3750 rpm
TRANSMISSION	TX-200-4A semi-automatic with 6 forward and 1 reverse gears
SUSPENSION	torsion bar
ELECTRICAL SYSTEM	24 V
BATTERIES	6 × 12 V
ARMAMENT (main)	1 × 7.62 mm MG
SMOKE-LAYING EQUIPMENT	2 × 3 smoke dischargers
AMMUNITION	1600 rounds of 7.62 mm (belted when fitted with GPMG) or 50 magazines each holding 28 rounds (when fitted with Bren LMG)
ARMOUR	6–12 mm

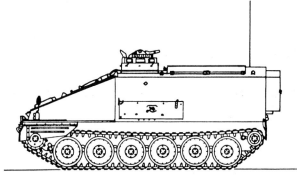

Alvis Stormer APC

Alvis Stormer APC with No 16 cupola

which commenced in 1982 with first deliveries made in 1983. Of the Stormer APCs, 12 vehicles will be fitted with Helio FVT 900 turrets armed with a 20 mm Oerlikon cannon and a 7.62 mm machine gun and the remainder with a Thyssen Henschel TH-1 turret armed with twin 7.62 mm machine guns.

Description

The hull of the Stormer is made of all-welded aluminium with the driver at the left front, engine compartment to his right and troop compartment at the rear.

The driver has an adjustable seat and a single-piece hatch cover that opens forwards. In front of him there is a single ×1 periscope which can be replaced by a passive night driving periscope.

The Perkins T6/3544 diesel is mounted to the right of the driver with air induction through armoured louvres and Dynacel air cleaners. Engine cooling is by a single mixed-flow fan drawing air through the radiator, over the engine and through the outlet louvres. The exhaust is also cooled by some of this air. The engine is coupled to a T300 hot shift, foot-operated, seven-speed gearbox with centrifugal clutch. An automatic operation for the transmission is available. The transmission contains a controlled differential steering system giving turning circle radii varying with the gear ratio, and a neutral or pivot turn when needed.

From the gearbox the drive goes to the front sprockets and then the tracks. It is anticipated that shock aborbers will be fitted to the first, second, fifth and sixth road wheel stations. Track adjustment is by hydraulic ram and hand pump.

The vehicle commander sits behind the driver and has a No 16 cupola with eight ×1 periscopes and a periscope with a magnification of ×1 and ×10 for aiming the 7.62 mm GPMG mounted on the right side of the cupola which can be aimed

and fired from within. The cupola has a single-piece hatch cover that opens to the left.

The section leader sits to the right of the vehicle commander and has four periscopes and a hatch cover.

The number of troops carried depends on the armament installation but would normally be eight seated four down either side of the troop compartment on bench seats that can be folded up to enable stores to be carried. The infantry enter and leave the vehicle through a large single door that opens to the right and incorporates a single vision block.

Over the top of the troop compartment there is a large two-piece hatch that opens either side of the hull. On the prototype there was no provision for the infantry to aim and fire their small arms from inside the vehicle, but this capability was provided on one of the later prototype Stormer vehicles.

The torsion bar suspension consists of six dual rubber-tyred aluminium road wheels with the drive sprocket at the front and the idler at the rear. Tracks are single pin, steel links, with rubber bushes and integrally-mounted rubber pads.

The Stormer has an NBC and/or air-conditioning system in the left side of the hull, below the commander's station and can be fitted with passive night vision equipment. Two four-barrelled electrically-operated smoke dischargers are mounted on the front of the hull. Appliqué armour can be added to the vehicle for increased protection.

The basic model can ford to a depth of 1.1 metres without preparation but, with a front flotation screen it is fully amphibious, propelled in the water by its tracks at a speed of 6.5 km/h. When fitted with an appliqué propeller kit its water speed is 9.6 km/h.

Variants

The prototype of the Stormer is fitted with a No 16 cupola armed with a 7.62 mm GPMG but the basic hull can be adapted to mount either a gun or missile turret, this is achieved by modification of the roof section and installation of compatible turret rings. Typical variants include:

Two-man turret armed with 76 mm or 90 mm gun

Two-man turret armed with 30 mm Rarden cannon and a 7.62 mm coaxial machine gun with both weapons having an elevation of +35 degrees, depression of −10 degrees, with turret traverse a full 360 degrees. A total of 165 rounds of 30 mm ammunition would be carried, of which 60 would be for ready use in the turret with remainder in the hull

ATGW vehicle with HOT, TOW or MILAN systems

Anti-aircraft vehicle, gun or missile

Alvis Stormer fitted with Helio FVT 200 turret armed with 20 mm cannon and 7.62 mm coaxial machine gun

Engineer vehicle
Load carrier
Minelayer, for example Royal Ordnance Bar minelaying system
81 mm mortar carrier
Recovery vehicle
Command vehicle

In 1984 the prototype of the Stormer air defence vehicle was shown for the first time. This is essentially the standard Stormer fitted with an American General Electric two-man power-operated turret armed with a 25 mm or 30 mm Gatling cannon with two Stinger surface-to-air missiles mounted above and an ESD surveillance radar at the rear. The chassis of Stormer is also being proposed for installation of the British Aerospace Dynamics Rapier Laserfire air defence system with four missiles in the ready to launch position.

Family concept

In June 1982 Alvis released outline drawings for 14 variants based on the chassis of the Stormer APC. These are anti-tank with Emerson TOW launcher, missile launcher platform, maintenance/recovery, engineer with front-mounted dozer blade, electronic warfare/battalion command and control, logistics, ambulance, light armoured squad carrier, mobile protected gun-near term/light assault, assault gun, low profile 75 mm, low profile 90 mm, air defence and mortar carrier. Since then Alvis has carried out extensive development and pre-production trials, supplementing the 32 187 km of testing by the US Marine Corps during the LAV programme. The first Stormer production vehicle with the 250 bhp engine was completed early in 1984.

MPWS/MPGS

Alvis has submitted three studies to the US Marine Corps and Army Tank Automotive Command for the Mobile Protected Weapon System (MPWS), and one for the Mobile Protected Gun System (MPGS). For the MPWS the company put forward the Sagitar chassis (a development of the Stormer) with a two-man turret armed with a 76 mm gun (L23A1) and a twin TOW ATGW launcher, another mounting a 75 mm ARES cannon and a conceptual design armed with a projected Royal Ordnance Nottingham 105 mm gun. Alvis also proposes the 75 mm ARES cannon or the Rheinmetall Rh 105-11 SLR gun for the MPGS requirement.

SPECIFICATIONS					
CREW	3 + 8	ACCELERATION		STEERING	regenerative triple differential system controlled by external disc brakes
MAX COMBAT WEIGHT	11 804 kg	(0–48 km/h)	19 seconds		
POWER-TO-WEIGHT		FUEL CAPACITY	332 litres		
RATIO	21.17 bhp/tonne	MAX ROAD RANGE	530 km	SUSPENSION	torsion bar
GROUND PRESSURE	0.43 kg/cm²	FORDING	1.1 m	HAND BRAKE	hand lever connected by
LENGTH	5.38 m	with preparation	amphibious		cable to contracting bands
WIDTH	2.4 m	GRADIENT	60%		operating on periphery of
over tracks	2.31 m	VERTICAL OBSTACLE	0.46 m		main brake discs
HEIGHT (top of MG)	2.49 m	TRENCH	1.8 m	FOOT BRAKE PEDAL	hydraulically-
GROUND CLEARANCE	0.425 m	ENGINE	Perkins T6/3544		connected to main brakes
TRACK	1.888 m		water-cooled 6-cylinder	ELECTRICAL SYSTEM	28.5 V
TRACK WIDTH	432 mm		turbo-charged diesel	BATTERIES	4 × 6TN (2 for automotive, 2
LENGTH OF TRACK			developing 250 bhp at		for radio) low-maintenance
ON GROUND	3.112 m		2600 rpm	ARMAMENT	depends on role
MAX ROAD SPEED	72 km/h	TRANSMISSION	T300 crossdrive,		
MAX WATER SPEED			semi-automatic hot-shift		
tracks	6.5 km/h		type, providing 7 speeds in		
propeller	9.6 km/h		each direction and pivot		
			turns		

Status: Stormer entered production in 1982 with first deliveries made to Malaysia in 1983. Three vehicles have been delivered to the USA.

Manufacturer: Alvis Limited, Holyhead Road, Coventry, West Midlands CV5 8JH, England. (A member of the United Scientific Group.)

Alvis Spartan Armoured Personnel Carrier

Development

The Spartan is the armoured personnel carrier member of the Alvis Scorpion Combat Vehicle Reconnaissance (Tracked) series which was accepted for service with the British Army in May 1970. Spartan entered service with the British Army of the Rhine in 1978 and is used to transport Royal Artillery Blowpipe SAM teams, as missile resupply vehicle for Swingfire and Blowpipe and for carrying Royal Engineer assault teams. It is not used in place of the FV432 APC as it can only carry four troops plus its three-man crew.

Description

The hull of the Spartan is made of all-welded aluminium armour and provides the crew with protection against attack over its frontal arc from 14.5 mm projectiles and against 7.62 mm armour-piercing rounds over the remainder of the vehicle. The hull is divided into three compartments: driver's at the front left, engine at the front right and the crew and troop compartment at the rear.

The driver is seated at the front of the hull on the left and has a single-piece hatch cover that opens forwards. He is provided with a single wide-angle periscope which can be replaced with a passive periscope for night driving.

The vehicle commander/gunner is seated behind the driver and has a No 16 cupola with eight periscopes, monocular sight with a magnification of ×1 or ×10 with the line of sight elevating with the machine gun. The ×1 mirror assembly can be replaced by a ×1.8 image intensifier. Mounted on the right side of the cupola is a 7.62 mm machine gun which can be aimed and fired from within the vehicle. The cupola has a single-piece hatch cover that opens to the rear.

To the right of the commander/gunner is the section

Alvis Spartan APC of the Belgian Army from the rear (C R Zwart)

Alvis Spartan fitted with Euromissile MILAN MCT turret

the rear. There are no track return rollers. Hydraulic lever type shock absorbers are provided for the first and last road wheel stations either side. Standard equipment includes an NBC system and night vision equipment.

The Spartan can ford to a depth of 1.067 metres without preparation. A flotation screen carried collapsed around the top of the hull can be erected by the crew in five minutes and the vehicle is then propelled in the water by its tracks.

SPECIFICATIONS

CREW	3 + 4
COMBAT WEIGHT	8172 kg
POWER-TO-WEIGHT	
RATIO	23.25 hp/tonne
GROUND PRESSURE	0.338 kg/cm²
LENGTH	5.125 m
WIDTH	2.257 m
WIDTH OVER TRACKS	2.134 m
HEIGHT OVERALL	2.28 m
GROUND CLEARANCE	0.356 m
TRACK	1.708 m
TRACK WIDTH	432 mm
MAX ROAD SPEED	80.5 km/h
FUEL CAPACITY	386 litres
MAX ROAD RANGE	483 km
FORDING	1.067 m
AMPHIBIOUS	with preparation
GRADIENT	60%
VERTICAL OBSTACLE	0.5 m
TRENCH	2.057 m
ENGINE	Jaguar J60 No 1 Mk 100B 4.2 litre 6-cylinder petrol developing 190 hp at 4750 rpm
TRANSMISSION	TN15 cross drive, semi-automatic hot-shift type providing 7 speeds forward and reverse
STEERING	Merritt system incorporated in transmission
SUSPENSION	torsion bar
ELECTRICAL SYSTEM	28.5 V
BATTERIES	4
MAIN ARMAMENT	1 × 7.62 mm MG
SMOKE DISCHARGERS	2 × 4
AMMUNITION	3000
ARMOUR	aluminium

Status: In production. In service with Belgium and the United Kingdom (Army and Royal Air Force).

Manufacturer: Alvis Limited, Holyhead Road, Coventry, West Midlands CV5 8JH (A member of the United Scientific Group).

Alvis Spartan APC of the British Army (Simon Dunstan)

commander/radio operator who is provided with three observation periscopes and a single-piece hatch cover that opens to the right.

Entry to the personnel compartment at the rear is via a single door in the hull rear that opens to the right and has an integral vision block. Over the top of the troop compartment are two roof hatches that open either side of the vehicle. Two periscopes are provided in the left side of the hull and one in the right but there is no provision for the crew to fire their weapons from inside of the vehicle. Three infantrymen are seated on the left side of the vehicle and a fourth to the rear of the vehicle commander/gunner and section commander/radio operator. If required a ZB 298 ground surveillance radar can be mounted on the roof of the vehicle.

Spartan is powered by a de-rated (from 265 to 190 bhp) and militarised Jaguar 4.2 litre engine with a Solex carburettor and compression ratio reduced from 9.1 to 7.75:1. The transmission, which has the same principle of operation as that installed in the Chieftain MBT, is a hot-shift, foot-operated, seven-speed gearbox with a controlled differential steering system. For engine cooling a single mixed flow fan draws in air through the radiator over the gearbox, over the engine and out through the louvres.

The torsion bar suspension consists of five rubber-tyred road wheels with the drive sprocket at the front and idler at

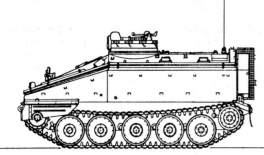

Alvis Spartan Armoured Personnel Carrier (FV103)

Variants

Anti-aircraft
Spartan can be fitted with the French ESD TA-20 twin 20 mm anti-aircraft turret or a turret with Blowpipe SAMs.

Anti-tank
The Spartan can be fitted with a Hughes TOW ATGW launcher, Euromissile MILAN Compact Turret with two MILAN ATGWs in ready to launch position or HOT Compact Turret with four HOT ATGWs in ready to launch position. The Spartan with MILAN Compact Turret has been adopted by the British Army.

Alvis Saracen Armoured Personnel Carrier

Development
Shortly after the end of the Second World War the Fighting Vehicles Research and Development Establishment (now the Military Vehicles and Engineering Establishment) began the design of the FV600 series of 6 × 6 vehicles. The first three models in this series were the FV601 Saladin armoured car, the FV602 command vehicle (which was cancelled in 1949 although the FV604 later took over its original role) and the FV603 Saracen APC. Owing to the situation in Malaya in the late 1940s, development of the FV603 was given precedence over that of the FV601 Saladin armoured car.

Design parent for the FV600 series was Alvis Limited of Coventry which completed the first prototype of the Saracen in 1952 and first production vehicles in December the same year. The first Mk 1s were powered by a Rolls-Royce B80 Mk 3A petrol engine which had BSF threads but later production Mk 1s were powered by a B80 Mk 6A petrol engine and had UNF threads. Early production vehicles had a slightly different turret: the rear of the turret opened either side rather than folding down horizontally as on later turrets.

Throughout the 1950s and early 1960s the Saracen was the standard APC of the British Army and was replaced from 1963 by the FV432 tracked APC. Today the Saracen is still in service with the British Army, mainly for internal security operations in Northern Ireland. Production continued for export until 1972. Production of the Saracen APC amounted to 1838 vehicles.

Description
The hull of the Saracen is made of all-welded steel with the engine at the front and the personnel compartment at the rear.

Air enters the engine compartment at the front of the vehicle through armoured louvres and is expelled through the four hatch covers over the engine compartment. Power is transmitted from the engine to the road wheels via a fluid coupling, five-speed pre-selective gearbox, transfer box with forward and reverse change, and differential transverse drive direct to each centre wheel hub through universally jointed shafts. Drive to the front and rear wheel hubs is by transmission shafts and bevel boxes. Each wheel hub houses an epicyclic train which provides the final gear reduction to the wheels. Steering of the front two and centre wheels is by positive mechanical linkage, hydraulically-assisted between the steering wheel and the road wheels. Hydraulic pressure for both steering and the foot brake is provided by an engine-driven hydraulic pump.

The suspension is of the double wishbone type with torsion bars and sleeves. Two telescopic double-acting hydraulic shock absorbers are fitted at each front and rear wheel station and the centre wheel stations each have a single telescopic double-acting hydraulic shock absorber. The gearbox and the transfer box are under the floor of the crew compartment in the centre and the fuel tank is under the floor of the crew compartment at the rear.

The driver sits at the front of the vehicle behind the engine compartment and has three No 17 periscopes, one in front and one either side of his position. The periscopes are mounted in hatch covers with the hatch cover to the driver's front folding forward onto the engine compartment for

Alvis Saracen APC with driver's front hatch, firing ports, rear doors and machine gun turret hatches open and 7.62 mm machine gun over rear troop compartment (Ministry of Defence)

Alvis Saracen modified for use in Northern Ireland fitted with screens against RPG-7 rockets (Ministry of Defence)

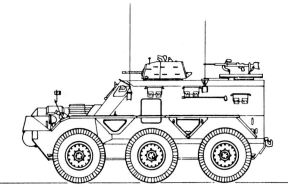

Alvis Saracen APC with reverse-flow cooling

increased visibility and those either side folding upwards on the outside.

The section commander sits behind the driver on the left with the radio operator in a similar position to his right. The eight infantrymen sit on individual seats, four down each side of the vehicle facing each other. They enter and leave the vehicle by two doors in the rear of the hull which open outwards and have a rectangular firing port that folds downwards on the outside. There are three similar firing ports in each side of the hull and a hull escape hatch over the second axle on each side.

The turret, which is similar to that fitted in the Ferret scout car Mk 2/3, has a basket type seat and is mounted in the forward part of the roof. The rear part of the turret roof folds forwards and can be locked horizontal if required while the turret rear folds downwards on the outside to form a seat for the gunner. The turret is armed with a 7.62 mm (0.30) Browning machine gun which has an elevation of +45 degrees and a depression of −12 degrees, except over the rear of the vehicle, and is fitted with a No 3 Mk 1 periscopic sight which is mounted in the forward part of the turret roof.

At the rear of the roof is a ring mount which is normally fitted with a 7.62 mm Bren LMG or sometimes a 7.62 mm (0.30) Browning machine gun. Three electrically-operated smoke dischargers mounted on each mudguard at the front of the vehicle launch smoke grenades to the front of the vehicle.

The Saracen APC is not fitted with an NBC system or any night vision equipment, although the latter could be fitted if required. A fresh air ventilation system is standard on all vehicles and pipes air from the outside (via two dome-shaped ventilators on the right side of the hull) to ducts that run down each side of the personnel compartment. The Saracen has no amphibious capability, although a deep fording kit was developed for the vehicle.

Variants

Saracen modified for use in Northern Ireland
Many of the Saracens used by the British Army in Northern Ireland have been fitted with wire screens for protection against Soviet RPG-7 rockets. The basic idea is that the HEAT warhead of the RPG-7 rocket will activate well away from the side of the vehicle. Some Saracens have also been uparmoured, especially around the firing ports and emergency exits, to stop bullet splash from entering the hull.

Saracen with Reverse-flow Cooling (FV603 (C))
This was designed by Alvis specifically for operations in the Middle East. On the basic model air is drawn in through the louvres at the front of the engine compartment and expelled

through the four hatch covers over the top. On the reverse-flow cooling model air is drawn in through raised louvres at the back of the engine compartment, passed forward over the engine by the fans the blades of which have been reversed, and then expelled through the radiators and front louvres. To prevent air rushing into the radiator and impeding passage of air through it in the opposite direction, a cowl has been mounted over the front of the vehicle.

Saracen with Open Roof
Some of the Saracens delivered to Kuwait in the 1960s were supplied with an open roof and a reverse-flow cooling system.

FV604 Command Vehicle
The FV604 is essentially the FV603 APC modified for use as a command vehicle.

The inside has been fitted with mapboards and modified to accommodate a crew of six: three staff officers, two radio operators and a driver. Externally, stowage baskets have been fitted as well as an auxiliary charging plant and additional batteries to power the communications equipment installed. Early vehicles retained the turret of the standard Saracen APC but most vehicles now have a ring-mounted machine gun in place of the turret. To increase the working area for the command staff a tent can be erected at the rear of the FV604. Loaded weight of the FV604 is 10 170 kg, length 4.851 metres, width 2.515 metres and height 2.057 metres.

FV610 Command Vehicle
The full designation of the FV610 is Armoured Carrier 6 × 6 Command GPO/CPO FV610(A). It has a crew of six which normally consists of three staff officers, two radio operators and a driver. Its main difference from the FV604 is a wider and higher hull as it is anticipated that it will be used in the static role for longer periods than the FV604. Equipment fitted to the FV610 includes additional mapboards, communications equipment, an auxiliary charging plant and additional batteries. Loaded weight of the FV610 is 10 700 kg, length 4.851 metres, width 2.515 metres and height 2.362 metres.

FV611 Ambulance
This has the same hull as the FV610 and can carry ten seated patients, or three stretcher and two seated patients, or two stretcher and six seated patients in addition to the crew of two which consists of the driver and the medical orderly.

FV610 command vehicle showing tent frame retracted

SPECIFICATIONS (FV603 (C) with reverse-flow cooling)

CREW	2 + 10	GRADIENT	42%	ARMAMENT		
CONFIGURATION	6 × 6	VERTICAL OBSTACLE	0.46 m	turret	1 × 7.62 mm MG	
COMBAT WEIGHT	10 170 kg	TRENCH	1.52 m	ring-mounted	1 × 7.62 mm MG	
UNLOADED WEIGHT	8640 kg	TURNING RADIUS	7 m	SMOKE-LAYING		
POWER-TO-WEIGHT		ENGINE	Rolls-Royce B80 Mk 6A	EQUIPMENT	2 × 3 smoke	
RATIO	15.73 hp/tonne		8-cylinder petrol developing		dischargers	
GROUND PRESSURE	0.98 kg/cm²		160 hp at 3750 rpm	AMMUNITION	3000	
LENGTH HULL	5.233 m	TRANSMISSION	pre-selector 5-speed	ARMOUR		
WIDTH	2.539 m	STEERING	recirculating ball,	Hull visor plate	12 mm at 40°	
HEIGHT			hydraulically-assisted	Hull skid plate	10 mm at 40°	
to turret top	2.463 m	CLUTCH	fluid coupling	Hull sides	12 mm at 20°	
to hull top	2 m	SUSPENSION	independent double	Hull top	8 mm	
GROUND CLEARANCE	0.432 m		wishbone and torsion bar,	Hull floor	12 mm	
TRACK	2.083 m		hydraulic shock absorbers	Turret front	16 mm at 15°	
WHEELBASE	1.524 m + 1.524 m	TYRES	12.00 × 20	Turret sides	16 mm at 15°	
ANGLE OF APPROACH/		BRAKES		Turret rear	16 mm at 15°	
DEPARTURE	53°/53°	main	hydraulic disc on all	Turret top	8 mm	
MAX ROAD SPEED	72 km/h		wheels			
FUEL CAPACITY	200 litres	parking	mechanical on all			
MAX RANGE	400 km		wheels			
FORDING	1.07 m	ELECTRICAL SYSTEM	24 V			
with preparation	1.98 m	BATTERIES	2 × 12 V			

Status: Production complete. In service with Hong Kong (police), Indonesia, Jordan, Kuwait, Lebanon, Libya, Nigeria, Qatar, South Africa, Sudan, Thailand, United Arab Emirates and the United Kingdom.

Manufacturer: Alvis Limited, Holyhead Road, Coventry, West Midlands CV5 8JH, England. (A member of the United Scientific Group.)

Vickers Valkyr Armoured Personnel Carrier

Development
The Valkyr APC has been developed as a private venture by Vickers Defence Systems in association with Beherman-Demoen of Belgium which built the BDX (4 × 4) APC which is described under Belgium.

Vickers was responsible for research, development and construction of the prototypes based on the initial Beherman Demoen design. A prototype APC version was shown at the 1982 British Army Equipment Exhibition. A production version of the APC was shown at the 1984 exhibition and a fire support vehicle with a two-man 90 mm Cockerill turret was demonstrated at the firepower display.

Valkyr has been designed specifically to form the basis of a vehicle family which fulfills a variety of internal security (IS) and battlefield roles as a personnel carrier and fire support vehicle.

Description
The monocoque hull of both versions of the Valkyr is all-welded high-hardness steel armour which gives immunity against 7.62 mm armour-piercing projectiles over the frontal arc, and elsewhere against 7.62 mm ball ammunition fired at point blank range. For the IS variant, or where specified, appliqué armour is used to give all-round armour-piercing protection; this enables one basic hull to meet two different threat levels.

The crew is also protected from shell splinters from 155 mm howitzer projectiles. The armoured glass windscreen and vision blocks afford similar protection, while the underside of the hull gives protection against anti-personnel mines.

The driver sits centrally at the front of the vehicle. He has access to the troop compartment through a small passageway on the left side of the hull.

A commander's cupola is fitted on the left side of the body between the front wheel arch and side door. A variety of cupolas are offered with various vision and weapon systems.

Access to the crew compartment is through two large rear-opening doors with a side door on the left for the commander and driver. A door on the right may be used for loading stores.

Vision blocks are fitted above the side door and in each rear door. Weapon firing ports can be fitted to suit the user's needs.

The engine compartment is to the rear of the driver on the right side with the air-inlet and air-outlet louvres in the roof and the exhaust pipe running alongside the upper part of the hull on the right side. The powerpack is fully enclosed by noise absorption panels. A PTO at the front of the engine provides hydraulic power for brake and steering

Latest model of Valkyr used in IS role with commander's cupola to left rear of driver

Vickers Defence Systems Valkyr Fire Support vehicle fitted with Belgian Cockerill two-man turret armed with 90 mm Cockerill Mk. 3 gun

actuation, fan operation and brake cooling oil circulation.

A two-stage 360 mm diameter air cleaner is fitted, protecting the engine from damage by dirt, dust and sand. The large particles are removed by the cyclonic first stage while a dry filter element removes the remainder. An electrical restriction indicator provides a visual warning to the driver when the filter element needs replacing.

The engine is water-cooled. The coolant flows through a gill-type radiator mounted horizontally above the engine. Air is drawn through the radiator by a hydraulically-driven mixed flow fan. A second gill-type radiator is mounted below the coolant radiator and cools the axle/disc coolant oil. Air is drawn from vents in the rear over the engine transmission casings and expelled through the roof.

A Graviner Firewire fire-detection system is fitted around the engine/transmission area, with a manually-operated extinguishing system which can be triggered by either crew or passengers.

The engine is directly coupled to a fully automatic gearbox with four forward and one reverse gears. For road use the rear axle is normally engaged, with the four-wheel drive being selected when travelling over rough country. For maximum tractive effort lockable differentials are used on both axles in low gear ratios.

The engine and transmission are all located within the armoured hull for maximum protection against disabling damage. Drive is provided through the constant velocity joints on the front and universal joints on the rear. Hub reduction units are employed on all wheels.

Fully independent suspension is fitted all round and each wheel is mounted on double wishbones with variable rate coil springs and coaxial telescopic dampers. The steering is Adwest servarak power assisted. Run-flat inserts are fitted to the 14.00 × 20 radial ply tyres. The large tyres reduce ground pressure and improve traction on soft ground.

The brakes are of the oil-immersed multiple disc type, heat generated by braking being dispersed into the oil which is continually cycled through a remote cooler. Two modes of brake operation are employed: the footbrake operates hydraulically on all four wheels, with full power assistance. A dual hydraulic circuit, split vertically into front and rear axle systems ensures braking capacity in the event of either circuit failing. Hydraulic accumulators incorporated into the brake

circuit provide a reserve of power to stop the vehicle even with the engine disabled. The mechanical handbrake operates on the rear brakes.

Valkyr as an APC can carry eight fully-equipped troops plus the driver and commander/gunner. Ample storage is provided behind the seats for a Light Anti-tank Weapon, ammunition, 48-hour survival kit, water and spare fuel. The main difference in the Fire Support hull is a lower silhouette which allows a crewed turret to be fitted. The Valkyr FSV has been designed to accept a complete range of turret and weapons including:
One-man turret with twin 7.62 mm machine guns
One-man turret with 7.62 mm and 12.7 mm machine guns
Two-man turret with 7.62 mm machine gun, 20 mm cannon and 60 mm gun/mortar
Two-man turret with 7.62 mm machine gun, 12.7 mm machine gun and 60 mm gun/mortar
Two-man turret with 90 mm gun. The vehicle has already been tested fitted with the Cockerill CM 90 90 mm turret and the ENGESA ET-90 90 mm two man turrets.
One-man anti-aircraft turret with twin 20 mm cannon

Optional equipment includes an air-conditioning system, NBC system, passive night vision equipment, appliqué armour, winch, anti-molotov cocktail system and water propulsion kit mounted at the rear of the hull for increased water speed. The basic model is fully amphibious, propelled in the water by its wheels.

Variants
In addition to being used as an APC the Valkyr can be used for a wide range of other roles including anti-tank with ATGW, close support, recovery, workshop, state vehicle, command post, field ambulance, 81 mm mortar carrier and internal security vehicle. For the last role a variety of equipment can be fitted including a barricade removal device, smoke grenade launchers, public address system, teargas bottles, ring-mounted machine-gun, water cannon and secondary glazing/armoured shutters.

Status: Development complete. Ready for production.

Manufacturer: Vickers Defence Systems, Armstrong Works, Newcastle-upon-Tyne NE99 1CP, England.

Latest version of the Vickers Defence Systems Valkyr APC, with commander's cupola fitted with 7.62 mm machine gun

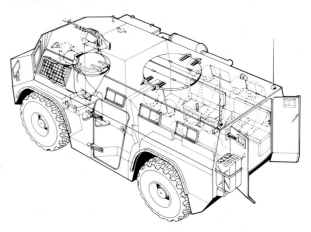

SPECIFICATIONS (Vickers Valkyr)

CREW	2 + 10	MAX SPEED	100 km/h	SUSPENSION	double wishbone
CONFIGURATION	4 × 4	FUEL CAPACITY	200 litres	TYRES	14.00 × 20
COMBAT WEIGHT	11 000 kg	MAX RANGE	700 km	BRAKES	
UNLOADED WEIGHT	8650 kg	FORDING	fully amphibious	main	hydraulic
POWER-TO-WEIGHT		GRADIENT	60%	parking	mechanical
RATIO	16.36 hp/tonne	SIDE SLOPE	40%	STEERING	power assisted rack and
LENGTH HULL	5.6 m	VERTICAL OBSTACLE	0.4 m		pinion
WIDTH	2.5 m	TURNING RADIUS	8 m	ELECTRICAL SYSTEM	24 V
HEIGHT TO HULL TOP		ENGINE	General Motors 4-53T diesel	BATTERIES	2 × 12 V, 100 Ah
APC	2.05 m		developing 180 hp at	ARMAMENT	see text
FSV	2.21 m		2800 rpm	ARMOUR	8 mm to 13 mm
GROUND CLEARANCE	0.38 m	TRANSMISSION	General Motors Allison		
WHEELBASE	3.1 m		Division AT-545 automatic		
ANGLE OF APPROACH/			with 4 forward and 1 reverse		
DEPARTURE	45°/45°		gears		

FS100 Simba Fighting Vehicle

Development

The FS100 Simba (4 × 4) family of AFVs has been designed as a private venture by the Fighting Vehicle Division of GKN Sankey Limited specifically for the export market and meets the requirement for a wheeled family of vehicles capable of mounting modern weapon systems up to 90 mm. The design offers a high level of reliability while retaining simplicity of operation and maintenance. A removable roof plinth enables weapon systems to be installed rapidly.

Description

Two armour options are available for the FS100 Simba range of light combat vehicles. The high mobility option of a lightweight high hardness ballistic steel hull gives immunity against 7.62 mm ball rounds at any angle and any range. The high protection option provides complete immunity against 7.62 mm AP or ball rounds fired from any distance or any angle between +40 degrees and −10 degrees. This option also gives improved protection against mine blast.

The hull of the FS100 is of all-welded steel armour construction that provides the crew with complete protection from small arms fire and shell splinters.

The driver sits at the front of the vehicle on the left and has two bullet-proof windows to his front and either side and a single-piece hatch cover that opens to the rear.

The engine is to the right of the driver with the air-inlet louvres at the front and the air-outlet louvres on the right side. The Perkins TV8.540 rated at 210 bhp is coupled to a Clark combined gearbox/transfer box which transmits power to the front and rear axles.

The troop compartment is at the rear of the Simba. Bullet-proof windows are provided in each side of the troop compartment with firing ports positioned between the windows.

The troops enter and leave the Simba via two doors in the rear of the hull, each of these has a bullet-proof vision block with a firing port underneath.

A wide range of armament installations can be fitted to the Simba. When used as an APC the vehicle normally transports up to a crew of 12 including the commander and driver. When a one-man turret with single or twin 7.62 mm GPMG is fitted a crew of ten is normally carried.

FS100 Simba Light Combat Group

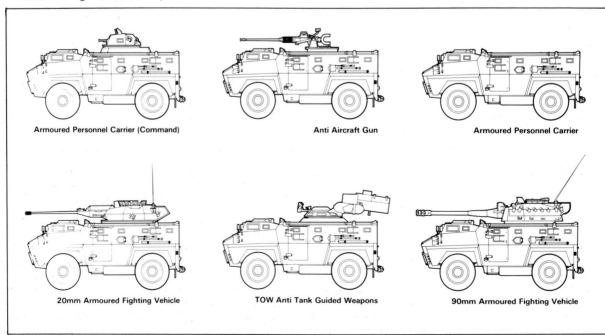

Armoured Personnel Carrier (Command)

Anti Aircraft Gun

Armoured Personnel Carrier

20mm Armoured Fighting Vehicle

TOW Anti Tank Guided Weapons

90mm Armoured Fighting Vehicle

GKN Sankey FS100 in basic armoured personnel carrier configuration without armament

Variants

FS100/20
Two-man turret armed with 20 mm Oerlikon cannon and coaxial 7.62 mm GPMG with crew of three consisting of commander, gunner and driver. Space is also provided for stowage and four passengers.

FS100/90
Two-man turret with 90 mm Cockerill Mk III gun and 7.62 mm coaxial GPMG with crew of three consisting of commander, gunner and driver. Space is also provided for stowage and four passengers. The Belgian Cockerill CM 90 turret is currently being offered for the FS100/90.

FS100/20 Anti-aircraft
20 mm Oerlikon HS 820 cannon in scarfe ring mount.

FS100/TOW/ATGW
Fitted with Emerson TOW mount as installed in M901 Improved TOW Vehicle.

FS100/HOT/ATGW
Fitted with the Euromissile HOT Compact Turret (HCT) with four HOT ATGW in ready to launch position.

FS100/CP
Command post configuration with facilities for multi-radio installations, map displays and watchkeeper consoles.

FS100/Ambulance
Equipped for ambulance role with up to three stretcher positions.

FS100/Recovery
Equipped for recovery role.

SPECIFICATIONS (APC)	
CONFIGURATION	4 × 4
CREW	12 max
COMBAT WEIGHT	10 000 kg
LENGTH	5.26 m
WIDTH	2.54 m
HEIGHT (hull top)	2.1 m
	(w/o armament)
GROUND CLEARANCE	
(axle)	0.33 m
WHEELBASE	2.9 m
TRACK	
front	2.08 m
rear	1.99 m
ANGLE OF APPROACH/	
DEPARTURE	40°/40°
FUEL CAPACITY	230 litres
MAX ROAD SPEED	100 km/h
ROAD RANGE	650 km
FORDING	1 m
GRADIENT	52%
SIDE SLOPE	35%
VERTICAL OBSTACLE	0.41 m
TURNING RADIUS	8.25 m
ENGINE	Perkins TV8.540 diesel, 210 bhp at 2500 rpm
TRANSMISSION	Clark 13.1 HR 28422 semi-automatic, 4 forward and 2 reverse gears
ARMAMENT	Pintle GPMG or one-man single or twin GPMG 7.62 mm turret
STEERING	power-assisted
SUSPENSION	semi-elliptical springs with hydraulic shock absorbers
TYRES	14.00 × 20 or 12.00 × 20
BRAKES	
main	drum, air-hydraulic (dual circuit)
parking	transmission brake
ELECTRICAL SYSTEM	24 V

Status: Development complete. Ready for production.

Manufacturer: GKN Sankey Limited, Defence Vehicle Operations, PO Box 20, Hadley Castle Works, Telford, Shropshire TF1 4RE, England.

AT105 Saxon Armoured Personnel Carrier

Development
The AT105 was developed by GKN Sankey as the successor to its earlier AT104. The first prototype of the AT105 was completed in 1974 and the first production vehicles in 1976.

Main improvements over the original AT104 can be summarised as: the armoured hull has been designed to give the same degree of protection to the radiator, engine and transmission as to the crew; redesigned hull floor to give increased protection against damage from mines; more powerful engine and a shorter wheelbase for improved mobility and turning.

Whereas the original AT104 was designed primarily for internal security operations, the new and redesigned AT105 is now being offered for a much wider range of applications such as reconnaissance, command/radio and recovery. In mid-1982 the AT105 was named the Saxon. Early in 1983 the British Ministry of Defence placed an order with GKN Sankey for an initial 47 Saxon APCs for the British Army, with first deliveries made in early 1984. GKN is now building the second production batch of 247 Saxons for the British Army who has an option on a further 200 vehicles to bring the total order book to 497 vehicles. There is also a requirement for 500 Saxons to equip Territorial Army units earmarked for BAOR.

Saxon APC as delivered to British Army with commander's hatch cover in open position but 7.62 mm machine gun not installed

AT105-E Saxon APC with turret armed with twin 7.62 mm GPMGs and electrically operated smoke dischargers

Each British Army Saxon will carry a fully-equipped rifle section of ten and be issued to UK-based infantry battalions that will reinforce BAOR in time of war. The British Army Saxons have a fixed observation cupola for the commander, with a socket in each corner of the cupola for a 7.62 mm GPMG DISA mount. British Army vehicles will have no door in the left side of the hull, a stowage rack on the roof and external fully-enclosed bins. Two variants are being supplied to the British Army, command and recovery. The latter has a side-mounted five-tonne hydraulic winch that can be used to the front or rear and is driven from a PTO from the gearbox. There are interior seats for a crew of four in addition to stowage for recovery equipment. From production vehicle 100, British Army Saxons will be fitted with two banks of electrically-operated smoke dischargers. These will be back-fitted to earlier vehicles.

By March 1984 the first group of the British Army's Saxon APCs had successfully completed the first familiarisation course at the Infantry Trials and Development Unit, School of Infantry, Warminster, and first deliveries had been made to the 1st Battalion The King's Own Border Regiment for operational training.

Description

(Right-hand drive model; left-hand drive also available)

The basic model has a hull of all-welded steel with the driver seated at the very front of the hull on the right side and the personnel compartment at the rear. The hull provides the crew with complete protection against small arms fire up to and including 7.62 mm armour-piercing rounds, and HE shell fragments up to 155 mm when burst at ten metres from the vehicle. The floor is V-shaped to give maximum protection against mine blast, except for the axles, which are outside the armoured section. The engine, transmission, fuel, batteries, as well as the vacuum servos and hydraulics are all contained within the armoured compartment. The engine, transmission and other automotive components are standard commercial items. British Army vehicles have a high degree of commonality in engine and axle components with other in-service vehicles.

The driver can reach his seat either from inside the vehicle or by a forward-opening hatch cover over his position. There are bullet-proof windscreens in front and on both sides.

The personnel sit four down each side of the hull on padded bench seats which are usually equipped with seat belts, and enter and leave the vehicle by two doors in the rear of the hull and a single door in each side of the hull. The British Army specification has minor differences from other in-service vehicles and these include exterior stowage bins and no left hand door. Each of the doors has a firing port and a vision block. There are additional firing ports in each side of the hull and a single firing port in the forward part of the hull on the left side. Specially designed ball mounts have also been developed which can be installed in the firing ports to allow the crew to fire their weapons from inside the vehicle in safety. The interior of the hull is lined with 26 mm thick thermal insulation and a forced air circulation system is fitted as standard on all vehicles.

The commander's cupola has four sides each with a vision block, and a single-piece hatch cover that opens forwards. A 7.62 mm machine gun can be pintle-mounted at this position if required. The commander's cupola is welded to an oblong sheet of armour which in turn is bolted to the roof of the vehicle. This allows the command module to be removed and replaced by another module with a different armament installation. When the engine needs replacement the roof module is removed first and the complete engine and transmission can be lifted through the roof. Run-flat cross-country tyres are fitted as standard and in a 'shot through' condition the vehicle can travel 96 km at 48 km/h.

Optional equipment for the AT105 includes air-conditioning systems, auxiliary power unit, barricade

AT105-E Saxon APC

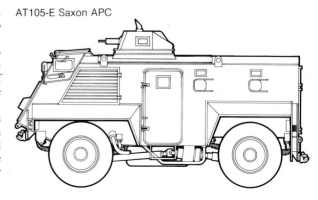

AT105 with one-man turret armed with ARWEN 37V weapon, barricade removal equipment on front of hull and wire mesh protection screen folded back on hull side

remover, door safety mechanism, grenade launchers, hand-operated searchlight, heater, rotating/flashing beacons and siren, loud speakers and a front-mounted winch.

Variants

AT105-E Armoured Personnel Carrier

This is as AT105-P but fitted with a turret armed with a single 7.62 mm GPMG with an elevation of +50 degrees and a depression of −15 degrees, or a turret armed with twin 7.62 mm GPMGs with identical elevation and depression. The AT105 can also be used to deploy and operate a remote-controlled EOD vehicle for bomb disposal duties.

Saxon Recovery Vehicle

This has a side-mounted 5000 kg hydraulic winch giving recovery facilities to the front or rear of the vehicle. The winch is hydraulically driven by a PTO from the gearbox. Interior configuration gives seating for a crew of four in addition to stowage for recovery equipment.

AT105-Q Command Vehicle

This has the commander's cupola as fitted to the AT-105P but can be fitted with a turret armed with single or twin 7.62 mm GPMGs. The interior is modified for use as a command vehicle: on the right side of the hull are staff positions with individual communication control modules, and on the left is a mapboard with strip lighting, and storage space behind. A teleprinter operator's position with seat and table behind are also provided. A similar configuration has been adopted for the British Army Command vehicles.

AT105-A Armoured Ambulance

This is as AT105-P with commander's cupola and can carry four stretcher patients, one or two orderlies, commander and driver, or two stretcher cases, four walking wounded, one orderly, commander and driver.

AT105 with ARWEN 37V

In February 1984 GKN Sankey announced that a new version of the AT105 had been developed for use in IS operations. This has a one-man turret fitted with the ARWEN 37V rapid fire weapon which can fire five rounds in quick succession before it needs reloading. It is mounted in a new turret design that allows high levels of visibility and the ability to follow the flight of CS or smoke rounds.

AT105 Water Cannon

The prototype of this version was tested in 1984.

AT105 Ambulance

This can carry four stretcher patients or a mixture of stretcher and seated patients and was shown for the first time in 1984.

SPECIFICATIONS	
CREW	2 + 8 (or 10)
CONFIGURATION	4 × 4
COMBAT WEIGHT	10 670 kg
UNLOADED WEIGHT	8640 kg
POWER-TO-WEIGHT RATIO	
(164 bhp engine)	13.68 bhp/tonne
LENGTH	5.169 m
WIDTH	2.489 m
HEIGHT	
to commander's cupola	2.628 m
top of turret, if fitted	2.86 m
GROUND CLEARANCE	
hull	0.41 m
axles	0.29 m
TRACK	
front	2.08 m
rear	1.99 m
WHEELBASE	3.073 m
ANGLE OF APPROACH/ DEPARTURE	48°/40°
MAX ROAD SPEED	96 km/h
FUEL CAPACITY	160 litres
MAX ROAD RANGE	510 km
FORDING	1.12 m
GRADIENT	60%
VERTICAL OBSTACLE	0.41 m
TURNING RADIUS	7.57 m
ENGINE	Bedford 500 6-cylinder diesel developing 164 bhp at 2800 rpm*
TRANSMISSION	Allison AT-545 automatic with 4 forward and 1 reverse gears
TRANSFER CASE	2-speed
STEERING	Burman, power-assisted
SUSPENSION	semi-elliptical springs and hydraulic shock absorbers
TYRES	12.00 × 20, 13.00 × 20 or 14.00 × 20
BRAKES	
main	drum, air/hydraulic (dual circuit)
parking	transmission brake
ELECTRICAL SYSTEM	24 V
BATTERIES	2 × 12 V, 100 Ah
ARMOUR	proof against 7.62 mm/ 0.30 AP rounds at point blank range

* It can also be fitted with a Perkins T6-354-4 diesel developing 195 bhp at 2500 rpm

Status: In production. In service with Bahrain, Kuwait, Malaysia (40 purchased in 1977 for $4.7 million), Nigeria, Oman (25 for Royal Guard and Police) and British Army.

Manufacturer: GKN Sankey Limited, Defence Vehicles Operations, PO Box 20, Hadley Castle Works, Telford, Shropshire TF1 4RE, England.

Note: About 30 AT104 internal security vehicles were built by GKN Sankey between 1972 and 1976 and these remain in service with the Dutch State Police and Royal Brunei Malay Regiment.

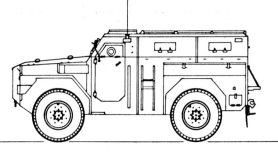

FV1611 one-ton armoured personnel carrier

Humber One-ton Armoured Personnel Carrier

Development

After the end of the Second World War, an entire range of one-ton (4 × 4) vehicles was developed specifically to meet the requirements of the British Army by Rootes under the Humber name, known as the FV1600 series. As insufficient Alvis Saracen (6 × 6) APCs were available in the early 1950s it was decided to produce an APC model of the FV1600 series. About 1700 were subsequently built with the chassis supplied by Rootes at Maidstone in Kent and the armoured bodies by GKN Sankey (which later built the FV432 tracked armoured personnel carrier) and the Royal Ordnance Factory at Woolwich.

By the late 1960s most of the vehicles had been withdrawn from service and scrapped but when the situation in Northern Ireland became worse the vehicles were brought back into service as internal security vehicles, in which role they remain in service today. It is estimated that about 500 are in service with the British Army.

FV1611 APC modified for use in Northern Ireland with searchlight and observation equipment on roof (Ministry of Defence)

Description

The basic APC is designated the FV1611 or Truck 1-ton Armoured 4 × 4 Humber, or more commonly the Pig. It has an all-welded hull with the engine at the front, commander and driver in the centre and the personnel compartment at the rear.

The driver sits on the right with the commander on the left, both with a windscreen to their front which when in action is covered by an armoured shutter hinged at the top, with an integral vision block. Most vehicles have had the windscreen removed. Both the driver and commander also have a side door which opens forwards, the top of which opens to the outside for increased visibility. The top part has an integral vision block. Over the top of the commander's and driver's position is a circular hatch that opens forwards.

The six men sit on bench seats, three down each side of the vehicle, although a maximum of eight can be carried in the rear. They enter and leave the vehicle by twin doors in the rear of the hull, each of which has a firing port. As originally built two rectangular firing ports, hinged at the bottom, were provided in each side of the troop compartment, but many vehicles have had a ventilator fitted over one of these firing ports in each side of the hull.

As a result of combat experience in Northern Ireland all vehicles have been uparmoured to enable them to withstand attack from 7.62 mm armour-piercing rounds, which has increased the vehicle's weight to about 7000 kg. Other modifications include the removal of external stowage boxes, a drop panel fitted under the rear of the hull to stop bullets going under the vehicle and striking the legs of troops standing at the rear and modifications to the rear doors: cutting off the top quarter and fitting a hinged flap to the top of the hull.

There are a number of specialised versions of the Pig in service in Northern Ireland, including vehicles with barricade-removing equipment at the front of the hull, special EOD equipment and some with a protected observation position in the roof. Some vehicles have been fitted with searchlights and tear gas launchers.

Variants

FV1609, original armoured version but the troop compartment at the rear has an open roof

FV1612, radio vehicle with crew of three (commander, driver and radio operator)

FV1613, ambulance with crew of two (driver and medical orderly) and accommodation for three stretchers or eight sitting patients or one stretcher and four sitting patients.

The basic truck version, the FV1601, is no longer in service with the British Army and the FV1620 armoured Hornet vehicle, which launched the Malkara ATGW, has also been withdrawn from service.

SPECIFICATIONS

CREW	2 + 6 (or 8)
CONFIGURATION	4 × 4
COMBAT WEIGHT	5790 kg
UNLOADED WEIGHT	4770 kg
POWER-TO-WEIGHT	
RATIO	20.72 bhp/tonne
LENGTH	4.926 m
WIDTH	2.044 m
HEIGHT	2.12 m
TRACK	1.713 m
WHEELBASE	2.743 m
MAX ROAD SPEED	64 km/h
FUEL CAPACITY	145 litres
MAX ROAD RANGE	402 km at 64 km/h
ENGINE	Rolls-Royce B60 Mk 5A
	6-cylinder petrol developing
	120 bhp at 3750 rpm
TRANSMISSION	manual with 5 forward and 1
	reverse gears
TRANSFER BOX	single speed
STEERING	re-circulating ball
CLUTCH	single dry plate
SUSPENSION	torsion bar and telescopic
	shock absorber for each
	wheel station
TYRES	11.00 × 20
BRAKES	
main	hydraulic, drum pattern
	on all wheels
parking	hand, mechanical

Status: Production complete. In service with United Kingdom.

Manufacturers: Chassis, Rootes Limited, bodies GKN Sankey and ROF Woolwich.

Hotspur Dragoon Armoured Personnel Carrier

Development

The Dragoon 6484 APC has been developed as a private venture by the Hotspur company and was shown for the first time at the 1984 British Army Equipment Exhibition. At that time it was expected that production of the Dragoon would begin in the near future.

Prototype of Hotspur Dragoon armoured personnel carrier

Description

The Dragoon APC is based on the chassis of the re[...] Land-Rover One Ten with an additional powered axle, [...]ified and strengthened to accommodate the weight of the armoured hull.

The Hotspur steel armoured hull, which fully encloses the engine and troop compartment, has been designed to provide ballistic immunity at 25 metres at a 90-degree attack angle from ball ammunition fired from 7.62 mm type weapons and from point-blank attack by lighter weapons such as the 9 mm Sterling SMG, M1 carbine and .44 Magnum. The floor armour protects the crew from mine fragments and grenades.

The engine and transmission are at the front of the vehicle with the troop compartment at the rear. A spare wheel and tyre are carried on the bonnet. The engine is coupled to a manual transmission and the driver can select either 6 × 6 or 6 × 4 (first and second axles) depending on the terrain encountered.

The commander and driver sit to the rear of the engine and each has a laminated armoured glass windscreen to his front and side with anti-splinter screens of polycarbonate. The screens can be activated from inside the vehicle either manually or electrically. In each side of the hull is a single door that opens to the front, in the upper part of this is a bullet-proof vision block with a firing port underneath.

The troop compartment is at the rear of the hull and the 12 troops sit on bench seats down either side of the hull and enter via the side doors or the two doors in the hull rear. In each side of the troop compartment are two vision blocks with a firing port underneath and each of the rear doors also has a firing port with vision block underneath. The troop compartment is 3.15 metres long, 1.44 metres wide and 1.194 metres high.

If required, a light armour turret or a fully-rotating machine gun hatch mounting a 7.62 mm machine gun can be fitted to the roof. The basic turret has manual traverse but powered traverse is an option.

Standard equipment for the Dragoon includes a full air-conditioning system for the troop compartment in addition to a forced draught ventilation system.

Optional equipment includes a 24-volt electrical system, winch, spot lamps, intercom/siren, public address system, two four-barrel smoke/grenade launchers on the turret, self-sealing fuel tank, fuel tank with an additional 45.5-litres

capacity, powered steering, run-flat tyres with split rims, night vison equipment for the driver and a diesel engine.

Variants

A number of variants of the Dragoon are under considera tion, these include a field ambulance and a commun-ications/command vehicle.

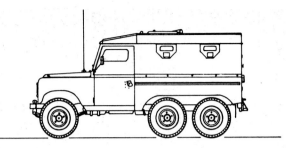

Hotspur Sandringham 6 APC without armament

SPECIFICATIONS

CREW	1 + 13
CONFIGURATION	6 × 6
COMBAT WEIGHT	4700 kg
POWER-TO-WEIGHT	
RATIO	24 hp/tonne
LENGTH	5.74 m
WIDTH	1.87 m
HEIGHT	
with turret	2.72 m
to hull roof	2.125 m
GROUND CLEARANCE	0.21 m
TRACK	1.486 m
WHEELBASE	3.81 m
ANGLE OF APPROACH/	
DEPARTURE	40°/30°
FUEL CAPACITY	98 litres
TURNING RADIUS	8.65 m
ENGINE	3.528-litre V-8, water-cooled petrol developing 114 hp at 4000 rpm
TRANSMISSION	manual, 4 forward, 1 reverse gears
STEERING	recirculating ball, worm and nut
CLUTCH	single dry plate
TRANSFER BOX	2-speed
SUSPENSION	
front	dual rate coil springs, live beam axle, double acting hydraulic dampers
middle and rear	A frame, live rear axle, single rate coil springs, double acting hydraulic dampers
BRAKES	
front	hydraulic, servo-assisted disc
rear and middle	hydraulic, servo-assisted drum
TYRES	7.50 × 16
ELECTRICAL SYSTEM	12 V
BATTERY	1 × 12 V, 58 Ah

Status: Development complete. Ready for production.

Manufacturer: Hotspur Armoured Products Limited, Ynysygerwn Avenue, Aberdulais, Neath, West Glamorgan SA10 8HH, Wales.

Hotspur Sandringham 6 Armoured Personnel Carrier

Development

The Hotspur Sandringham 6 APC has been developed as a private venture and was shown for the first time at the British Army Equipment Exhibition held in June 1980. By early 1981 the prototype had successfully completed its trials and production began in 1982.

The vehicle is based on the chassis of the Sandringham 6 (6 × 6) vehicle manufactured by Hotspur Cars Limited. This in turn is essentially a 6 × 6 version of the new 4 × 4 V-8 powered LWB Land-Rover with greatly increased load carrying capability.

The Sandringham 6 APC has over 90 per cent common-ality of spares with the standard Land-Rover and full spare parts back up is therefore available from the extensive net-work of Land-Rover distributors all over the world. Servicing is no more difficult than with the Land-Rover and all routine maintenance points are readily accessible and major items such as the engine or gearbox are easily removed and replaced. The conversion is fully approved by Land-Rover Limited.

Description

The layout of the Hotspur Sandringham 6 APC is similar to the LWB Land-Rover with the engine at the front, driver and commander to the rear of the engine and the troop compart-ment at the rear. The chassis has been modified, reinforced and internally rustproofed.

The opaque steel armour is resistant to multi-impact all-round attack from high velocity rifles at 25 metres and shell splinters. The fully welded body unit, complete with seats, is bolted to the chassis and is detachable.

The V-8 engine is coupled to a manual transmission with four forward and one reverse gears, two speed transfer box with permanent six wheel drive, and a lockable central differential.

The radiator grille and engine compartment sides are armoured and the integral welded steel floor with angled sections gives protection against sub-surface mine fragments and grenade attack.

The commander and driver have side doors that open forwards, the upper part of the doors have transparent armour of multi-laminated glass construction with separate polycarbonate anti-spall screens resistant to attack from high velocity rifles and lesser weapons to British Standard Specification 5051 level G3. The windscreens to the front of the commander and driver are also of transparent armour with a similar level of protection. Both windscreen and front door windows can be provided with additional protection by hinged armour screens which incorporate vision slots. The commander and driver each have a Land-Rover de-luxe seat complete with seat belt.

The eight fully equipped infantrymen sit at the rear, four down each side of the hull and enter and leave via two doors in the rear. Locking bars are provided on all doors of the vehicle. Rear steps, spring loaded, assist the infantrymen in leaving the vehicle and a grab rail runs down the centre of the roof. The floor of the troop compartment is non-slip.

Six firing ports with vision blocks, two in each side of the hull and two in the rear doors, allow some of the infantry to fire their small arms from within the vehicle.

The on/off road tyres are fitted with safety run-flat bands.

Standard equipment includes fan ventilation system, interior lights, reversing lights, twin wing mirrors, locking fuel cap, lamp guards and 80-litre long range explosion-proof fuel tank.

Two Hotspur Sandringham 6 APCs as supplied to Finland for use in Lebanon, with vehicle on left showing visor lowered

Optional equipment includes automatic engine fire-extinguishing system, auxiliary 50-litre petrol tank, barricade ram, CS gas/smoke dischargers, diesel engine, driving siren, external spotlamps, four wheel drive only (e.g. 6 × 4), front-mounted twin spotlamps (internally-controlled), front-mounted power winch, full air-conditioning, full harness seat belts in rear, fully adjustable Bostrum shock-absorbing driver's seat, heavy duty alternator, helicopter lifting lugs, hostile fire indicator, high-power solvent screen wash, roof-mounted lightweight armoured machine gun cupola with periscope to accept 7.62 mm GPMG or Minimi and mount, lightweight fully rotating armoured machine gun turret, public address system, radio base or slave equipment, self-sealing petrol tank, twin driving spotlamps, two-way intercom and various communications systems.

Variants

The manufacturer has other body options including command/communication vehicle, field ambulance, long distance patrol vehicle and a fuel or water tanker. The basic vehicle has also been adapted as a mobile platform for several anti-aircraft weapon systems and as a tractor for artillery.

SPECIFICATIONS

CONFIGURATION	6 × 6
CREW	2 + 8
COMBAT WEIGHT	3700 kg
UNLOADED WEIGHT	2690 kg
GROUND PRESSURE	
(unloaded)	1.16 kg/cm²
LENGTH	4.445 m
WIDTH	1.69 m
HEIGHT	
(without armament)	2.083 m
GROUND CLEARANCE	0.209 m
WHEELBASE	2.706 m + 0.939 m
TRACK	1.334 m
FUEL CAPACITY	82.81 litres
ENGINE	V-8 petrol developing 92 bhp (DIN) at 3500 rpm
TRANSMISSION	manual, 4 forward and 1 reverse gears
TRANSFER BOX	2-speed
STEERING	re-circulating ball
SUSPENSION	heavy duty dual comprising semi-elliptic leaf road springs assisted by progressive rubber springs on front and rear axles, telescopic heavy duty shock absorbers
ELECTRICAL SYSTEM	12 V
BATTERY	1 × 12 V, 120 Ah

Status: In production. In service with Finland (two for use with United Nations Forces), Sri Lanka (six) and an undisclosed Gulf state army (six).

Manufacturer: Hotspur Armoured Products Limited, Ynysygerwn Avenue, Aberdulais, Neath, West Glamorgan SA10 8HH, Wales.

Shorland SB 401 Armoured Personnel Carrier

Development

The first Shorland armoured personnel carrier, the SB 301, was developed as a private venture by Shorts with the prototype completed in 1973 and the first production vehicle the following year. It has been designed specifically for internal security operations and is based on operational experience obtained with the Shorland armoured patrol car, with which it shares many common components. The latest version, the SB 401, is fitted with the V-8 Land-Rover engine, offering higher power and performance.

Description

The SB 401 is based on the chassis of the well-tried 2.768-metre (109-inch) long wheelbase Land-Rover chassis strengthened to take the all-welded armour body. Trials carried out by the British Army on the Shorland armoured personnel carrier have shown that the armour cannot be penetrated by fire from a 7.62 mm FN rifle or a 7.62 mm GPMG down to 23 metres firing at right angles to the plate. Servicing and 85 per cent of the spares are identical to the Land-Rover's. Major automotive differences are the stronger axles and the different final drives.

The engine is at the front of the vehicle and is protected by armour plate on the front, sides, rear and top, with the bonnet being opened from inside the vehicle. The engine is provided with an extra capacity radiator for tropical use.

A gutter under the junction of the bonnet cover and windscreen assembly ensures that burning fuel from petrol

Rear view of Shorland SB 401 armoured personnel carrier with back doors open

Shorland SB 401 armoured personnel carrier with observation/
firing ports open and roof-mounted smoke dischargers

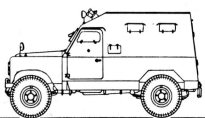

Shorland SB 401 armoured personnel carrier

bombs thrown against the windscreen is diverted to the ground without entering the engine compartment.

The driver sits on the left side of the vehicle with the commander to his right (right-hand drive models are also available with the positions reversed). The windscreens are Triplex safety glass and can be quickly covered by internally-controlled drop-down armoured visors containing laminated glass observation windows. Both the driver and the commander are provided with a side door with a drop-down vision port in the upper part. Mounted in the forward part of the roof, between the driver's and commander's seats, is a searchlight that can be controlled from within the vehicle. The roof is angled to ensure that hand grenades and other missiles thrown onto it roll off.

The passenger compartment is at the rear of the hull and the six passengers sit on bench seats, three down each side of the hull. All personnel have individual seat belts. A grab rail, suspended from the roof, assists the rapid exit of the passengers from the vehicle. Normal means of entry and exit for the passengers is through the two doors in the rear of the hull, each of which has an observation/firing port that opens on the outside. There are another two observation/firing ports in each side of the passenger compartment. The vehicle is insulated internally with washable plastic polyurethane foam and the floor is made of reinforced glass fibre which protects

against blast, nail and pipe bombs. The built-in ventilation system is adequate for operations in a tropical climate.

The heavy-duty front axle has spiral differential for all-wheel drive. The rear axle is similar but has floating shafts.

The SB 401 is unarmed although two four-barrelled smoke dischargers can be mounted on the forward part of the roof if required.

Variants

In 1984 the prototype of a Shorland with a ring-mounted 7.62 mm machine gun was announced. In this model the gunner is provided with a single-piece hatch cover that opens to the rear and lateral armour protection.

Status: In production. The SB 401 is in service in 17 countries including Malaysia.

Manufacturer: Short Brothers Limited, Montgomery Road, Belfast BT6 9HN, Northern Ireland.

SPECIFICATIONS		FUEL CAPACITY	100 litres	SUSPENSION	semi-ellip
CREW	2 + 6	MAX RANGE	368 km		and hydrau
CONFIGURATION	4 × 4	VERTICAL OBSTACLE	0.23 m		absorbers, a
COMBAT WEIGHT	3545 kg	TURNING RADIUS	8.84 m		fitted front an
POWER-TO-WEIGHT		ENGINE	V-8 water-cooled petrol,	TYRES	9.00 × 16
RATIO	26.4 hp/tonne		4-stroke, developing 91 bhp	BRAKES	
LENGTH	4.292 m		at 3500 rpm	main	hydraulic, servo-
WIDTH	1.778 m	TRANSMISSION	manual with 4 forward and 1		assisted
HEIGHT	2.159 m		reverse gears	parking	mechanical, operatii
GROUND CLEARANCE	0.324 m	TRANSFER CASE	2-speed		on transfer box output
TRACK	1.358 m	STEERING	recirculating ball, worm and	ELECTRICAL SYSTEM	12 V (24 V optional)
WHEELBASE	2.768 m		nut	BATTERY	1 × 12 V, 57 Ah
MAX ROAD SPEED	104.6 km/h	CLUTCH	single dry plate		

UNITED STATES OF AMERICA

M2 Infantry Fighting Vehicle

Development

The United States Army has had a requirement for a Mechanised Infantry Combat Vehicle since the early 1960s. The first vehicle designed to meet this requirement was the XM701 (also known as the MICV-65), five of which prototypes were completed by Pacific Car and Foundry in 1965. These vehicles used automotive and suspension components of the M107/M110 series of self-propelled guns which were developed by Pacific Car and Foundry in the late 1950s. The XM701 was not developed past the prototype stage as it was considered that the chassis was too large for use as an MICV.

In 1967, under contract to the United States Army, the Ordnance Division of FMC Corporation built two MICVs under the designation XM765. This was not adopted by the Army but further development by the company, as a private venture several years later, resulted in the Armoured Infantry Fighting Vehicle which is currently in service with the Netherlands, Philippines and Belgium. There is a separate entry for the Armoured Infantry Fighting Vehicle.

In April 1972 the United States Army issued a Request For Proposals for a new MICV. A number of companies submitted proposals to meet this requirement and three companies were short-listed: Chrysler Corporation, FMC Corporation and Pacific Car and Foundry.

In November 1972 an Engineering Development and Advanced Production Engineering contract was awarded to Ordnance Division of FMC Corporation. The total value of this contract was $29.3 million which covered the cost of the design, development and fabrication of three prototype vehicles, a ballistic vehicle, 12 pilot vehicles and associated systems engineering, product assurance and test support.

The prototypes, called the XM723, had a crew of three (commander, gunner and driver) and carried eight fully-equipped infantrymen. The driver sat at the front on the left, with the commander to his rear and the gunner in the turret on the right side of the hull. The turret was armed with a 20 mm cannon and a coaxial 7.62 mm machine gun. The troop compartment was at the rear of the hull and the infantrymen could aim and fire their weapons from inside the vehicle. All prototypes were completed by the summer of 1975.

In August 1976 an MICV Task Force was formed by the United States Army to make an independent examination of the whole XM723 programme to determine whether the vehicle would meet the future requirements of the Army. The Task Force made a number of recommendations, of which

the following were accepted by the Army in October 1976:

A common vehicle would be developed for both the infantry and scout roles as the Armored Reconnaissance Scout Vehicle (prototypes of which were built by the FMC Corporation and Lockheed Missile and Space) had been cancelled

The vehicle would be fitted with TOW ATGW system and 25 mm cannon in a two-man TOW/Bushmaster Armored Turret (TBAT-II)

A two-tube TOW ATGW launcher would be mounted on the left side of the turret to give the vehicle an anti-tank capability

The firing ports would be retained

The vehicle would be amphibious

The vehicle would have the same level of armour protection as the XM723

The vehicle would be issued on the scale of four per platoon, 13 per company and 41 per battalion.

The complete programme was then renamed the Fighting Vehicle System (FVS) which consisted of two vehicles, the XM2 Infantry Fighting Vehicle and the XM3 Cavalry Fighting Vehicle. The responsibility of the Fighting Vehicle

Hughes TOW ATGW being launched from M2 Bradley Infantry Fighting Vehicle

Infantry dismounting via power-operated ramp in hull rear of Bradley M2 Infantry Fighting Vehicle

Systems Manager was expanded in June 1977 to include a carrier for the General Support Rocket System (now known as the Multiple Launch Rocket System).

The first two prototypes of the XM2 Infantry Fighting Vehicle were handed over to the United States Army at San Jose, California in December 1978, and the remaining six were completed by March 1979. In December 1979 the XM2 was type classified as the M2 and the XM3 as the M3. In February 1980 the US Army announced that it planned to produce 100 M2/M3s with fiscal year (FY) 1980 funds. The first production vehicles were handed over in May 1981, despite an 11-week strike at FMC Corporation. The first production contract deliveries of 100 vehicles were completed on schedule in July 1982, and 400 second year deliveries were completed in May 1983. Two subsequent contracts of 600 vehicles each for FY82 and FY83 were awarded. The FY84 request was for 600 vehicles at a cost of $815.5 million, the FY85 request for 710 at a cost of $1056.4 million. The anticipated FY86 request is for 900 at a cost of $1256.9 million.

The first battalion was equipped with the M2 at Fort

M2 Bradley Infantry Fighting Vehicle with TOW launcher retracted and hatches propped

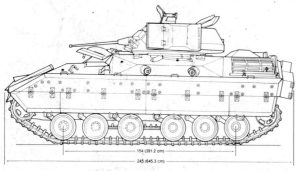

154 (391.2 cm)
245 (645.3 cm)

Dimensions in inches (metric)

Hood, Texas in March 1983, with deliveries to the 7th Army training centre in Vilseck, West Germany, in September 1983. The United States Army has a total requirement for 6882 M2s and M3s. The M2 will not replace the M113 one-for-one, but will replace them for specific roles such as the APC in the mechanised infantry battalions.

On 20 October 1981, the M2 IFV/M3 CFV was dedicated the Bradley Fighting Vehicle after the late General of the Army, Omar N Bradley.

When being airlifted in the C-141 Starlifter the head of the gunner's integral sight and the skirt plates are removed and the front two roadwheels have to be lowered by jacking up the suspension trailing arms.

The M2 Bradley IFV has been tested in Saudi Arabia together with the M1 MBT.

Description

The hull of the M2 Infantry Fighting Vehicle is made of all-welded aluminium armour with spaced laminate armour fitted to the hull, sides and rear. According to FMC the armour of the M2 can defeat 95 per cent of all of the types of ballistic attack encountered on the battlefield under IFV/CFV doctrine.

The driver sits at the front of the vehicle on the left and has a single-piece hatch cover that opens to the rear and four periscopes, three to the front and one to the left side. The centre front periscope can be replaced by an AN/VVS-2 passive night periscope.

The engine compartment is to the right of the driver. The engine is coupled to a General Electric HMPT-500 hydro-mechanical transmission. The transmission design incorporates two hydraulic pump/motor assemblies that utilise radial ball pistons and a unique gearing arrangement to provide both steer and propulsion ratios. There are three speed ranges with overall transmission ratios infinitely variable in all ranges. There is a 3.2 kg Halon fixed fire extinguisher in the engine compartment and two 2.3 kg ones in the

M2 Bradley Infantry Fighting Vehicle with all hatches closed and TOW launcher retracted alongside turret

personnel compartment. In addition there is also a 1.2 kg portable Halon fire extinguisher.

The turret, which is of welded steel and aluminium armour construction, is mounted in the centre of the vehicle on the right side with the gunner seated on the left and the commander on the right. Each crew member is provided with a single-piece hatch cover that opens to the rear. The gunner has a combined day/thermal sight with an optical relay for the commander with magnifications of ×4 and ×12, and both crew members have periscopes for front and side observation. In addition, production vehicles are fitted with a fixed power, daylight back-up sight which will allow the gunner or commander secondary sighting capability in the event of primary sight failure.

Main armament consists of a Hughes M242 25 mm Chain Gun with a 7.62 mm M240C machine gun mounted coaxially to the right of the main armament. The Hughes weapon was chosen after an extensive evaluation between the M242 Chain Gun and a self-powered XM241 which was similar to the Oerlikon KBA-BO2 entered by Ford Aerospace and Communications Corporation. The Ordnance Division of Hughes Helicopters was awarded an initial $5.4 million contract in January 1979 to proceed with production engineering work. The 25 mm cannon has dual feed and the gunner can select single shots, 100 or 200 rpm rates of fire. The cannon will fire both Oerlikon 25 mm and American M790 series of ammunition including M791 APDS-T, M792 HEI-T and M793 TP-T. The empty cartridge cases are automatically ejected outside the turret. An APFSDS-T round for the M242 Hughes Helicopters Chain Gun is now under development.

The turret has 360-degree electric traverse and the weapons can be elevated from −10 to +60 degrees. The General Electric turret drive and stabilisation system allows the armament to be laid and fired while moving across rough country. The system consists of a traverse drive assembly for positioning and holding the turret, gun elevation drive assembly for positioning and holding the weapon, TOW elevation drive assembly for positioning and holding the TOW missile launcher, a TOW lift mechanism for raising and lowering the TOW launcher, electronic control assembly, three gyro blocks, gunner's handstation, commander's handstation and cabling.

The TOW weapon sub-system has been developed by the Hughes Aircraft Corporation under a contract worth $16.5

million. When travelling the twin tube TOW launcher is retracted and lies along the left side of the turret. The TOW system enables the M2/M3 vehicles to engage enemy armour out to a maximum range of 3750 metres. The TOW missile launcher has an elevation of +30 degrees and a depression of −20 degrees.

Two electrically-operated smoke dischargers, with four smoke grenades in each, are mounted on the forward part of the turret, one on either side of the main armament. In addition production vehicles are fitted with an engine smoke-generating system similar to that on most Soviet vehicles.

The M2 carries seven infantrymen: one sits forward of the turret on the left side facing the rear, one to the left of the turret facing the front, one at the left rear of the vehicle facing inwards, two sit at the right rear facing the back and two sit to the back of the turret facing the front.

The infantrymen enter and leave the vehicle via a large hydraulically-operated ramp at the rear of the hull, which has an integral door in the left side in case the ramp fails to open. A single-piece hatch cover that opens to the rear is provided over the top of the troop compartment. Six firing ports, two in each side of the hull and two at the rear, each with a periscope over it, enable the infantrymen to fire their M231 5.56 mm weapons from inside the vehicle.

The suspension system includes torsion bars, and on each side there are six dual rubber-tyred road wheels with the drive sprocket at the front and the idler at the rear. There are two track return rollers that support the inside of the track only, and one double roller. Hydraulic shock absorbers are fitted to the first, second, third and sixth road wheel stations. The tracks are of the single-pin type with replaceable rubber pads.

In production vehicles a central M13A1 gas particulate filter system is provided for the commander, gunner and driver but the infantrymen have to wear individual masks.

The M2 is fully amphibious, being propelled in the water by its tracks. Before entering the water a special water barrier can be erected in approximately 15 minutes by a trained crew.

During the development of the M2/M3 a considerable amount of effort was placed on maintenance and logistical support; diagnostic equipment falls into two main categories, organisational and direct support. The former is built on the Army's standard Simplified Test Equipment/Internal Com-

Fighting Vehicle Systems Carrier, M987

bustion Engine (STE/ICE) concept to provide a common system for both the M1 MBT and the M2/M3. This equipment can isolate faults in the engine, transmission, electrical or fire-control sub-systems to the responsible line replaceable unit (LRU). The faulty part can be replaced from stock so the vehicle can be returned to service, the faulty LRU will be repaired elsewhere.

The Direct Support Electrical System Test Set (DSESTS) provides an automatic test set for both the M1 and M2/M3 and can check the LRU that was removed by organisational level maintenance and identify the specific printed circuit board (PCB) or module causing the malfunction. Once identified, the PCB or module can be replaced into the LRU which is then returned to stock for future use.

Variants

Improvements
It is likely that the following improvements will be incorporated by 1985: Hughes TOW 2 ATGW, ventilated facepiece and an improved 25 mm round (APFSDS-T).

In the longer term the following may also be incorporated: driver's thermal viewer, heading reference unit, low profile antenna, biological/chemical protection, nuclear hardening, improved maintenance/diagnostic capabilities and 25 mm cannon ammunition improvements.

M3 Cavalry Fighting Vehicle
This is almost identical to the M2 except that it has a crew of five. It has no firing ports and has greater ammunition capacity than the M2; however from the exterior, the M2 and M3 appear identical.

M2 Bradley with 35 mm cannon
Undergoing trials in late 1984 was an M2 Bradley fitted with a new two-man turret armed with an ARES 35 mm Talon rapid-fire cannon.

M2 Bradley Air Defence Vehicle
This is the basic Bradley M2 with its original turret removed and replaced by a General Electric Blazer two-man turret armed with a 25 mm GAU-12/U five-barrelled Gatling Gun, four Stinger surface-to-air missiles, ESD RA-20 search/acquisition radar and a passive electro-optical fire control system. This is a private venture development.

Vickers Mechanised Infantry Combat Vehicle
Vickers Defence Systems of the United Kingdom have proposed purchasing M2 Bradley hulls from the United States and installing the following turrets in the United Kingdom:
   M30 two-man power-operated turret armed with 30 mm Rarden cannon and 7.62 mm coaxial machine gun
   M25 two-man power-operated turret armed with 25 mm Hughes Helicopters Chain Gun and 7.62 mm coaxial machine gun

Multiple Launch Rocket System
The Vought Multiple Launch Rocket System (MLRS) in service with the United States Army and selected by Britain, France, Italy, West Germany and the Netherlands is designated the M933 and based on the Fighting Vehicle Systems Carrier M987, a member of the Fighting Vehicle Systems which includes the M2 and M3. A prototype of the Armored,

Forward Area, Rearm Vehicle (AFARV), which is used to rearm AFVs in the forward area, has been developed to the prototype stage and based on the M987 chassis.

SPECIFICATIONS (M2, data in square brackets relates to M3 where different)	
CREW	3 + 7 [3 + 2]
COMBAT WEIGHT	22 590 [22 443] kg
UNLOADED WEIGHT	19 005 [18 824] kg
AIRPORTABLE WEIGHT	20 055 [19 732] kg
POWER-TO-WEIGHT RATIO	20.38 [20.51] hp/tonne
GROUND PRESSURE	0.54 [0.53] kg/cm²
LENGTH	6.453 m
WIDTH	3.2 m
over tracks	2.972 m
HEIGHT	
to gunner's sight	2.972 m
to turret roof	2.565 m
reduced	2.634 m
GROUND CLEARANCE	0.432 m
TRACK WIDTH	533 mm
LENGTH OF TRACK ON GROUND	3.912 m
MAX SPEED	
road	66 km/h
water	7.2 km/h
FUEL CAPACITY	662 litres
CRUISING RANGE	483 km
FORDING	amphibious
GRADIENT	60%
SIDE SLOPE	40%
VERTICAL OBSTACLE	0.914 m
TRENCH	2.54 m
ENGINE	Cummins VTA-903T turbo-charged 8-cylinder diesel developing 500 hp at 2600 rpm
TRANSMISSION	General Electric HMPT-500 hydro-mechanical
STEERING	hydrostatic
SUSPENSION	torsion bar
ELECTRICAL SYSTEM	28 V
BATTERIES	4 × 12 V 6TN
ARMAMENT	
main	1 × 25 mm cannon
coaxial	1 × 7.62 mm MG
ATGW	2-tube TOW launcher
firing port guns	5.56 mm
SMOKE-LAYING EQUIPMENT	2 × 4 smoke dischargers plus exhaust generator
AMMUNITION	
25 mm	300 ready, 600 reserve [300/1200]
7.62 mm	800 ready, 1540 reserve [800/3740]
5.56 mm firing port	4200 reserve [n/app]
TOW missiles	2 in launcher, 5 in reserve [10]
LAW (M72A2)	3 stowed
FIRE-CONTROL SYSTEM	
Turret power control	electric
by commander	yes
by gunner	yes
Max rate power traverse	60°/s
Max rate power elevation	60°/s
Gun elevation/depression	+60°/−10°
Turret traverse	360°
TOW launcher elevation/depression	+30°/−20°
Gun stabiliser	yes
ARMOUR	
Top and front slopes	5083 aluminium
Vertical sides and rear	spaced laminate
Bottom	5083 aluminium with anti-mine appliqué (IFV only)
Side slopes	7039 and 5083 aluminium

Status: In production. In service with the US Army. US Army forecasts show total procurement costs of the IFV/CFV to be more than $11 000 million.

Manufacturer: FMC Corporation, Ordnance Division, 1105 Coleman Avenue, San Jose, California 95108, USA.

Armoured Infantry Fighting Vehicle

Development
In 1967, under contract to the United States Army, the Ordnance Division of the FMC Corporation built two MICVs under the designation XM765. These were based on the proven M113 APC modified to incorporate firing ports and a fully-enclosed weapon station. Further development of the XM765 by FMC as a private venture resulted in the Product Improved M113A1, the first prototype of which was completed in 1970. This had a fully-enclosed weapon station in the centre of the hull, behind the driver and engine, and the commander's cupola to the rear of the turret. This arrangement gave the commander very little forward vision so the vehicle was redesigned with the commander sitting behind the driver on the left and the turret to the rear of the engine on the right. This model, called the Armoured Infantry Fighting Vehicle, has been tested by Belgium, West Germany, Italy, the Netherlands, Norway, the Philippines and Switzerland.

The first country to order the AIFV was the Netherlands which placed an order for 880 vehicles in 1975; the first deliveries were made in 1977. Many of the components for the Dutch vehicles are made in the Netherlands under the terms of an offset arrangement. In 1981 the Dutch Army ordered an additional 840 AIFVs of which 119 will be in the Improved TOW Vehicle configuration, DAF and RSV will be involved in the production/final assembly of these vehicles. The Philippines has placed an order for 45 AIFVs. In July 1979 Belgium placed an order for 514 AIFVs and 525 M113A2s which are built under licence in Belgium by Belgian Mechanical Fabrication and replace M75 and AMX VCIs at present in service with the Belgian Army. First production vehicles were completed in 1982 and production is expected to run at the rate of 20 to 25 vehicles (AIFV and M113A2) a month until 1988. Additional details of Belgian vehicles are given under Belgium earlier in this book.

Armoured Infantry Fighting Vehicle of Netherlands Army (YPR 765) (Netherlands Army)

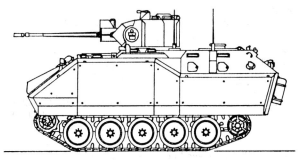

FMC Armoured Infantry Fighting Vehicle

Description
The hull of the AIFV is made of welded aluminium armour with an additional layer of FMC-developed and patented spaced laminate steel armour bolted onto the hull. The composite armour provides better protection for less weight than any other armour material. Closed cell polyurethane foam within the armour system gives increased buoyancy for amphibious operations.

The driver sits at the front of the hull on the left and has a single-piece hatch cover that opens to the right. To the front and left side of his position are four M27 day periscopes, the centre one of which can be replaced by a passive periscope for driving at night.

The commander sits to the rear of the driver and has a single-piece hatch cover that opens to the rear and five periscopes, four standard M17 periscopes and an M20A1 with a magnification of ×1 and ×6, which can be replaced by a passive night periscope if required.

The engine is to the right of the driver and is coupled to the three-speed automatic transmission by a transfer gear case. The complete powerpack can be removed through a hatch in the front of the hull, which can also be used for daily maintenance tasks. Normal steering and braking are by oil-cooled band-type brakes in the controlled differential. There is a set of air-cooled disc brakes on the differential output shafts for low-speed tight turns on land and for more efficient manoeuvring in the water. A large radiator and a belt-driven high-capacity fan mounted in the top of the engine compartment provide cooling at high ambient temperatures.

The power train is similar to the M113A1s except for improved features such as the engine turbo-charger, larger capacity radiator, transmission modified with heavy-duty components, heavy universal joints and final drives as fitted to the M548 tracked cargo carrier.

The enclosed weapon station is on the right side of the hull behind the engine. It is all welded with an additional layer of spaced laminate armour as fitted to the hull. The gunner has a single-piece hatch cover that opens to the rear, four M27 day periscopes (two either side), a Philips sight with a magnification of ×2 for day use and ×6 for night use and an open anti-aircraft/emergency gun sight. Coupled to the 25 mm cannon is a 150-watt searchlight.

Main armament consists of an Oerlikon 25 mm KBA-B02 cannon with dual feed, which has 180 rounds of ready-use ammunition and another 144 rounds in reserve. Mounted coaxially to the left of the main armament is a Belgian 7.62 mm MAG machine gun with 230 rounds of ready-use ammunition and a further 1610 rounds in reserve in the hull. Turret traverse and gun elevation are electro-hydraulic, elevation is from −10 degrees to +50 degrees at a speed of

60 degrees a second and turret traverse is through a full 360 degrees at 60 degrees a second. Although developed and manufactured by FMC, some weapon stations for the Dutch vehicles were manufactured and integrated by DAF. Certain interior modifications have also been carried out by DAF for a number of AIFVs. Dutch vehicles also have six smoke dischargers mounted on the front of the hull.

The seven infantrymen sit in the troop compartment at the rear of the hull. One man sits between the commander and the turret facing the rear and the remaining six sit three each side, back to back. Over the top of the troop compartment is a single-piece hatch cover that opens to the rear and contains the troop compartment ventilator. There are five firing ports, two in each side of the hull and one in the ramp at the rear. Over each of the side firing ports is an M17 periscope and over the rear firing port an M27 periscope. To reduce accidental damage inside the vehicle, holders support the individual weapons during firing. Spent brass catching bags prevent ejected cartridge cases from hitting adjacent men.

The infantrymen enter and leave the vehicle by a power-operated ramp at the rear of the hull which opens downwards. An emergency door is provided in the left side of the ramp.

The two armoured fuel tanks at the rear of the vehicle, one either side of the ramp, are separated from the vehicle interior by armour plate.

The new torsion bar-in-tube spring arrangement, which almost doubles the effective length of the torsion spring, gives a much improved ride compared with the M113A1 APC. The track, roadwheels and most of the other suspension elements are proven M113A1 components. The suspension either side consists of five dual rubber-tyred road wheels with the drive sprocket at the front and the idler at the rear. There are no track return rollers. The first, second and last road wheel stations either side have a hydraulic shock absorber. The track is a T130E1 steel block, rubber-bushed pin type with removable rubber pads.

The AIFV is fully amphibious, being propelled in the water by its tracks. Before entering the water a trim vane, which is stowed flat on the glacis plate when not in use, is erected at the front of the hull.

Optional equipment includes a Hughes 25 mm Chain Gun or a 12.7 mm (0.50) M2 HB machine gun in place of the

Armoured Infantry Fighting Vehicle from rear with all hatches closed

Netherlands Army Armoured Infantry Fighting Vehicle fitted with Emerson ITV turret

25 mm cannon, an M36 sight for the gunner with magnifications of ×1 and ×7, an NBC system, a heater for the personnel/cargo area and a heater for the engine coolant and battery.

Variants

Belgian Vehicles
Details of these are given under Belgium.

Netherlands Models
The basic AIFV is designated the YPR 765 PRI by the Netherlands Army and variants in service are:

YPR 765 PRCO-B command vehicle, crew nine, combat weight 13 700 kg

YPR 765 PRCO-C1 to C5, crew nine, combat weight 12 400 kg, armed with 12.7 mm (0.50) M2 machine gun. The C1 is a battalion commander's vehicle, C2 a battalion gunnery centre, C3 a mortar fire-control vehicle, C4 an AA command vehicle and C5 an observation vehicle with a crew of four. All these versions have an M113 type cupola with a 12.7 mm M2 HB pintle-mounted machine gun

YPR 765 PRRDR radar vehicle fitted with the British ZB 298 battlefield surveillance radar

YPR 765 PRRDR-C radar/command vehicle

YPR 765 PRGWT ambulance, crew four, weight 11 600 kg, unarmed

YPR 765 PRI/I squad vehicle fitted with M113 type cupola with 12.7 mm (0.50) M2 machine gun, carries nine men plus driver

YPR 765 PRMR mortar tractor (tows 120 mm Brandt mortar), crew seven, combat weight 13 000 kg, armament one 12.7 mm (0.50) M2 machine gun pintle-mounted on a standard M113 type cupola

YPR 765 PRVR-A and PRVR-B cargo vehicles, crew two, combat weight 13 400 kg, armament one 12.7 mm (0.50) M2 machine gun pintle-mounted on a standard M113 type cupola

YPR 765 PRAT fitted with the Emerson TOW launcher system as fitted to the M901 Improved TOW Vehicle. The

PRAT (Pantser Rups Anti-tank) entered service with the Dutch Army in 1982, and has a crew of four
YPR 806 PRBRG armoured recovery vehicle, crew four, weight 12 200 kg, armament one 12.7 mm (0.50) M2 machine gun. Details of this model are given later in this entry.

With the addition of a variety of kits, developed by FMC, the basic AIFV Universal Vehicle Chassis can be converted to the following roles:

Command Post
This has revised seating arrangements for a command staff of six plus its crew of three (commander, gunner and driver), and is fitted with additional communications equipment, table and stowage rack for 12.7 mm (0.50) ammunition. It is normally armed with a 12.7 mm (0.50) M2 HB machine gun on a pintle mount.

Mortar Prime Mover
This tows a 120 mm Brandt or similar mortar and has racks at the rear of the troop compartment on the right side for 51 mortar bombs. A crew of seven is normally carried: three vehicle crew plus four mortar crew. It is normally armed with a 12.7 mm (0.50) M2 HB machine gun on a pintle mount, but this can be replaced by an M26 weapon station fitted with a 12.7 mm (0.50) M2 HB machine gun.

TOW ATGW Vehicle
In addition to being fitted with the Emerson ITV kit, other TOW installations are possible and the vehicle can also be fitted with other types of ATGW system such as the HOT.

Cargo Carrier
This model can carry up to 2040 kg of cargo and has a crew of two, driver and gunner. Armament consists of a 12.7 mm (0.50) M2 HB machine gun. The cargo kit includes protective grating behind the driver and gunner and tie-down devices to secure the load while travelling across country.

Ambulance
Four stretchers suspended from hanger harnesses are fitted in the troop compartment at the rear and two seats are provided for medical assistants. This model is unarmed.

Recovery Vehicle
This is similar to the XM806 which is a member of the M113A1 family but the Dutch vehicles have smoke dischargers mounted on the front of the hull, a HIAB crane mounted on the roof and additional buoyancy pods attached to the hull sides. This vehicle features the same suspension and power train as the AIFV. The trim vane at the front of the hull also has an additional buoyancy attachment.

Philippines Models
In 1979 the Philippine Government procured 45 AIFVs which have basically the same configuration as the Netherlands YPR 765 PRI vehicles. Although the enclosed weapon station was delivered ready to accept the Oerlikon 25 mm KBA-BO2 cannon, a kit was developed to convert the station to accept the 12.7 mm (0.50) M2 HB machine gun in place of the Oerlikon 25 mm cannon. Six armoured recovery vehicles were also procured (see previous variant entry).

SPECIFICATIONS						
CREW	3 + 7	ACCELERATION		SUSPENSION	torsion bar in tube
COMBAT WEIGHT	13 687 kg	0 to 32 km/h	10 s	ELECTRICAL SYSTEM	28 V
UNLOADED WEIGHT	11 405 kg	0 to 48 km/h	23.1 s	BATTERIES	4 × 12 V 6TN
POWER-TO-WEIGHT		FUEL CAPACITY	416 litres	ARMAMENT	
RATIO	19.29 hp/tonne	MAX ROAD RANGE	490 km	main	1 × 25 mm cannon
GROUND PRESSURE	0.67 kg/cm²	FORDING	amphibious	coaxial	1 × 7.62 mm MG
LENGTH	5.258 m	GRADIENT	60%	SMOKE-LAYING	
WIDTH	2.819 m	SIDE SLOPE	30%	EQUIPMENT	6 smoke dischargers
WIDTH OVER TRACKS	2.54 m	VERTICAL OBSTACLE	0.635 m	AMMUNITION	
HEIGHT		TRENCH	1.625 m	25 mm	180 ready +
to top of periscopes	2.794 m	TURNING RADIUS	7.62 m		144 reserve
turret roof	2.619 m	ENGINE	Detroit Diesel 6V-53T	7.62 mm	230 ready +
to hull top, front	1.854 m		V6 liquid-cooled		1610 reserve
to hull top, rear	2.007 m		diesel developing		
FIRING HEIGHT	2.33 m		264 hp at 2800 rpm	FIRE-CONTROL SYSTEM	
GROUND CLEARANCE	0.432 m	TRANSMISSION	Allison TX100-1A	Turret power control	electro-hydraulic/
TRACK WIDTH	381 mm		automatic with 3		manual
LENGTH OF TRACK			forward and 1 reverse	Max rate power traverse	60°/s
ON GROUND	2.667 m		gears, torque converter	Max rate power elevation	60°/s
MAX SPEED			and lock-up clutch	Gun elevation/depression	+50°/−10°
road	61.2 km/h	STEERING	FMC DS 200 mechani-	Gun stabiliser	optional
on 10% grade	28.2 km/h		cally controlled		
water	6.3 km/h		differential and		
			pivot steer		

Status: In production. In service with Belgium, the Netherlands and Philippines.

Manufacturer: FMC Corporation, Ordnance Division, 1105 Coleman Avenue, San Jose, California 95108, USA.

M113 Armoured Personnel Carrier Family

Development
In January 1956 development began of an air-transportable, armoured, multi-purpose vehicle family: 'To provide a lightweight, armored personnel carrier for armor and infantry units capable of amphibious and air-drop operation, superior cross-country mobility and adaptation to multiple functions through applications of kits and/or modifications of its superstructure'.

Prototypes of both aluminium (T113) and steel (T117) were built and tested but development of the T117 was cancelled in favour of further development of the T113. This became the T113E1 which was standardised as the M113 in

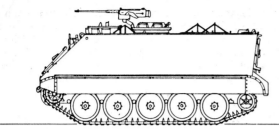

M113A1 armoured personnel carrier armed with 12.7 mm (0.50) M2 HB machine gun

M113A1 armoured personnel carrier of the US Army with roof-mounted 12.7 mm M2 HB machine gun (US Army)

1960 and entered production at FMC's San Jose facility in early 1960. Trials of a diesel-engined model called the T113E2 showed a substantial improvement in operating range (from 321 to 483 km) as well as a reduction in fire risk. This model was standardised as the Carrier, Personnel, Full-Tracked, Armored, M113A1, in May 1963. After standardisation ten pre-production vehicles were built and the M113A1 replaced the M113 in production from September 1964.

By early 1980 70 000 members of the M113 family of armoured vehicles had been built with 4000 being built under licence in Italy by OTO Melara.

Recent production figures for the M113 family of tracked vehicles are:

	US Army	FMS	FMC direct sales
1977	769	2084	528
1978	1250	1646	853
1979	1424	677	378
1980	864	1559	828
1981	461	1241	487
1982	382	1228	481
1983	385	609	112

Description

The all-welded aluminium hull of the M113 protects the crew from small arms fire and shell splinters.

The driver sits at the front of the hull on the left side and has a single-piece hatch cover that opens to the rear. To his front and left side are four M17 periscopes and there is also an M19 periscope in his roof hatch. An infra-red or passive periscope can replace one of the day periscopes for driving at night.

The engine compartment to the right of the driver's position is fitted with a fire-extinguishing system that can be operated by the driver or from outside the vehicle. The air-inlet and air-outlet louvres and the exhaust pipe outlet are in the roof and there is an engine access door in the front of the hull that hinges forwards.

The power train consists of the power plant (engine, transfer gear case and transmission), steering control differential, pivot steer, final drive and associated drive shafts and universal joints.

The commander sits to the rear of the engine compartment and has a cupola that can be traversed through a full 360 degrees, five M17 periscopes and a single-piece hatch cover. Pintle-mounted on the forward part of the commander's cupola is a 12.7 mm (0.50) Browning M2 HB machine gun with an elevation of +53 degrees, a depression of −21 degrees and a total traverse of 360 degrees. One hundred rounds of ready-use ammunition are carried for this weapon.

The infantrymen enter and leave the M113 via a power-operated ramp in the rear of the hull that opens downwards and has a door in the left side. Behind the commander's cupola is an oblong hatch cover that opens to the rear, behind which is a domed ventilator. The infantrymen travel on seats down each side of the hull, which can be folded up to enable the vehicle to be used as an ambulance or to carry cargo.

The torsion bar suspension either side consists of five dual rubber-tyred road wheels with the drive sprocket at the front and the idler at the rear. There are no track return rollers and the first and last road wheel stations are fitted with a hydraulic shock absorber. A rubber track shroud on each side of the hull controls the flow of water over the tracks when the vehicle is afloat. The M113 is fully amphibious, being propelled in the water by its tracks. Steering when afloat is the same as on land. Before entering the water the two bilge pumps are switched on and the trim vane, which folds back onto the glacis plate when not in use, is extended at the front of the hull.

The following kits are available for members of the M113 family: anti-mine armour bolted on front half of vehicle bottom (includes buoyancy aids), anchor kit (set of two for use with capstans for self-recovery), buoyant side pods, combination bulldozer/snow plough, NBC detector and automatic alarm, diesel engine to replace existing petrol engine, full width buoyant trim vane, gun shields, heater for personnel and cargo areas, heater for engine coolant and battery, stretcher kit which provides support for four stretchers when the vehicle is being used as an ambulance, M8A3 gas-particulate unit (includes M2A2 air purifier with flexible hoses to fit M14A1 tank gas masks of driver and commander and up to two others), non-skid ramp plate kit and windscreen for driving with hatch open.

M113A2 (formerly Product Improved M113A1)

Following successful trials with prototype vehicles the United States Army in 1978 decided to carry out a product improvement programme on its fleet of M113 (5300) and M113A1 (12 700) APCs, all of which are to be brought up to the new standard by 1989. The conversions will be carried out at the Red River Army Depot Texas, Daewood Industries in South Korea and Mainz Army Depot, West Germany. The Army plans to have 19 242 Product Improved M113A1s (M113A2) in service by the end of fiscal year 1989. The US

Army also ordered an initial batch of 2660 M113A2s at a cost of $154 million, the first of which were completed at FMC's San Jose facility in July 1979. These improvements can be summarised as follows:

Improved engine cooling design that reverses the position of the fan and radiator and incorporates a new radiator and surge tank and a new cooling fan. This new cooling system draws in ambient air through the radiator providing increased cooling efficiency for both the engine and transmission, reduces oil film and dust build-up on the core of the radiator, provides a negative pressure engine compartment which reduces the possibility of exhaust fumes leaking into the crew compartment and finally provides a longer engine life and greater tractive effort at reduced temperatures.

The improved suspension system incorporates high-strength steel torsion bars that provide 228 mm of roadwheel travel, improved shock absorbers on the first, second and fifth road wheel stations, stronger rear idler assembly which has also been raised to reduce the chance of ground impact and finally increased ground clearance to minimise sprocket ground contact on rough terrain.

Other M113A2 variants such as the M577A2 and the M125A2 are currently available. The M548 cargo carrier with A2 improvements has been redesignated the M548A1 and first production vehicles were completed in 1982.

Rear-mounted, armoured fuel cells are a current production option and many non-United States orders are calling for their installation. This option provides more interior space and reduces the danger of fire. M113A1 vehicles have now been phased out of production.

The United States Army procured 254 M548A1 vehicles in fiscal year 1981, 69 M113A2 type vehicles in fiscal year 1982 and 520 M113A2 type vehicles in fiscal year 1983. The fiscal year 1984 request was for 400 M113A2s at a cost of $73.2 million after which the US Army will have procured 20 939 M113 series APCs. The fiscal year 1985 request is for 50 M113A2s at a cost of $8.9 million.

M113A3

In mid-1980 a Development-In-Process Review consisting of DARCOM, TRADOC and Logistics Evaluation Agency members recommended to the Department of the Army that the improved M113A1E1, developed by TARADCOM at Warren, Michigan, should be type classified for US Army use. It is expected that depot conversions of M113A1/M113A2s to the M113A3 configuration will begin in 1987.

The M113A1E1 incorporates the cooling and suspension improvements of the M113A2 but also has better performance and reliability. Major improvements include the replacement of the 6V-53 (212 hp) diesel engine by the

turbo-charged 6V-53T (275 hp) and the replacement of the present TX100-1 transmission, transfer gearcase, steering differential and pivot brakes with the X200-3 Detroit Diesel Allison transmission which provides four forward speeds instead of the present three, hydrostatic steering to provide smoother turning with less effort and reduced shock loading on the suspension system and greater power efficiency which results in more horsepower and fuel savings.

The driver's controls have also been changed and the conventional sticks have been replaced by a steering wheel and brake pedal.

The US Army refers to this improvement as the RISE power train (Reliability Improvement of Selected Equipment). During development tests, a significant improvement for the M113A1E1 over the M113A1 was achieved including acceleration of 0 to 32 km/h in 8.1 seconds compared with 11.7 seconds, braking from a speed of 32 km/h in 7.3 compared with 10 metres, cross-country speed of 33.7 km/h compared with 26 km/h. For 48 270 km of development tests the M113A1E1 went 3047 km between failures as opposed to 1298 km for the standard M113A1. At a speed of 35.4 km/h, the vehicle used 22 per cent less fuel than the M113A1. When standardised the M113A1E1 will become the M113A3. It will also have armoured external fuel tanks and internal spall protection liners. The three improvements (RISE, AEFT and spall liners) will be applied to the M901A1 and M981 vehicles which will become the M901A2 and M981 PI.

Possible additional improvements

Several other improvements are being investigated for the M113 family. The electrical system will need more charging power and easier diagnosis to cope with the increased power loads of the new electronics systems to be installed. A high output and heavy duty electrical system with built-in test equipment is being evaluated. New ballistic liners inside the vehicles to increase crew survivability from shaped charge spalling have been tested. Each member of the M113 is now being studied by the US Army for both active and passive NBC protection. It is planned to install smoke grenade launchers on the M113A2 APC.

Stretched M113A1

In 1976 two prototypes of a stretched M113A1 were built and tested between 1977 and 1978. The hulls are approximately 0.66 metre longer than the standard vehicles and have an additional set of road wheels each side, and are also fitted with the General Motors Corporation 6V-53T turbo-charged diesel engine, hydrostatic steering, the new cooling system and the improved suspension. The stretched M113A1 has a gross vehicle weight of 14 968 kg, a maximum payload of 4218 kg, maximum road speed of 64 km/h, range of 483 km and can carry 14 men plus the driver. The single hatch cover over the troop compartment has been replaced by two hatch covers hinged in the centre that open either side of the vehicle. Other improvements being investigated include a variable-speed fan drive, a new track, a night sight system, infra-red suppressor and laser target designator.

Variants

M113/M113A1 with Dozer Kit

The bulldozer kit adapts the M113A1 APC to carry out general bulldozing work, improvement of water entrances

M113A3 APC showing fuel tanks at hull rear

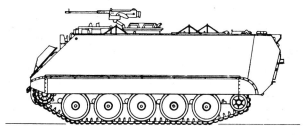

M106A1 showing position of 107 mm (4.2-inch) mortar

and grading. The installation of the kit does not change the basic vehicle or its load-carrying ability. It is fully amphibious as the front-mounted buoyant blade acts as a trim vane when raised during amphibious operations, after removal of the standard trim vane.

M106/M106A1 107 mm Mortar Carrier

Full designation is Carrier, Mortar, 107 mm, Self-propelled. This is the basic APC with a 4.2-inch (107 mm) M30 mortar mounted on a turntable in the rear of the hull that fires to the rear through a opening in the roof covered by a three-part hatch. The mortar has a traverse of 43 degrees right and 46 degrees left and 88 (M106A1) or 93 (M106) rounds of mortar ammunition are carried. Mounted externally on the left side of the hull is a mortar baseplate and bridge that allows the mortar to be fired away from the vehicle if required. The 12.7 mm (0.50) M2 HB machine gun is retained.

M125/M125A1/M125A2 81 mm Mortar Carrier

Full designation is Carrier, Mortar, 81 mm, Self-propelled. This is the basic APC with an 81 mm M29 mortar mounted on a turntable with a 360-degree traverse in the rear of the hull. That fires through an opening in the roof, covered by a three-part hatch. The mortar can also be deployed away from the vehicle and 114 mortar bombs are carried. The 12.7 mm (0.50) M2 HB machine gun is retained.

The US Army did not request any funds for the M125A2 in fiscal year 1981 or 1983 but the 1982 request was for 42 vehicles at a total cost of $6.9 million, these being earmarked for the National Guard.

M163 Vulcan Self-propelled Anti-aircraft Gun

This is essentially an M113A1 chassis fitted with a one-man electrically-driven turret which is armed with a 20 mm M168 Vulcan gun, Navy Mk 20 Mod. A gyro lead-computing sight and a range-only radar are mounted on the right side of the turret. The chassis is designated the M741.

M132/M132A1 Flamethrower

This model is obsolete and no longer in service with the US Army.

M548 Cargo Carrier

This unarmoured cargo carrier was designed from 1960 under the designation XM548 and uses many automotive components of the M113A1 APC. The XM548 was followed by a diesel-engined version called the XM548E1 which was subsequently standardised as the M548. First production vehicles were completed early in 1966 by the FMC Corporation at its Charleston, West Virginia, facility. The current M548A1 vehicles are being produced with M113A2 improvements, such as suspension and cooling system. The chassis is used as the basis for a number of other vehicles:
Chaparral low-altitude surface-to-air missile system (M730).
HAWK self-propelled surface-to-air missile system (M727) is no longer in service with the US Army.
Tracked Rapier self-propelled surface-to-air missile system.
Oerlikon twin 35 mm GDF-CO2 SPAAG.
MSM-Fz: This is a modified M548 with anti-tank mine-laying system for the West German Army.
Lance surface-to-surface tactical nuclear missile system uses two variants of the M548 chassis, the M752 launch vehicle (chassis designation M667) and the M688 loader transporter which carries additional missiles.

The basic M548 can carry 5443 kg of cargo but currently undergoing trials is a stretched M548 which has a payload of 7258 kg. This has an additional road wheel each side and all the improvements mentioned in the stretched M113A1 described previously.

M577/M577A1/M577A2 Command Post

Full designation is Carrier, Command Post: Light Tracked, M577 or M577A1. The first four prototypes were built at Detroit Arsenal under the designation XM577 and were conversions of existing M113 APCs. The XM577 was standardised as the M577 in March 1963, after the vehicle was already in production. The first order was for 270 vehicles which were completed between December 1962 and May 1963 and the second order was for 674 vehicles which were completed between November 1963 and July 1964. The US Army did not request any funds for the M577A2 in fiscal year 1981, but the fiscal year 1982 request was for 27 vehicles at a cost of $4.4 million for the National Guard. By fiscal year 1983 the US Army had procured 4130 M577 series command

M125A1 showing turntable-mounted 81 mm mortar

United States Army M577A1 armoured command vehicle in travelling configuration (United States Army)

post carriers with a further 652 being requested in fiscal year 1984 at a cost of $130 million. The fiscal year 1985 request is for 167 vehicles at a cost of $33.4 million.

The M577/M577A1 is essentially an M113/M113A1 with a higher roof to the rear of the driver's position. In the static role a tent can be erected at the rear of the hull to increase the work area. A generator is mounted externally to provide power for the additional communications equipment installed. In addition to being used as a command post the vehicle can also be used as a fire direction centre, communications vehicle and as a mobile medical treatment facility.

M113A2 Recovery Vehicle

Full designation is Recovery Vehicle: Full Tracked, Light Armored M113A2 (previously called the XM806) and is essentially an M113A2 fitted with a hydraulically-driven winch and a fairlead assembly for recovering disabled vehicles. Mounted either side of the ramp at the rear of the hull are spades which are lowered to the ground during recovery operations. An auxiliary spade unit, carried on the roof when not required, can be used between the two spades in soft soil. The winch has a capacity of 5103 kg on a full drum and 9070 kg on a bare drum. Mounted on the top of the hull on the left side is an auxiliary crane which can lift a maximum load of 1361 kg at a radius of 1.53 metres. There is also a fitter's model of the M113/M113A1/M113A2 which has an HIAB crane mounted on the left side of the roof which can lift a maximum load of 3085 kg.

M901 Improved TOW Vehicle

This entered service with the United States Army in 1979 and is essentially an M113A2 APC fitted with the ground TOW launching system designed by Emerson which consists of an M27 cupola equipped with an image transfer assembly, an armoured launcher, missile guidance set, and an auxiliary battery pack. The launcher assembly contains two TOW launch tubes, TOW sight assembly, and an acquisition sight mounted on top of two elevating arms. In addition to the two ready-to-launch missiles another ten are carried in the hull. A 7.62 mm machine gun is mounted on the cupola for local defence and 1000 rounds of ammunition are carried for it. The United States Army has a requirement for 2526 ITVs of which 1100 were deployed to Europe by 1981. Emerson has also developed to the prototype stage the Armoured Cavalry Cannon Vehicle (ACCV) which is armed with an

externally-mounted 25 mm cannon, and the Fire Support Team Vehicle (FISTV) based on the M901 and fitted with the AN/TVQ-2 GLLD with north-finding module and line of sight sub-system, AN/TAS-4 night sight, land navigation system and extensive communications equipment.

Three pre-production units were used in the engineering development tests with an additional three vehicles completed late in 1982. Sixty-four vehicles were ordered in fiscal year 1983 with 200 projected for fiscal year 1984. A total requirement of 1314 FISTVs is foreseen by the US Army.

Armoured Infantry Fighting Vehicle

This has been developed from the M113A1 as a private venture by the FMC Corporation and is fully described in its own entry earlier.

Lynx Command and Reconnaissance Vehicle

This uses many automotive components of the M113 APC but has a lower profile hull and only four road wheels. It is used only by Canada and The Netherlands.

Thyssen Henschel M113

Thyssen Henschel has completed trials of an M113 series APC fitted with HL-113 hydrostatic steering gear and improved brake system. This, according to Thyssen Henschel, has a number of advantages over the torque-controlled differential steering system currently fitted to the M113 series. The advantages include easier operation as the driver has a steering wheel and footbrake in place of the conventional steering brake levers, increased safety through stable straight ahead travel and continuous steering, increased safety through low loss steering and a resulting high manoeuvrability (the vehicle can turn on its vertical axis in nine seconds) through higher average speeds and especially when turning curves, increased safety through dual circuit brakes, and through well dimensioned air-cooled disc brakes and a continuous regulating mechanism which automatically adjusts to wear on the brake linings, increased safety through improved weight balance in the space for the drive mechanism, and easier maintenance.

The powerpack consisting of the engine, PTO and gearbox which remain unchanged and the HL-113 hydrostatic steering gear and improved brake system replaces the standard

M901 Improved TOW Vehicle with launcher extended

177

DA 200 differential steering gear. In order to drive the hydrostatic axial piston transmission it is necessary to flange an intermediate PTO gear between the engine and the gearbox. The conversion can be undertaken by a normal repair workshop although Thyssen Henschel can undertake this if required.

Thyssen Henschel appliqué armour

Thyssen Henschel have developed an appliqué armour kit for the M113 APC which weighs a total of 650 kg. When fitted the armour provides the following protection:

Hull front   14.5 mm projectiles at a range of 100 metres
20 mm (DM 43) projectiles at a range of 200 metres

Hull sides   14.5 mm projectiles at a range of 100 metres at an angle of 45 degrees
20 mm (DM 43) projectiles at a range of 200 metres at an angle of 35 degrees

Air Defence Anti-Tank System

The prototype of the private venture Air Defence Anti-Tank System (ADATS) developed by Oerlikon-Bührle is mounted on M113A2 chassis, although it can also be fitted to other chassis such as the V-300 Commando (6 × 6). A total of eight missiles are carried in the ready to launch position.

Infantry Armoured Fighting Vehicle

This is a further development of the M113A1 by OTO Melara of Italy and is fully described under Italy.

M113 with Tadpole sight

The Orlando Division of Martin Marietta has developed, as a private venture, the Tadpole vehicle-mounted sight, which has undergone trials at the US Army Field Artillery School at Fort Sill. Tadpole consists of a 15.24-metre telescoping mast on top of which is a sight. It can be mounted on other types of AFV and provides day, night and limited adverse weather target information while remaining concealed. The sight, which is similar to the helicopter Mast Mounted Sight (MMS) already successfully flight tested by the company, has a laser rangefinder/designator and a silicon vidicon tv, gimballed mirror to line-of-sight stabilisation system.

M113 Fire Support Vehicle

This is essentially an M113A2 APC fitted with the Cadillac Gage two-man turret armed with a 90 mm Cockerill Mark III gun, coaxial 7.62 mm machine gun, 7.62 mm anti-aircraft machine gun and, if required, smoke dischargers. Forty-two rounds of 90 mm (10 ready use and 32 stowed) and 2000 rounds of 7.62 mm ammunition would be carried. This model has yet to enter production.

Other variants of the M113 family

Almost every M113 user has developed variants of the M113/M113A1 family, including:

Australia: following trials with three prototypes of the M113A1 fitted with the turret of the British Scorpion CVR (T) vehicle armed with a 76 mm gun, a further 45 vehicles have been delivered to the Australian Army. The vehicle is used for fire support and retains its amphibious capability as additional buoyancy aids are fitted to the hull sides and front. This model is 4.864 metres long, 2.69 metres wide and 2.73 metres high. The Australian Army also has in reserve 18

Australian Army M113A1 fitter's vehicle in travelling configuration (Australian Army)

Australian M113A1 fitted with turret of British Alvis Scorpion CVR(T) vehicle armed with 76 mm gun (Paul Handel)

M113A1s fitted with the turret of the Saladin (6 × 6) armoured car which were withdrawn from service in the 1960s. Other M113 variants include a light reconnaissance vehicle with the American Cadillac Gage turret T50 armed with a 7.62 mm (0.30) and a 12.7 mm (0.50) machine gun, with 2500 rounds of 7.62 mm and 3000 rounds of 12.7 mm ammunition carried. Many Australian M113 APCs have a T50 turret armed with twin 7.62 mm (0.30) machine guns, with 5000 rounds of ammunition carried for them.

The Australian Army has applied the following designations to its M113 family vehicles:

M113A1 APC/LRV (armoured personnel carrier/light reconnaissance vehicle)
M113A1 APC(A) (ambulance)
M113A1 FSV (Scorpion) (fire support vehicle – Scorpion turret)
M113A1 FSV (Saladin) (fire support vehicle – Saladin turret)
M577A1 ACV (armoured command vehicle)
M125A1 APC(M) (carrier mortar)
M806A1 (armoured recovery vehicle, light)
M113A1 APC(F) (carrier, repair fitters)
M548 TLC (tracked load carrier)

Belgium: Belgian Mechanical Fabrications is building 525 M113 series vehicles under licence for the Belgian Army, additional details are given under Belgium.

Brazil: the Brazilian Army has about 700 M113 series vehicles and Moto Pecas SA of Sorocaba, São Paulo State, is overhauling these and replacing the original petrol engine with a Brazilian-built Mercedes-Benz OM-352-A diesel.

Canada: This country has about 900 M113A1 series vehicles in service including the basic M113A1 armoured personnel carrier, M577A1 command post vehicle, M113A1 engineer vehicle with hydraulically-operated dozer blade at front of hull, M548 tracked cargo carrier, and the Lynx command and reconnaissance vehicle.

In 1984 two variants of the M113A1 were tested by the Canadian Armed Forces and are expected to be adopted in the near future. Both variants have been developed by the Diesel Division of General Motors Canada. The M113 Engineering Variant Specially Equipped Vehicle is the M113A1 with the dozer blade but in addition has an hydraulic earth auger, hydraulic power tools, ramp restraining system and external fuel tanks either side of the hull. An M113A1 has also been fitted with the two-man power-operated turret as mounted on the LAV-25 vehicles being built by General Motors Canada for the United States

Australian Army M113A1 armoured personnel carrier/light reconnaissance vehicle (Australian Army)

Canadian Armed Forces M113A1 fitted with two-man LAV-25 turret armed with 25 mm Hughes Helicopters Chain Gun, 7.62 mm coaxial machine gun and two banks of four smoke dischargers

West German M113 APC fitted with Green Archer mortar-locating radar in operating position (C R Zwart)

West Germany Army battery fire-control vehicle based on M577A1 hull with antenna lowered on roof

Marine Corps. This is armed with a 25 mm Chain Gun, 7.62 mm coaxial and 7.62 mm anti-aircraft machine guns.

Egypt: This country placed an order for 500 M113A2s in 1980 and in 1984 the Pentagon announced a letter of offer to Egypt for the supply of 354 M113A2, 13 M577A2, 19 mortar carriers, 23 M113A2 armoured ambulances, 33 M548A1 ammunition carriers, 52 fitters vehicles and 43 M806E1 recovery vehicles. To meet the requirements of the Egyptian Army Thomson-CSF and ESD of France have each designed and built prototypes of a M113A2 twin 23 mm self-propelled anti-aircraft gun system with another M113A2 being used as a fire control vehicle. Egypt has also developed an appliqué armour kit for the M113A2 and uses a Soviet 120 mm mortar in place of the original American 4.2 inch mortar as used in the M106A1 mortar carrier.

Germany, Federal Republic: West Germany is one of the main users of the M113 outside the United States and has developed a number of versions to meet specific requirements, including radar vehicles fitted with the RATAC battlefield artillery radar and the Green Archer mortar-locating radar, an artillery observation post vehicle, 120 mm mortar carrier and modifications to the basic APC. The artillery observation vehicle is called the Beobachtungspanzer Artillerie and the first 26 of a planned procurement of 320 were delivered by Thyssen Henschel in 1982. The vehicle is fitted with a Peri D11 double periscopic sight, incorporating a laser rangefinder, FNA615 land navigation system and

Israeli Army M113 fitted with appliqué armour

a data input/output terminal linking it with the battery fire-control centre. Thyssen Henschel have also delivered 115 battery fire-control vehicles to the West German Army based on a modified M557A1 hull. The mortar carrier, of which some 500 are in service, is fitted with a Tampella 120 mm mortar in the back which fires to the rear and has a traverse of 18½ degrees left and 25 degrees right, elevation limits being from +45 degrees to +80 degrees. A total of 63 120 mm mortar bombs is carried, but when afloat only 23 can be carried. Most West German M113/M113A1 vehicles are fitted with eight smoke dischargers on the front of the hull and are armed with a single 7.62 mm MG3 machine gun. M113s are now being retrofitted with a diesel engine to bring them up to M113A1 standard.

Israel: most M113s have had their trim vanes removed from the front of the hull and an extension fitted to the exhaust outlet so that exhaust does not blow back into the troop compartment when the vehicle is being driven with its roof hatches open. Other modifications include mounting up to four 7.62 mm or 12.7 mm (0.50) machine guns on the top of the hull and racks fitted on either side of the hull to enable personnel kit and other stores to be carried outside the vehicle thus giving more room inside the troop compartment. The Israelis call the M113 the Zelda. In addition to the basic APC, the Israeli Army uses many specialised versions of the M113A1 including anti-tank fitted with the Hughes TOW ATGW system, forward ambulance, forward engineer, modified M577 command vehicles, 60 mm Soltam mortar carriers and technical support. Rafael Armament and Development Authority has developed a new type of armour that can be fitted to the front, sides and rear of the M113 to give a high degree of protection against attack from HEAT projectiles. Many Israeli M113s, especially those used in Southern Lebanon, have now been fitted with the kit.

New Zealand: New Zealand purchased 72 members of this family including the M113A1 armoured personnel carrier (some of which have the T50 turret as on Australian vehicles), M125A1 mortar carrier, M577A1 command vehicle, M579 fitters' vehicle and the M806A1 armoured recovery vehicle. The Ministry of Works and Development (MWD) is rebuilding 64 of these over a six-year period beginning in 1980 at a cost of $6 million.

Norway: to meet the requirements of the Norwegian Army the NM 135 has been developed. This is an M113A1 fitted with a new Swedish Hägglunds turret armed with a West German Rheinmetall 20 mm Rh 202 cannon with a 7.62 mm machine gun mounted coaxially with the main armament on the right of the turret. This turret is mounted behind the engine compartment on the left side, with the commander's hatch moved to the immediate rear of the driver. The conversion has been carried out by the Norwegian company of Kongsberg Våpenfabrikk A/S.

Singapore: To meet the requirements of the Singapore Army, Chartered Industries of Singapore has designed a modification kit to convert the M113 to a 120 mm or 81 mm mortar carrier. This is now in service and offered for export. The 120 mm mortar has a traverse of 18.5 degrees left and 25 degrees right with elevation being from 800 mils to 1422 mils.

Spain: Spain uses the M113, M113A1, M113A2, M548 tracked cargo carrier, M577 command post vehicle, M113 series recovery vehicle and the M125 81 mm mortar carrier. Talbot carries out the complete overhaul of M113s in Spain and can also bring M113 petrol-engined vehicles up to the M113A1/M113A2 standard. In place of the M106 107 mm mortar carrier the Spanish Army uses a similar vehicle with a Spanish-built 120 mm mortar which fires to the rear of the hull. A baseplate is carried externally on the left side of the hull to allow the mortar to be dismounted for use away from the vehicle.

Switzerland: the basic APC is called the Schützenpanzer 63 by the Swiss Army but many have been fitted with the Swedish Hägglund turret armed with a 20 mm cannon as fitted to the Pbv 302 APCs of the Swedish Army. When fitted with this turret the vehicle is known as the Schützenpanzer 63/73. Other versions in service include the bulldozer model (called the Geniepanzer 63), a command vehicle (Schützenpanzer Kdo Spz-63), 120 mm mortar carrier (designated the Minenwerferpanzer 64), command vehicle (designated the Kommandopanzer 63), command vehicle with turret-mounted 20 mm cannon (designated the Kommandopanzer 63/73), repair vehicle (designated the Kranpanzer 63), wireless vehicle (designated the Übermittlungspanzer 63) and an artillery command vehicle (designated the Feuerleitpanzer 63).

NM 135 developed for Norwegian Army by Kongsberg Våpenfabrikk A/S with Swedish Hägglunds turret armed with West German Rheinmetall 20 mm cannon

Model	M106A1	M113	M113A1	M113A2	M125A1	M577A1
CREW	6	2 + 11	2 + 11	2 + 11	6	5
COMBAT WEIGHT	11 996 kg	10 258 kg	11 156 kg	11 341 kg	11 261 kg	11 513 kg
UNLOADED WEIGHT	9005 kg	8960 kg	9702 kg	9926 kg	10 539 kg	10 865 kg
POWER-TO-WEIGHT RATIO	17.92 hp/tonne	20.37 hp/tonne	19.27 hp/tonne	18.51 hp/tonne	19.09 hp/tonne	18.67 hp/tonne
GROUND PRESSURE	0.59 kg/cm²	0.5 kg/cm²	0.55 kg/cm²	0.56 kg/cm²	0.55 kg/cm²	0.57 kg/cm²
LENGTH	4.926 m	4.863 m	4.863 m	4.863 m	4.863 m	4.863 m
WIDTH	2.863 m	2.686 m	2.686 m	2.686 m	2.686 m	2.686 m
over tracks	2.54 m	2.54 m	2.54 m	2.54 m	2.54 m	2.54 m
HEIGHT						
overall	2.5 m	2.5 m	2.5 m	2.52 m	2.5 m	2.68 m
to hull top	1.828 m	1.828 m	1.828 m	1.85 m	1.828 m	2.469 m
GROUND CLEARANCE	0.41 m	0.41 m	0.41 m	0.43 m	0.41 m	0.41 m
TRACK	2.159 m	2.159 m	2.159 m	2.159 m	2.159 m	2.159 m
TRACK WIDTH	381 mm	381 mm	381 mm	381 mm	381 mm	381 mm
LENGTH OF TRACK ON GROUND	2.667 m	2.667 m	2.667 m	2.667 m	2.667 m	2.667 m
MAX SPEED						
road	67.59 km/h	64.37 km/h	67.59 km/h	67.59 km/h	67.59 km/h	67.59 km/h
water	5.8 km/h	5.6 km/h	5.8 km/h	5.8 km/h	5.8 km/h	5.8 km/h
FUEL CAPACITY	360 litres	302 litres	360 litres	360 litres	360 litres	454 litres
MAX CRUISING RANGE	483 km	321 km	483 km	483 km	483 km	595 km
FORDING	amphibious	amphibious	amphibious	amphibious	amphibious	amphibious
VERTICAL OBSTACLE	0.61 m	0.61 m	0.61 m	0.61 m	0.61 m	0.61 m
GRADIENT	60%	60%	60%	60%	60%	60%
TRENCH	1.68 m	1.68 m	1.68 m	1.68 m	1.68 m	1.68 m
ENGINE	GMC Detroit Diesel model 6V-53 6-cylinder water-cooled diesel developing 215 bhp at 2800 rpm	Chrysler 75M V-8 petrol developing 209 bhp at 4000 rpm	GMC Detroit Diesel model 6V-53 6-cylinder water-cooled diesel developing 215 bhp at 2800 rpm			
TRANSMISSION	GMC, Allison TX-100-1 with 4 forward and 1 reverse ranges	GMC, Allison TX-200 with 2 forward and 1 reverse gears	GMC, Allison TX-100-1 with 4 forward and 1 reverse ranges	GMC, Allison TX-100-1 with 4 forward and 1 reverse ranges	GMC, Allison TX-100-1 with 4 forward and 1 reverse ranges	GMC, Allison TX-100-1 with 4 forward and 1 reverse ranges
SUSPENSION	torsion bar	torsion bar	torsion bar	torsion bar	torsion bar	torsion bar
ELECTRICAL SYSTEM	24 V	24 V	24 V	24 V	24 V	24 V
BATTERIES	2 × 12 V 6TN	2 × 12 V 6TN	2 × 12 V 6TN	2 × 12 V 6TN	2 × 12 V 6TN	2 × 12 V 6TN
ARMAMENT	1 × 12.7 mm MG	1 × 12.7 mm MG	1 × 12.7 mm MG	1 × 12.7 mm MG	1 × 12.7 mm MG	1 × 7.62 mm MG
AMMUNITION	1000	2000	2000	2000	1000	1000
ARMOUR	12–38 mm	12–38 mm	12–38 mm	12–38 mm	12–38 mm	12–38 mm

Status: In production. In service with Argentina, Australia, Belgium, Bolivia, Brazil (army and marines, including M577 command), Canada, Chile, Costa Rica, Denmark, Ecuador, Egypt (including M125A2, M577A2; in March 1980 Egypt ordered 550 M113A2 APCs at a cost, with spares and training equipment of $82·8 million), El Salvador, Ethiopia, West Germany, Guatemala, Greece (in 1982 Greece ordered 110 M113A2s at a cost of $26 million including spares), Haiti, Iran, Israel, Italy, Jordan, Kampuchea, South Korea, Kuwait, Laos, Lebanon (in January 1980 an order was placed for 70 M113A2 APCs and four M577A2 command post vehicles at a cost of $10·7 million), Libya, Morocco, Netherlands, New Zealand, Norway, Pakistan, Peru, Philippines, Portugal, Saudi Arabia (in November 1983 the US Department of Defense notified Congress of a letter of offer to Saudi Arabia for the supply of 24 M106A2 mortar carriers, 62 M125A1 mortar carriers, 80 M577A2 command post vehicles and 156 M113A2 APCs), Singapore, Somalia, Spain, Sudan, Switzerland, Taiwan (late in 1982 the DoD informed Congress of a letter of offer to Taiwan for the sale of 164 M113A2s, including 24 ambulance models, 75 M125A2 mortar carriers, 31 command post vehicles, 90 M106A2 mortar carriers, plus spares at a cost of $97 million), Thailand (including M113A2), Tunisia (including M125A1, M557A1), Turkey, USA, Uruguay, Viet-Nam, Yemen Arab Republic (North) and Zaïre.

Manufacturer: FMC Corporation, Ordnance Division, 1105 Coleman Avenue, San Jose, California 95108, USA.

M59 Armoured Personnel Carrier

Development

In 1951 the FMC Corporation of San Jose, which was then building the M75 APC, designed another full tracked APC under the designation T59. This was powered by two Cadillac engines and was followed by the T59E1 which was powered by two General Motors Corporation model 302 petrol engines. The T59E1 was standardised as the M59 (Carrier, Personnel, Full Tracked: Armored, M59) in December 1953. Just over 4000 M59s were built by the FMC Corporation between February 1954 and March 1959. The M59 replaced the expensive and non-amphibious M75 APC and was in turn replaced by the M113 APC in the United States Army from 1961. The M59 was regarded as a considerable improvement over the M75 but it was underpowered and capable of amphibious operations only in very calm waters.

Description

The hull of the M59 is made of all-welded steel with the driver seated at the front of the hull on the left and the commander to his right. The driver has a single-piece hatch cover that opens to the rear with an integral M17 periscope which can be replaced by an M19 infra-red periscope. Forward of the driver's position are another three M17 periscopes.

On vehicles numbered 7 to 1312 the commander has a cupola which can be traversed through a full 360 degrees, a single-piece hatch cover that opens to the rear, six periscopes and a 12.7 mm (0.50) machine gun which can be aimed and fired by the commander with his head and shoulders exposed.

On vehicles 1313 to 2941 the commander has a cupola with four periscopes, a single-piece hatch cover and an externally-mounted 12.7 mm (0.50) machine gun which can be aimed and fired by the commander with his head and shoulders exposed.

On vehicles numbered 2942 and onwards, which are designated the M59A1, the commander has an M13 cupola which can be traversed through a full 360 degrees and is armed with a 12.7 mm (0.50) M2 machine gun which can be elevated to +58 degrees and depressed to −10 degrees, both elevation and traverse being manual. The cupola has an M28 roof-mounted periscope sight for aiming the machine gun, four vision blocks and a single-piece hatch cover that opens to the rear.

The ten infantrymen sit in the troop compartment at the rear, five down each side of the hull on bench seats that can be folded down to enable cargo to be carried. They enter and leave by a power-operated ramp at the rear of the hull, which is hinged at the bottom and has an emergency hatch in its centre in case of ramp failure. Over the top of the infantry compartment are two roof hatches, the forward one opening to the right and the rear one to the left.

The two engines are mounted in the space between the hull sides and the troop compartment. Over the top of each engine compartment are an air-intake grille, radiator filler cap, exhaust-outlet grille and an engine access hatch. The M59 is powered by two 127 bhp petrol engines through a GMC model X300M Hydramatic transmission mounted directly to each engine. Power is transmitted from the transmission through right-angle gearboxes on each side of the forward section of the vehicle to a two-speed transfer case and controlled differential in the forward centre section of the hull. Steering and braking are accomplished by wet drum brakes in the controlled differential, which transmits power through universal joints to the final drive. The controlled differential enables the M59 to make sharp turns but does not allow it to pivot.

The torsion bar suspension consists of five dual rubber-tyred road wheels with the drive sprocket at the front, idler at the rear and three track return rollers. The first and last road wheel stations are provided with a hydraulic shock absorber.

The M59 is fully amphibious, being propelled in the water by its tracks. Before entering the water the trim vane is erected at the front of the hull and the bilge pump switched on. The vehicle has no NBC system although a slight pressurisation of the personnel compartment reduces the amount of dust that enters the vehicle. Infra-red driving lights are standard.

Variants

The basic M59 can be used as an ambulance, command vehicle, load carrier, reconnaissance vehicle and weapons carrier armed with a 106 mm M40 recoilless rifle. The only variant of the M59 to enter service was the M84 4.2-inch (107 mm) mortar carrier which was developed under the designation of the T84 and was standardised in November 1955. The M84 was fitted with the same M13 cupola as the M59A1 and had a crew of six which consisted of the driver, commander, gunner, loader and two ammunition members.

The M30 4.2-inch (107 mm) mortar is mounted in the rear of the hull and fires to the rear. A baseplate is carried externally on the left side of the ramp to enable the mortar to be dismounted and used away from the vehicle if required. Major external differences are that the rear ramp has an emergency hatch in the right side rather than the centre, the roof hatch which covers the troop/mortar compartment is of a different design and is in two parts that fold forwards, and when afloat rectangular screens are erected around the four air-inlet/exhaust grilles to stop water entering the engine compartment. The screens have to be erected when afloat as the M84 has a loaded weight of 21 364 kg compared with the M59 which weighs 19 232 kg. A total of 88 4.2-inch (107 mm) mortar bombs is carried.

SPECIFICATIONS (M59A1)	
CREW	2 + 10
COMBAT WEIGHT	19 323 kg
UNLOADED WEIGHT	17 916 kg
POWER-TO-WEIGHT	
RATIO	13.14 bhp/tonne
GROUND PRESSURE	0.51 kg/cm²
LENGTH	5.613 m
WIDTH	3.263 m
over tracks	3.149 m
HEIGHT	
to top of cupola sight	2.768 m
to hull top	2.387 m
GROUND CLEARANCE	0.457 m
TRACK	2.616 m
TRACK WIDTH	533 mm
LENGTH OF TRACK	
ON GROUND	3.079 m
MAX SPEED	
road	51.5 km/h
water	6.9 km/h
FUEL CAPACITY	518 litres
MAX RANGE	164 km
FORDING	amphibious
GRADIENT	60%
VERTICAL OBSTACLE	0.46 m
TRENCH	1.676 m
ENGINES	2 × General Motors Corporation model 302 6-cylinder water-cooled in-line petrol developing 127 hp at 3350 rpm
TRANSMISSION	2 × Hydramatic with 4 forward and 1 reverse gears in two ranges (high and low)
SUSPENSION	torsion bar
ELECTRICAL SYSTEM	24 V
BATTERIES	2 × 12 V
ARMAMENT	1 × 12.7 mm MG
SMOKE-LAYING	
EQUIPMENT	none
AMMUNITION	2205
FIRE-CONTROL SYSTEM	
Turret power control	manual
Gun elevation/depression	+58°/−10°
Turret traverse	360°
ARMOUR	
Hull front	16 mm
Hull sides	12.7 mm
Hull top	10 mm
Hull floor	12.7 mm
Hull rear	12.7 mm

Status: Production complete. In service with Brazil, Greece and Turkey.

Manufacturer: FMC Corporation, Ordnance Divison, 1105 Coleman Avenue, San Jose, California 95108, USA.

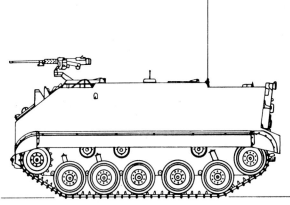

M59 APC with pintle-mounted 12.7 mm (0.50) Browning M2 HB machine gun

M59A1 APC with M13 cupola armed with 12.7 mm (0.50) Browning M2 HB machine gun (US Army)

M75 Armoured Personnel Carrier

A total of 1729 M75 full-tracked armoured personnel carriers were built by International Harvester between 1951 and 1954. Some of these remain in service with the Belgian Army but all of these are expected to be withdrawn from service by 1988 and replaced by the M113A2 and AIFV which are now being built in Belgium by BMF (qv under Belgium).

United States Light Armored Vehicle Competition (LAV)

The LAV programme resulted from a US military requirement for a lightly armoured weapon system for rapid deployment with tactical mobility, reasonable survivability and assault capability. These requirements will be filled by a family of vehicles. All mission role vehicles (MRVs) will use the same chassis, power train and suspension components and will have similar hulls. Current requirements are for eight versions of the LAV: LAV-25 (25 mm Hughes Chain Gun weapon), assault gun (requires 75–105 mm main armament), anti-tank (TOW), command and control, 81 mm mortar, maintenance/recovery, logistics, and air defence.

The specific capabilities, which apply to all variants of the LAV, are as follows: **(1)** RAM-D (limited to automotive chassis components), reliability 0.9 (322 km mission), availability 0.85 and durability 32 200 km overhaul **(2)** transportable by tactical and strategic aircraft including CH-53E helicopter, C-130, C-141 and C-5A aircraft **(3)** per cent no go: ten per cent maximum Germany dry conditions **(4)** cross-country V80 speed: 28 km/h minimum **(5)** road speed: 100 km/h minimum **(6)** cruise range: 644 km minimum **(7)** swim capability **(8)** NBC protective system: individual, growth to collective **(9)** protection level: NATO 7.62 mm ball, minimum (0° obliquity, 0 range) **(10)** diesel engine **(11)** automatic transmission **(12)** driver's night vision **(13)** smoke capability (grenade launchers) **(14)** intercom **(15)** receiver, transmitter, receiver **(16)** secure voice **(17)** 70 per cent minimum gradient capability **(18)** 30 per cent minimum side slope capability **(19)** 0.457-metre vertical obstacle **(20)** personnel heater **(21)** slave capability **(22)** ventilation of vehicle interior.

The LAV programme had two phases, the competitive test and evaluation followed by production. The first phase began in April 1981 with a request for proposals (RFP) to buy prototype vehicles for testing. In September 1981 three companies, Alvis Limited (UK), General Motors (Canada) and Cadillac Gage (USA) were awarded contracts; Cadillac Gage was awarded two.

In November 1981 each contractor delivered two LAV-25 vehicles with two-man turrets armed with a 25 mm Hughes Chain Gun, a coaxial 7.62 mm M240 machine gun and two banks of four smoke dischargers, and one assault gun vehicle with a 90 mm Cockerill Mk III gun, a coaxial 7.62 mm M240 machine gun and two banks of four smoke dischargers. A third LAV-25 vehicle was received in April 1982. Alvis, teamed with Martin Marietta, supplied three Alvis Stormer vehicles to meet the LAV-25 requirement and one Alvis Scorpion vehicle to meet the assault gun requirement; General Motors provided four 8 × 8 versions of the MOWAG Piranha vehicle, and Cadillac Gage supplied four V-150 S (4 × 4) and four V-300 (6 × 6) vehicles.

The production phase began in December 1981 with the release of an RFP to buy production vehicles and prototypes of other versions not tested in the first phase. It was announced in September 1982 that the Diesel Division, General Motors Canada had won the LAV competition and two separate contracts resulted.

A five-year, multi-year contract was awarded for LAV-25 production, with each programme year to be called up separately. In the first year 60 LAV-25s were bought for the US Marine Corps; in the second, called up in March 1983, 170 vehicles were bought. The first production vehicle was completed in November 1983. To ensure that the LAV meets all requirements four initial production vehicles were scheduled for 32 200 km of testing between April and October 1984.

The second contract was for the development and testing of five specialised mission role vehicles, anti-tank (TOW), 81 mm mortar carrier, logistics (cargo), command and control, and maintenance/recovery. Two of each have been delivered and tested. Early in 1984 the US Army withdrew from the LAV programme; future details of the actual vehicles are given in this section under Canada.

In the US Marine Corps the LAV will be issued to the Light Armored Assault Battalion for use in reconnaissance in force, co-ordinated attacks, exploitation and pursuit operations. When used in a defensive role the mobility and firepower of the LAV will be used to disrupt, delay and deceive the enemy.

At present the US Marine Corps plans to form three Light Armored Assault battalions, one at 29 Palms, California, one

np LeJeune, North Carolina, and one at Camp Pendle-
alifornia. An additional company will be stationed in
wa for use in the Far East.

Cadillac Gage Commando V-300 Armoured Vehicle Range

Development

The Commando V-300 (6 × 6) range of armoured vehicles has been developed as a private venture by the Cadillac Gage Company which has already designed and built the highly successful Commando V-150 (4 × 4) range of vehicles now in service with over 20 countries. The first two prototypes of the V-300 were completed in 1979 and the vehicle entered production in 1983. Late in 1982 Panama placed an order worth over $6 million for 12 V-300 Commando vehicles in four different configurations including fire support vehicle with 90 mm Cockerill Mk III gun, APC with twin 7.62 mm machine guns and recovery. All of these were delivered by the end of 1983. The company also supplied a number of vehicles for the Light Armored Vehicle compeition including models fitted with the two-man turret armed with a Cockerill 90 mm Mk III gun, two-man 25 mm Chain Gun turret and two-man 25 mm Chain Gun turret fitted with a stabilisation system. In 1984 Kuwait ordered 62 V-300 Commando vehicles.

Description

The hull of the V-300 Commando is of all-welded unitised construction of special high hardness steel ballistic plate that protects the crew from small arms fire and shell splinters.

The driver sits at the front of the hull on the left side and has a single-piece square hatch cover that opens to the rear. To his front are three periscopes for forward observation and one of these can be replaced by a passive periscope for driving at night. In the side of the hull to the left of the driver is a bullet-proof vision block with a firing port underneath. To the rear of this is a small half-door that opens to the rear, this has a bullet-proof vision block underneath which is a firing port.

The engine compartment is to the right of the driver with the air inlet and air outlet in the roof and the exhaust pipe in the right side of the hull. Power from the engine is transmitted to the final drives via an Allison MT-643 four-speed automatic gearbox. The transfer box contains a two-speed system with a spline engagement clutch for the axle drive.

On the glacis plate is a receptacle for a shovel and pick axe and under the nose is an internally-mounted hydraulic winch

Cadillac Gage V-300 Commando with two-man turret armed with 90 mm Cockerill Mark III gun

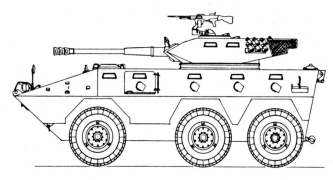

Cadillac Gage V-300 Commando fitted with Cadillac Gage turret armed with 20 mm Oerlikon cannon, 7.62 mm coaxial machine gun and 7.62 mm anti-aircraft machine gun

Cadillac Gage V-300 Commando fitted with two-man turret armed with Cockerill 90 mm Mk III gun, 7.62 mm coaxial machine gun and 7.62 mm anti-aircraft machine gun

which has a maximum capacity of 9072 kg, this is provided with 45 metres of 12.7 mm diameter steel core cable.

The V-300 can be fitted with a number of armament installations, these are mounted in the centre of the hull over the second axle and include:
Cadillac Gage two-man turret with 90 mm Cockerill Mk III gun (described in V-150 entry)
Cadillac Gage two-man turret with 76 mm Royal Ordnance L23A1 gun (described in V-150 entry)
Turret armed with 25 mm M242 Hughes Chain Gun, 7.62 mm coaxial and 7.62 mm anti-aircraft machine guns and smoke dischargers
Cadillac Gage two-man turret with 20 mm Oerlikon cannon (described in V-150 entry)
Cadillac Gage one-man turret with 20 mm Oerlikon cannon (described in V-150 entry)
Cadillac Gage one-man 1-metre machine gun turret (described in V-150 entry)
Cadillac Gage one-man machine gun turret (described in V-150 entry).
Ring mount with 7.62 mm or 12.7 mm machine gun.

The troop compartment is at the rear of the V-300 and in each side of the hull are three bullet-proof vision blocks each with a firing port underneath. Over the top of the troop compartment are two rectangular roof hatches hinged on the outside. The infantry enter and leave the vehicle through two doors in the rear of the hull, each of these has a bullet-proof vision block underneath which is a firing port. As an alternative to the two-part hatch cover a circular hatch cover with provision for mounting a 7.62 mm pintle-mounted GPMG can be fitted.

The front suspension is a swing-mounted solid axle with rear suspension being independent with coil springs at each wheel station. The front solid axle is restrained longitudinally by trailing arms and laterally by stabilising rods attached to the axle and hull. The two rear axles consist of short drive shafts extending from the hull-mounted differentials to the independently-sprung trailing arms-mounted wheel stations. The road wheels have a combined wheel travel of 30 cm, a jounce of 17.5 cm and a rebound of 12.5 cm. All the swing-mounted axles are of the double-reduction top-mounted type. The front and rear axles have positive No-Spin differentials to maintain traction in off road operations. The central axles contain the inter-axle differential. All wheels have hydraulic brakes and steering is power assisted on the front wheels. All wheels have run-flat tubeless tyres.

The V-300 is fully amphibious without preparation, being propelled in the water by its wheels at a speed of 4.8 km/h.

A wide range of optional equipment is available including night vision devices, heater kit, air-conditioning system, NBC system, wiper kit for the driver and a slave cable.

Variants

TOW Anti-tank
This would be fitted with the same mount as used in the M901 Improved TOW Vehicle based on the M113 chassis with two missiles in the ready to launch position and reserve missiles carried in the hull.

TOW Anti-tank
Fitted with an external top-mounted swing-up launcher with an elevation of +30 degrees, depression of −10 degrees and traverse of 360 degrees. Ten TOW ATGW missiles are carried plus a 7.62 mm machine gun and 2000 rounds of ammunition.

Cadillac Gage V-300 Commando with turret armed with Hughes Helicopters 25 mm Chain Gun, coaxial 7.62 mm machine gun and smoke dischargers. The 7.62 mm anti-aircraft machine gun is not installed

81 mm Mortar
Fitted with turntable-mounted 81 mm mortar with elevation from +42 to +85 degrees, total traverse of 360 degrees, range of 150 to 4400 metres with a total of 60 mortar bombs carried. Also fitted with 7.62 mm machine gun for which 2000 rounds of ammunition are carried.

Ambulance
This model would unarmed and be fitted with a raised roof and ramp in place of twin doors at the rear to facilitate the loading of stretchers and walking wounded.

Others
These could include cargo carrier, command vehicle, recovery vehicle and anti-aircraft with a missile system such as ADATS, or a gun system such as the General Electric 20 mm Vulcan as installed on a number of V-150 Commando 4 × 4 vehicles supplied to Saudi Arabia.

SPECIFICATIONS

CREW	3 + 9 (max)	MAX SPEED		SUSPENSION	solid front axle, middle and
CONFIGURATION	6 × 6	road	92 km/h		rear independent with coil
COMBAT WEIGHT	13 137 kg	water	5 km/h		springs, direct acting
POWER-TO-WEIGHT		ACCELERATION			telescopic shock absorber
RATIO	17.88 bhp/tonne	0 to 32 km/h	8 s		acting at each wheel station
LENGTH	6.4 m	FUEL CAPACITY	265 litres	TYRES	14.5 × 21
WIDTH	2.54 m	MAX RANGE	700 km	BRAKES	
HEIGHT		FORDING	amphibious	main	hydraulic (all wheels) power
MG turret	2.59 m	GRADIENT	60%		booster with electric back up
20 mm turret	2.692 m	SIDE SLOPE	30%	parking	drum and shoe hand-
ITV	2.756 m	VERTICAL OBSTACLE	0.609 m		operated
hull top	1.981 m	TURNING RADIUS	10 m	ELECTRICAL SYSTEM	24 V
GROUND CLEARANCE		ENGINE	VT-504 V-8 turbo-charged	BATTERIES	2 × 12 V, 100 Ah
hull	0.533 m		diesel, 235 hp at 3000 rpm		
axle	0.355 m	TRANSMISSION	Allison MT-643 automatic, 4		
TRACK			speeds forwards and 1		
front	2.167 m		reverse		
rear	2.198 m	TRANSFER CASE	2-speed with spline		
WHEELBASE	2.209 m + 1.524 m		engagement clutch for axle		
ANGLE OF APPROACH/			drive		
DEPARTURE	45°/78°	STEERING	variable ratio power		

Status: In production. In service with Panama. On order for Kuwait.

Manufacturer: Cadillac Gage Company, PO Box 1027, Warren, Michigan 48090, USA.

lac Gage Commando V-150 Armoured cle Range

opment

In 1962 the Cadillac Gage Company, as a private venture, started design work on a 4 × 4 armoured vehicle which could undertake a wide range of roles such as armoured personnel carrier, convoy escort vehicle or reconnaissance vehicle. The first prototype of the vehicle, called the V-100 Commando, was completed in March 1963 and the first production vehicles the following year.

The V-100 was widely used in Viet-Nam for both convoy escort work and for patrolling air bases and other high value targets. The V-100 was powered by a Chrysler 361 V-8 petrol engine which developed 200 hp and gave the vehicle a maximum road speed of 100 km/h. Gross vehicle weight was 7370 kg and a maximum of twelve men including the crew could be carried. The V-100 was supplemented in production by the larger V-200, which was powered by a Chrysler 440 CID engine which developed 275 hp and gave the vehicle a maximum road speed of 96 km/h. Gross vehicle weight of the V-200 is 12 730 kg. The V-200 is believed to have been sold only to Singapore and is no longer being produced. Versions of the V-200 used by Singapore include anti-aircraft with the Swedish Bofors RBS-70 surface-to-air missile system, recovery fitted with A frame at front of hull, fire support fitted with two-man turret armed with 90 mm Mecar gun in two-man turret with 7.62 mm coaxial and 7.62 mm anti-aircraft machine guns and APC fitted with two-man turret armed with 20 mm Oerlikon cannon, 7.62 mm coaxial and 7.62 mm anti-aircraft machine guns.

The United States Air Force still uses a number of original V-100 Commando vehicles at the Tactical Fighter Weapons Centre at Nellis Air Force Base in Nevada. Typical roles include simulating the Soviet SA-9 SAM system and command and control systems associated with the Soviet air defence systems.

In October 1971 the V-150 was introduced and has now replaced the V-100 and V-200 in production. Production of the V-100, V-150 and V-200 has now reached well over 4000 units.

The vehicles have been exported to over 20 countries and have been used in some numbers both by the United States Army and the United States Air Force. As a result of experience in use the vehicle has been constantly updated and improved.

There is a separate entry for the Cadillac Gage V-300 (6 × 6) armoured vehicle range.

There are two other vehicles on the market today which are very similar in appearance to the Commando, the American Dragoon 300 series and the Portuguese Chaimite, which is known to have been sold to Lebanon, Libya, Peru, Philippines and Portugal. Both these vehicles are described in this book.

Cadillac Gage has delivered two V-150 S Commando vehicles for evaluation in the LAV competition. One was fitted with a two-man turret armed with a 90 mm Cockerill Mark III gun, 7.62 mm coaxial and 7.62 mm anti-aircraft machine gun, the second armed with a 25 mm M242 Chain Gun, 7.62 mm coaxial and 7.62 mm anti-aircraft machine guns. In 1984 Kuwait placed an order for 20 V-150 S Commando vehicles.

Description

The all-welded hull of the V-150 Commando armoured personnel carrier protects the crew from small arms fire up to 7.62 mm in calibre, overhead blast, shell splinters and Molotov cocktails.

The driver sits at the front of the hull on the left side and has two vision blocks in front of him and one on his left. The vehicle commander sits on the driver's right and has one vision block to his front and one on his right. Both crew members have a single-piece hatch cover over their position that opens to the outside. Early production vehicles had a firing port just behind the driver's and commander's side vision block, but current vehicles do not.

The troop compartment is behind the commander's and driver's position with three infantrymen seated down each side of the hull and one to the rear of the machine gunner's position. They enter and leave the vehicle by two doors in the side of the hull, one on each side. The lower part of the door folds downwards and the upper part, which contains the vision block and firing port, opens to the rear. In each side of the hull, forward of the side door, is a firing port with a vision block over the top. All vision blocks in the V-150 have crash pads and spall shields for additional protection.

In centre of the troop compartment roof is a cupola which can be traversed manually through 360 degrees and has a single-piece hatch cover that opens to the rear. On the forward part of the cupola, which has no observation devices, is a pintle-mounted 7.62 mm machine gun with 200 rounds of ready-use ammunition and another 3000 rounds in reserve in the hull.

There is also a door at the rear of the hull on the right side, with the lower part folding downwards and the upper part, which contains the firing port and vision block, opening upwards. Over the top of the passageway that connects the troop compartment with the rear door is a single-piece circular hatch that opens forwards. A further two seats are provided in this passageway.

The engine compartment is at the rear of the hull on the left side with access panels in the top and side of the hull. The engine cooling system is a conventional automotive water-cooled system utilising a fin and tubed radiator with an additional surge tank for reserve capacity. The engine fan and venturi are designed for maximum air flow efficiency and minimum horsepower draw. The cooling system is capable of

V-150 Commando with two-man turret armed with 20 mm Oerlikon cannon, 7.62 mm coaxial machine gun and 7.62 mm anti-aircraft machine gun

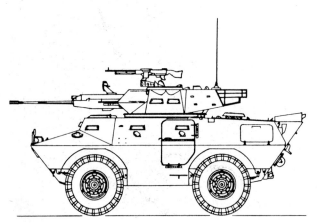

V-150 Commando fitted with turret armed with 20 mm Oerlikon cannon, 7.62 mm coaxial machine gun, 7.62 mm anti-aircraft machine gun, six smoke dischargers fitted to turret side

V-200 Commando 120 mm mortar carrier of Singapore Army with roof hatches, side and rear doors open

operating in ambient temperatures of 130° F. The engine compartment has a fire-extinguishing system that is operated manually by the driver.

Wherever possible, standard military automotive components are used in the V-150 Commando, such as the engine, transmission and axles. When originally introduced the Commando V-150 was powered by a Chrysler 361 V-8 petrol engine developing 200 hp at 4000 rpm coupled to a manual transmission with five forward and one reverse gears and a single-speed transfer case. Current production vehicles have a V-8 diesel that develops 202 hp at 3300 rpm coupled to an automatic transmission and a two-speed transfer case.

The solid axles have silent locking differentials and the suspension consists of semi-elliptical springs and hydraulic double-acting shock absorbers with rebound control at each wheel station. Jounce control is by hollow rubber springs at each wheel station. The run-flat tyres, which are capable of operation for a distance of 40 km, have self-cleaning treads. Mounted internally at the front of the hull is a winch with a capacity of 4536 kg, which has 48.76 metres of 9.5 mm diameter cable. All members of the Commando family are fully amphibious, being propelled in the water by their wheels.

Standard equipment on all vehicles includes fuel and water cans, two hand-held fire extinguishers, pioneer tool set, tow cable, breaker bar and lug wrench, first aid kit, snatch block, vehicle tool kit (including 8000 kg hydraulic jack stowed

inside the vehicle), pamphlet bag, oddment box, slave cable, wiper kit, spare vision blocks and an air compressor with hose.

Optional equipment for the Commando includes smoke or smoke/fragmentation launchers, fixed pintle socket for rear, rear ring mount with 7.62 mm pintle and cradle, ring mount and cradle for 0.30 calibre, 0.50 calibre machine guns or 40 mm automatic grenade launcher, gun shield for fixed pintle socket or ring mount weapon, spotlight for fixed pintle socket or ring mount weapon with or without shield, night vision equipment, periscope for ring mount (standard on 20 mm, 76 mm and 90 mm turret ring mounts), spare periscope and stowage, weapons (where applicable), extra spare barrel stowage, hand held weapon stowage, M26 hand grenade stowage, smoke hand grenade stowage, binocular stowage, radios and associated mountings, canopy with poles (pod type vehicles only), vision blocks in pod (standard on Police ERV), gun ports in pod (standard on police ERV), sight M28C × 5.6 power (machine gun turret vehicles only), land navigation system and /or vehicle heading reference system, NBC system, public address system (standard on Police ERV), heater kit, air-conditioning system, wiper kit for driver, blackout covers, handbrake warning light, cooker kit and lifting boom.

Variants

Commando with MG Turret
Basic vehicle fitted with Cadillac Gage one-man turret which can mount twin 7.62 mm or twin 0.30 calibre machine guns or a combination of 7.62 mm/0.50 calibre machine guns or 0.30/0.50 calibre machine guns. Laying and control of the weapons are mechanical with a hand-operated gearbox that allows 360 degrees continuous traverse, and a gunner's handle at the rear of the balanced gun cradle which allows elevation from −13 degrees to +55 degrees. The turret has a single-piece hatch cover that opens to the rear, eight vision blocks and an M28C sight with a magnification of ×1.5. Mounted coaxially with the weapon is a 500 000 candle-power spotlight. When fitted with twin 7.62 mm machine guns 3800 rounds of ammunition are carried of which 800 rounds are in the turret for ready use and 3000 in the hull. This model has a crew of three and can carry seven infantry-

V-100 Commando with turret armed with 0.30 and 0.50 machine guns

ght to top of turret is 2.54 metres and gross vehicle
8981 kg.

ando with One-metre MG Turret
vehicle fitted with Cadillac Gage one-metre turret
which can be armed with twin 7.62 mm, twin 0.30 calibre or
twin 0.50 calibre machine guns, or a combination of these
weapons. The turret has a manual traverse through 360
degrees and the guns have an elevation of +55 degrees and a
depression of −10 degrees. The turret has a single-piece
hatch cover that opens to the rear, an M28C sight with a
magnification of ×1.5, eight vision blocks and a 500 000
candlepower spotlight. Depending on the armament installed 1400 rounds of 0.50 calibre ammunition are carried, of
which 400 are for ready use in the turret, or 3800 rounds of
0.30 or 7.62 mm ammunition of which 800 are for ready use
in the turret. This model has a crew of three and can carry
seven infantrymen. Height to the top of turret is 2.59 metres
and gross vehicle weight is 8754 kg.

Commando with One-metre 20 mm Turret
Basic vehicle with one-man turret armed with 20 mm Oerlikon 204 GK cannon with provision for coaxial 7.62 mm
machine gun. Gun can be elevated from −8 to +55 degrees at
40 degrees a second and turret traversed through 360 degrees
at 60 degrees a second. Traverse is electro-hydraulic with
manual back up. Turret has eight vision blocks and a sight
with a magnification of ×8 and ×1, and a 500 000 candlepower searchlight that moves in elevation with the armament
and a blower for removing turret fumes.

Four hundred rounds of 20 mm ammunition are carried,
200 in the turret ready to use and 200 in hull, and 3200 rounds
of 7.62 mm ammunition, 220 for ready use and the remainder
in hull.

This model has a crew of three consisting of commander,
gunner and driver and can carry five men, a loaded weight of
9072 kg and a height of 2.895 metres.

Commando with 20 mm Turret
Basic vehicle fitted with a two-man turret armed with a
20 mm Oerlikon 204 GK cannon, with a 7.62 mm machine
gun mounted coaxially to the left of the main armament and a
7.62 mm anti-aircraft machine gun mounted on the turret
roof. The cannon has an internally-controlled hydraulic
charger, emergency firing trigger for the commander and rate
controller which allows firing of one, two or four rounds per
second or fully automatic. Turret traverse is a full 360 degrees
at 60 degrees a second with elevation from −8 to +60 degrees
at 40 degrees a second. The electro-hydraulic controls are the
same as in the 76 mm and 90 mm turrets and are scaled down
versions of the Cadillac Gage system used in the M60 and
Leopard 1 MBTs. Either the commander or the gunner can
aim and fire the armament. Turret vision equipment consists
of four vision blocks (two in each side of the turret), commander's periscope that can be traversed through a full 360
degrees and a gunner's sight with a magnification of 8 and a
periscope with a projected graticule. In addition to the main
sights the turret has an external anti-aircraft sight. It is also
provided with a 500 000 candlepower spotlight and a turret
blower. Of 400 rounds of 20 mm ammunition carried 200 are
for ready use and of 3200 rounds of 7.62 mm ammunition 400
are in the turret for ready use and 200 at the anti-aircraft gun
for ready use. This model has a crew of three and can carry

V-200 Commando of Singapore Army fitted with two-man Cadillac Gage turret armed with 20 mm Oerlikon cannon and two
7.62 mm machine guns

two infantrymen. The gross vehicle weight is 9888 kg and the
height to the top of the turret is 2.54 metres.

Commando with 25 mm Turret
This turret was installed on the V-150 S Commando entered
in the Light Armored Vehicle competition. It is armed with a
25 mm M242 Hughes Helicopters Chain Gun, 7.62 mm
M240 coaxial MG and a similar weapon on the turret roof for
anti-aircraft defence. Two hundred and thirty 25 mm ready
rounds (170 HE and 60 AP) are carried in the turret with a
further 400 in the vehicle. There are 400 rounds of 7.62 mm
ready use ammunition in the turret, 200 at the anti-aircraft
station and a further 1000 rounds in the vehicle.

The turret has powered traverse (360 degrees at 30 degrees
a second) and elevation (from −8 degrees to +60 degrees at
30 degrees a second). Vision equipment includes an M36E1
day/night sight for the gunner and eight periscopes for the
commander. The commander can also have an M36E1 day/
night sight but only six periscopes are then fitted.

Commando with 40 mm/12.7 mm Turret
This is fitted with a one-man turret armed with a 40 mm
Mk 19 Mod 1 grenade launcher on the left, a 12.7 mm M2
HB machine gun on the right and four smoke dischargers
mounted either side of the turret at the rear. The weapon can
be elevated from −8 degrees to +45 degrees and turret
traverse is a full 360 degrees.

Commando V-150 S
This was announced in 1981 with two vehicles being delivered for evaluation in the LAV competition late in the same
year. Both vehicles had a two-man turret, one armed with a
90 mm Cockerill Mk III gun and the second with a 25 mm
M242 Hughes Chain Gun, both having a 7.62 mm coaxial
and a 7.62 mm anti-aircraft machine gun. The V-150 S is
very similar to the V-150 but is slightly heavier, has a longer
hull and longer wheelbase.

Commando Air Defence Vehicle
This is the basic vehicle fitted with the same turret as
mounted on the M167 towed system. This entered production for Saudi Arabia in 1981.

Commando with 76 mm Turret-mounted Gun

This model is fitted with a two-man power-operated turret armed with the 76 mm L23A1 gun as installed on the British Scorpion CVR(T), with a 7.62 mm machine gun mounted coaxially to the left of the main armament and a 7.62 mm anti-aircraft machine gun on the turret roof. As of 1985 the 76 mm version had not been placed in production.

Commando with 90 mm Turret-mounted Gun

This was originally armed with the Belgian Mecar gun but is now offered with the Cockerill Mk III gun. Mounted coaxially with the main armament is a 7.62 mm machine gun and a similar weapon is fitted on the turret roof for anti-aircraft defence. Turret traverse is a full 360 degrees at 30 degrees a second, and elevation is from −8 to +28 degrees at 30 degrees a second. The electro-hydraulic control equipment is identical to that installed in the 20 mm turret. Vision equipment consists of three vision blocks (two in left and one in right side of the turret), commander's periscope that can be traversed through 360 degrees, gunner's periscope with a magnification of ×8 and a unity periscope with projected graticule. A 500 000 candlepower spotlight is mounted coaxially with the main armament. Of 39 rounds of 90 mm ammunition carried, eight are for ready use in the turret and

Cadillac Gage V-150 Commando with Cockerill 90 mm Mk III gun and Marconi Command and Control Systems Digital Fire-control System, during trials in 1983

V-150 fitted with two-man Cadillac Gage turret armed with 90 mm Mecar gun, 7.62 mm coaxial and 7.62 mm anti-aircraft machine guns and smoke dischargers at turret rear

V-150 Commando fitted with command pod and externally-mounted 7.62 mm machine gun

of 3200 rounds of 7.62 mm machine gun ammunition 400 are for ready use in the turret and 200 for the anti-aircraft machine gun. This model has a crew of three and can carry four infantrymen, gross vehicle weight being 9888 kg. In 1983 the V-150 Commando with the Marconi Command and Control Systems Digital Fire-control System was successfully demonstrated. This gives a high first round hit probability and is suitable for installation in a wide range of other tracked and wheeled vehicles.

Commando with 81 mm Mortar

This is armed with an 81 mm M29 turntable-mounted mortar that fires through the roof of the vehicle, and can be traversed through a full 360 degrees and elevated from +42 degrees to +85 degrees. Its minimum range is 150 metres and maximum range 4400 metres. When not in action the roof is covered by concertina doors that open either side of the vehicle. Provision is made for mounting a 7.62 mm machine gun at any one of four positions around the top of the hull and 2000 rounds of ammunition are carried for it. Sixty-two 81 mm mortar bombs are carried and if required the mortar can be removed from the vehicle and fired from the ground. This model has a crew of five and a gross vehicle weight of 8845 kg.

Commando with TOW ATGW System

This is almost identical to the above model but is fitted with a Hughes TOW ATGW system which has an elevation of +30 degrees, a depression of −10 degrees and 360-degree traverse. Seven TOW missiles are carried. When not in action the top of the vehicle is covered by hatches that open to the front and rear. Provision is made for mounting a 7.62 mm machine gun at any one of four positions around the top of the hull and 2000 rounds of ammunition are carried for this weapon. This model has a crew of four and can also carry two infantrymen. Gross vehicle weight is 8958 kg.

Commando Command Vehicle

This is the standard vehicle fitted with a fixed armoured pod mounted at the roof opening. In each of the four sides of the pod is a firing port and in the roof is a single-piece hatch cover that opens to the rear, forward of which is a 7.62 mm pintle-mounted machine gun. Of 2000 rounds of 7.62 mm ammunition carried, 200 are for ready use. Internally the vehicle has a rd, table and additional communications equipment. In addition to the crew of three, seven staff members [are carried]. Overall height without the machine gun is 2.311 [m].

Base Security Vehicle
This was originally developed for the United States Air Force and like the mortar carrier has concertina hatch covers that open either side of the vehicle. Provision is made for mounting 7.62 mm machine guns or 40 mm grenade launchers in four positions at the front, sides and rear. A total of 3000 rounds of 7.62 mm ammunition is carried. This model has a crew of three and can carry eight fully-equipped infantrymen, weighs 9072 kg and is 2.311 metres high.

Police Emergency Rescue Vehicle (ERV)
This model has a fixed pod with six vision blocks and eight vertical gun ports. In the roof is a single-piece hatch cover that opens to the rear and in front of which is a 7.62 mm or a 12.7 mm machine gun. This model has a crew of three and can carry nine additional men and weighs 9162 kg. It is used by a number of police authorities and a large number was purchased by Turkey.

Recovery Vehicle
This is fitted with a heavy-duty winch with a maximum capacity of 11 340 kg which is provided with 60.9 metres of 19 mm diameter cable. The boom is pivoted at the front of the vehicle and when required hinges forward to the front of the vehicle. When it is being used two stabilisers are lowered at the front. The boom has a maximum capacity of 4536 kg with the stabilisers in position. Armament consists of a 7.62 mm or a 12.7 mm machine gun with 2200 rounds of ammunition.

SPECIFICATIONS (Commando V-150 with turret-mounted 20 mm cannon. Specifications in square brackets relate to V-150 S Commando)

CREW	3 + 9	VERTICAL OBSTACLE	0.609 [0.91] m
CONFIGURATION	4 × 4	TURNING RADIUS	8.382 [8.5] m
COMBAT WEIGHT	9888 [10 433] kg	ENGINE	V-8 diesel developing 202 bhp at 3300 rpm
POWER-TO-WEIGHT RATIO	20.42 [19.36] hp/tonne	TRANSMISSION	automatic, 4 forward, 1 reverse gears
LENGTH	5.689 [6.14] m	CLUTCH	single plate, hydraulically-actuated
WIDTH	2.26 m	TRANSFER CASE	2-speed (with spline engagement for front axle drive)
HEIGHT			
to turret roof	2.54 m		
to hull top	1.981 m	STEERING	power-assisted
GROUND CLEARANCE		SUSPENSION	semi-elliptical springs and double-acting hydraulic shock absorbers
axles	0.381 m		
hull	0.648 m		
TRACK			
front	1.914 m	TYRES	14.50 × 21
rear	1.943 m	BRAKES	
WHEELBASE	2.667 [3.12] m	main	hydraulic, dual circuit
MAX SPEED			
road	88.54 km/h	parking	drum acting on output shaft of transmission
water	4.828 km/h		
ACCELERATION		ELECTRICAL SYSTEM	24 V
(0–32.2 km/h)	10 s	BATTERIES	2 × 12 V, 100 Ah
FUEL CAPACITY	303 litres	ARMAMENT	
MAX RANGE	643 km	main	1 × 20 mm cannon
FORDING	amphibious	coaxial	1 × 7.62 mm MG
GRADIENT	60%	anti-aircraft	1 × 7.62 mm MG
SIDE SLOPE	30%		

SMOKE-LAYING EQUIPMENT	optional		
AMMUNITION			
main	400		
7.62 mm	3200		
FIRE-CONTROL SYSTEM			
Turret power control	electro-hydraulic/manual		
by commander	yes		
by gunner	yes		
Max rate power traverse	60°/s		
Max rate power elevation	40°/s		
Gun elevation/depression	+60°/−8°		
Turret traverse	360°		

In 1982 Cadillac Gage announced that it had developed a Cummins V-6 diesel conversion kit as a direct replacement for the V-8 diesel installed in the V-150. When fitted with this engine the V-150 has an operational range of 800 km compared to the standard V-8 model with 644 km, with an acceleration of 0 to 32 km/h in nine seconds. This kit can be installed with no special tools or other equipment at base workshop level.

Status: In production. In service with Bolivia (V-100), Botswana (V-150), Cameroon (V-150, additional 24 ordered in 1983 at a cost of $13.1 million), Dominican Republic (V-150), Ethiopia (V-150)*, Haiti (V-150), Gabon (V-150), Guatemala (V-150), Indonesia (V-150), Jamaica (V-150), Kuwait (V-150 S ordered in 1984), Malaysia (V-100 and V-150), Oman (V-150)*, Panama (V-150), Philippines (V-150), Saudi Arabia (ambulance, APC, ARV, 20 mm anti-aircraft, 81 mm mortar, 90 mm gun and Hughes TOW), Singapore (V-150 and V-200), Somalia (V-100 and V-150), Sudan (V-150), Taiwan (V-150), Thailand (V-150), Tunisia (V-150), Turkey (V-150), USA (V-100) Venezuela (V-150), and Viet-Nam (V-100). Note: the United States Army designation for the V-100 is the M706.

*probably out of service

Manufacturer: Cadillac Gage Company, PO Box 1027, Warren, Michigan 48090, USA.

Dragoon 300 Armoured Vehicle Family

Development
The Dragoon 300 armoured vehicle family was originally designed to meet a requirement issued in 1976 by the United States Army Military Police for a vehicle which would be airportable in a Lockheed C-130 Hercules transport aircraft and be suitable for convoy and air base protection.

Although this request subsequently lapsed the Verne Corporation of Detroit went ahead and built two prototypes which made their first public appearance in 1978. Following successful trials, both in the United States and overseas, a pre-production batch of 17 vehicles was built by the Dominion Manufacturing Company, near Washington DC. World-wide marketing of the Dragoon 300 armoured vehicle family is undertaken by the Arrowpointe Corporation.

The Dragoon 300 armoured vehicle family has already been evaluated by a number of countries in South America and first production vehicles were completed for the United States Army and Navy in 1982 (see under Variants).

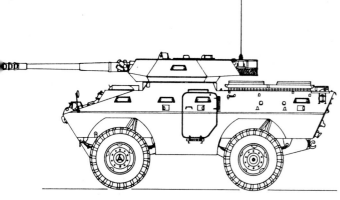

Dragoon 300 fitted with two-man Arrowpointe turret armed with 90 mm Cockerill Mk III gun and coaxial 7.62 mm machine gun

From the early concept stage, logistics and life-cycle costs were the main criteria in the development of the Dragoon. Some 70 per cent of the components of the vehicle are common to the M113A2 full tracked armoured personnel carrier and the M809 (5 × 5) 5-ton truck. Components of the former include the engine, starter, alternator, cold start, periscopes, bilge pumps, interior and exterior lighting, gauges, switches, electrical and hydraulic system components. M809 components include axles, suspension, brakes, steering, electrical and hydraulic system components.

Description

The all-welded hull of the Dragoon is of XAR-30 high hardness steel ballistic plate which meets the requirements of MIL-A-12560 and is of monocoque construction with welded seams. XAR-30 is approximately 30 per cent superior to US Specification MIL-A-12560 homogeneous steel armour against small calibre ball and armour piercing ammunition, in addition XAR-30 has threshold penetration velocities in excess of that specified by US Mil Spec 46100B.

The driver sits at the front of the vehicle on the left with the vehicle commander/co-driver to his right. The driver has three vision blocks to his front which provide him with a 180-degree field of view, while the commander has one, each having a single-piece hatch cover that opens to the outside and a vision block in the side of the hull. A firing port is provided below the commander's vision block. Both also have a seat which is adjustable front/rear and up/down with the back folding forward for access.

In each side of the hull, between the front and rear axles, is a side door, the lower part folds down to form a step while the upper part, which contains a vision block with a firing port underneath, swings backwards through 180 degrees and can be locked open.

Forward of the side door is a vision block underneath which is a firing port. All vision blocks are fitted with spall shields and crash pads and the firing ports have covers that can be secured from within the vehicle and have quick cam levers for opening and closing.

When being used as an APC, a maximum of eleven fully-equipped men, plus a crew of two, can be carried, each of the latter being provided with an individual seat with a back rest.

The engine compartment is at the rear of the Dragoon on the right side. Thermal and acoustic insulation are provided between the engine compartment and the personnel area on interchangeable close-out panels. Quick access is provided to the engine compartment from the interior and exterior of the vehicle, the panels do not have to be in place for correct engine running.

The air intake louvres are in top of the hull and the air outlet louvres and exhaust outlet are in the right side of the hull and have been designed to prevent the entry of flaming liquids such as petrol bombs. A counter-balanced tilt hood gives access to the engine compartment and fluid level checks. Access doors are provided for servicing the filters.

Power is transmitted from the engine and gearbox via a chain case and rear propeller shaft to the rear differential, then via an intermediate propeller shaft to the disconnect clutch in the centre of the hull. From there it is transmitted to the front differential and front axle via a forward propeller shaft. All of the drive train components are enclosed. The transmission employs a torque converter active through the three lowest forward gear reductions, and direct drive (lock-up) in fourth and fifth forward gears.

The cooling system is at the rear of the engine compartment on the right side and provides the maximum possible engine and transmission cooling and incorporates a hydraulically-driven fan.

Both waterproof axles are designed so that in the event of an axle shaft failure, a wheel will not come off.

The Dragoon has power-assisted hydraulic brakes and a separate electrically-actuated hydraulic override braking system permits braking in the event of a primary hydraulic system failure. A parking brake is included as part of the primary brake system.

Power-assisted steering is provided and permits manual steering in the event of failure of the hydraulic system, with variable steering ratios for both cross-country and high speed road operations. After a loss of air pressure the tyres are capable of continuing operations for a minimum of 80 km on a concrete road surface at a speed of 56 km/h.

The heavy duty suspension consists of semi-elliptical springs and direct action hydraulic shock absorbers. Special wrap is provided on the second leaf for added safety and the front and rear springs are interchangeable. The shock absorbers have built-in shock valves for good balance between cross-country and high speed road operation. Jounce stops are installed at each spring position to prevent the suspension components from striking the hull. The stops sustain all the imposed loads without damage to the rubber portion.

In the rear of the hull on the left side is another door, the lower part of which folds down to form a step while the upper part, which contains a vision block and a firing port, opens to the right. In the left side of the hull, towards the rear, is a single vision block.

A tow hook at the rear enables the Dragoon 300 to tow a trailer or other vehicles up to a maximum weight of 11 338 kg. Mounted internally at the front of the hull is a winch with a capacity of 9078 kg, this is operated off the main vehicle hydraulic circuit which enables the vehicle to be in gear while winching and during recovery operations. This has 52 metres of cable.

The Dragoon is fully amphibious, being propelled in the water by its wheels; when afloat, steering is by turning the front wheels as on land. Three bilge pumps, each with a capacity of 190 litres a minute, expel any water that seeps into the hull through the rubber door seals.

Standard equipment on all vehicles includes a heater, run-flat tyres and a dry fire extinguisher. A wide range of optional equipment is available including active or passive night vision equipment, air conditioning, smoke dischargers,

d firewire detection/fire suppression system, NBC and various spotlights.

s

re four distinct groups of Dragoon 300 vehicles:
Personnel carrier may be outfitted as a basic APC, reconnaissance, command, recovery, security, escort or a command/communications vehicle. Each of these may be fitted with ring- or pintle-mounted machine guns up to 12.7 mm in calibre, and a variety of communications systems. Command version could have a raised roof with additional vision blocks. Light weapons carrier may be fitted with a single machine gun up to 12.7 mm calibre, twin machine guns up to 12.7 mm calibre, or machine guns in combination such as 7.62 mm/12.7 mm. Special weapons carrier such as 81 mm mortar, TOW missile carrier (with Improved TOW system), Dragon ATGW carrier and anti-personnel rocket launcher.

Heavy weapons carrier which may be equipped with various armament installations including turret-mounted 20 mm or 25 mm cannon, 76 mm or 90 mm gun, all of which may have coaxial, ring- or pintle-mounted machine guns. The two-man Arrowpointe-designed turrets have the same degree of protection as the basic vehicle with the commander seated on the left and the gunner on the right, both with an individual hatch cover that opens to the rear, two periscopes, one facing the front and the other the rear, and a vision block in each side of the turret. The gunner has an M36 sight, also used in the M60 MBT, with ×1 and ×7 optics with provision for active or passive night vision equipment.

Turret power is provided by the primary vehicle hydraulic system and is supported by a secondary manual back-up. The turret has an independent 24-volt dc power source to prevent draw on the vehicle's power system in silent watch and to ensure turret and weapon operations in case the basic vehicle becomes disabled or there is a failure in the primary hydraulic or electrical system. Exhaust blowers are fitted in the turret to expel fumes.

Control of turret and weapons operations is provided by a single cyclic control grip. This self-contained grip includes elevation, depression, traverse, weapon selection (main or coaxial), cyclic rate of fire and firing. All functions of the weapon system are provided with emergency back up.

Dragoon 300 in APC configuration with twin doors in side of hull and 7.62 mm machine gun with shield. This model used by US Navy to protect nuclear weapon storage facilities

Dragoon 300 fitted with AN/MSQ-103A Teampack system (left) and video optical surveillance system (right) as used by US Army's 9th Infantry Division

Dragoon 300 with Arrowpointe-designed two-man turret armed with 90 mm Cockerill Mark III gun, 7.62 mm coaxial machine gun and two banks of four smoke dischargers (Christopher F Foss)

For the Light Armored Vehicle competition, Arrowpointe proposed the following models of the Dragoon 300 vehicle:
Basic vehicle with pintle-mounted 7.62 mm M60 machine gun
Fitted with one-man turret armed with 7.62 mm and 12.7 mm machine guns
Fitted with two-man turret armed with 20 mm or 25 mm cannon and 7.62 mm coaxial machine gun, weapons have elevation of +60 degrees and depression of −10 degrees
Fitted with two-man turret armed with 90 mm Cockerill Mark III gun and 7.62 mm coaxial machine gun, weapons have elevation of +35 degrees and depression of −8 degrees
Fitted with two-man turret armed with 90 mm Mecar gun and 7.62 mm coaxial machine gun, weapons have elevation of +45 degrees and depression of −8 degrees
Command and control vehicle equipped with various antenna and communications equipment
Service and control vehicle with barricade ram/debris blade at front of hull, 7.62 mm or 12.7 mm machine gun at front and 7.62 mm machine gun at rear of hull
Ambulance or utility vehicle, unarmed
Mortar carrier with 7.62 mm machine gun
Self-loading logistics vehicle with boom with capacity of 2268 kg
Maintenance, recovery and engineer vehicle with boom crane and front mounted dozer blade or scoop bucket

US Army and US Navy Vehicles

Between March and November 1982 the Dragoon was in production to meet contracts placed by the US Army and Navy.

Six Dragoons were supplied for the 9th Infantry Division High Technology Test Bed (HTTB) with two provided for the electronic warfare role, each fitted with the Emerson AN/MSQ-103A Teampack and a video optical surveillance vehicle.

The EW variant carries out advanced battlefield direction finding and high speed communications jamming and is fitted with an antenna that can be quickly raised well above the vehicle. The video optical surveillance vehicle has a modified Arrowpointe 25 mm two-man turret which in its forward part has been fitted with a long range day/night surveillance system that can be retracted quickly under armour protection. This provides the field commander with a highly mobile, armour protected observation capability,

which, when connected to an on-board data link, gives a clear, front line view of the battlefield for rear area commanders. The Teampack electronic detection system is normally carried in the horizontal position on the left side of the vehicle at the rear protected by a brush guard and a weather shield. When required for action it can be erected quickly into the vertical position. A 7.62 mm M60 machine gun is mounted on the forward part of the roof on the right side.

The US Navy versions are used to patrol three nuclear weapon storage facilities on the east coast of the USA and at one facility in Alaska. These are fitted with a 7.62 mm machine gun with a ballistic shield and a floodlight above. This model also has a double width door each side which are in three parts, the lower part dropping down to form a step and the upper parts, each with a vision block with a firing port underneath, opening either side. This enables personnel to be disembarked quickly.

SPECIFICATIONS					
CREW	3 + 6	MAX ROAD SPEED	115.9 km/h	TRANSFER CASE	single-speed
CONFIGURATION	4 × 4	MAX WATER SPEED	4.83 km/h	STEERING	hydraulic
COMBAT WEIGHT	12 700 kg	FUEL CAPACITY	341 litres	SUSPENSION	semi-elliptical springs and
UNLOADED WEIGHT	9430 kg	MAX ROAD RANGE	1045 km		hydraulic shock absorbers
POWER-TO-WEIGHT		FORDING	fully amphibious	TYRES	14.00 × 20
RATIO	23.62 bhp/tonne	GRADIENT	60%	BRAKES	
LENGTH	5.588 m	SIDE SLOPE	30%	main	internal expanding
WIDTH	2.438 m	VERTICAL OBSTACLE			shoe
HEIGHT		forwards	0.99 m	parking	integral
over turret periscopes	2.642 m	reverse	0.61 m	ELECTRICAL SYSTEM	24 V
hull top	2.133 m	TURNING RADIUS		BATTERIES	2 × 12 V, 100 Ah
GROUND CLEARANCE		land	8.788 m	ARMAMENT	
hull centre	0.692 m	water	8.839 m	main	1 × 20 mm cannon
axles	0.381 m	ENGINE	Detroit Diesel Allison 6V-53T	coaxial	1 × 7.62 mm MG
TRACK	1.981 m		6-cylinder, liquid-cooled,	SMOKE-LAYING	
WHEELBASE	2.794 m		turbo-charged diesel	EQUIPMENT	optional
ANGLE OF APPROACH/			developing 300 bhp at	FIRE-CONTROL SYSTEM	
DEPARTURE	60°/45°		2800 rpm	Turret power control	hydraulic/manual
ACCELERATION		TRANSMISSION	Allison MT-653 DR	Gun elevation/depression	+60°/−10°
(0 to 35 km/h)	4.5 s		automatic, 5 forward and 1	Turret traverse	360°
			reverse gears		

Status: Production. In service with the US Army and Navy.

Manufacturer: Dominion Manufacturing Company, marketed by the Arrowpointe Corporation, 4000 Town Center, Southfield, Michigan 48075, USA.

Mark 44 Armoured Personnel Carrier

Development

The Mark 44 armoured personnel carrier, designed as a private venture by Emergency One Incorporated, a subsidiary of the Federal Signal Corporation, was announced in 1983.

Description

The hull of the Mk 44 is of all-welded steel armour construction which gives complete protection against 7.62 mm ball attack, overhead blast and anti-personnel mines. The sides, front, rear and roof are of 6.35 mm thick armour, the floor is of 9.52 mm thick armour. All powertrain components as well as axles, suspension and shock absorbers are attached to the hull.

The driver sits at the front of the hull on the left with the vehicle commander to his right. Both crew members have a bullet-proof window to their front and sides and a single-piece hatch cover that opens to the outside. Their seats can be hydraulically adjusted vertically to put them in the head-out

position. The seats can be quickly retracted from this position into the safety of the vehicle.

The troop compartment is to the rear of the hull and has three doors, one in each side and one in the right rear. Each of the doors is in two parts, lower part folding down to form a step and the upper part, with an integral firing port and bullet-proof observation window, folding to one side. The number of troops carried depends on the armament installed, but can be as many as eleven. Eight vision blocks and firing ports are provided.

A wide range of armament installations can be mounted over the troop compartment including the Emerson TAT-251 and TAT-252 systems and the Improved TOW mount as fitted to the M901 Improved TOW Vehicle.

The Deutz air-cooled diesel engine is mounted at the rear of the hull on the left side with five hatches in the roof for maintenance. The air-inlet and air-outlet louvres are in the roof and the exhaust pipe is on the left side of the hull. The engine transmits power to the Twin Disc automatic transmission with integral transfer case and front axle disconnect, heavy duty drive lines and universal joints transmit power to the Rockwell Military front and rear axles. The front axle is

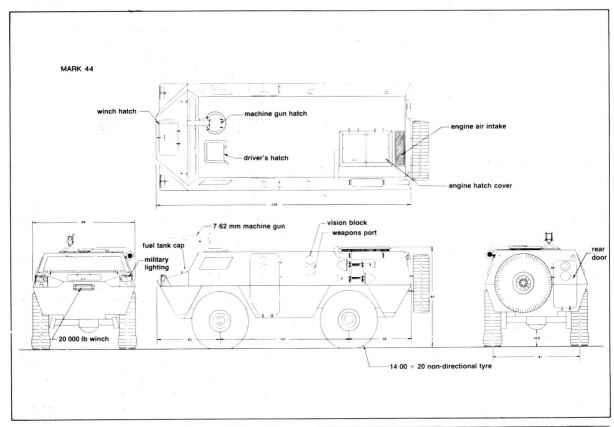

MARK 44

winch hatch

machine gun hatch

driver's hatch

engine air intake

engine hatch cover

7·62 mm machine gun

vision block

weapons port

fuel tank cap

military lighting

rear door

20 000 lb winch

14·00 × 20 non-directional tyre

General arrangement of Mark 44 APC (not to 1/76th scale)

rated at 5443 kg, the rear axle at 6310 kg.

The suspension at each wheel station consists of semi-ellipitical multi-leaf springs with shackles, shock absorbers and jounce stops.

Standard equipment on all vehicles includes a front-mounted Ramsey hydraulic winch with a capacity of 9072 kg and 84 metres of cable, six-metre towing cable stowed internally, fire extinguishers, four bilge pumps, spare wheel and tyre, snatch block, first aid kit and ammunition lockers. The basic vehicle is fully amphibious, propelled in the water by its wheels. Optional equipment includes night vision equipment, grenade stowage, air compressor, run-flat tyres, full air-conditioning and propellers for increased water speed. In place of the commander's right-opening roof hatch a cupola with a rear-opening roof hatch and a 7.62 mm or 12.7 mm machine gun mounted on the forward part can be installed.

Mark 44 APC at speed without armament

Variants

Depending on the armamen installed, the Mark 44 can be adapted for a wide range of roles.

SPECIFICATIONS

CREW	2 + 7 (or 11)	FUEL CAPACITY	378 litres	STEERING	integral hydraulic
CONFIGURATION	4 + 4	MAX ROAD RANGE	1287 km	SUSPENSION	semi-elliptical leaf springs
UNLADEN WEIGHT	9299 kg	FORDING	amphibious		and hydraulic shock
POWER-TO-WEIGHT RATIO		GRADIENT	60%		absorbers
(unladen)	27.5 hp/tonne	SIDE SLOPE	30%	BRAKES	
LENGTH	6.045 m	VERTICAL OBSTACLE	0.609 m	main	hydraulic, electric
WIDTH	2.438 m	TURNING RADIUS	9 m		back up
HEIGHT		ENGINE	Deutz F8L413F air-cooled	parking	mechanical
(without armament)	2.286 m		V-8 diesel developing 256 hp	TYRES	14.00 × 20
GROUND CLEARANCE	0.686 m		at 2650 rpm	ELECTRICAL SYSTEM	24 V
MAX ROAD SPEED	105 km/h	TRANSMISSION	Twin Disc Model 1130,	ARMOUR	6.35 mm to 9.52 mm
ACCELERATION			automatic with 4 forward and		
0 to 32 km/h	10.5 seconds		4 reverse gears and integral		
0 to 80 km/h	24 seconds		transfer case		

Manufacturer: Emergency One Incorporated, 1701 S.W. 37th Avenue, P O Box 2710 Ocola, Florida 32678, USA.

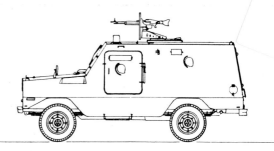

Cadillac Gage Commando Ranger fitted with 7.62 mm machine gun and shield to protect gunner

Cadillac Gage Commando Ranger Armoured Personnel Carrier

Development

The Commando Ranger has been developed by the Cadillac Gage Company as a private venture to meet a requirement for a low-cost vehicle capable of transporting troops at a high road speed but still retaining an off-road capability.

Late in 1977 the United States Air Force issued a requirement for a Security Police Armored Response/Convoy Truck for patrolling air bases. The Air Force decided to initiate a two-step procurement, technical and price. In April 1978 a number of American manufacturers submitted detailed technical proposals in response to the requirement and in October the same year the US Air Force selected three manufacturers' proposals as meeting the technical requirements: the Cadillac Gage Company, Oshkosh Truck Corporation and the Vehicle Systems Development Corporation.

In March 1979 the US Air Force chose the Cadillac Gage Commando Ranger and in June 1979 the company was awarded a contract worth $4.4 million for the supply of a number of vehicles plus technical and administrative data.

The first Cadillac Gage Commando Ranger, called the Peacekeeper by the United States Air Force, was handed over in April 1980. By early 1981 480 vehicles had been ordered by the US Air Force and the US Navy with the former having a requirement for 810 vehicles for delivery by 1985. By late 1982 over 600 Cadillac Gage Commando Ranger armoured personnel carriers had been built. The US Navy uses them for base security.

Description

The hull of the Commando Ranger is made of all-welded 'CADLOY' high hardness armour which provides the crew

United States Air Force Cadillac Gage Commando Ranger without armament installed (Terry J Gander)

with complete protection from small arms fire. The crew and vital components are protected from the effects of grenades exploding under the vehicle by bolt-on armour shields.

The Commando Ranger armoured personnel carrier is based on a standard Chrysler truck chassis but with a shorter wheelbase.

The engine is at the front of the hull and is coupled to an automatic transmission with three forward and one reverse gears which is equipped with an auxiliary oil cooler. Coupled to the transmission is a two-speed transfer case. The manually-selected four-wheel drive case with an interaxle differential delivers proportionalised torque to both front and rear axles. The interaxle differential enables the wheels on one axle to travel at a different speed from those on the other. Both axles are of the full floating type.

The vehicle has a dual hydraulic service brake system and a foot/lever actuated parking brake. The service brake system consists of two separate brake fluid lines and a split, front and rear, master cylinder. Power assist is supplied by means of a tandem-diaphragm brake booster that utilises engine vacuum for power. The front brakes are disc with self-adjusting calipers and the rear are drum with self-adjusting shoes.

The suspension, front and rear, consists of leaf springs with double-acting shock absorbers and jounce stops at each wheel station. The combat tyres are filled with foam and when penetrated by small arms fire allow the vehicle to travel up to 80 km at 56 km/h.

The driver sits at the front of the vehicle on the left with the commander to his right. The steering wheel can be tilted to assist the driver in entering and leaving the vehicle. Both crew members have a bullet-proof windscreen in front of them with a wiper. There is a firing port between the two windscreens. Each also has a rear-opening side door with a bullet-proof vision block in its upper half under which is a firing port.

The troop compartment is at the rear of the hull with the men seated three down each side facing each other. They enter the vehicle through two doors in the rear of the hull which open outwards. Both doors have a firing port and the left one has a vision block. In each side of the troop compartment is a vision block with a firing port underneath. The top of the hull is angled to allow hand grenades to roll off before they explode. If required the vehicle can be delivered with a roof hatch on which can be fitted a variety of light armament installations such as a pintle-mounted 7.62 mm M60 machine gun with a shield and 200 rounds of ready-use ammunition and a further 800 rounds carried in the hull.

The interior of the Commando Ranger is insulated, which reduces noise, retains cool air as the vehicle is fitted with an air-conditioning system and also aids crew safety. The air-conditioning system is fitted as standard and there is also provision for exhausting air. Standard equipment includes two-speed wipers, heater, windscreen defogger and internal dome light.

Optional equipment includes flashing lights, public address system, radios, spotlight, Wegmann grenade launchers, front-mounted winch and a 24-volt electric system in place of the standard 12-volt system.

Variants

In addition to being used as an APC the Commando Ranger can be used as a command vehicle (crew of two plus two command staff), ambulance (crew of two and carrying two stretcher plus three seated patients) and as a light reconnaissance vehicle which can be fitted with a Cadillac Gage one-man turret armed with twin 7.62 mm (or 0.30) or one 7.62 mm (0.30) and one 12.7 mm (0.50) machine guns. These have an elevation of +50 degrees, depression of −14 degrees, and 360-degree turret traverse, which is manual. The turret has an M28C roof-mounted sight with a

Cadillac Gage Commando Ranger from rear showing firing ports (Terry J Gander)

magnification of ×1.5, eight vision blocks and a single-piece hatch cover that opens to the rear.

SPECIFICATIONS

CREW	2 + 6	MAX ROAD SPEED	112.65 km/h	TRANSFER CASE	2-speed
CONFIGURATION	4 × 4	FUEL CAPACITY	121 litres	STEERING	integral power with
COMBAT WEIGHT	4536 kg	MAX RANGE (at 72 km/h)	556 km		pump assistance
POWER-TO-WEIGHT		GRADIENT	60%	SUSPENSION	leaf springs and
RATIO	40 hp/tonne	SIDE SLOPE	30%		double-acting hydraulic
LENGTH	4.699 m	VERTICAL OBSTACLE	0.254 m		shock absorbers
WIDTH	2.019 m	ENGINE	Dodge 360 CID V-8	BRAKES	
HEIGHT	1.981 m		liquid-cooled petrol	main	hydraulic, dual circuit
GROUND CLEARANCE			developing 180 hp at	parking	foot/lever actuated
front axle	0.203 m		3600 rpm	ELECTRICAL SYSTEM	12 V
rear axle	0.209 m	TRANSMISSION	Dodge model A727	BATTERY	1 × 12 V 70 Ah
TRACK	1.689 m		automatic with 3	ARMAMENT	see text
WHEELBASE	2.946 m		forward and 1		
ANGLE OF APPROACH/			reverse gears		
DEPARTURE	25°/24°				

Status: In production. In service with the United States Air Force and Navy and Indonesia. Luxembourg has a small number of vehicles fitted with a one-man turret armed with twin 7.62 mm GPMGs.

Manufacturer: Cadillac Gage Company, Post Office Box 1027, Warren, Michigan 48090, USA.

Landing Vehicle Assault and Landing Vehicle Tracked Experimental

Development

A requirement for a new vehicle to replace the current LVTP7A1 from 1989/90 was issued by the United States Marine Corps in 1973. Between 1974 and 1975 detailed definition of the requirement was carried out and conceptual designs were formulated, model tested and refined. At the same time sub-system work began on the armour, armament and suspension.

In January 1976 the United States Navy awarded contracts for the conceptual design of the Landing Vehicle Assault (LVA) to Bell Aerospace Division of Textron, Buffalo, New York; FMC Corporation of San Jose, California; and the Pacific Car and Foundry Company of Renton, Washington.

In February 1977 the Curtiss-Wright Corporation of Wood-Ridge, New Jersey, was awarded a contract worth $24.5 million for the development of a stratified charge rotary combustion engine designated the Model RC 4-350. Other major sub-contractors included the Allison Division of

General Motors (transmission), National Water Lift (land running gear and primary weapon system design), Carborundum Corporation (armour) and Alcoa Corporation (armour).

The FMC Corporation and PACCAR Corporation concepts used a planing hull with retractable tracks while the Bell Aerospace concept used an air-cushion, inflating-deflating air bag and non-retractable tracks.

The United States Marine Corps requirement was for a vehicle with a water speed of between 40 and 64 km/h, a land speed of between 64 and 88 km/h, water range of 121 km, land range of 402 km, maximum length of 10.058 metres, maximum width of 3.352 metres, maximum height of 3.352 metres, and able to carry between 18 and 22 fully equipped marines or 2722 kg of cargo. Loaded weight was to be between 24 948 kg and 17 210 kg and armament was to be a 25 mm cannon with a 7.62 mm coaxial machine gun, both of which would be mounted in a fully stabilised turret.

It was intended that two of the three designs would then be selected in 1979 for a more detailed design, additional model testing, the refinement of full-scale mockups and limited examination of critical sub-systems.

In February 1979, General Louis H Wilson made the following statement before the House Armed Services Committee about the Landing Vehicle Assault programme:

'Today I would like to inform the Committee that I have cancelled our planned $1.7 billion development and procurement of the assault amphibian that we refer to as the Landing Vehicle Assault (LVA). The LVA was to have been a tracked vehicle that would carry about 20 troops and plane on top of the water at speeds between 25 and 40 miles per hour.

'For the past several years we have been conducting R & D on this vehicle. The requirement was driven by the need of the amphibious ships carrying these amphibians to standoff up to 25 miles from a defended beach. I have concluded that such a distance is not required for the initial assault waves. Admiral Hayward agrees with me.

'In addition to being a very costly vehicle I felt that the Marine Corps simply could not afford, the high water speed required of the LVA would have resulted in a complex vehicle design that would have been difficult to maintain in the field. The LVA by necessity would have been a large vehicle, and thus I believe that it would have been vulnerable to anti-armor weapons when engaged in land combat.

'The Marine Corps will proceed with a much cheaper alternative to replace our present assault amphibian, the LVTP7. This alternative will be the LVT(X), a low water speed amphibian, which we would plan to introduce into the Fleet Marine Force in 1986 or earlier. The LVT(X) will be designed to maximise maintainability and projection of combat power ashore.

'The RDT & E funds provided by this Committee for the LVA in the past years will not have been wasted. Of the approximate $20 million spent to date, over half has been spent on rotary engine development. The development of this rotary engine should continue, since this engine at 750 horsepower will have application to both the LVT(X) and our Mobile Protected Weapon System. Based on equal horsepower the rotary engine in development will be much smaller and will weigh about half as much as a current diesel engine. The rotary will be a multi-fuel engine with fuel economy competitive with the diesel. Of the remaining RDT & E funds, only about $3 million has been used in development unique to the LVA.

'Three short-term contracts for the preliminary conceptual design of the LVT(X) have been awarded to Bell Aerospace, Niagara Falls, New York; Booze-Allen Applied Research,

Model of Bell Aerospace Textron LVT(X) (Terry J Gander)

Bethesda, Maryland; and the FMC Corporation of San Jose, California. The characteristics will not be finalised until these evaluations and other analytical efforts have been completed.'

It is expected that the LVT(X) will be introduced into service in the 1990s and will be optimised for land warfare and have improved cross-country mobility, greater agility, improved troop protection, reduced vehicle vulnerability and increased firepower.

Both 13- and 21-troop versions of the LVT(X) are being considered with each configuration characterised by a significant reduction in silhouette. A two-year contract for the advanced development phase of the LVT(X) engine was signed by the Curtiss-Wright Corporation in August 1980.

In mid-1982 the US Naval Sea Systems Command, which acts for the US Marine Corps, awarded Bell Aerospace, Textron, FMC Corporation and General Dynamics Land Systems Division, each a $2 million study contract for the LVT(X) and final reports were submitted in December 1983. An RFP was issued to the concept study contractors to begin the demonstration and validation phase in 1984. Two contractors are to be selected to develop and validate prototypes based on the studies.

During the summer of 1984 Bell Aerospace Textron and General Dynamics Land Systems Division showed models of their entries in the LVT(X) programme for the US Marine Corps. It is believed that the FMC entry is based on its M2/M3 vehicles currently in production for the US Army.

Bell Aerospace

The Bell Aerospace Textron entry has the engine at the front right, driver at the front left and the troop compartment at the hull rear. Entry to the troop compartment is via a power-operated ramp with an integral door in the hull rear.

Mounted over the forward part of the troop compartment is a two-man (gunner and commander), power-operated turret armed with an externally-mounted 25 mm cannon, 7.62 mm coaxial machine gun and six smoke dischargers.

To the right of the turret is a low-profile cupola for the troop commander and mounted externally on each side of the troop compartment roof is a 7.62 mm machine gun aimed and fired from within the vehicle.

Suspension is of the hydro-pneumatic type with six dual rubber-tyred road wheels, drive sprocket at the front, idler at the rear and two track return rollers. Water propulsion is via two 533 mm diameter water jets at the hull rear, one either side of the troop compartment.

In addition to the basic LVT(X), specialised versions would include a command and communications vehicle, 105 mm assault vehicle, an engineering vehicle (including mine clearance) and a recovery vehicle.

General Dynamics

This vehicle has a similiar layout to the Bell Aerospace entry's but is fitted with a two-man, power-operated turret armed with a fully-stabilised 35 mm cannon and a coaxial 7.62 mm machine gun. The fire-control system is of the hunter-killer type for rapid target engagement. It includes a day/thermal night sight, integrated laser rangefinder and an independent 360-degree panoramic sight for the commander. The troop commander has forward observation periscopes to the right of the turret and mounted each side of the troop compartment roof at the very rear is a 7.62 mm externally-mounted machine gun which is video-sighted from within the

Model of General Dynamics Land Systems Division LVT(X)
(Terry J Gander)

vehicle. The suspension either side consists of seven road wheels, drive sprocket at the front, idler at the rear and track return rollers; it is of the hydro-pneumatic type.

The vehicle would weigh about 32 tonnes, have a crew of three consisting of the commander, gunner and driver and carry 17 fully-equipped marines. the 1200 hp disel would be coupled to a fully-automatic transmission and give a maximum road speed of 72 km/h. When afloat it would be propelled by two water jets, one either side of the hull, at a maximum speed of 19.3 km/h. Standard equipment would include an NBC system and a Halon fire suppression system.

Variants

In addition to the basic personnel carrier it is expected that the family will include command and control, engineering, assault gun and recovery vehicle variants.

Status: Conceptual design.

Manufacturer: Not selected.

LVTP7 Armoured Amphibious Assault Vehicle

Development

In the early 1960s the standard LVTP of the United States Marine Corps was the LVTP5A1. This however had a short land and water range, low water speed and was difficult to maintain.

In March 1964 the United States Marine Corps issued a requirement for a new LVTP and, after evaluating a number of submitted proposals, a contract for the development of a new LVTP was awarded to the Ordnance Division of the FMC Corporation. Overall project management of the programme was under the direction of the Naval Ship Systems Command.

Engineering development began in February 1966 and the first of 15 prototypes was completed in September 1967 and delivered to the Marine Corps the following month. Trials with the prototypes, designated the LVTPX12, were completed in September 1969.

In June 1970 FMC was awarded a contract worth $78.5 million for the production of 942 vehicles without weapon

stations. When the government-supplied weapon stations were included the unit cost was about $129 000. The first production vehicles, which were designated the LVTP7 (Landing Vehicle, Tracked, Personnel, Model 7) were handed over to the United States Marine Corps in August 1971 and the first unit was equipped with the vehicle by March 1972. Final deliveries were made in September 1974 after which the LVTP5A1 and its variants were phased out of service. Main improvements over the LVTP5 series can be summarised as follows:

MODEL	LVTP7	LVTP5
MAX ROAD SPEED	64 km/h	48 km/h
MAX ROAD RANGE	482 km	305 km
OPERATING COSTS (per hour, at 1974 prices)	$40	$72
TRACK LIFE	600 hours	200 hours
MAINTENANCE HOURS (for 100 hours of operating)	6	22
NUMBER OF GREASE POINTS	29	152

In the United States Marine Corps, LVTP7s are issued to Assault Amphibian Battalions which consist of a Headquarters and Service Company, and four Assault Amphibian Companies. The Headquarters and Service Company has 15 LVTP7s, three LVTC7s and one LVTR7. The Assault Amphibian Company has four platoons of LVTP7s, each platoon having 10 LVTP7s. The company Headquarters section has one LVTR7, three LVTC7s and three LVTP7s. This gives the battalion a total of 187 LVTP7s, 15 LVTC7s and 5 LVTR7s. Both the 1st Marine Division (based in California) and the 2nd Marine Division (based in North Carolina) each have one Assault Amphibian Battalion. The

LVTP7 from above showing arrangement of roof hatches

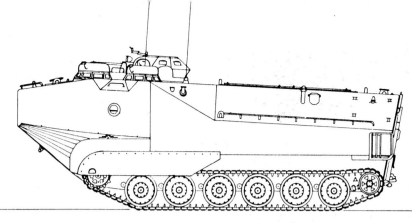

Landing Vehicle, Tracked, Model 7 (LVTP7)

3rd Marine Division is based in the Far East and has two companies of LVTP7s.

In addition to being adopted by the United States Marine Corps, the LVTP7 has been exported to a number of other countries including Argentina, Italy, Spain, South Korea, Thailand and Venezuela:

MODEL	LVTP7	LVTC7	LVTR7
Argentina	19	1	1
Italy	24	1	nil
South Korea	53	5	3
Spain	16	2	1
Thailand	22	nil	1
USA	855	77	54
Venezuela	9	1	1

Note: The above figures do not include the more recent LVT7A1.

Description

The all-welded aluminium hull of the LVTP7 protects the crew from small arms fire, shell splinters and flash-burns.

The driver sits at the front of the hull on the left side and has a single-piece hatch cover that opens to the right rear and seven vision blocks for all-round observation. An M24 infrared periscope can be fitted in the forward part of the driver's hatch cover for driving at night.

The commander sits behind the driver and has a single-piece hatch cover that opens to the rear and seven vision blocks for all-round observation. Forward of the commander's station is an M17C periscope which can be extended to enable the commander to see forward over the driver's hatch cover.

The engine is in the forward part of the hull on the centre-line and power is transmitted to the FMC HS-400 transmission via a torque converter with lock-up. The transmission combines shifting, steering and braking functions in one unit and gives four gears forward and two in reverse. The engine can be removed from the vehicle in 45 minutes and can be run outside for test purposes if required. Power is transmitted to the drive sprockets through hull-mounted final drives. A PTO mounted on the converter housing supplies power for the water jets and the cooling fan through electro-hydraulically controlled clutches.

Mounted over the powerpack is a fan and radiator. Air is drawn in and discharged through ballistic grilles in the roof. When afloat hydraulically-actuated doors below the grilles seal off the air openings. Air for the engine and troop com-partment then enters the vehicle through a hydro-dynamically-actuated air valve mounted on the top of the hull to the right of the driver. Cooling takes place in the contact cooler which is an integral part of the hull floor.

The armament installation is beside the engine on the right side of the hull. The turret has a single-piece hatch cover that opens to the rear, nine vision blocks, a sight with a magnification of ×1 and ×8 and one direct ring sight. The turret is armed with a 12.7 mm (0.50) M85 machine gun with two rates of fire, 1050 rpm (high) and 450 rpm (low). Of 1000 rounds of 12.7 mm ammunition carried 400 are for ready use. The machine gun has an elevation of +60 degrees and a depression of −15 degrees. Turret traverse, which is electro-hydraulic, is a full 360 degrees. Prototype vehicles were fitted with a turret armed with a 20 mm cannon and a 7.62 mm coaxial machine gun.

The 25 fully-equipped marines sit on three bench seats in the troop compartment at the rear of the hull, one in the centre and one on either side. The centre seat can be removed and the two side ones folded up to allow up to 4536 kg of cargo to be carried. The removable centre seat stows on the left bulkhead when not required. The marines enter and leave the vehicle through a power-operated ramp at the rear of the hull, which has a door in the left side of the ramp in case of ramp failure and a single vision block. Over the top of the troop compartment are three torsion-spring-balanced roof hatches.

The tube-over-bar suspension consists of six dual rubber-tyred road wheels with the drive sprocket at the front and the idler at the rear. There are no track return rollers. The first and last road wheel stations have a hydraulic shock absorber. The single pin, rubber bushed tracks have a moulded rubber top surface and replaceable rubber pads.

The LVTP7 is fully amphibious without preparation, being propelled in the water by two water jets, which are mounted one either side of the hull at the rear. The water jets are driven through right-angled gearboxes on top of the sponsons and drive shafts that extend to the rear of the hull. The water jets, which are aluminium, are mixed flow pumps with special exhaust nozzles to maximise thrust and each pumps 52 990 litres of water per minute. At the rear of each pump is a hinged steering deflector which reverses the direction of the jet when closed. Maximum speed forwards is 13.5 km/h and maximum speed in reverse is 7.2 km/h. The tracks can also be used to propel the vehicle when afloat.

Four bilge pumps are fitted: two electric (each with a capacity of 379 litres a minute) and two hydraulic (each with a capacity of 435 litres a minute).

The LVTP7 has no NBC system but is fitted with infra-red driving lights. A number of kits have been developed for use

LVTP7A1 fitted with Cadillac Gage one-man turret armed with 40 mm Mk 19 grenade launcher and 12.7 mm M2 HB machine gun

with the LVTP7, including one for converting the vehicle to an ambulance that can carry six stretcher patients, navigation kit, visor kit for the driver and a winterisation kit which keeps the crew and personnel compartment heated when the outside temperature is down to −54°C, the normal heater being effective down to −32°C.

Modernisation

LVTP7A1 (now called LVT7A1)

In March 1977 the FMC Corporation was awarded a contract to convert 14 LVTP7s into prototypes of a new configuration known as the LVTP7A1. It is planned that the entire Marine Corps LVTP7 fleet will be converted between 1982 and 1985. The emphasis on the conversion is to increase the vehicle's reliability, availability, maintainability and durability while reducing life cycle costs. New items being added to the LVTP7 to bring it up to the LVTP7A1 standard are:

A powerpack using the Cummins VT400 engine
Off-board and on-board diagnostic instrumentation (fault isolation)
Smoke-generating capability
Passive night driving and night firing devices
Improved fire suppression system
Secure voice radio installation
Provision to mount Position Location and Reporting System (PLARS) installation (being developed by Hughes)
Improved troop/crew compartment ventilation
Improved hydraulic and electrical system
Improved electric weapon station.

In addition to previously announced improvements, the LVTP7A1 will have a non-integral fuel tank, watertightness improved by reworking seals which surround air intakes, exhaust plenums and cargo hatches, main wiring harness segmented for rapid repair without requiring an entirely new harness, removable headlights, troop commander's hatch and vision block are higher for better visibility over the more forward driver's hatch.

Under development is a modular line-charge system which will be bolted into the cargo compartment of the LVTP7A1. This is a modified M125 mine-clearance system which uses a Mark 22 rocket motor fired from an elevated launcher rail. When launched the rocket pulls a linear charge to a range of about 550 metres. Once the charge is on the ground it is fired

and should detonate 80 per cent of the mines for seven metres on either side of the line. The M125 carries three shots.

The programme is known as the LVTP7 Service Life Extension Program (SLEP) with $10.5 million requested in fiscal year 1980, $47.3 million in fiscal year 1981 (25 conversions plus $7.2 million for RDT & E), $171.3 million in fiscal year 1982 (149 conversions), $116 million in fiscal year 1983 (307 conversions), $150.5 million in fiscal year 1984 (263 conversions), and $115.9 million in fiscal year 1985 (240 conversions).

In addition to the conversion of LVTP7 to LVTP7A1 configuration (this conversion programme also applies to the other three members of the family, eg LVTC7A1 and LVTR7A1), funding is being provided to build new vehicles to LVTP7A1 configuration, $12 million in fiscal year 1981, $61.6 million (30 vehicles) in fiscal year 1982, $116.0 million (146 vehicles) in fiscal year 1983 and $115.3 million (153 vehicles) in fiscal year 1984. With the later funding the additional 329 LVTP7A1s for the Maritime Prepositioning Ships (MPS) should be completed. In fiscal year 1985 a further four vehicles were ordered at a cost of $3.5 million.

As the LVTP7A1 is now in production a number of additional foreign sales have been made. Early in 1983 Brazil ordered 12 vehicles. In 1982 the US Department of Defense notified Congress of letters of offer to South Korea for 41 LVTP7A1 and one LTVC7A1 vehicles at a cost of $50 million and Philippines for 55 LVTP7A1s at a cost of $64 million. In October 1983 the Department of Defense notified Congress of a letter of offer to Spain for the sale of nine LVTP7A1 and two LVTC7A1 vehicles at a total cost of $16 million. The first production LVTP7A1 was handed over to the US Marine Corps in October 1983.

Further Improvements

The US Marine Corps is considering a number of additional improvements for the LVTP7A1 including:

Driver-operated extendable/retractable bow flap for increased water speed
Improving the turret-mounted M85 machine gun feed chute to reduce stoppage rates and reload times
Adding 40 mm grenade launcher in turret.
Universal weapon mount for TOW or Dragon ATGW, 40 mm grenade launcher, M2 12.7 mm (0.50 calibre) or 7.62 mm M60/M60D machine gun.

Landing Vehicle, Tracked, Personnel Model 7 (LVTP7) with driver's hatch closed

LVTR7A1 showing crane with jib extended

Variants

LVTC7 (Landing Vehicle, Tracked, Command, Model 7)

This had the development designation LVTCX2 and is similar to the basic LVTP7 except that its machine gun turret has been replaced by a simple hatch cover similar to that fitted at the driver's and commander's position. Armament consists of a pintle-mounted 7.62 mm M60D machine gun with 1000 rounds of ammunition. To increase the working area for the crew of 12 (commander, driver, assistant driver/gunner, five radio operators and the four command staff) a tent can be erected at the rear of the hull. To provide power for the additional communications equipment installed an APU powered by a four-cylinder air-cooled petrol engine is fitted as standard. The LVTC7 also has a navigation system, a loaded weight of 20 008 kg and an unloaded weight of 18 228 kg.

LVTR7 (Landing Vehicle, Tracked, Recovery, Model 7)

This had the development designation of the LVTRX2 and like the LVTC7 has had the machine gun turret replaced by a 7.62 mm M60D machine gun. Equipment carried includes benches, tools, air compressor, battery charger, generator and a portable welding kit. Mounted on the roof of the LVTR7 is a hydraulic crane with an extending boom which can lift 2722 kg. The boom can be elevated from 0 to +65 degrees. The vehicle also has a recovery winch with 84.73 metres of 19 mm diameter cable with a breaking strength of 22 044 kg. The two-speed (high and low) winch has a maximum capacity of 13 636 kg on a bare drum at a low speed and 1978 kg on a full drum at high speed. The LVTR7 has a crew of five, a loaded weight of 24 339 kg and an unloaded weight of 23 334 kg.

LVTE7 (Landing Vehicle, Tracked, Engineer, Model 7)

The prototype of an engineer vehicle was completed in 1970 under the designation LVTEX3 but was never placed in production. It is based on the hull of the LVTP7 but had a hydraulically-operated dozer blade at the front of the hull and was provided with a rocket-propelled line charge for clearing minefields.

LVTH7 (Landing Vehicle, Tracked, Howitzer, Model 7)

This development was a project only and did not reach the prototype stage. It would have been armed with a 105 mm

SPECIFICATIONS [data in square brackets relates to LVTP7A1 where different from basic vehicle]	
CREW	3 + 25
COMBAT WEIGHT	22 838 [23 936] kg
UNLOADED WEIGHT	17 441 [18 566] kg
POWER-TO-WEIGHT RATIO	17.51 [17.31] hp/tonne
GROUND PRESSURE	0.57 [0.55] kg/cm²
LENGTH	7.943 m
WIDTH	3.27 m
HEIGHT	
overall	3.263 m
to turret roof	3.12 m
GROUND CLEARANCE	0.406 m
TRACK	2.609 m
TRACK WIDTH	533 mm
LENGTH OF TRACK ON GROUND	3.94 m
MAX SPEED	
road, forwards	64 [72.42] km/h
water, waterjets	13.5 km/h
water, tracks	7.2 km/h
FUEL CAPACITY	681 [647] litres
MAX RANGE (land at 40 km/h)	482 km
MAX ENDURANCE (water)	7 hours at 2600 rpm
FORDING	amphibious
GRADIENT	60%
SIDE SLOPE	60%
VERTICAL OBSTACLE	0.914 m
TRENCH	2.438 m
TURNING RADIUS	pivot
ENGINE	Detroit Diesel model, 8V-53T, 8-cylinder, water-cooled, turbo-charged diesel developing 400 hp at 2800 rpm [Cummins VT400, 8-cylinder, water-cooled, turbo-charged diesel developing 400 hp at 2800 rpm]
TRANSMISSION	HS-400 [HS-400-3A1] with hydraulic torque converter, 4 forward and 2 reverse ratios
SUSPENSION	tube-over-bar
ELECTRICAL SYSTEM	24 V
BATTERIES	4 × 12 V 6TN
ARMAMENT (main)	1 × 12.7 mm MG
SMOKE-LAYING EQUIPMENT	none [yes]
AMMUNITION (main)	1000
FIRE-CONTROL SYSTEM	
Turret power control	electro-hydraulic/ manual [electric/ manual]
by commander	no
by gunner	yes
Gun elevation/depression	+60°/−15°
Turret traverse	360°
Gun stabiliser	none
ARMOUR	
Hull sides	31–45 mm
Hull top	30 mm
Hull floor	30 mm
Hull rear	35 mm
Ramp outer	12.7 mm
Ramp inner	6.72 mm

Status: Production of the LVTP7 has been completed. Current production model is LVT7A1. In service with Argentina, Italy, Korea, Republic (South), Spain, Thailand, USA and Venezuela. The LVT7A1 has also been ordered by Brazil, South Korea, Spain and the Philippines and is already in service with the US Marine Corps.

Manufacturer: FMC Corporation, Ordnance Division, 1105 Coleman Avenue, San Jose, California 95108, USA.

turret-mounted howitzer and would have replaced the LVTH6, which was retired without replacement.

Mobile Test Rig
The Mobile Test Rig was built under the High Energy Laser Research Program and was tested between 1974 and 1976 at Redstone Arsenal, Huntsville, Alabama and at White Sands Missile Range, New Mexico. It is at present in storage.

LVTP7 with 40 mm/12.7 mm Turret
Late in 1982 LVTP7s were undergoing trials fitted with a one-man turret designed by Cadillac Gage armed with a 40 mm Mk 19 grenade launcher on the left and a 12.7 mm (0.50) M2 HB machine gun on the right. The weapons have an elevation of +45 degrees, depression of −8 degrees and turret traverse of 360 degrees at a maximum of 45 degrees a second. Mounted above the 12.7 mm machine gun is a 500 000 candlepower spotlight that moves in elevation with the weapon.

LVTP5A1 Armoured Amphibious Assault Vehicle

Development
In December 1950 the then Ingersoll Products Division of the Borg-Warner Corporation was contracted by the Bureau of Ships as Design Agent for the design, construction of mock-up and prototypes, development and prime contractor for the production of a new family of amphibious vehicles to replace the amphibians of the Second World War still used by the Marine Corps at that time.

Design studies began in January 1951 and the first prototype, designated the LVTPX1, was completed in August the same year. Production of the LVTP5 (Landing Vehicle, Tracked, Personnel, Model 5) began in 1952 and continued to 1957 by which time 1124 had been built. These were built by Baldwin-Lima-Hamilton (91), FMC Corporation (313), Ingersoll (239), Pacific Car and Foundry (56) and St Louis Car Manufacturing Company (425).

In the 1960s all vehicles were fitted with a box type snorkel over the engine compartment, which together with other minor modifications, resulted in the designation being changed from the LVTP5 to the LVTP5A1. Although the vehicle was a considerable improvement over the earlier amphibians it was never considered a satisfactory design, not only because of its short operating range, but also because of the excessive maintenance required to keep it operational.

LVTP5A1 with bow ramp lowered (US Marine Corps)

LVTP5A1 armoured amphibious assault vehicle (US Marine Corps)

Various experiments were tried to improve the performance of the LVTP5 but in the end a new vehicle called the LVTP7 was designed by the FMC Corporation. This entered service in 1971 and by 1974 the LVTP5 family had been phased out of service. Some were transferred to the Philippines and Taiwan where they remain in service today. More recently Chile has acquired a quantity of these vehicles. A brief summary of the main improvements of the LVTP7 over the LVTP5 are given in the entry for the LVTP7.

Description
The hull of the LVTP5 is of armour plate ranging from 6.35 to 15.87 mm thick welded and reinforced with internal framing members to form a rigid, watertight unit. The hull is barge shaped and has an inverted V-shaped bow and bottom for more efficient water operation. The ramp mounted in front of the LVTP5 is hydraulically operated and is composed of an inner and outer steel plate separated by equally spaced webs. The ramp is hinged to the hull and heavy live rubber seals, cemented around the hull opening, provide a watertight seal when the ramp is closed.

The driver sits at the front of the hull on the left and has four M17 periscopes, one M17C periscope and a single-piece hatch cover. The commander sits at the front of the hull on the right and also has four M17 periscopes, one M17C periscope and a single-piece hatch cover. The machine gun turret is between and slightly forward of the commander's and driver's positions and is armed with a 7.62 mm (0.30) M1919A4 machine gun with an elevation of +60 degrees, a depression of −15 degrees and a total traverse of 360 degrees. The gunner has five vision blocks and an M25C periscope sight for aiming the machine gun. Forward and either side of the machine gun turret is a single M17 periscope facing forwards.

All ventilation openings, bilge discharge outlets and access hatches are in the top deck. In each side of the hull is an emergency escape hatch and a single vision block.

Over the top of the troop compartment is the cargo hatch, which is 2.438 metres long and 2.108 metres wide and is made up of two double folding sections which are hinged to the outer sides of the top deck and spring-loaded to assist in opening.

The 34 marines sit on four troop seats of eight each with the remaining two men seated on the machine gunner's platform. In an emergency 45 standing marines can be carried. When being used for cargo the LVTP5 can carry 5443 kg when afloat and 8165 kg when on land, or a 105 mm towed howitzer, its crew and 90 rounds of ammunition. The crew compartment is ventilated by three manually-operated vents and an electric blower mounted in the roof.

The engine compartment is at the rear of the hull and contains the engine, cross-drive transmission, drop gears, final drives and all the accessories necessary for the operation of the engine. Limited access to the engine compartment is via a hatch in the transverse bulkhead. The main engine hatch is bolted to the top deck over the engine compartment and may be removed to permit the complete powerpack (engine and transmission) to be removed from the vehicle.

The engine is mounted on the vehicle's centreline in the engine compartment and is coupled to an Allison model CD-850-4 transmission which is a combined transmission, differential and steering unit. Torque received from the engine is delivered through the cross-drive transmission, drop gears, and single-speed final drives to the track driving sprocket.

The suspension consists of nine pairs of dual steel bogie wheels suspended from rubber torsion spring suspension assemblies on each side of the vehicle. Each wheel of each pair of road wheels consists of a hub with one steel rim and one demountable solid rubber-tyred rim. Within each underwater track return channel are the adjustable front idler, five track return rollers, track return skids and rear drive sprocket.

In the water the LVTP5 is propelled by its tracks, each of which is made of 134 blocks held together by inner and outer 25 mm diameter pins. Each track block has an inverted water grouser.

Kits available for the LVTP5A1 included infra-red, stretcher (carrying 12 stretcher patients), navigation and winterisation.

Variants

LVTH6 (Landing Vehicle, Tracked, Howitzer, Model 6)

This is fitted with a turret armed with a 105 mm M49 howitzer, a 7.62 mm (0.30) machine gun mounted coaxially with the main armament and a 12.7 mm (0.50) M2 HB machine gun mounted on the roof for anti-aircraft defence. When afloat, 100 rounds of 105 mm, 1000 rounds of 7.62 mm and 1050 rounds of 12.7 mm ammunition are carried. A total of 210 were built between 1953 and 1957, 175 by Ingersoll and 35 by Pacific Car and Foundry. They were retired from the United States Marine Corps without replacement as the howitzer version of the LVTP7 was never built.

LVTC5 (Landing Vehicle, Tracked, Command, Model 5)

This is similar to the basic LVTP5 but has a modified cargo compartment fitted with additional communications equipment, tables and mapboards. It has a command crew of nine plus its normal crew of three, and is distinguishable from the basic vehicle by its additional radio antennas. Fifty-eight LVTC5s were converted from basic LVTP5s by Ingersoll in 1955 and are also known as the LVTP5 (CMD).

LVTR1 (Landing Vehicle, Tracked, Recovery, Model 1)

Sixty-five of these were built by FMC Corporation from 1954. The vehicle is used for the recovery and maintenance of other members of the LVTP5 family and is fitted with a generator, welding equipment, air compressor, boom with a capacity of 3175 kg and a winch with a maximum capacity of 20 412 kg. This model does not have a machine gun turret.

LVTE1 (Landing Vehicle, Tracked, Engineer, Model 1)

This was a specialised model and was fitted with a special dozer blade at the front of the hull and a rocket-propelled mine-clearing system. It is no longer in service and was retired without replacement. There were many experimental models of the LVTP5 family including the LVTAAX1 anti-aircraft system armed with the turret of the M42 twin 40 mm self-propelled anti-aircraft gun.

Taiwanese LVTP5/LVTP6

In 1982 it was reported that Taiwan was to replace the LV-1790-1 V-12 petrol engine of the LVTP5/LVTP6 with a diesel engine and that initial trials with vehicles fitted with three different powerpacks had already commenced in Taiwan. These are believed to include NAPCO (GM Detroit Diesel 12V-71 with existing transmission), Summit Engineering (12V-71 diesel with CD-50-6 transmission) and Teledyne Continental (Teledyne Diesel with CD-50-6 transmission).

Landing Vehicle Tracked Amphibious Vehicles

A few of these vehicles, which were designed and built during the Second World War, are still in service with the Philippines and Taiwan.

Status: Production complete. In service with Chile, the Philippines and Taiwan.

Manufacturers: Baldwin-Lima Hamilton, FMC Corporation, Ingersoll, Pacific Car and Foundry and St Louis Car Manufacturing Company.

YUGOSLAVIA

BVP-M80A Mechanised Infantry Combat Vehicle

Development

The BVP-M80A mechanised infantry combat vehicle is a further development of the M-980 and was shown in public for the first time at the Cario defence equipment exhibition held late in 1984. At that time it was said to be in production and was being offered for export.

Description

The overall layout of the BVP-M80A is identical to the M-980 but is slightly heavier (14 tonnes against 13 tonnes), slightly wider and higher, greater ground clearance (0.4 m against 0.3 m) and have a slightly higher road speed (64 km/h against 60 km/h). It has a more powerful engine which in addiiton to giving the higher road speed gives an improved power-to-weight ratio.

Variants

There are no known variants of the BVP-M80A.

BVP-M80A mechanised infantry combat vehicle (Christopher F Foss)

Close up of twin Sagger type ATGW launcher on BVP-M80A mechanised infantry combat vehicle (Christopher F Foss)

Status: Production.

Manufacturer: Yugoslav state arsenals. Enquiries to Federal Directorate of Supply and Procurement, Beograd, Knez Mihailova 6, POB 308, Yugoslavia.

M-980 Mechanised Infantry Combat Vehicle

Development

The M-980 Mechanised Infantry Combat Vehicle was seen for the first time in public during a parade in Belgrade in May 1975. It has been designed in Yugoslavia but uses a number of foreign components; for example the engine is the same as in the French AMX-10P armoured infantry carrier, the ATGW is the Soviet Sagger and the 20 mm cannon is manufactured under licence from Switzerland.

Description

The hull of the M-980 is made of all-welded steel, although some reports have indicated that aluminium is used in some non-critical areas. Over the front arc of the M-980 its armour provides complete protection against 20 mm armour-piercing projectiles at a range of 100 metres while the remainder of the vehicle's armour provides protection against 7.62 mm armour-piercing projectiles fired from a range of 100 metres. The M-980 carries ten men: driver and turret gunner who remain with the vehicle at all times, vehicle commander, and seven fully equipped infantrymen. The driver sits at the front of the hull on the left and has a single-piece hatch cover that lifts and swings to the right to open. In front of his hatch are three periscopes, the centre one of which can be replaced by an infra-red or image intensification periscope for driving at night.

The squad commander sits behind the driver and has a cupola that can be traversed through a full 360 degrees, in the forward part of which is a single periscope. The cupola has a single-piece hatch cover that opens forwards and can be locked vertical if required. An infra-red searchlight mounted externally on the forward part of the commander's cupola can be operated from inside the vehicle.

The engine is mounted to the right of the driver with the air-inlet and air-outlet louvres in the roof and the exhaust outlet in the right side of the hull. It is assumed that the transmission is the same as that fitted to the French AMX-10P.

M-980 MICV from rear showing two ready-to-launch Sagger ATGWs mounted above turret rear

Close-up of turret of M-980 with two Saggers on launcher rails to rear of turret. Slits in turret front allow 20 mm cannon and 7.62 mm machine gun high elevation

The one-man turret is to the rear of the engine compartment and offset to the right of the vehicle's centreline. The turret is armed with an HS 804 20 mm cannon which has a cyclic rate of fire of 800 rounds a minute and is fed from a 50-round drum magazine. The cannon fires an HE projectile weighing 0.122 kg with a muzzle velocity of 880 metres a second or an AP projectile weighing 0.142 kg with a muzzle velocity of 880 metres a second which will penetrate 18 mm of armour at an incidence of 0 degrees at a range of 500 metres. Maximum anti-aircraft range is 1500 metres and maximum range when used in the ground/ground role is 2000 metres.

Mounted coaxially to the right of the 20 mm cannon is a 7.62 mm machine gun with a cyclic rate of fire of 1200 rpm, which is fed from a 50- or 300-round belt. Both weapons have a maximum elevation of +75 degrees and a depression of −5 degrees.

Mounted to the rear of the turret on the right side are two launcher rails for the Soviet Sagger ATGW. This missile weighs 11.29 kg and has a maximum range of 3000 metres. It is estimated that a further two to four missiles are carried in reserve in the hull, although the gunner has to expose himself in order to load another missile.

The turret is provided with a day sight for engaging ground targets (magnification of ×1.1 and a 40-degree field of view), night sight (magnification of ×5.3 and a 10-degree field of view) and a passive night sight (range of 800 metres, magnification of ×7.3 and 7-degree field of view). There are three vision blocks in the left side and rear of the turret. In the turret roof on the left side are two forward-facing periscopes and a single-piece hatch cover that opens to the rear.

The troop compartment is at the rear of the vehicle and the infantrymen enter and leave by two doors in the rear of the

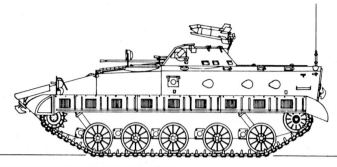

SPECIFICATIONS

CREW	2 + 8
COMBAT WEIGHT	13 000 kg
UNLOADED WEIGHT	11 000 kg
POWER-TO-WEIGHT	
RATIO	20 hp/tonne
GROUND PRESSURE	0.64 kg/cm²
LENGTH	6.4 m
WIDTH	2.59 m
HEIGHT	
over missile launcher	2.5 m
to turret roof	2.3 m
to hull roof	1.8 m
GROUND CLEARANCE	0.4 m
TRACK	2.47 m
TRACK WIDTH	300 mm
LENGTH OF TRACK	
ON GROUND	3.484 m
MAX SPEED	
road	60 km/h
water	7.5 km/h
MAX RANGE	
road	500 km
cross-country	300/350 km
FORDING	amphibious
GRADIENT	60%
VERTICAL OBSTACLE	0.8 m
TRENCH	2.2 m
ENGINE	HS 115-2 V-8 water-cooled turbo-charged diesel developing 260 hp at 3000 rpm
TRANSMISSION	pre-selector gearbox with hydraulic torque converter, 4 forward and 1 reverse gears
SUSPENSION	torsion bar
ELECTRICAL SYSTEM	24 V
ARMAMENT	
main	1 × 20 mm cannon
coaxial	1 × 7.62 mm MG
other	twin Sagger ATGW launcher
AMMUNITION	
20 mm	400
7.62 mm	2250
Sagger	4
FIRE-CONTROL SYSTEM	
Turret power control	n/av
by commander	no
by gunner	yes
Gun elevation/depression	+75°/−5°
ARMOUR	
Hull front	25-30 mm
Hull sides	15 mm
Hull top	8 mm
Hull floor	12 mm
Hull rear	12 mm
Turret front	20 mm

Status: In production. In service with Yugoslavia.

Manufacturer: Yugoslav state arsenals. Enquiries to Federal Directorate of Supply and Procurement, Beograd, Knez Mihailova 6, POB 308, Yugoslavia.

hull, each of which has a firing port and a vision block. In each side of the hull are three firing ports each with a periscope in the roof of the vehicle for aiming the weapon. Over the top of the troop compartment are two oval roof hatches hinged in the centre, which can be locked vertical.

The torsion bar suspension consists of five single rubber-tyred road wheels that are similar to those used on the French AMX-10P, with the drive sprocket at the front and idler at the rear. There are two track return rollers and the top of the track is covered by a skirt. Hydraulic shock absorbers are fitted at the first and last road wheel stations.

The M-980 is fully amphibious, being propelled in the water by its tracks. Before entering the water a trim vane, which is stowed on the glacis plate when not in use, is erected at the front of the hull. Standard equipment includes an NBC system which allows the vehicle to stay in a contaminated area for ten hours, smoke-laying system, central fire-extinguishing system with automatic and manual operation and internal temperature at +15°C at ambient temperature of −15°C.

Variants
There are no known variants of the M-980.

M-60P Armoured Personnel Carrier

Development
The M-60P armoured personnel carrier was first seen in public during a parade held in Yugoslavia in 1965, and for a short period was called the M-590.

In concept, the M-60P is similar to Western armoured personnel carriers of this period such as the American M59 and M113 and the British FV432. Its engine is an Austrian Steyr diesel which also powers the Yugoslav GJ-800 artillery tractor (which in turn is based on the Hungarian K-800 light tracked artillery tractor), and its suspension is based on the Soviet SU-76 self-propelled gun's which was supplied to Yugoslavia in the immediate post-Second World War period.

Description
The hull is made of all-welded steel which provides the crew with protection from small arms fire and shell splinters.

The driver sits at the front of the hull on the left side and has a single-piece rear-opening hatch cover with an integral periscope which can be replaced by an infra-red periscope for driving at night. The co-driver is seated on the right side of the hull and also has a hatch cover with an integral periscope that opens to the rear. The co-driver also operates the bow-mounted 7.92 mm machine gun which is based on the German MG42.

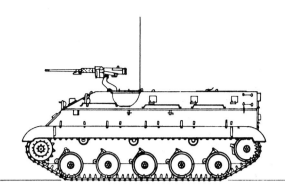

M-60P APC with 12.7 mm machine gun

The commander sits to the rear of the driver and has a single-piece hatch cover. The machine gunner sits to the rear of the co-driver and has a cupola which can be traversed through 360 degrees. The cupola has a two-piece hatch cover that opens either side of the machine gunner to give him some protection when he is using the 12.7 mm (0.50) M2 HB machine gun which is mounted on the forward part of his cupola. A tripod carried on the right side of the hull enables the 12.7 mm machine gun to be removed from the vehicle and used in the ground role.

The infantrymen sit on bench seats down either side of the hull and enter and leave the vehicle by twin doors in the hull rear. There are also hatches in the roof of the troop compartment. Three firing/observation ports are provided in each side of the hull and one in each of the rear doors. A spare road wheel is carried on the left side of the hull rear and a jerrican is carried on the right side of the hull rear.

The torsion bar suspension consists of five single rubber-tyred road wheels with the drive sprocket at the front and the idler at the rear, and three track return rollers. The running gear is outside the hull armour and its top part is covered by a light sheet metal guard.

The M-60P APC is not amphibious and is not fitted with an NBC system.

Variants

M-60PB Anti-tank

Mounted on top of the hull on the left side are two 82 mm recoilless rifles on a rotating mount with a mechanical traverse and elevating mechanism. The gunner has a suspended seat which moves with the rifles and a single-piece hatch cover that opens forwards. To the right of the mount is a hatch for the loader. The M-60PB has also been observed with the recoilless rifles mounted on the right side of the hull top.

The recoilless rifles have a maximum range of 4500 metres and a maximum rate of fire of four to five rounds a minute and have an elevation of +6 degrees, depression of −4 degrees 30 minutes with a prohibited zone of action of 76 degrees in the plane of the anti-aircraft machine gun and 135 degrees to the rear of the vehicle.

Effective range when engaging stationary targets is 1500 metres, and 1000 metres when engaging moving targets. The HEAT projectile will penetrate 250 mm of armour at an angle of 90 degrees with dispersion being two metres at 500 metres and four metres at 1000 metres. The HEAT projectile itself weighs 4.2 kg, with the complete round weighing 7.2 kg; ten rounds are carried. The M-60PB carries one fewer crew member than the basic M-60P APC.

It is also probable that there are other versions of the M-60 such as ambulance, command and radio vehicles.

M-60P armoured personnel carrier with commander's, gunner's and driver's hatches open

CREW	3 + 10
COMBAT WEIGHT	11 000 kg
POWER-TO-WEIGHT	
RATIO	12.73 hp/tonne
GROUND PRESSURE	0.7 kg/cm²
LENGTH	5.02 m
WIDTH	2.77 m
HEIGHT	
without armament	1.86 m
including MG	2.385 m
MG at max elevation	3.51 m
GROUND CLEARANCE	0.4 m
TRACK	2.385 m
TRACK WIDTH	400 mm
LENGTH OF TRACK	
ON GROUND	2.94 m
MAX ROAD SPEED	45 km/h
FUEL CAPACITY	150 litres
MAX RANGE	
road	400 km
cross-country	250 km
FUEL CONSUMPTION	
(road)	0.38 litre/km
FORDING	
still water	1.35 m
running water	1.25 m
GRADIENT	60%
SIDE SLOPE	40%
VERTICAL OBSTACLE	0.6 m
TRENCH	2 m
ENGINE	FAMOS 6-cylinder in-line water-cooled diesel developing 140 hp
TRANSMISSION	manual, 5 forward, 1 reverse gears
SUSPENSION	torsion bar
ELECTRICAL SYSTEM	24 V
BATTERIES	2 × 12 V
ARMAMENT	
anti-aircraft	1 × 12.7 mm MG
bow	1 × 7.92 mm MG
ARMOUR	
Max	25 mm
Min	10 mm

Status: Production probably completed. In service with Yugoslavia.

Manufacturer: Yugoslav state arsenals. Enquiries to Federal Directorate of Supply and Procurement, Beograd, Knez Mihailova 6, PO Box 308, Yugoslavia.

Yugoslav Wheeled Armoured Personnel Carrier

Yugoslavia has recently introduced into service a 4 × 4 anti-aircraft vehicle called the BOV-3 which utilises many proven commercial automotive components in its design.

Although an APC version of this vehicle probably exists, the only other known variant is an anti-tank model which is known as the BOV-1. This has a pod containing six ATGWs (probably based on the Soviet Sagger) which when travelling is within the hull of the vehicle and when required for action is raised above the roof of the vehicle. A further six missiles are carried within the hull and are manually loaded. Two missiles are capable of being launched every minute.

Description of BOV-3

The hull of the BOV-3 is of all-welded steel contruction with the driver being seated at the front left and the commander to his right, both with a single-piece hatch cover that opens to

BOV-1 anti-tank vehicle with pod containing six ATGWs raised

the rear. The driver has three periscopes for forward observation and a single vision block and firing port in the left side of the hull while the commander has a single forward facing periscope. There is also a crew entry hatch in the left side of the hull and a single roof hatch to the rear of the driver. The other two crew members, the gunner and loader, are normally seated inside the vehicle when not manning the anti-aircraft weapons.

The engine compartment is at the rear of the hull with air inlet and air outlet louvres on the top and an engine access door at the rear. The vehicle is powered by a West German Deutz type F 6L 413 F six-cylinder diesel developing 148 hp at 2650 rpm, this being coupled to a manual gearbox with five forward and one reverse gears and a two-speed transfer case. Steering is power-assisted and a central tyre pressure regulation system allows the driver to adjust the tyre pressure from 0.7 to 3.5 bars to suit the ground being crossed. Main brakes are air/hydraulic with a hand operated parking brake. Suspension consists of leaf type springs with telescopic shock absorbers. The differential locks are controlled electro-pneumatically.

Standard equipment includes a Jugo-Webasto 7.5 kW heater, day and infra-red night vision equipment, intercom and radios.

Mounted in the centre of the roof is the open-topped turret with an external turret basket at the rear. Access to the turret is only from outside of the vehicle with extension pieces being provided on the hull top either side of the turret for reloading purposes.

The turret is based on the standard towed 20/3 mm gun M55 A4 B1 which has been in service with the Yugoslav Army in its towed configuration for many years. The turret has full 360 degree hydraulic traverse at a speed of 80 degrees a second with weapon elevation from −4.5 to +83 degrees at 50 degrees a second. Each of the three 20 mm barrels is provided with a drum type magazine that holds 60 rounds of ammunition. A total of 1500 rounds of ammunition are carried. Maximum anti-aircraft engagement altitude is quoted as 2000 metres although effective anti-aircraft range is between 1000 and 1500 metres. The weapons can also be used in the direct fire support role against ground targets when maximum range is about 2000 metres.

The BOV-3 is a clear weather system only with no provision for external fire control, although general warning targets approaching could be given over the radio net.

SPECIFICATIONS

CREW	4
CONFIGURATION	4 × 4
COMBAT WEIGHT	9400 kg
POWER-TO-WEIGHT RATIO	15.7 hp/tonne
LENGTH	5.791 m
WIDTH	2.525 m
HEIGHT OVERALL	3.21 m
GROUND CLEARANCE	0.325 m
TRACK	1.9 m
WHEELBASE	2.75 m
MAX ROAD SPEED	93.4 km/h
RANGE ROAD	500 km
FORDING	1.1 m
GRADIENT	55%
SIDE SLOPE	30%
TRENCH	0.64 m
ENGINE	Deutz F 6L 413 F six-cylinder diesel developing 148 hp at 2650 rpm
TRANSMISSION	manual, five forward and one reverse gears
TRANSFER CASE	two-speed
STEERING	power-assisted
SUSPENSION	leaf type springs with telescopic shock absorbers
BRAKES	
main	air/hydraulic
parking	mechanical, hand-operated
ELECTRICAL SYSTEM	24 V
BATTERIES	2 × 12 V, 143 Ah
ARMAMENT	2 × 20 mm cannon
AMMUNITION	1500 rounds

Status: In production and service with the Yugoslav Army.

Manufacturer: Yugoslav state factories. Enquiries to Federal Directorate of Supply and Procurement, Beograd, Knez Mihailova 6, PO Box 308, Yugoslavia.

Close up of turret of BOV-3 showing 3 × 20 mm anti-aircraft guns (Christopher F Foss)

BOV-3 self-propelled 20 mm anti-aircraft gun in travelling configuration with weapons covered

Abbreviations

AA anti-aircraft
AAG anti-aircraft gun
ACCV Armored Cavalry Cannon Vehicle
ACEC Ateliers de Constructions Electriques de Charleroi
ACV Armored Cannon Vehicle
ADATS Air Defence Anti-Tank System
AFV armoured fighting vehicle
Ah ampère hour
AIFV armoured infantry fighting vehicle
AML Automitrailleuse Légère (light armoured car)
AMR Auto Mitrailleuse de Reconnaissance
AMX Atelier de Construction d'Issy-les-Moulineaux
AOI Arab Organisation for Industrialisation
AP armour-piercing
APC armoured personnel carrier
APC armour-piercing capped
APC-T armour-piercing capped tracer
APDS armour-piercing discarding sabot
APDS-T armour-piercing discarding sabot tracer
APE Amphibisches Pionier-Erkundungsfahrzeug
APERS anti-personnel
APERS-T anti-personnel tracer
APFSDS armour-piercing fin-stabilised discarding sabot
APFSDS(P) armour-piercing fin-stabilised discarding sabot (practice)
APFSDS-T armour-piercing fin stabilised discarding sabot tracer
APG Aberdeen Proving Ground
APHE armour-piercing high explosive
API armour-piercing incendiary
APIT armour-piercing incendiary tracer

APT armour-piercing tracer
APU auxiliary power unit
APV armoured patrol vehicle
ARE Atelier de Construction Roanne
ARMSCOR Armament Manufacturing Corporation (South Africa)
ARV armoured recovery vehicle
ASA Advanced Security Agency
AT anti-tank
ATDU Armoured Trials & Development Unit
ATG anti-tank gun
ATGW anti-tank guided weapon
AVGP Armoured Vehicle General Purpose
AVLB armoured vehicle launched bridge
AVR armoured vehicle reconnaissance

BAOR British Army of the Rhine
bhp brake horsepower
BITE built-in test equipment
BL blank
BLR Blindado Ligero de Ruedas (light wheeled armoured vehicle)
BL-T blank tracer
BMR Blindado Medio de Ruedas (medium wheeled armoured vehicle)

CAF Canadian Armed Forces
CCV Close Combat Vehicle
CFV Cavalry Fighting Vehicle
CRR Carro de Reconhecimento Sobre Rodas (wheeled reconnaissance vehicle)
CTRA Carro de Transporte Sobre Rodas Anfibro (amphibious wheeled transport vehicle)
CVR(T) Combat Vehicle Reconnaissance (Tracked)
CVR(W) Combat Vehicle Reconnaissance (Wheeled)
CWS cupola weapon station

DARCOM US Army Materiel Development and Readiness Command
DARPA Defense Advanced Projects Agency
DIA Defense Intelligence Agency
DoD Department of Defense
DSO Defence Sales Organisation
DS/T practice discarding sabot/tracer
DTAT Direction Technique des Armaments Terrestres

EBG Engin Blindé Génie (armoured engineer vehicle)
EBR Engin Blindé de Reconnaissance (armoured engineer vehicle)
EMC Engin Blindé Mortier Cannon
ENGESA Engesa Engenheiros Especializados
ERC Engin de Reconnaissance Cannon
ESD Electronique Serge Dassault
ERV emergency rescue vehicle
EW electronic warfare
EWK Eisenwerke Kaiserslautern Göppner
EWS external weapon station

FCE fire-control equipment
FCS fire-control system
FISTV Fire Support Team Vehicle
FLIR forward looking infra-red
FMC Food Machinery Corporation
FMS Foreign Military Sales
FN Fabrique Nationale
FOV field of view
FROG free rocket over ground
FSED full-scale engineering development
FUG Felderitó Usó Gépkosci (amphibious reconnaissance vehicle)
FV fighting vehicle
FVRDE Fighting Vehicles Research and Development Establishment
FVS Fighting Vehicle System
FY Fiscal Year

G gendarmerie
GAO General Accounting Office
GIAT Groupement Industriel des Armements Terrestres
GLS Gesellschaft für Logistischen Service
GMC General Motors Corporation
GPMG general purpose machine gun
GSRS General Support Rocket System
GST Gesellschaft für System-Technik
GW guided weapon

HB heavy barrel
HE high explosive
HE-APERS-FRAG high explosive anti-personnel fragmentation
HEAT high explosive anti-tank
HEAT-FS high explosive anti-tank fin-stabilised
HEAT-MP high explosive anti-tank multi-purpose
HEAT-MP(P) high explosive anti-tank multi-purpose (practice)
HEAT-T high explosive anti-tank tracer
HEAT-T-HVY high explosive anti-tank tracer heavy
HEAT-TP-T high explosive anti-tank target practice tracer
HEAT-T-MP high explosive anti-tank tracer multi-purpose
HEDP high explosive dual purpose
HE-FRAG high explosive fragmentation
HEI high explosive incendiary
HEIT high explosive incendiary tracer
HEP high explosive plastic
HEPD high explosive point detonating
HE/PR high explosive practice
HEP-T high explosive practice tracer
HESH high explosive squash head
HESH-T high explosive squash head tracer
HE-T high explosive tracer
hp horsepower
HPT high-pressure test
HVAP high velocity armour-piercing
HVAPDS-T high velocity armour-piercing discarding sabot tracer
HVAPFSDS high velocity armour-piercing fin stabilised discarding sabot
HVAP-T high velocity armour-piercing tracer
HVMS Hyper-Velocity Support Weapon
HVTP-T high velocity target practice tracer

IAFV infantry armoured fighting vehicle

IFV infantry fighting vehicle
ILL illuminating
IMI Israel Military Industries
IOC initial operational capability
IR infra-red
IS internal security
ITV Improved TOW Vehicle

JGSDF Japanese Ground Self-Defence Force
JPO Joint Project Office
JSDFA Japanese Self-Defence Force Agency

KE kinetic energy
LAD light aid detachment
LADS light air defense system
LATS Light Armoured Turret System
LAV Light Armoured Vehicle
LAV Light Assault Vehicle
LAW light anit-tank weapon
LLLTV low-light level television
LMG light machine gun
LVA landing vehicle assault
LVT landing vehicle tracked
LVTC landing vehicle tracked command
LVTE landing vehicle tracked engineer
LVTP landing vehicle tracked personnel
LVTR landing vehicle tracked recovery
LWT light weapon turret

MAC Medium Armoured Car
MAP Military Aid Programme
MG machine gun
MICV mechanised infantry combat vehicle
MILAN Missile d'Infanterie Léger Antichar (light infantry anti-tank missile)
MMBF mean miles between failures
MMS mast mounted sight
MoD Ministry of Defence
MoU memorandum of understanding
MPGS Mobile Protected Gun System
MPWS Mobile Protected Weapon System
MRS multiple rocket system
MV muzzle velocity
MVEE Military Vehicles and Engineering Establishment

NATO North Atlantic Treaty Organisation
NBC nuclear, biological, chemical

PAT power-assisted traverse
PE Procurement Executive
PM porte mortier (mortar carrier)
POS Postes Optiques de Surveillance

PRAC practice
PRAC-T practice tracer
PTO power take off
PWI-SR(GR) Panser Wagen Infanterie-Standaard (Groep)

RAC Royal Armoured Corps
RAM-D reliability, availability, maintainability and durability
RARDE Royal Armament Research and Development Establishment
RATAC Radar for Field Artillery Fire
RDT&E Research Development Test and Evaluation
REME Royal Electrical and Mechanical Engineers
RFP request for proposals
ROC required operational characteristics
RoC Republic of China
ROF Royal Ordnance Factory
ROF rate of fire
RSAF Royal Small Arms Factory
RTT Roues Transporteur de Troupes (wheeled troop armoured transport)
RUC Royal Ulster Constabulary

SAE Society of Automotive Engineers
SAM surface-to-air missile
SAMM Société d' Applications des Machines Motrices
SAPI-SD semi-armour piercing incendiary self destruct
SFIM Societe de Fabrication d'Instrument de Mesure
SH/PRAC squash head practice
SKOT Sredni Kolowy Opancerzny Transportér (medium wheeled armoured transport vehicle)
SLEP Service Life Extension Program
SMG sub-machine gun
SP self-propelled
SPAAG self-propelled anti-aircraft gun
SPAG self-propelled assault gun
STE/ICE Simplified Test Equipment/Internal Combustion Engine

TACOM Tank Automotive Command
TAM Tanque Argentino Mediano
TAT-251 Tactical Armament Turret 25 mm, 1 man
TBAT TOW/Bushmaster Armoured Turret
TI thermal imaging
TOPAS Transporter Oberneny Pasovy (wheeled armoured transport vehicle)
TOW tube-launched optically-tracked wire-guided
TP target practice
TPFSDS-T target practice fin-stabilised discarding sabot tracer
TP-T target practice tracer

TT transpory de troupes (troop transporter)
TUA TOW under armour
TUR Tiefflieger-Überwachungs-radar

UDR Ulster Defence Regiment
USMC United States Marine Corps

VAB Véhicule de l'Avant Blindé (front-armoured car)
VADAR Véhicule Autonome de Défense Antiaérienne Rapproché (autonomous close-action anti-aircraft vehicle)
VADS Vulcan Air Defense System
VAE Vehiculo Armado Exploracion (armoured reconnaissance vehicle)
VAPE Vehiculo Apoyo y Exploracion (support and reconnaissance vehicle)
VBC Véhicule Blindé de Combat (armoured fighting vehicle)
VBL Véhicule Blindé Léger (light armoured vehicle)
VCA Véhicule Chenillé d' Accompagnement (tracked support vehicle)
VCC Veicolo Corazzato de Combattimento (armoured fighting vehicle)
VCG Véhicule de Combat du Genie (armoured engineer vehicle)
VCI Véhicule de Combat d'Infanterie; Véhiculo combate infanteria (infantry combat vehicle)
VCR Véhicule de Combat à Roues (wheeled combat vehicle)
VCR/AT Véhicule de Combat à Roues/Atelier Véhicule (wheeled fighting vehicle)
VCR/IS Véhicule de Combat à Roues/Intervention Sanitaire (wheeled fighting vehicle/ambulance)
VCR/PC Véhicule de Combat à Roues/Post de Commandement (wheeled fighting vehicle/command post)
VCR/TH Véhicule de Combat à Roues/Tourelle HOT (wheeled fighting vehicle/HOT turret)
VCR/TT Véhicule de Combat à Roues/Transport de Troupes (wheeled fighting vehicle/troop transport)
VCTP Véhicule de Combate Transporte de Personal (armoured personnel carrier)
VDA Véhicule de Defense Antiaérienne (anti-aircraft defence vehicle)
VDAA Véhicule d'Auto-Défense Antiaérienne
VDSL Vickers Defence Systems Ltd
VEC Véhiculo de Exploración de Caballerie (cavalry reconnaissance vehicle)
VIB Véhicule d'Intervention du Base
VTP Véhicule transport de personnel
VTT Véhicule transport de troupe
VXB Véhicule Blindé à Vocations Multiples (multi-purpose armoured car)

WAPC Wheeled Armoured Personnel Carrier
WARPAC Warsaw Pact
WFSV Wheeled Fire Support Vehicle
WMRV Wheeled Maintenance and Recovery Vehicle

Index

Armoured Personnel Carriers and Infantry Fighting Vehicles and their variants in alphabetical order of countries

Note: Type designations in bold print indicate principal models; page numbers in bold print relate to detailed descriptions.

Other AFVs